**01**
Alexanderplatz
*Berlin-Mitte*

**02**
Gedenkstätte Berlin-
Hohenschönhausen
*Genslerstraße 66*
*Berlin-Hohenschönhausen*

**03**
Bundeskanzleramt
*Willy-Brandt-Straße 1*
*Berlin-Tiergarten*

**04**
Luftfahrtmuseum Finowfurt
Museumsstraße 1
*Schorfheide*

**05**
Gedenkstätte Berliner Mauer
*Bernauer Straße 111*
*Berlin-Wedding*

**06**
Historische Westernstadt
*Paulsternstraße 18*
*Berlin-Siemensstadt*

**07**
Kolonie Gemütlichkeit
*Heckerdamm 195*
*Berlin-Charlottenburg*

**08**
Checkpoint Charlie
*Friedrichstraße 43*
*Berlin-Mitte*

**09**
Café Keese
*Bismarckstraße 108*
*Berlin-Charlottenburg*

**10**
Amaras Shop
*Seestraße 43*
*Berlin-Wedding*

**11**
Olympiastadion
*Olympischer Platz 3*
*Berlin-Charlottenburg*

**12**
Tiergarten
*Straße des 17. Juni*
*Berlin-Tiergarten*

**13**
Operationsbunker
*Teichstraße*
*Berlin-Reinickendorf*

**14**
FriedrichstadtPalast Berlin
*Friedrichstraße 107*
*Berlin-Mitte*

**15**
Stern und Kreisschifffahrt
*Station Pergamonmuseum*
*Berlin-Mitte*

**16**
Kunststoffe
*Invalidenstraße 1*
*Berlin-Mitte*

**17**
Clärchens Ballhaus
*Auguststraße 24*
*Berlin-Mitte*

**18**
Bebauung an der Leipziger Straße
*Leipziger Straße*
*Berlin-Mitte*

**19**
Restaurant Himmelspagode
*Oranienburger Straße 3*
*Hohen Neuendorf*

**20**
Stadtbad Wedding
*Gerichtstraße 65–69*
*Berlin-Wedding*

**21**
Kunsthaus Tacheles
*Oranienburger Straße 54–56a*
*Berlin-Mitte*

**22**
Nachtclub Bel Ami
*Flatowallee 14*
*Berlin-Charlottenburg*

**23**
Fernsehturm am Alexanderplatz
*Panoramastraße 1a*
*Berlin-Mitte*

**24**
Haus des Berliner Verlags
*Karl-Liebknecht-Straße 29*
*Berlin-Mitte*

**25**
Club Avalon
*Zitadellenweg 20e*
*Berlin-Spandau*

**26**
Café Lumumba
*Karl-Marx-Allee 35*
*Berlin-Mitte*

**27**
Kino International
*Karl-Marx-Allee 33*
*Berlin-Mitte*

**28**
Stasimuseum Berlin
*Ruschestraße 103*
*Berlin-Lichtenberg*

**29**
Potsdamer Platz
*Berlin-Tiergarten*

**30**
Ehemaliger Grenzturm
*Erna-Berger-Straße*
*Berlin-Mitte*

**31**
Messe Berlin
*Messedamm 22*
*Berlin-Charlottenburg*

# IMPRESSUM

Fotografie, Art Direction, Design, Satz /
*Photography, Art Direction, Design, Typesetting:*
Dennis Orel, Benjamin Tafel

Lektorat / *Copyediting:*
Anja Breloh (Deutsch / *German),*
Ingrid Nina Bell (Englisch / *English)*

Übersetzungen ins Englische /
*Translated by:*
Michael Wolfson

Schrift / *Typeface:*
Molot, Bodoni, Univers

Verlagsherstellung / *Production:*
Christine Müller

Papier / *Paper:*
LuxoArt Samt, 135 g/m²

Buchbinderei / *Binding:*
Bramscher Buchbinder Betriebe, Bramsche

Gesamtherstellung / *Printed by:*
Dr. Cantz'sche Druckerei, Ostfildern

© 2010 Hatje Cantz Verlag, Ostfildern,
Dennis Orel, Benjamin Tafel

© 2010 für die Fotografien / *for the photographs:*
Dennis Orel, Benjamin Tafel

Erschienen im / *Published by*
Hatje Cantz Verlag
Senefelderstrasse 12
73760 Ostfildern-Ruit
Deutschland / Germany
Tel. +49 711 4405-200
Fax +49 711 4405-220
www.hatjecantz.com

*Hatje Cantz books are available internationally at
selected bookstores. For more information about our
distribution partners, please visit our homepage at
www.hatjecantz.com.*

ISBN 978-3-7757-2616-0

*Printed in Germany*

Ebenfalls bei Hatje Cantz erschienen /
*Also published by Hatje Cantz:*

Stuttgart!
Eine Stadt im Süden Deutschlands /
*A Place in Southern Germany*

Von / *By* Dennis Orel und / *and* Benjamin Tafel
288 Seiten / *pages,* 264 farbige Abbildungen /
*color illustrations*
Broschur / *Softcover,* ISBN 978-3-7757-2287-2
(Deutsch–Englisch / *German–English)*

# BERLINER LUFT

## BENJAMIN TAFEL & DENNIS OREL

HATJE
CANTZ

**»ICK MUSS SAGEN, SIEHST RICHTICH SCHNIEKE AUS, BERLIN.«**

*"I just gotta say that you really look lovely, Berlin."*

**»NU MAL SACHTE MIT DE JUNGEN FERDE.«**

*"Just go easy with the young horses."*

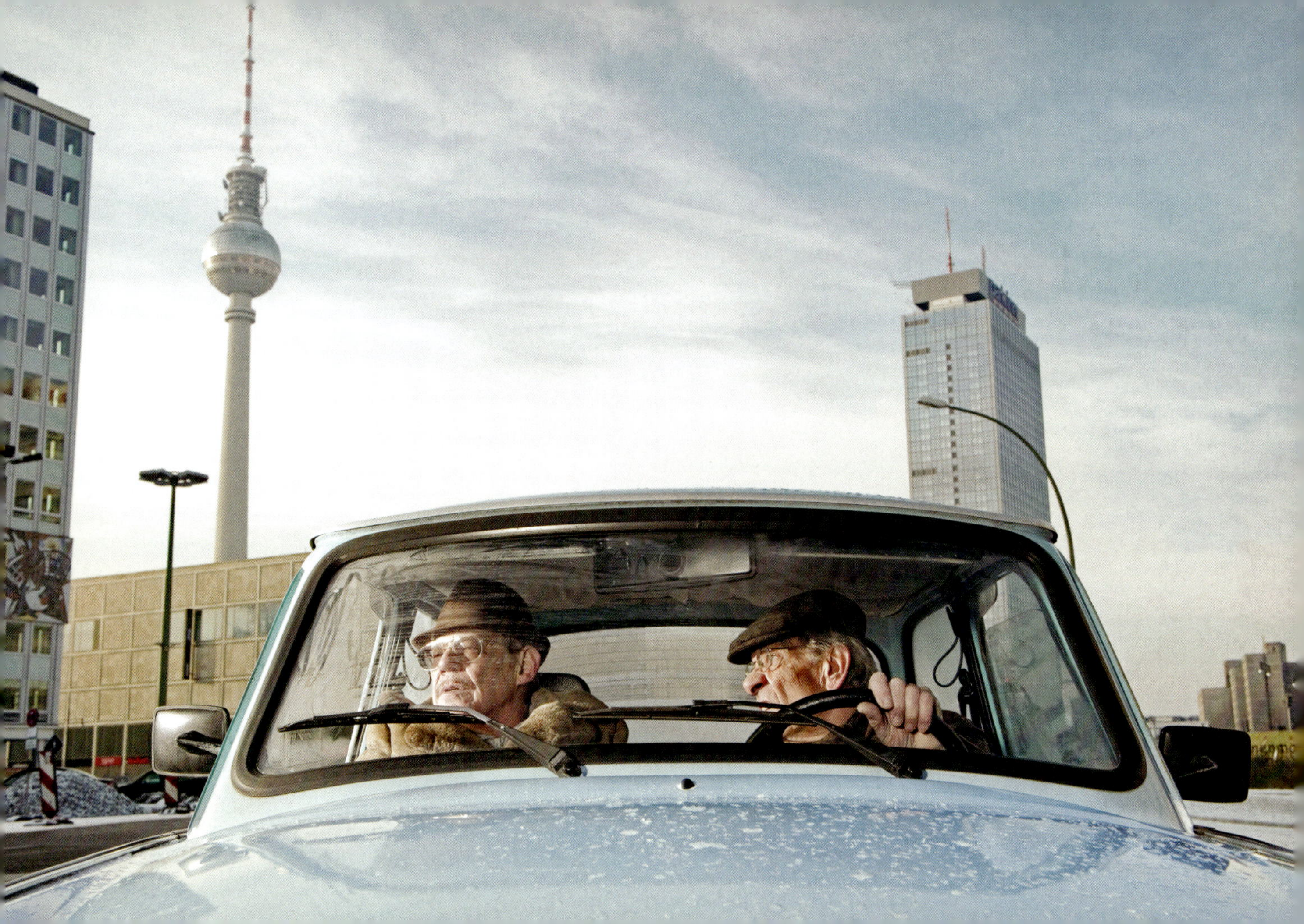

»DA DENKSTE, DU BIST DET ORIGINAL.«
*"You think that you're the original."*

»ES JIBT HIER SONE UND SOLCHE,
UND DANN JIBT ES NOCH JANZ ANDERE.«
*"There are all sorts of people here in this city,
and then there are the others."*

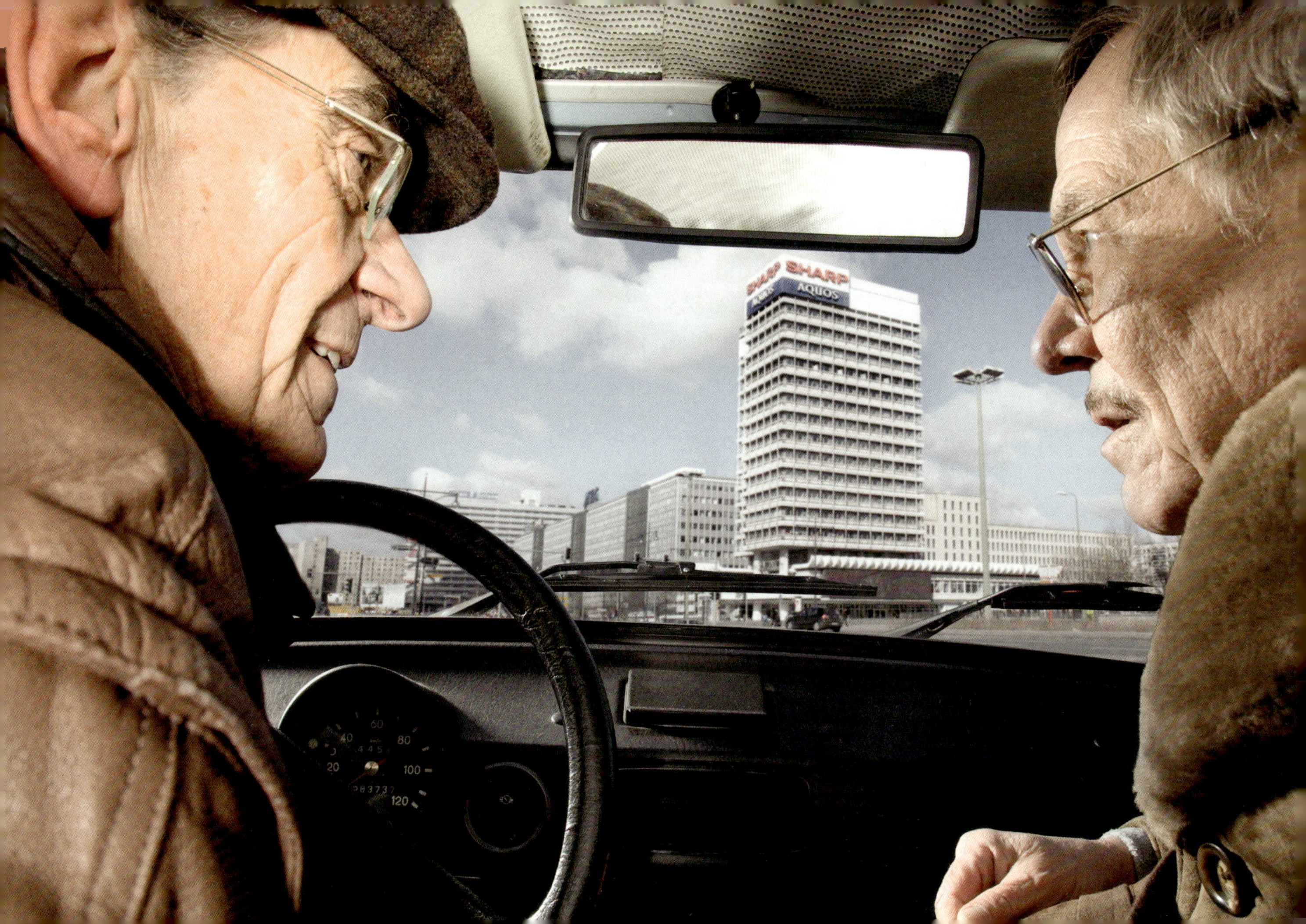
SHARP SHARP
AQUOS

**»RIECHSTE DET? DET IS DIE BERLINER LUFT. EN JANZ BESONDERER DUFT.«**

*"Smell that? That's Berlin air. A very special fragrance."*

**»JA, ABGASE UND FRITTENFETT.«**

*"Right, auto fumes and french-fries fat."*

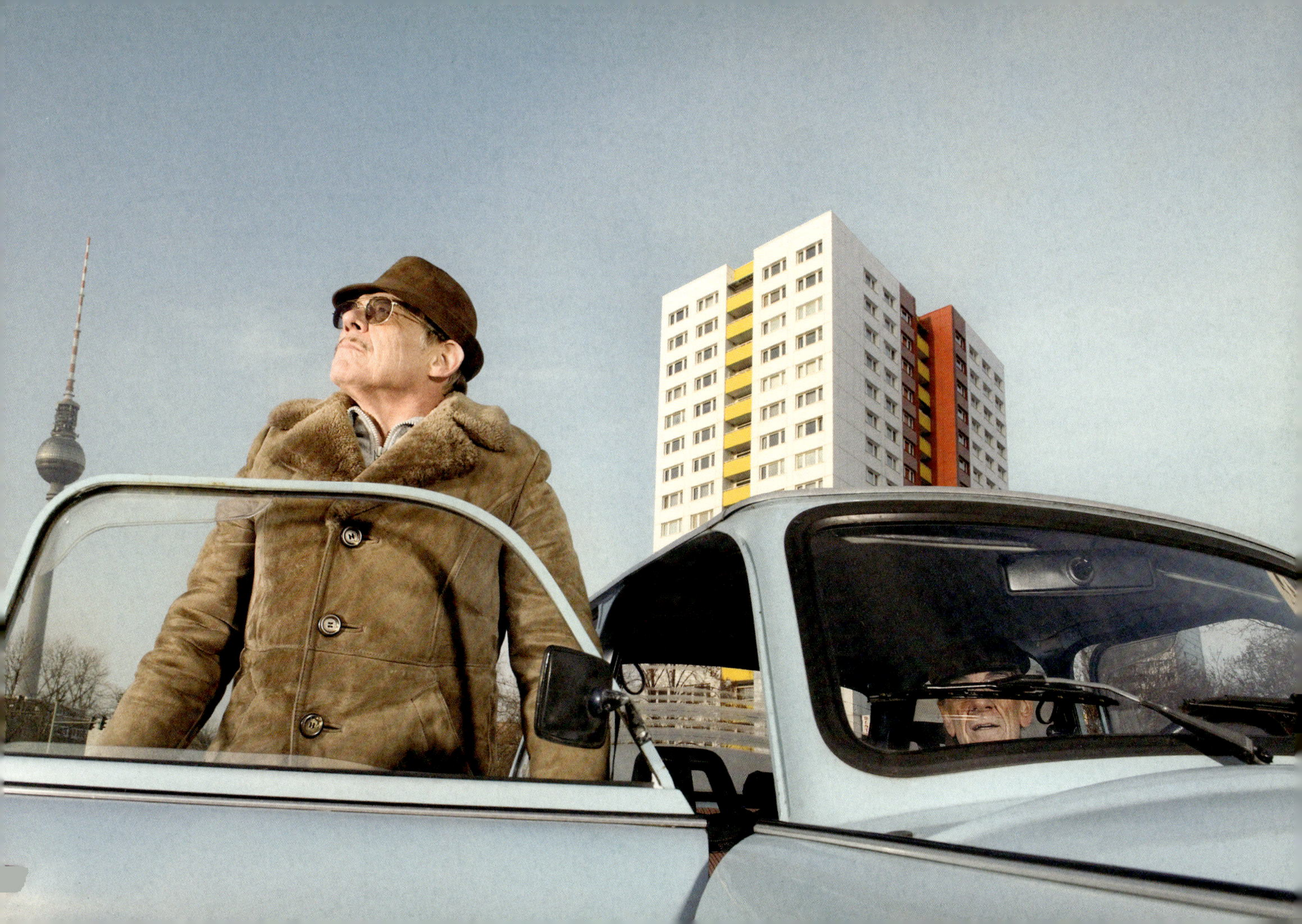

**»ACH, GRÜSS MIR DEENE KEULE.«**

"Hey, say hi to your brother for me."

**»LIEBA VALOOFE ICK MIA.
SCHEENEN DANK OOCH FÜR DET BACKOBST.«**

"I'd rather get lost. Thanks for nothing."

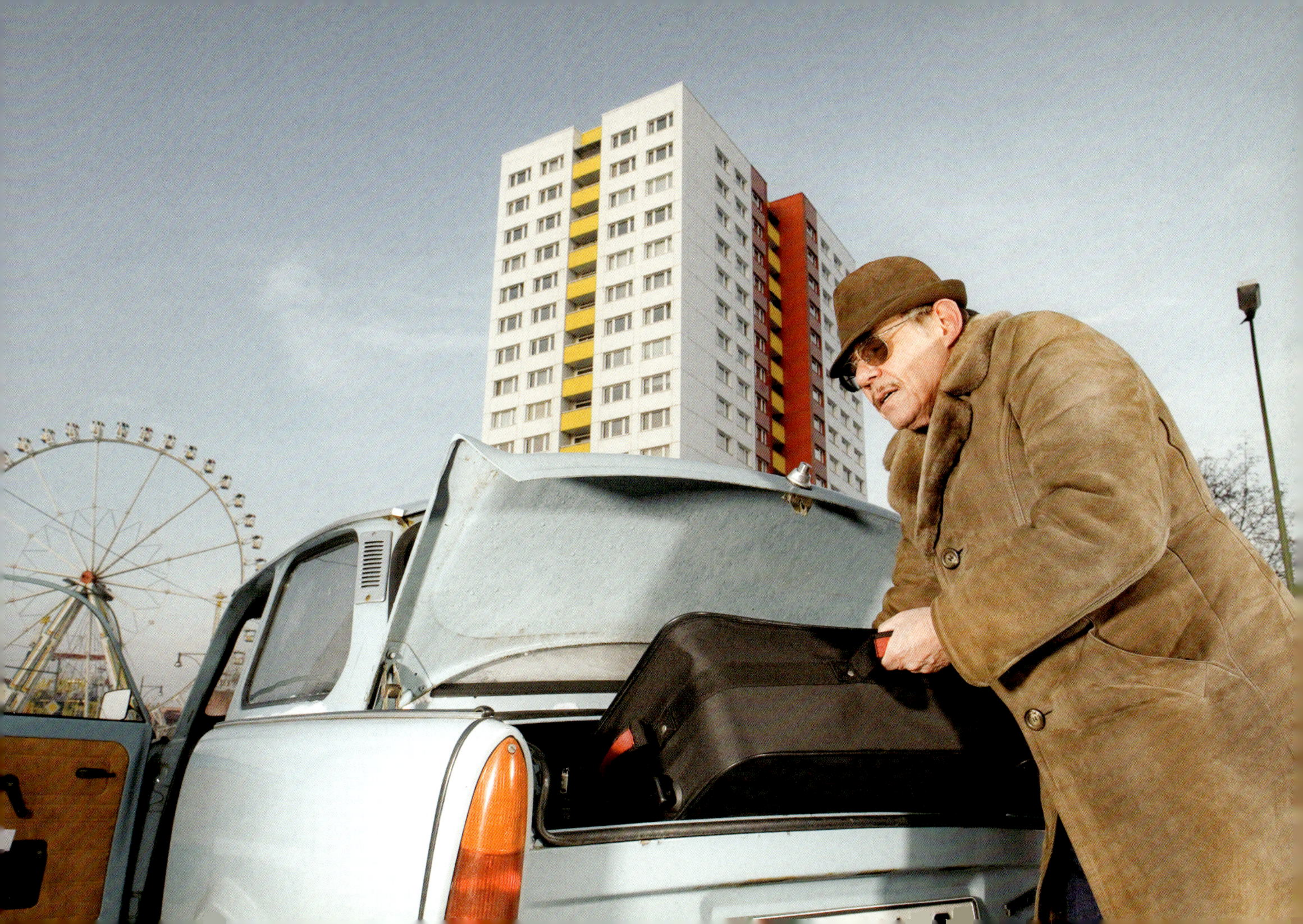

# ORGELN AM ALEX
## *Hurdy-gurdy on Alex*

**01** **Alexanderplatz**
*Berlin-Mitte*

Der Duft gebratener Würste steigt vom Bauchladengrill des mobilen Würstchenstands mit gelbem Regenschirm auf. Eine Gruppe spanischer Schüler steht an der Weltzeituhr und lässt sich von ihrer Lehrerin Berliner Geschichte gestenreich erläutern. An den Terrassenbrunnen unter dem Fernsehturm finden sich vier Punker mit frisch gefärbter Haarpracht ein, die sich sogleich mit Pappbechern bewaffnet auf die Jagd nach spendablen Touristen machen. Ein Herr in beigefarbener Safarijacke spendiert einen Euro und versucht sodann, unter wilden Verrenkungen den hohen Turm in den richtigen Aus-schnitt zu rücken. An dessen Ausgang erscheint ein Schwabe, der seiner Reisebegleitung zuraunt: »Des Geld hätte ma' anders investiere könne!«

*The smell of fried sausages rises from the mobile vendor's grill under a yellow umbrella. A group of Spanish school kids stand at the world-time clock listening to their teacher explaining something about the history of Berlin accompanied by numerous gesticulations. Four punks with freshly dyed hair show up at the terrace fountains at the foot of the television tower and, paper cup in hand, immediately start off in search of munificent tourists. A gentleman wearing a beige-colored safari jacket contributes a Euro and then wildly contorts himself to get the perfect detail of the high tower in his viewfinder. A fellow from Swabia emerges who whispers to his traveling companion, "You could have invested the money otherwise!"*

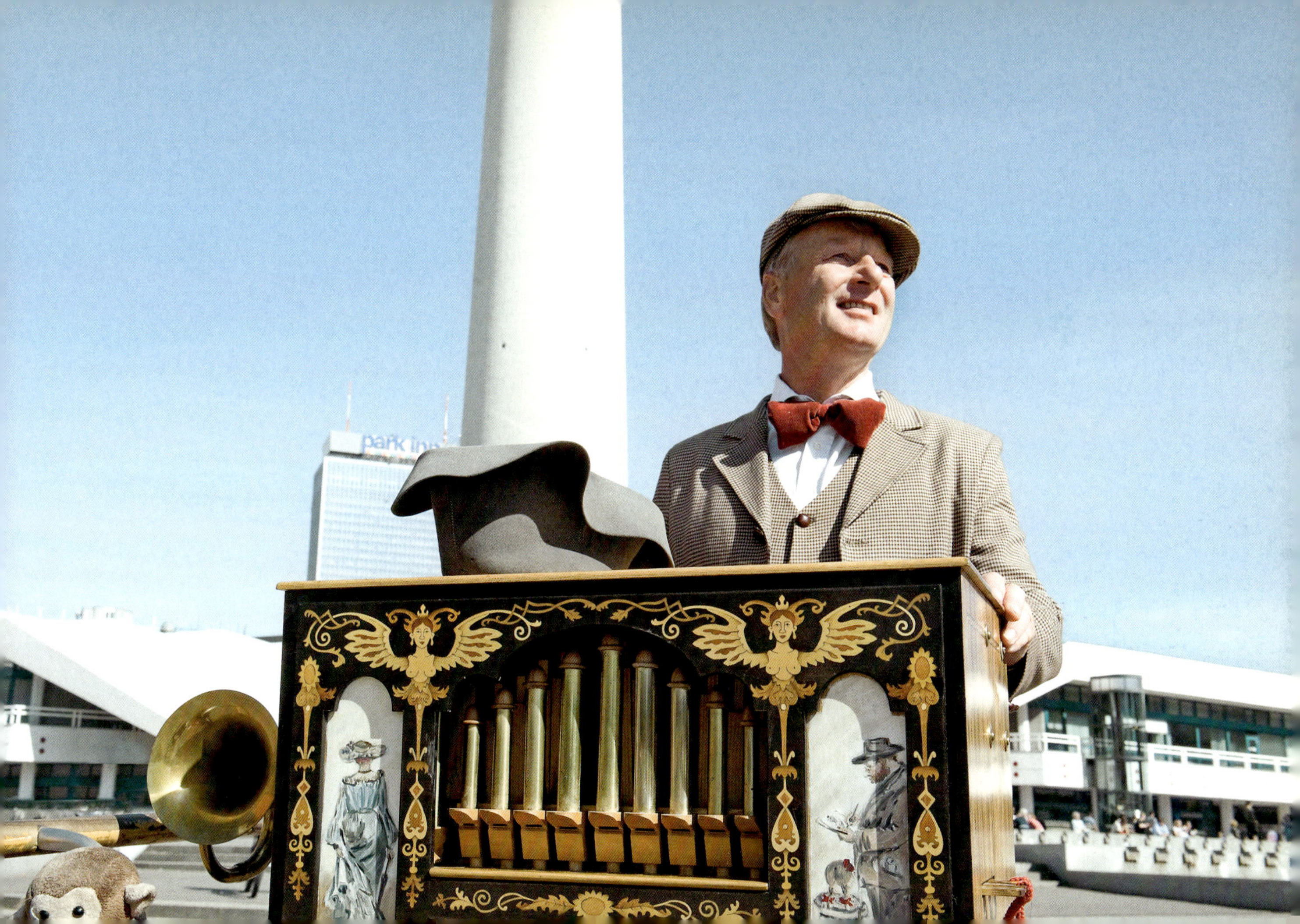

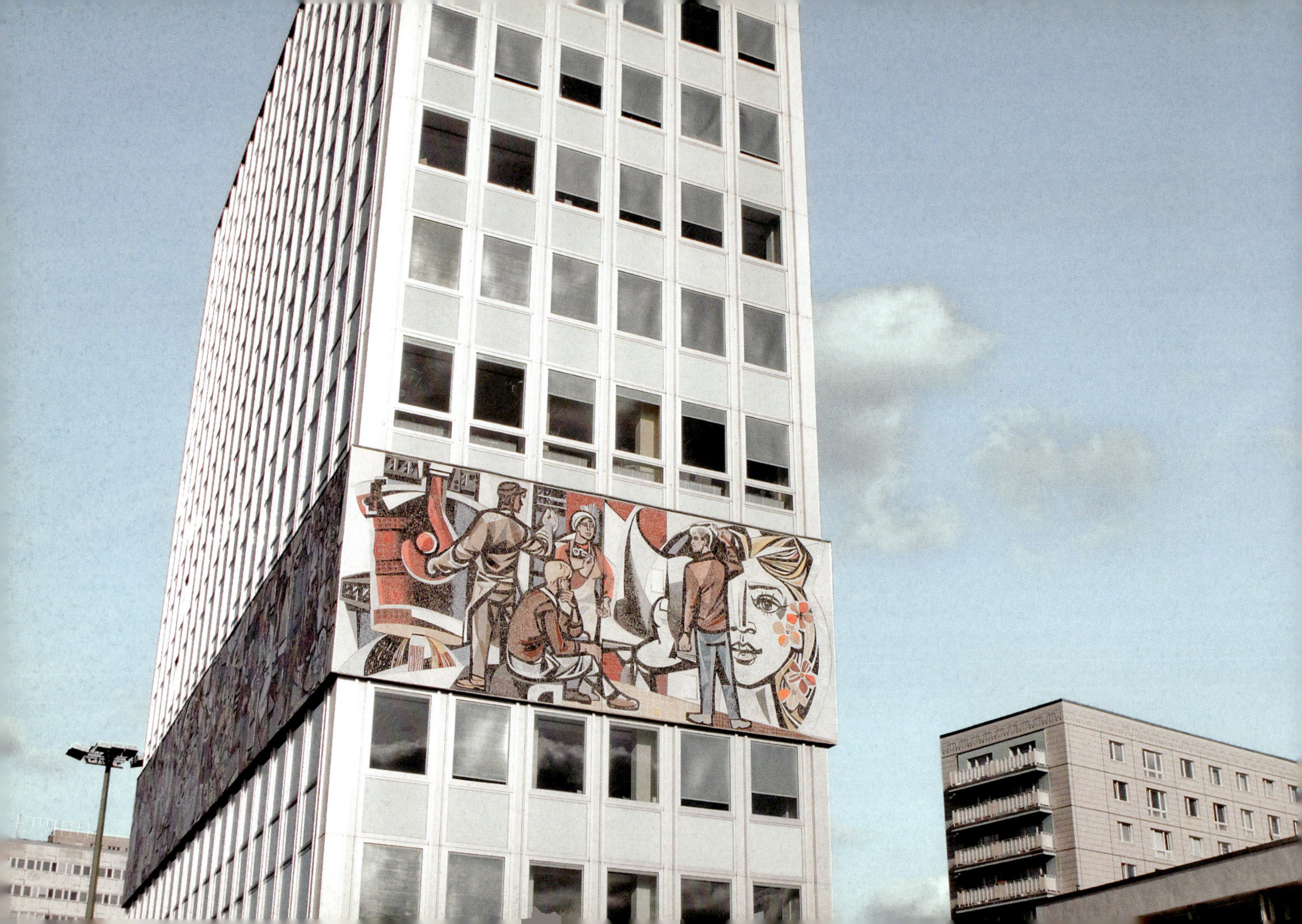

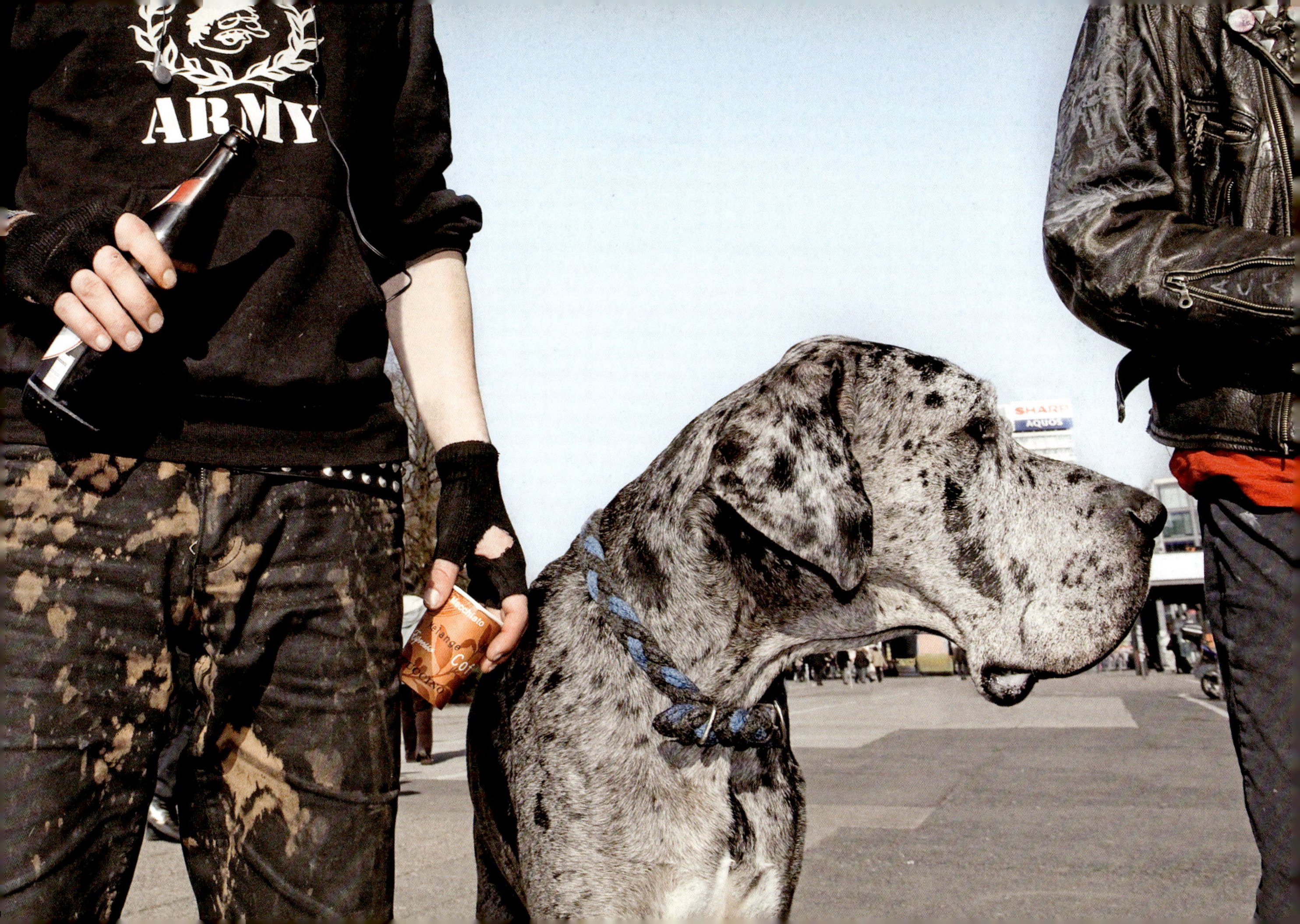

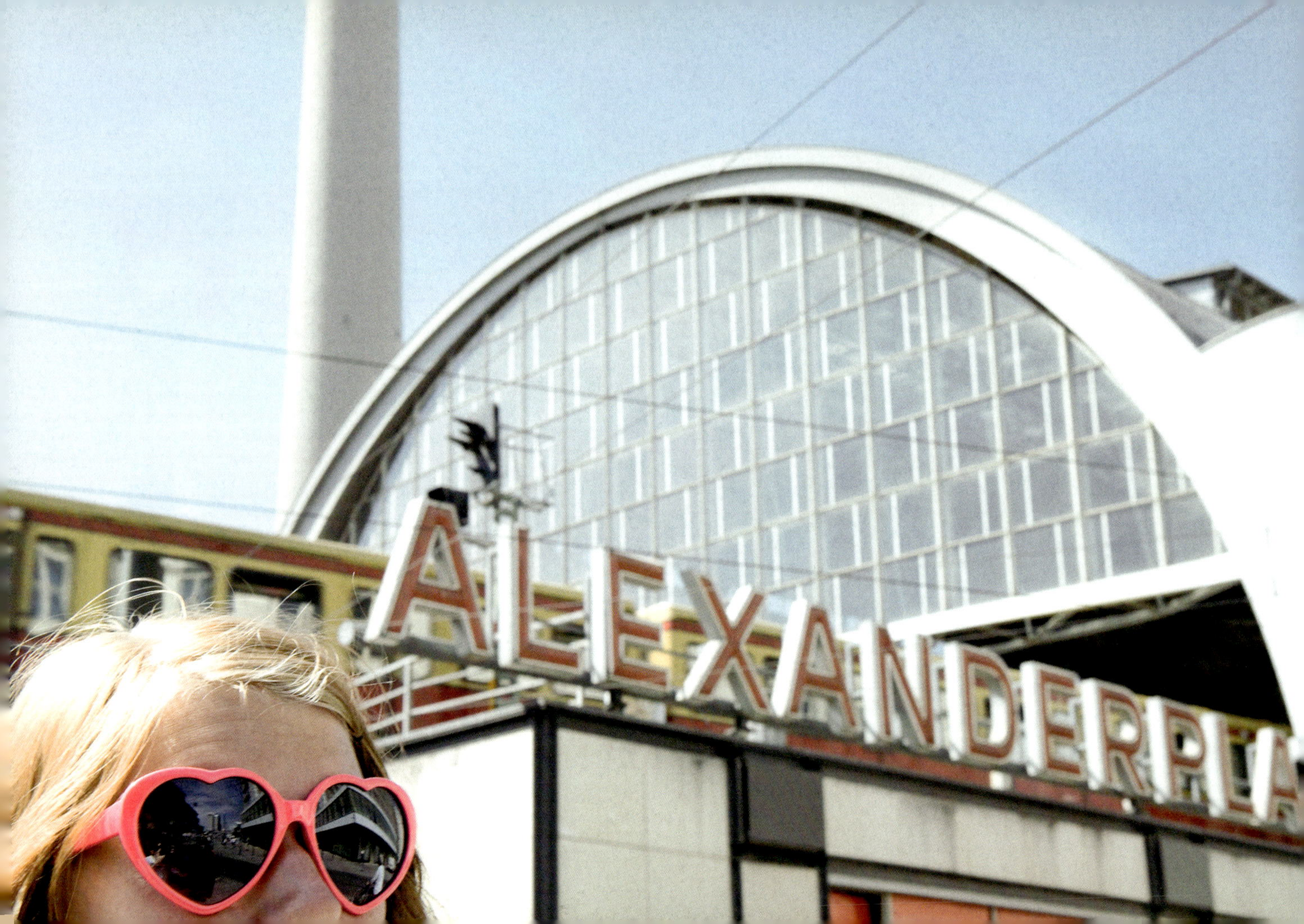
ALEXANDERPLA

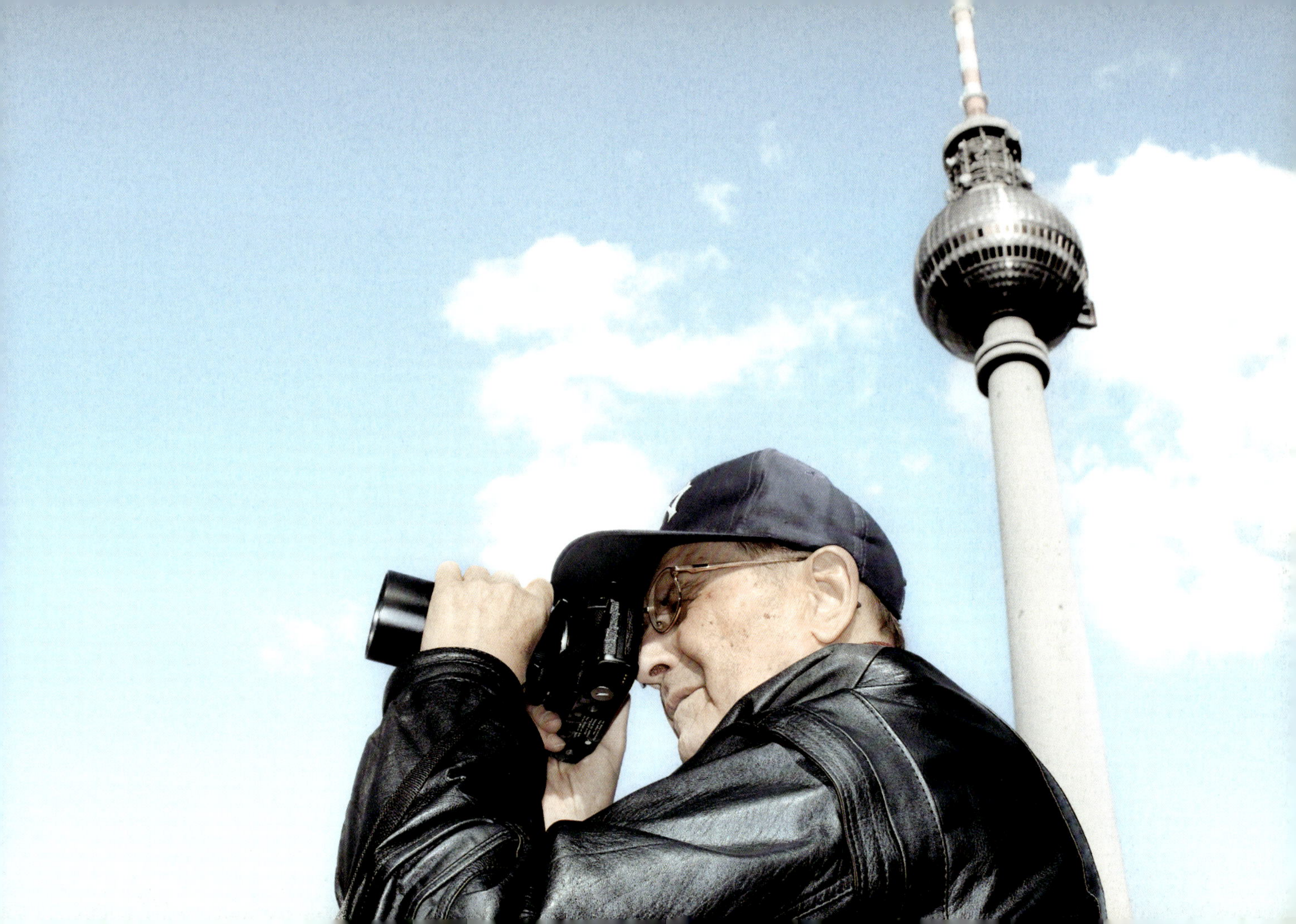

# DIE GEHEIME STADT
## *The secret city*



Die Besucher betreten den sechsstöckigen Plattenbau direkt hinter der Untersuchungshaftanstalt des Ministeriums für Staatssicherheit. Sie gelangen in den Vernehmungstrakt mit seinen langen Fluren und Zimmern, einheitlich ausgestattet mit Tischlampe und einem Telefonapparat. Hin und wieder blickt Erich Honecker von den Wänden. Die Schilderungen eines ehemaligen Insassen der Haftanstalt dringen nur gedämpft durch die grün gepolsterten Doppeltüren. Der von der Außenwelt hermetisch abgeschlossene Sperrbezirk war zu Zeiten des Kalten Krieges auf keiner Karte verzeichnet. Ein mausgrauer Transporter erinnert an eine der Verschleierungstaktiken. Getarnt mit der Aufschrift »Frischer Fisch«, sorgten diese Wagen für Gefangenentransporte.

*The visitors enter the six-story prefabricated building behind the detention center of the Ministry for State Security. They reach the interrogation tract with its long corridors and rooms that are uniformly equipped with a table lamp and a telephone. Every so often, Erich Honecker looks down from the walls. The muffled narrative of a former detention center inmate penetrates the green upholstered double doors. The restricted area that was hermetically sealed from the outside world was not shown on any map during the Cold War era. A mouse-gray van recalls one of the cover-up tactics. Camouflaged with the inscription "fresh fish," these delivery trucks were used to transport prisoners.*

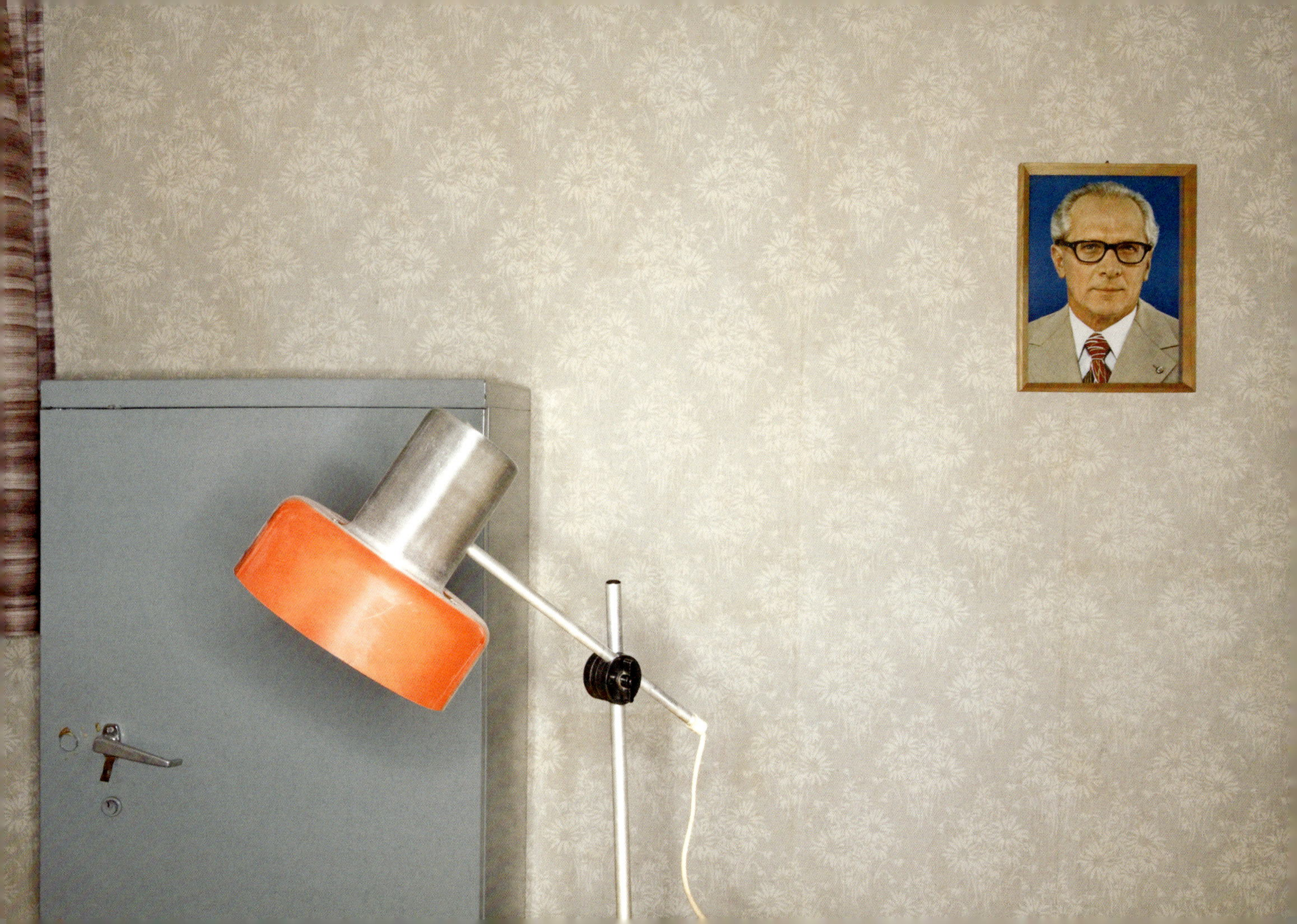

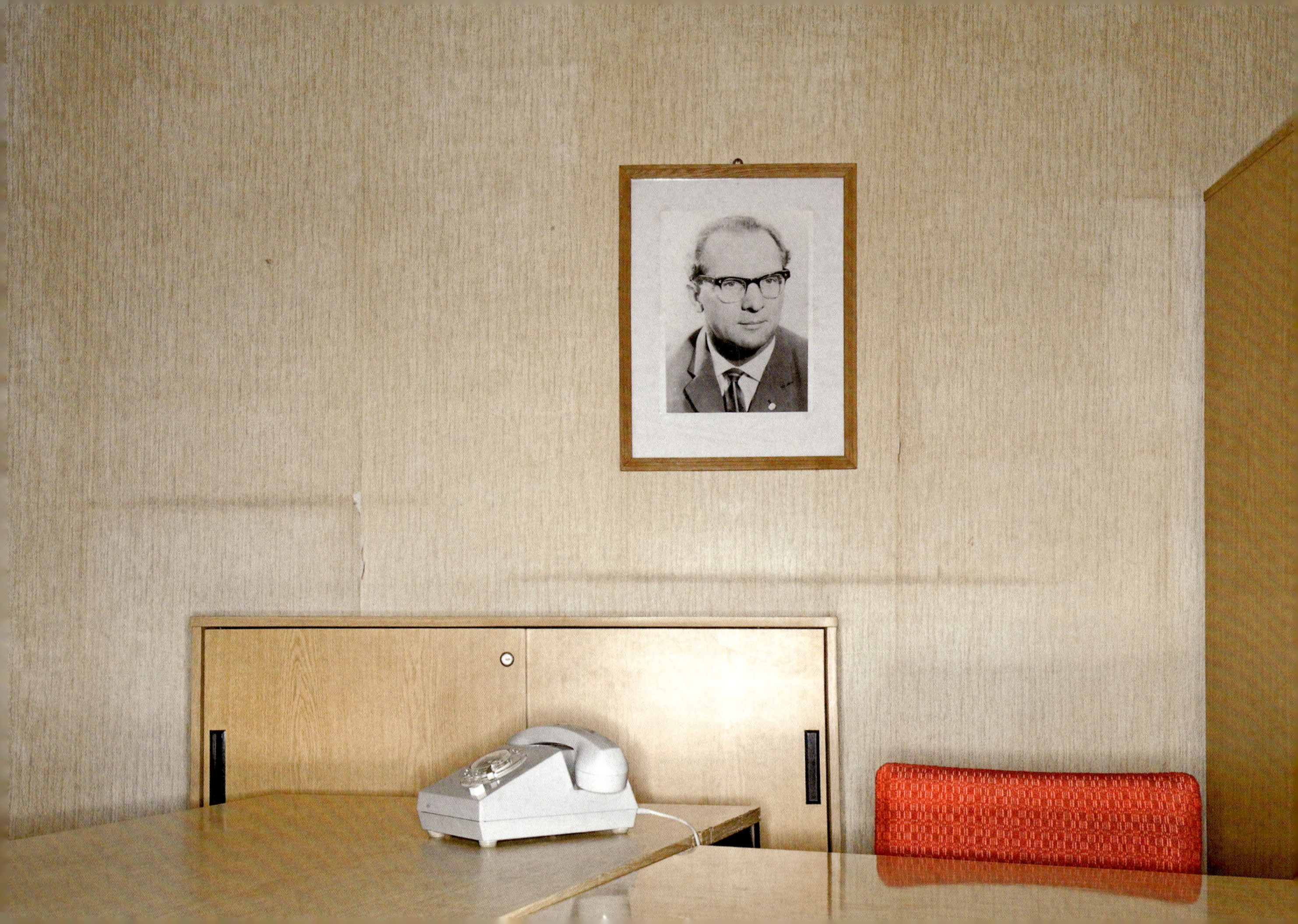

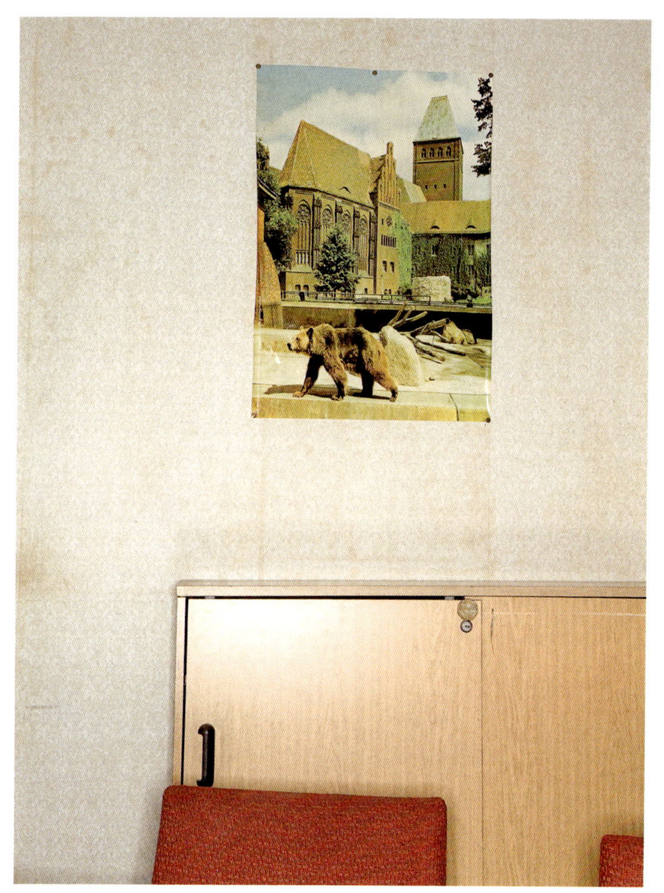

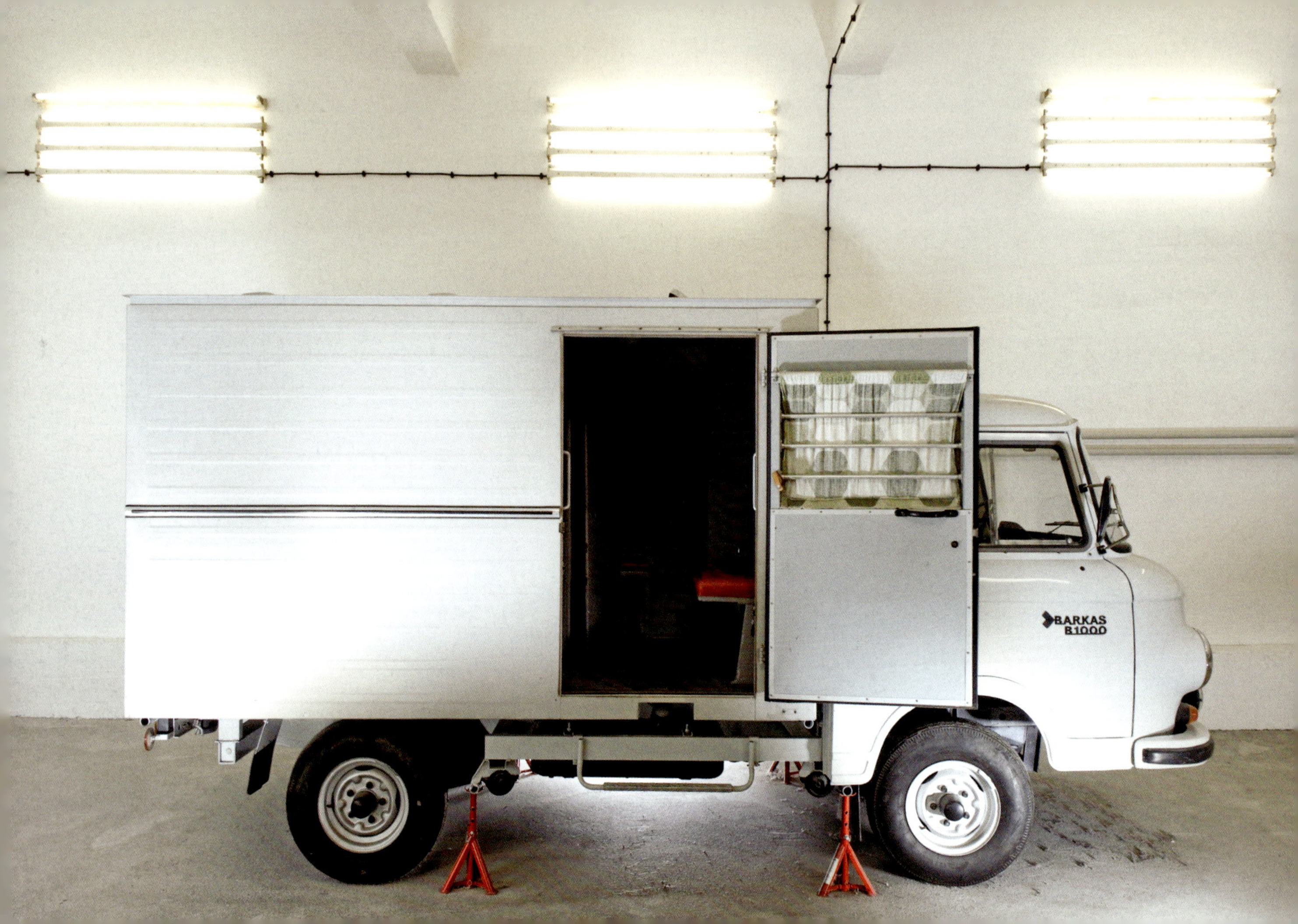

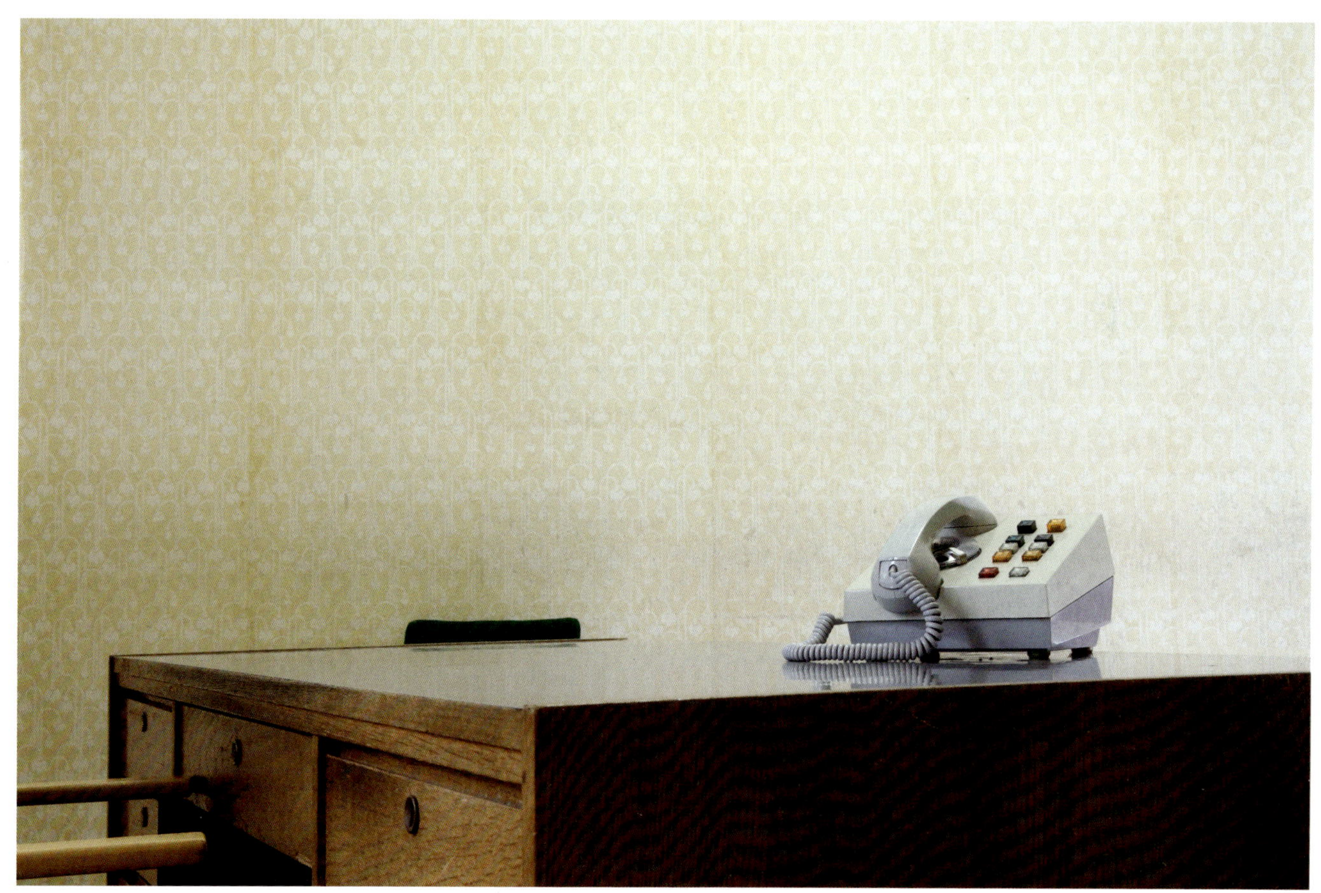

**IM INNEREN HERRSCHT DIE RUHE DER MACHT. SICHERHEITSBEAMTE EMPFANGEN DEN IM KANZLERGARTEN GELANDETEN HUBSCHRAUBER – RÜCKKEHR VON DER SPRITZTOUR AUS POLEN.**

The interior is dominated by the calm of power. Security officials meet the helicopter that has landed in the chancellery garden—the return from a joyride to Poland.

**03** Bundeskanzleramt
*Willy-Brandt-Straße 1 . Berlin-Tiergarten*

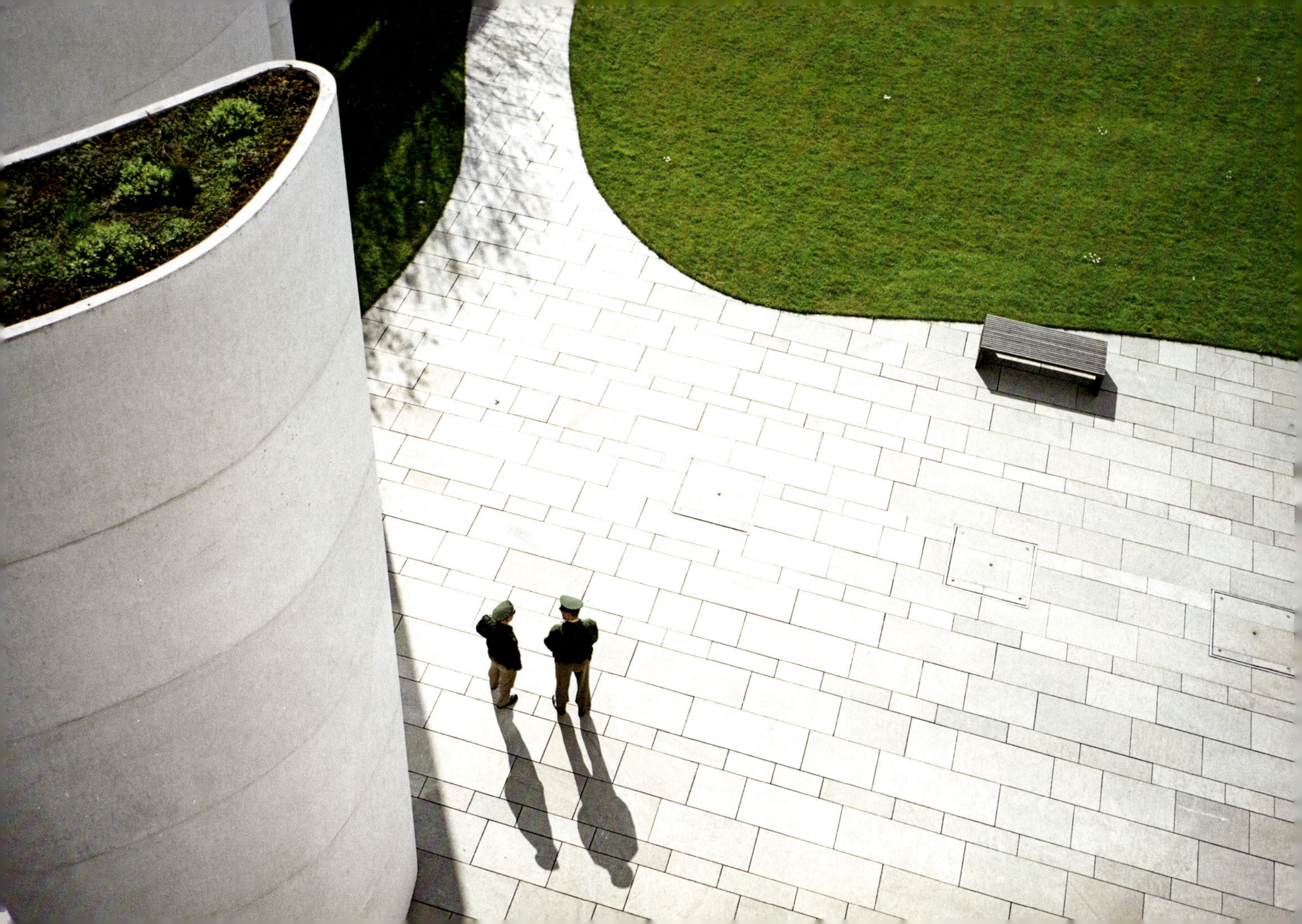

# GRILLEN UNTERM STRAHLTRIEBWERK
## Grilling under the jet engine

**04** **Luftfahrtmuseum Finowfurt**
*Museumsstraße 1 . Schorfheide*

Auf der Startbahn, auf der einst sowjetische MiGs gen Himmel schossen, liefern sich ein Ford Mustang und ein Ford Thunderbird ein Rennen. Die Startflagge fällt. Unter lautem Knattern der V8-Motoren brennt sich das schwarze Gummi in den Asphalt. Nach einer Meile ist das Rennen entschieden – Sieg für den Mustang. Der Rockabilly, der das Spektakel beobachtet hat, grillt vor seinem Armeezelt. In der Luft hängen weißer Rauch und der Geruch von Benzin. Zwischen den ehemaligen Kampfjets der Volksarmee liegt ein Pärchen auf einem Ledersofa. Mittlerweile hat der Fahrer des Ford Mustang seine umherstreunende Dogge eingesammelt und bugsiert sein Gefährt vom Areal. Der Blick ist grimmig, die Tankanzeige steht auf Null.

*On the runway where Soviet MiGs used to take off for the skies, a Ford Mustang is now racing a Ford Thunderbird. The starting flag drops. Black rubber burns its way into the asphalt amidst the loud crackling sound of the V8 motors. The race is decided after a mile; it's a victory for the Mustang. The rockabilly fan observing the spectacle is grilling in front of his army tent. White smoke and the scent of gasoline hang in the air. A couple is lying on a leather sofa between the fighter jets of the former People's Army. The driver of the Ford Mustang has in the meanwhile gathered up his Great Dane that has been roaming about and steers his vehicle away from the area. His glance is grim; the fuel gage shows that he's running on empty.*

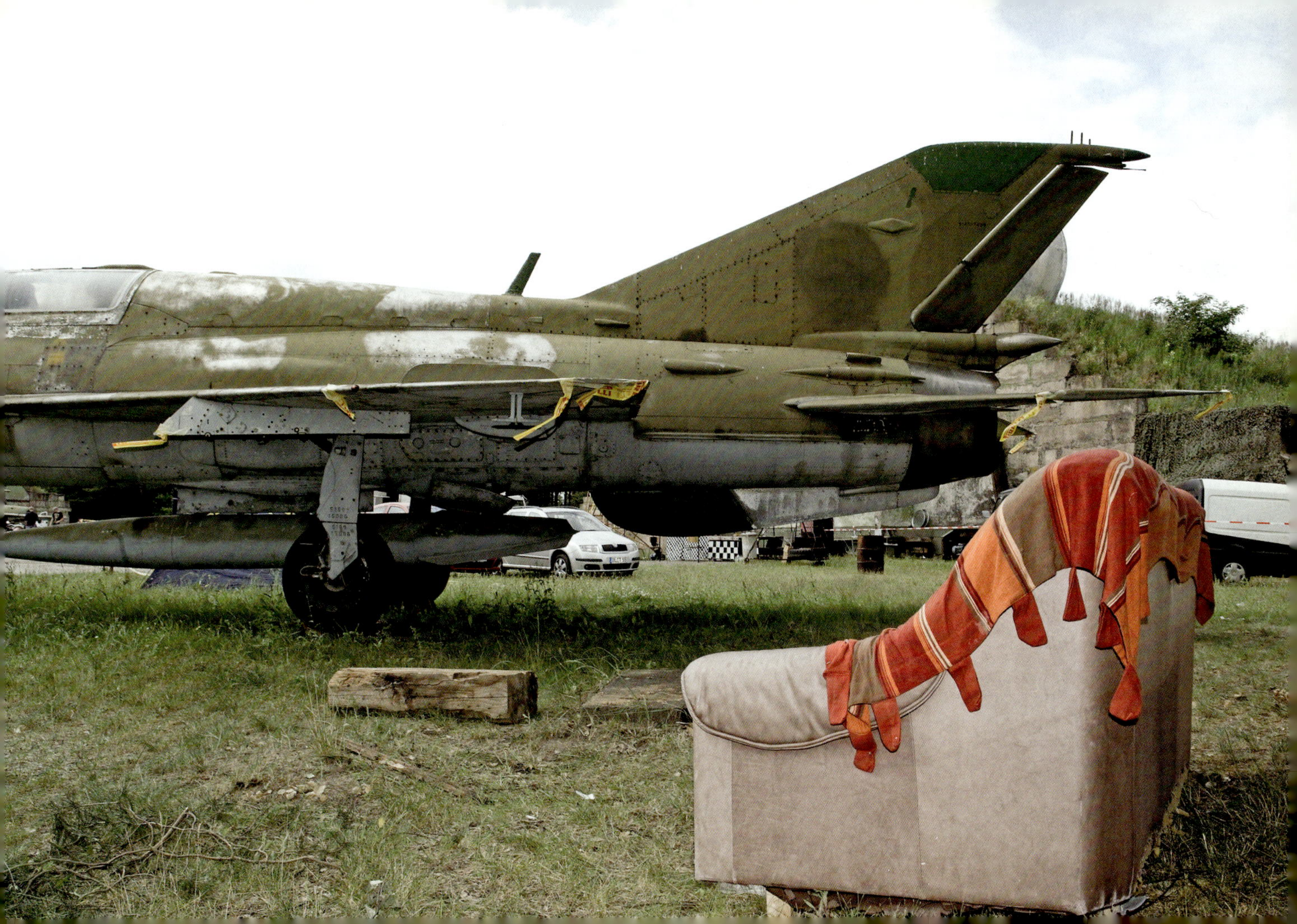

**■■■ MAN ERHASCHT EINEN KURZEN BLICK DURCH
DIE MAUERSCHLITZE. DIE DIESEL LAUFEN, DIE EAST SIDE
GALLERY WARTET.**

*One catches a brief glimpse through the slit in the wall.
The Diesel engines are running; the East Side Gallery waits.*

**05** Gedenkstätte Berliner Mauer
*Bernauer Straße 111 . Berlin-Wedding*

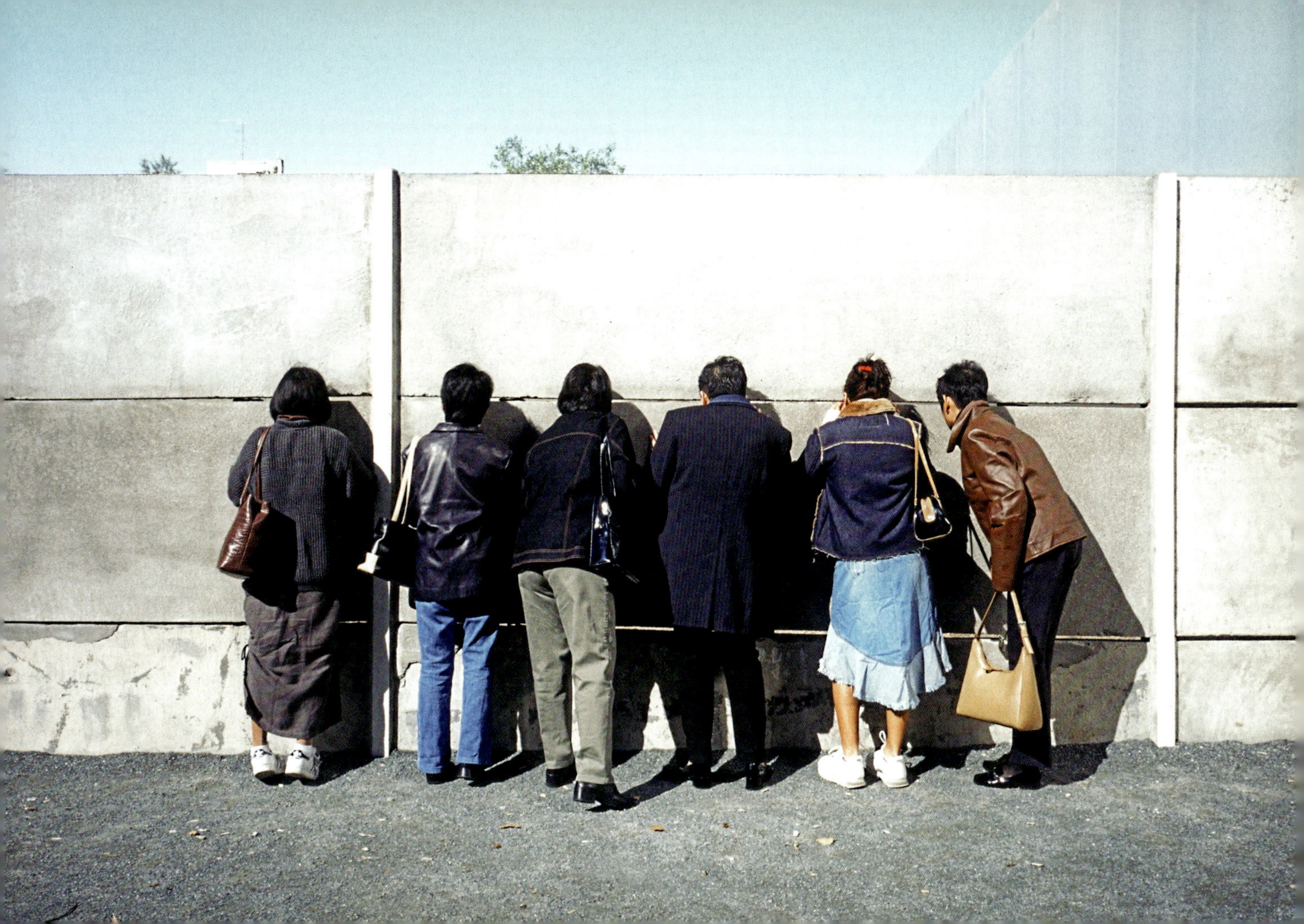

**BÜRGERMEISTER JACK HUNTER HAT OLD TEXAS TOWN FEST IM GRIFF. DAS JAILHOUSE STEHT LEER, UND IM SALOON WIRD SQUAREDANCE GETANZT. RAUCHZEICHEN STEIGEN AUS DER NACHBARSCHAFT AUF — DAS HEIZKRAFTWERK BERLIN-SPANDAU IST UM DIE ECKE.**

*Mayor Jack Hunter runs Old Texas Town like a tight ship. The jail house is vacant and there is square-dancing in the saloon. Smoke signs are rising from the neighborhood—the Berlin-Spandau heat and power station is around the corner.*

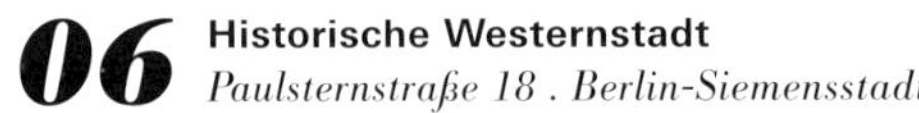

**06** Historische Westernstadt
*Paulsternstraße 18 . Berlin-Siemensstadt*

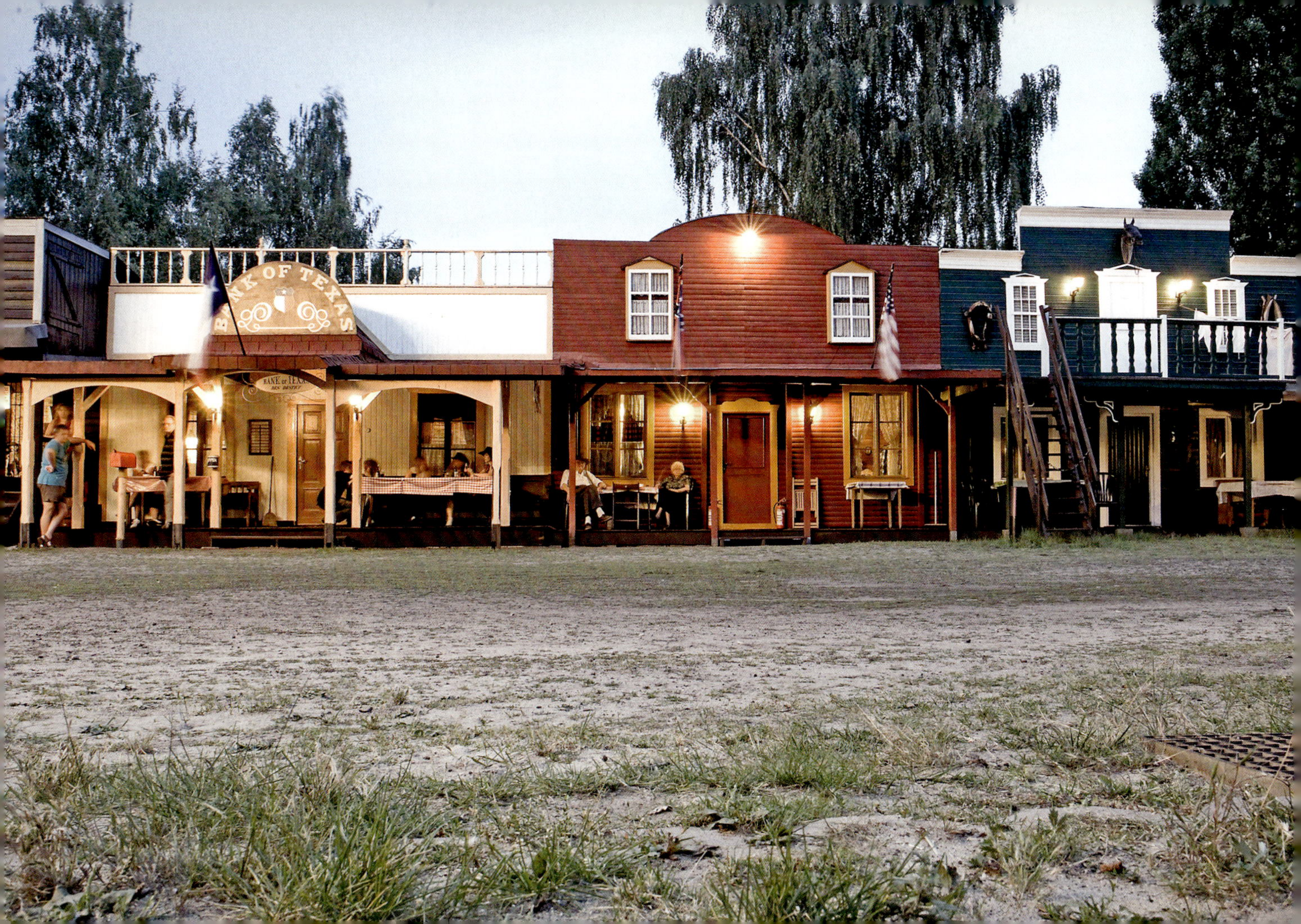

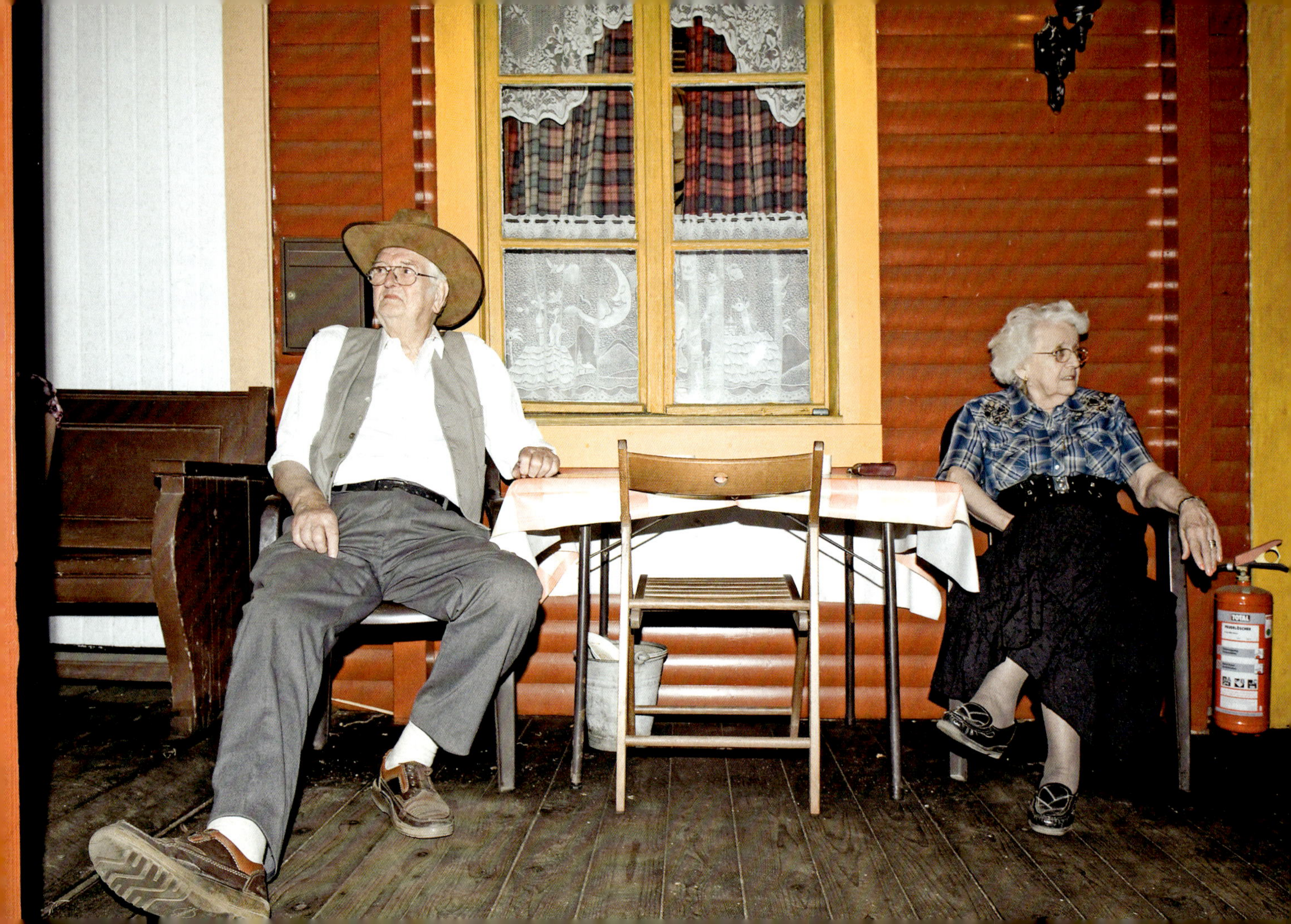

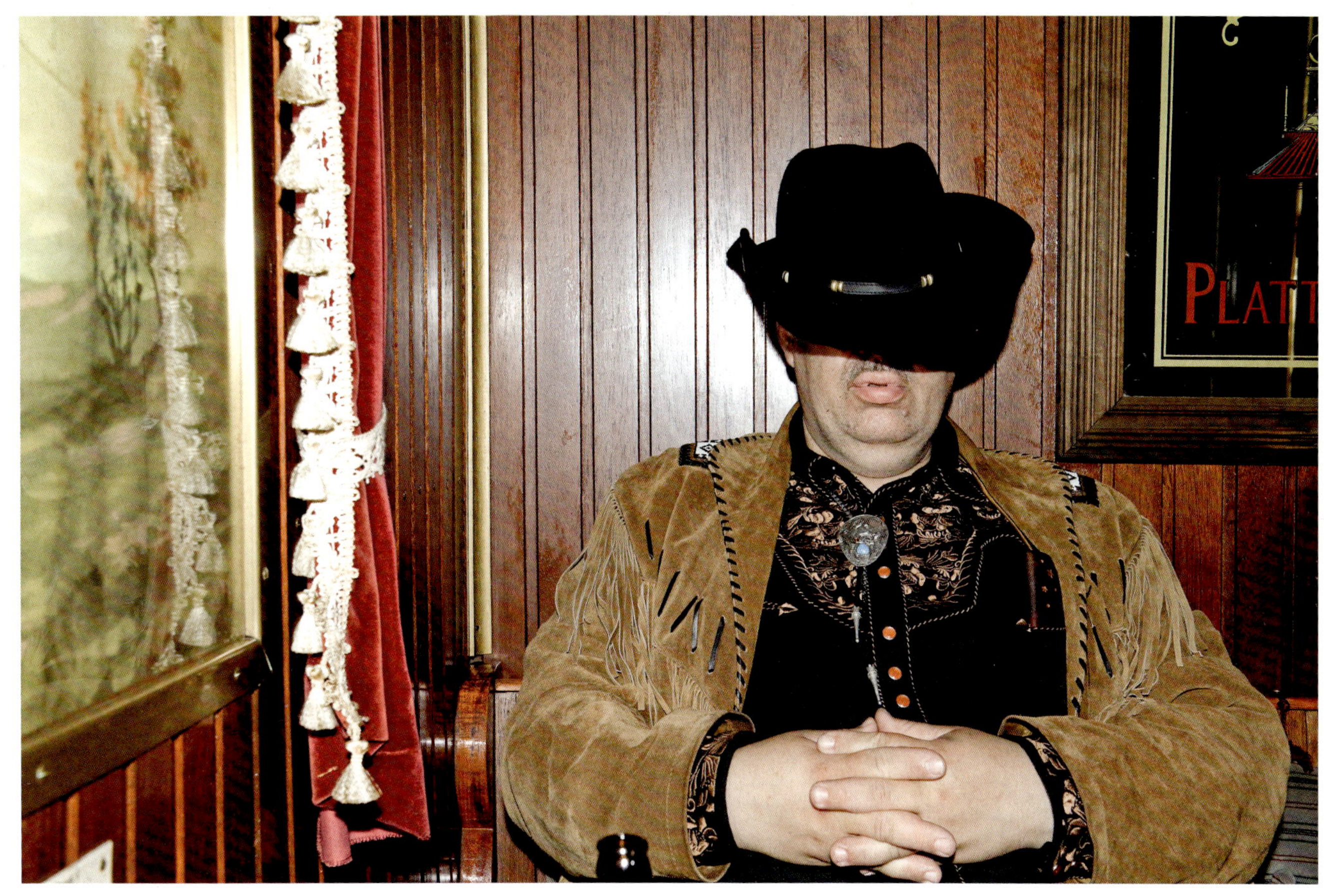
C
PLATT

# KOLONIE GEMÜTLICHKEIT

## Coziness Colony



In einer Berliner Kleingartenanlage: Ein Pächter wirft seinen Rasenmäher an und bearbeitet liebevoll seine Rasenfläche. Der Nachbar regt sich derweil lautstark über das Bundeskleingartengesetz auf, weil seine neu errichtete Laube zwei Quadratmeter mehr misst als gestattet. Seine Frau erkundigt sich inzwischen nach der Verordnung für Massenaufstiege von Kinderballons. Im Vereinsheim einige Lauben weiter hört man vom dröhnenden Rasenmäherlärm und dem Gebrüll nichts. Gelassen sitzt die wöchentliche Diskussionsrunde der Kleingärtner bei Bier und Holunderschorle und plant das Sommerfest mit großer Tombola, als einer laut schreit: »Mensch Udo, meene Bratwürste uf'm Grill, mit denen kann ick jetzt enen verkloppen.«

*On a Berlin allotment site: A tenant fires up his lawnmower and lovingly treats his lawn. The neighbor is simultaneously audibly agitated about the Federal Allotment Garden Law because his recently constructed summer cottage measures two square meters more than is allowed. His wife has informed herself in the meanwhile about the ordinance regarding the mass soaring of children's balloons. The droning of the lawn mower and the bellowing is not audible in the club house a few cottages down the path. The weekly discussion group of allotment gardeners sits calmly over beer and elderberry spritzer and plans the summer party and raffle when someone yells: "Jeez Udo, my sausages on the grill, I can give someone his comeuppance with them."*

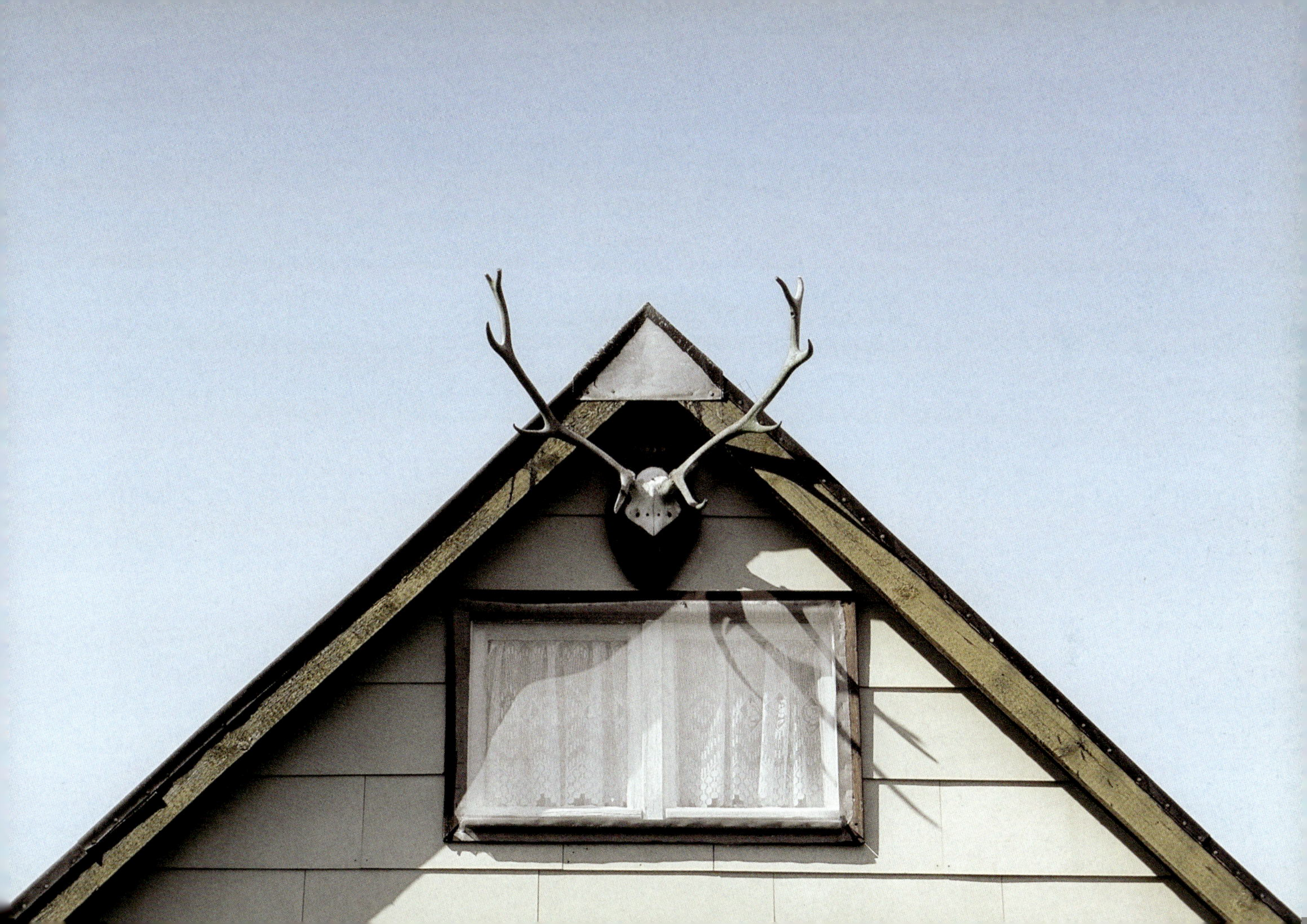

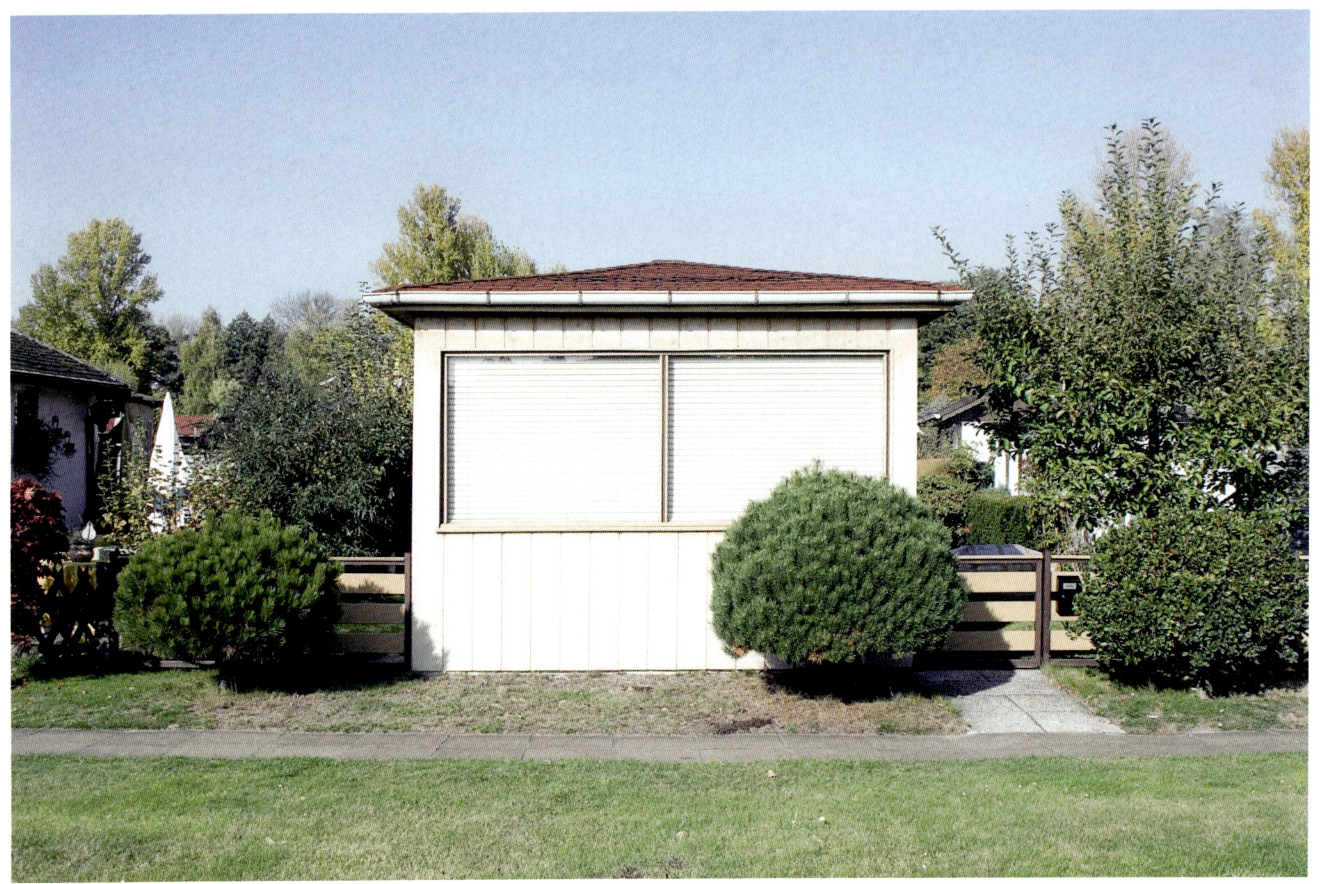

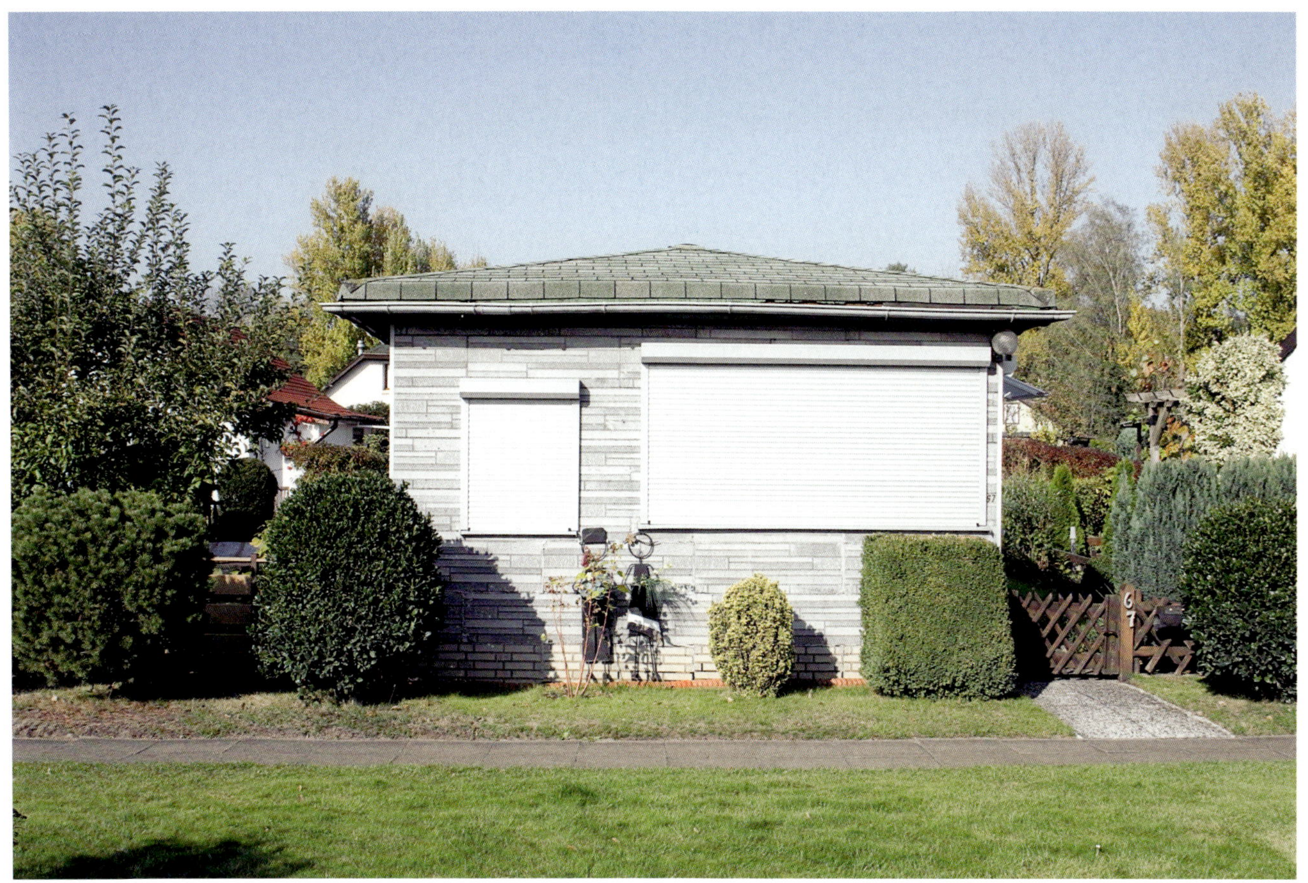

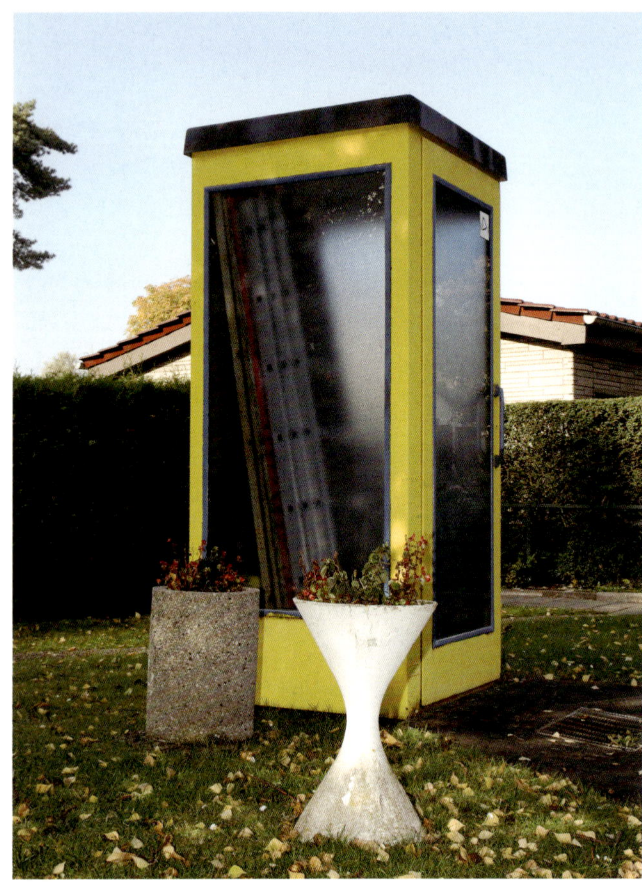

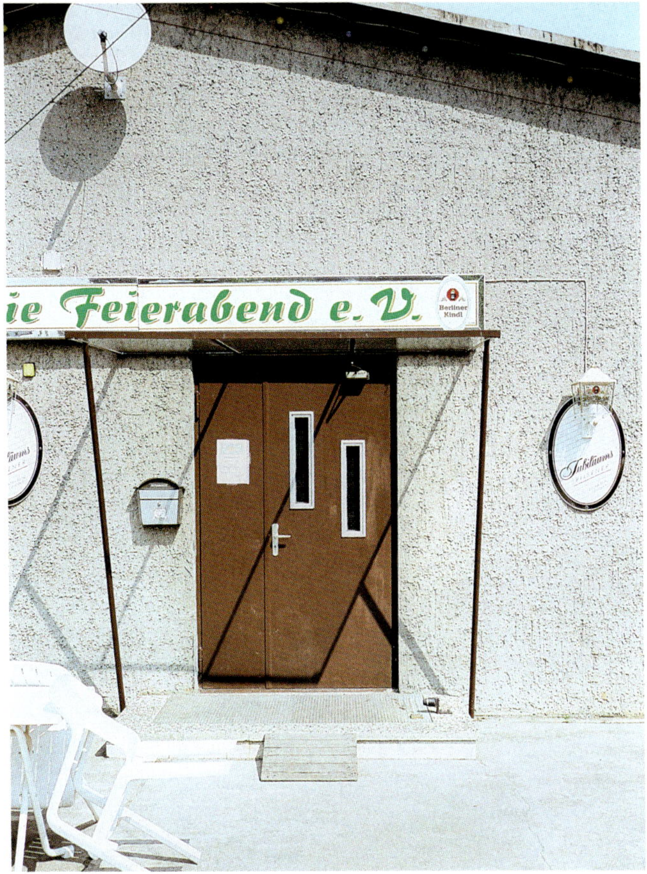

ie Feierabend e. V.
Berliner Kindl

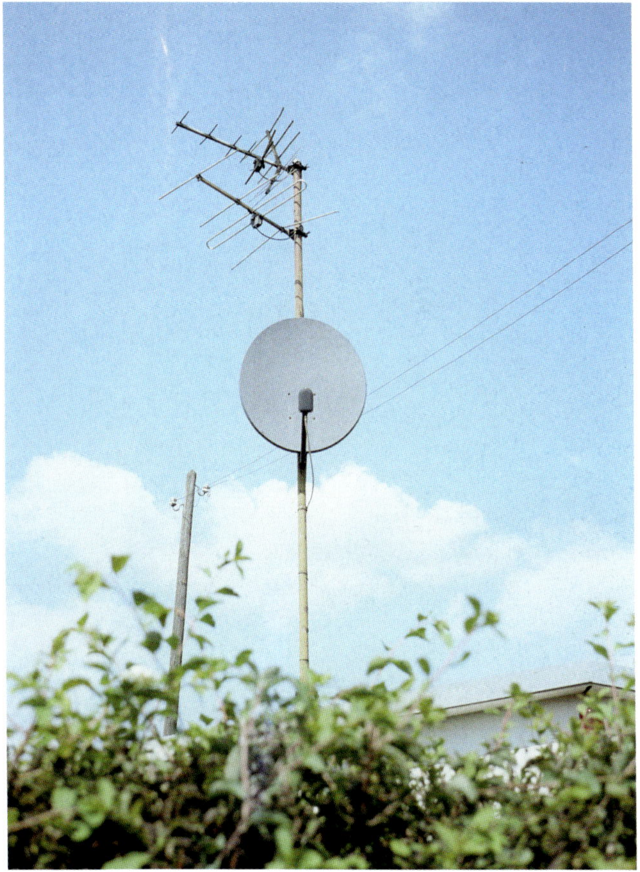

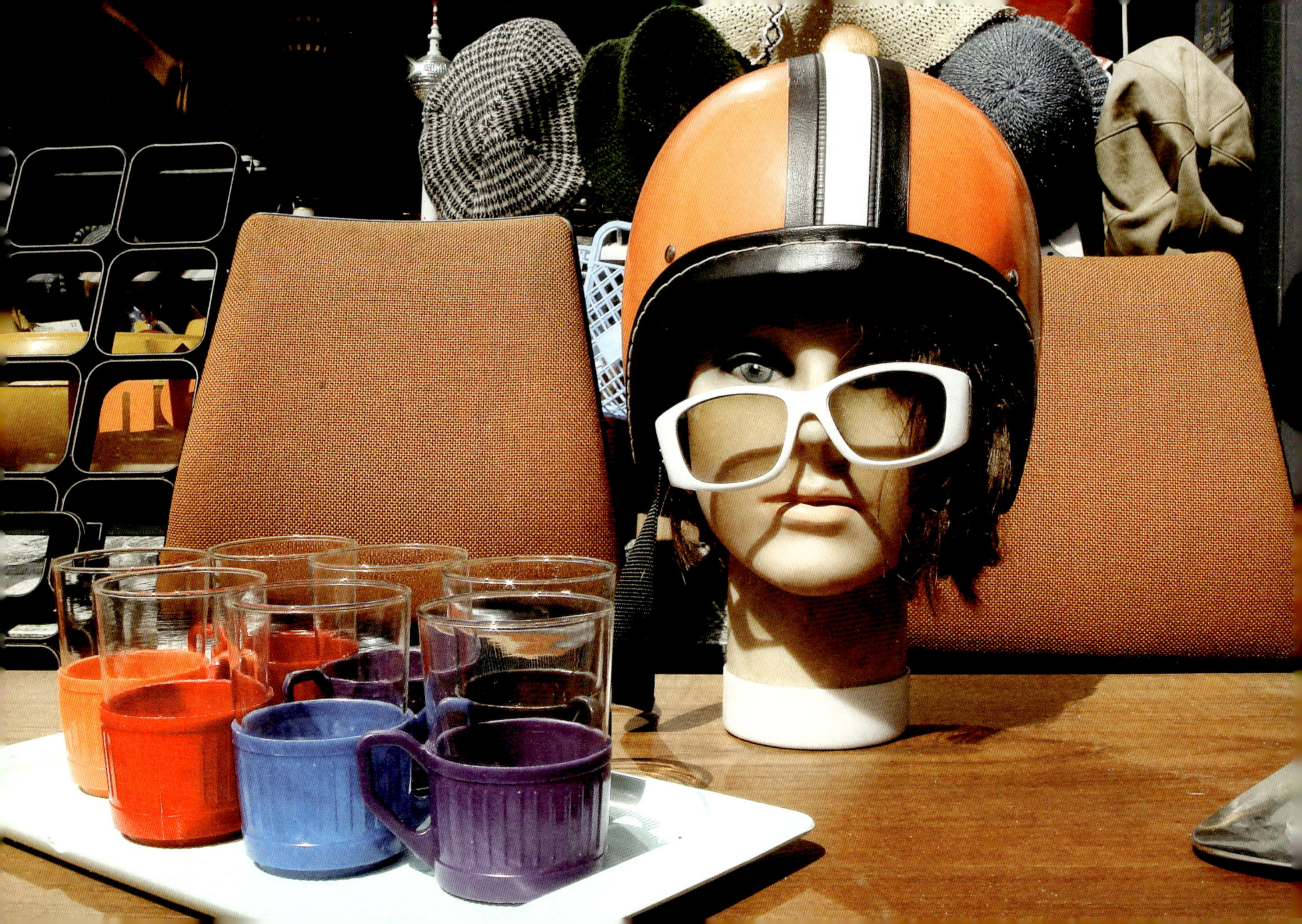

# PRENZLAUER BERG: SCHWÄBISCHE INVASIONEN UND SECOND HAND AM MAUERPARK

## Prenzlauer Berg: Swabian invasions and second-hand shops at Mauerpark

Karaoke und Homorodeln im Mauerpark, Diabolospiel und Biosupermarktketten, Gulaschkanone am Kollwitzplatz, Kitas und junge Familien, Junggesellenabende bei Bonner Zahnärzten, Anti-Schwabendemos und Walpurgisnachtfeuer, Bummeln in der Castingallee, Partyrausch im LSD-Viertel.

*Karaoke and gay tobogganing in Mauerpark, diabolo juggling and organic-food supermarket chains, field kitchens at Kollwitzplatz, daycare centers and young families, stag parties at dentists from Bonn, anti-Swabian demonstrations and Walpurgis Night bonfires, strolling on Castingallee, intoxicating partying in the LSD district at Lychener, Schliemann, and Duncker Streets.*

# IN DEN FENSTERN DES EHEMALIGEN WACHHÄUSCHENS SPIEGELT SICH DIE NEONREKLAME DER UMLIEGENDEN SCHNELLIMBISSE. AN DEN SOUVENIRSTÄNDEN KAUFEN SICH BESUCHER RUSSISCHE OFFIZIERSMÜTZEN.

*The neon signs of the neighboring fast-food restaurant reflect in the former guardhouse windows. Visitors buy Russian officers' caps at the souvenir stands.*

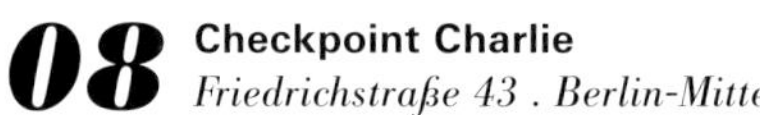

**08 Checkpoint Charlie**
*Friedrichstraße 43 . Berlin-Mitte*

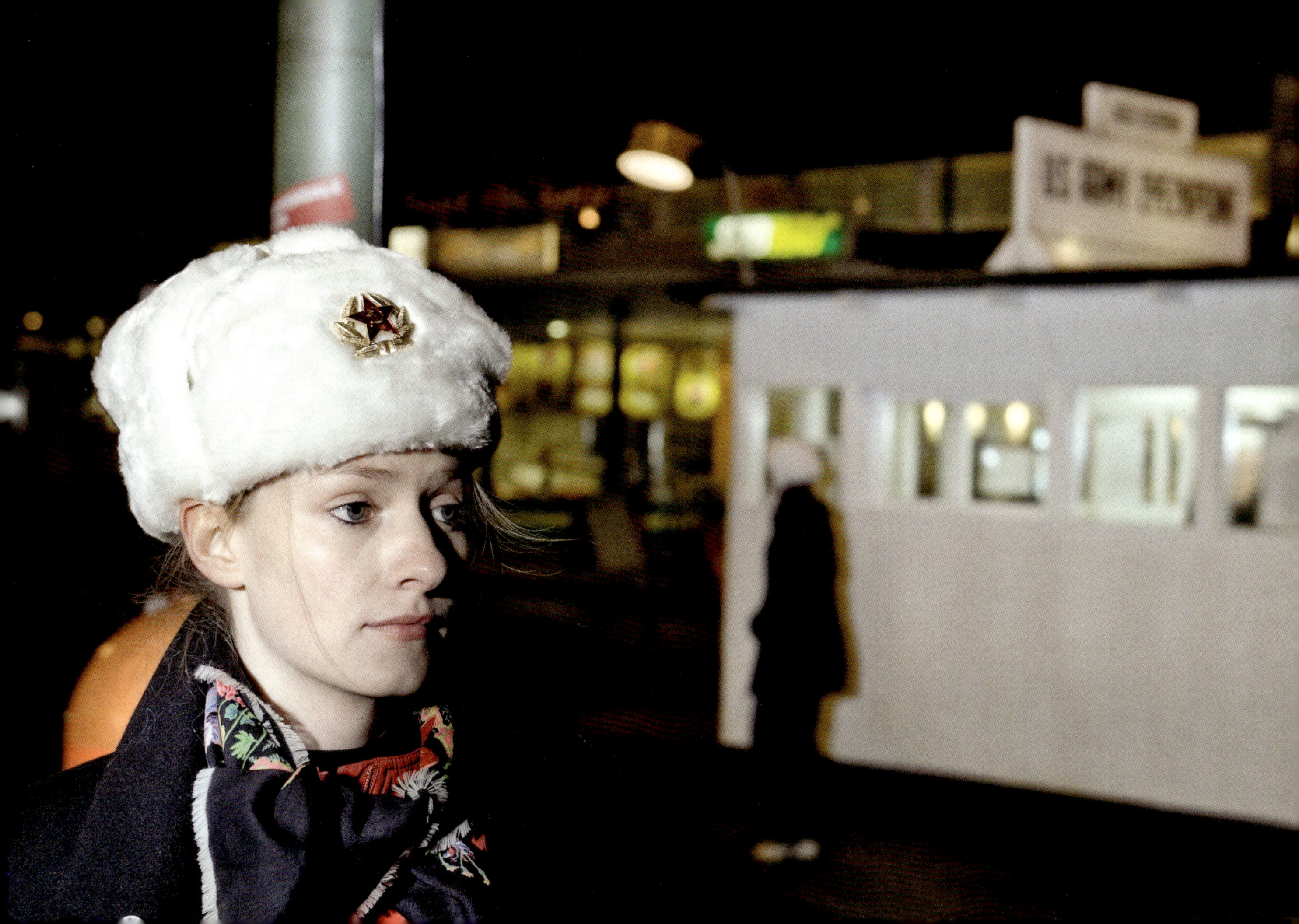

# BALL PARADOX IM CAFÉ KEESE
## Paradox Ball at Café Keese

**09** **Café Keese**
*Bismarckstraße 108 . Berlin-Charlottenburg*

»Ball Paradox, das heißt hier, seit 1966 haben die Damen das Sagen«, ruft ein Mittfünfziger und verschwindet im Eingang des Tanzcafés. Drinnen tanzen Pärchen im 1960er-Jahre-Interieur. Aus dem Mikrofon ertönt es sanft: »Meine Herren, lassen Sie die Damen spüren, dass Sie führen.« Die Herren zeigen nun ihr Können mit den Tanzschritten Achterbahn, Expander und Körbchen. Die Damen quietschen vergnügt. An den schwach beleuchteten Tischen wirft man sich derweil sehnsuchtsvolle Blicke zu. Ein Herr im grünen Anzug überwindet sich und greift zum Tischtelefon, um die Dame an Tisch 48 zum Tanz aufzufordern, während deren Nachbarin freudig mitteilt: »Meine Schwiegermutter bevorzugt den Tanztee für die Junggebliebenen.«

*"Paradox Ball, that means here that women have had the say around here since 1966," a gentleman in his mid-fifties calls out and disappears into the entrance of the dance café. Inside, couples are dancing in a nineteen-sixties interior. A soft voice speaks into the microphone: "Gentlemen, let the ladies feel that you're leading." And so the gentlemen now display their prowess with the rollercoaster, expander and box steps. The ladies squeal with pleasure. Yearning glances are being exchanged in the meanwhile at the dimly illuminated tables. A gentleman dressed in a green suit musters up all his courage and reaches for the table telephone to ask the lady at table 48 for the next dance while her neighbor joyfully exclaims: "My mother-in-law prefers the tea dances for the young-at-heart."*

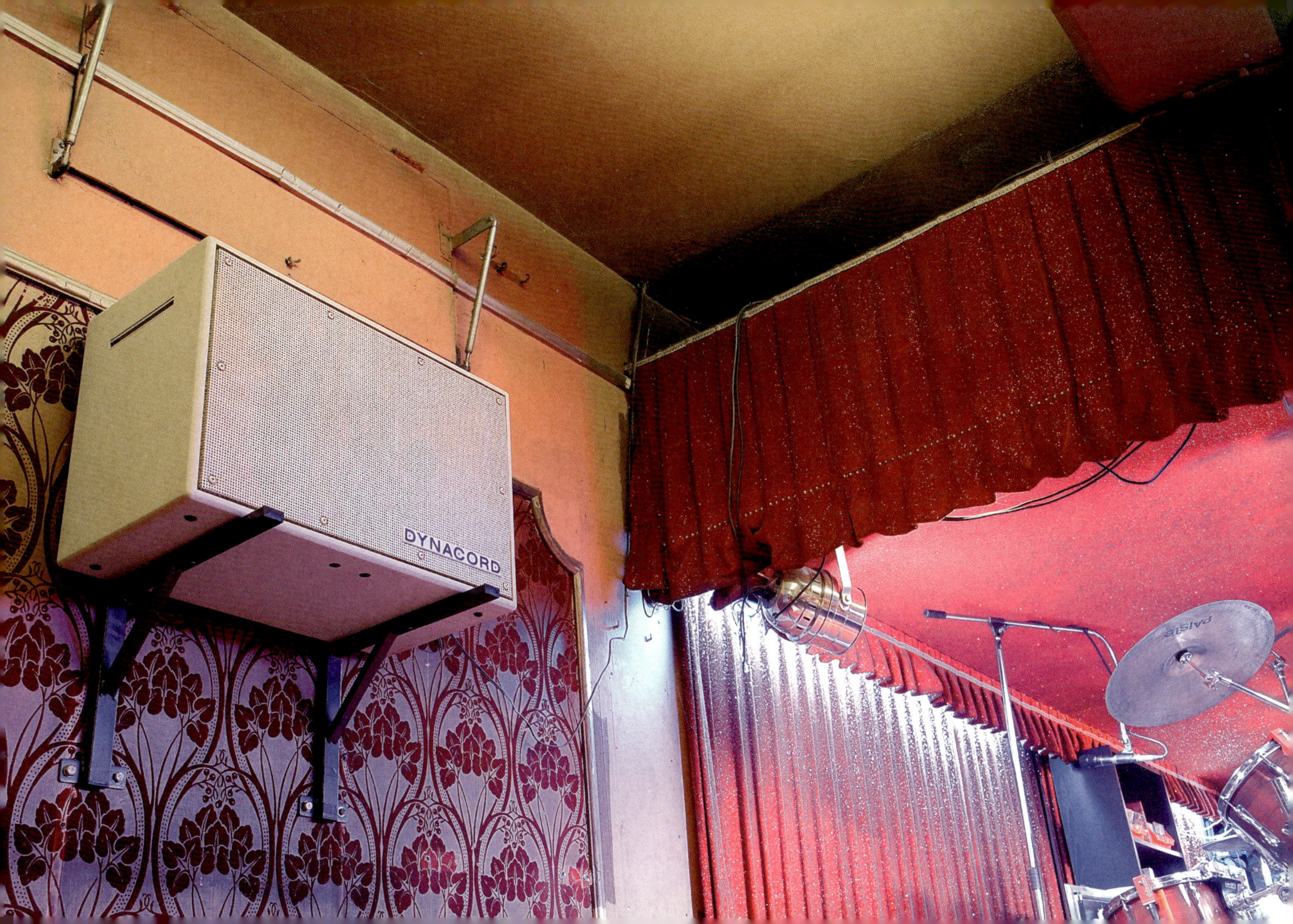

DYNACORD

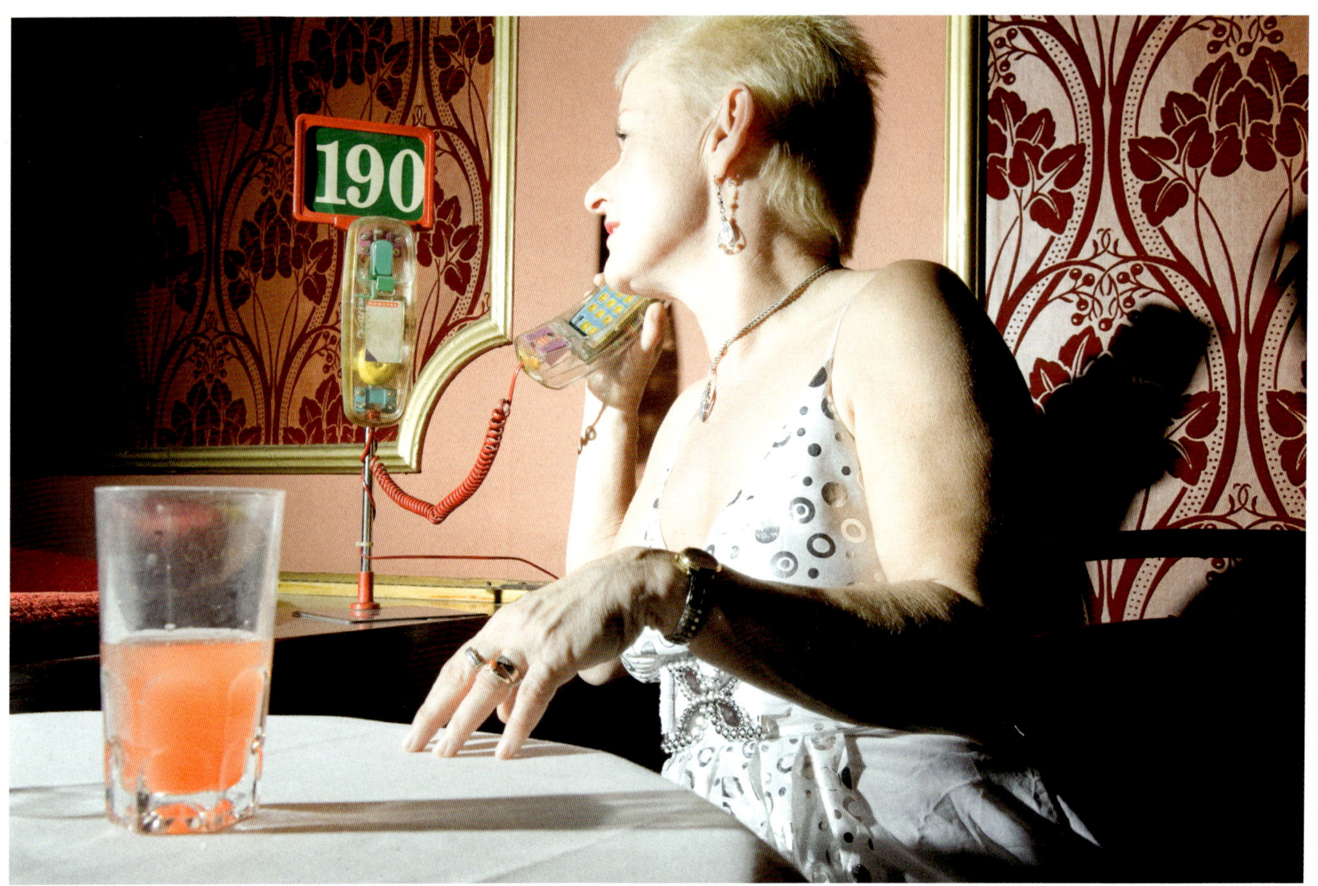
190

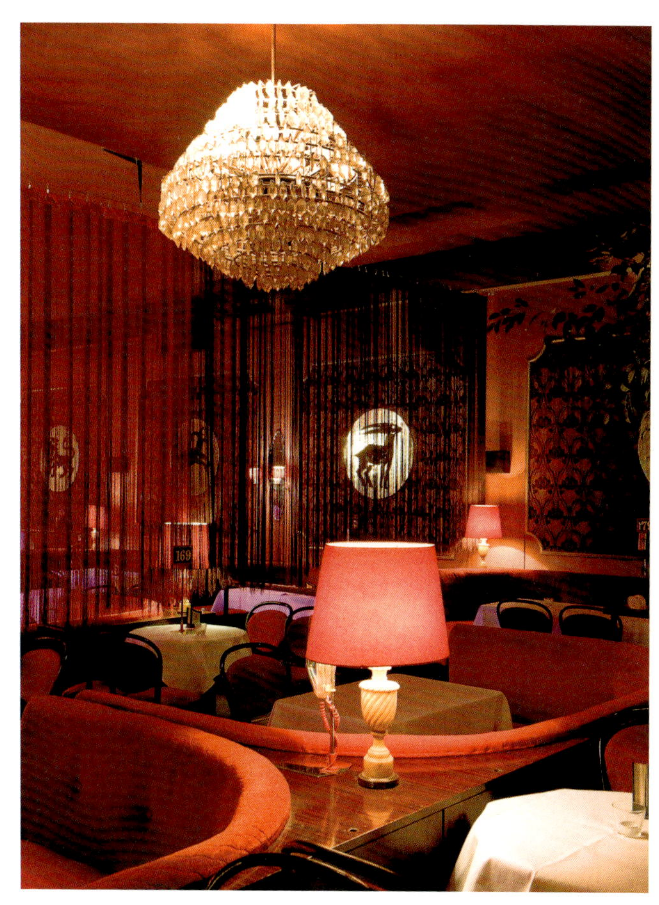

# »JETZT LEG ICH 'NEN SCHÖNEN LANGSAMEN DISCOFOX AUF.«

*"I'm now going to put on a nice slow discofox."*

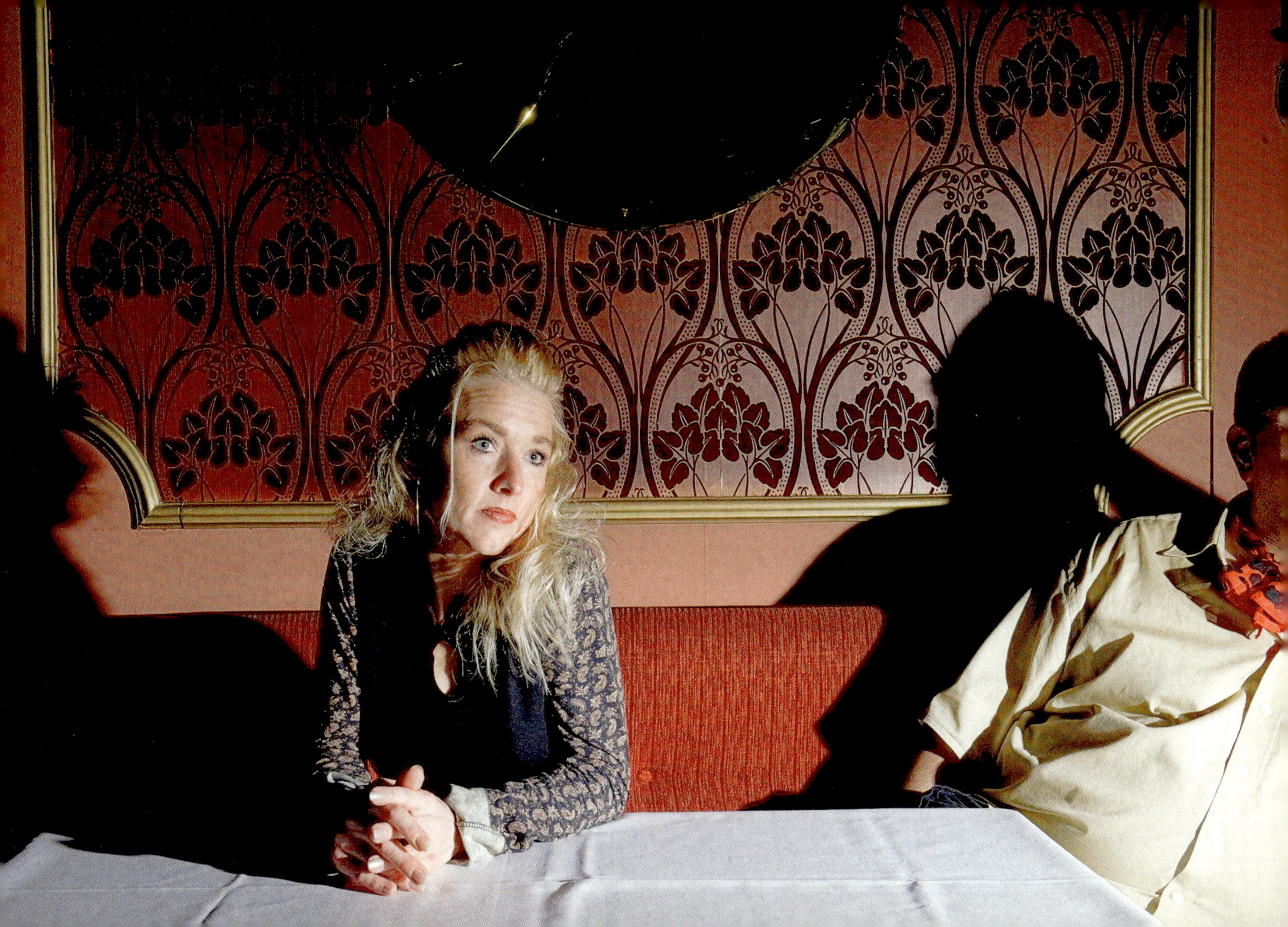

# OB TÜRKISCHE HOCHZEIT ODER SWINGERCLUB: WEDDINGER PRÊT-À-PORTER

*Whether Turkish wedding or swinger club:*
*prêt-à-porter in Wedding*

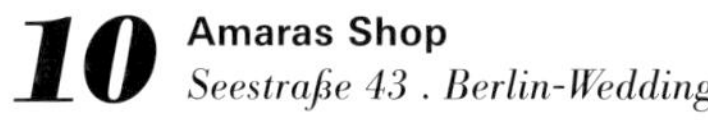

**10** **Amaras Shop**
*Seestraße 43 . Berlin-Wedding*

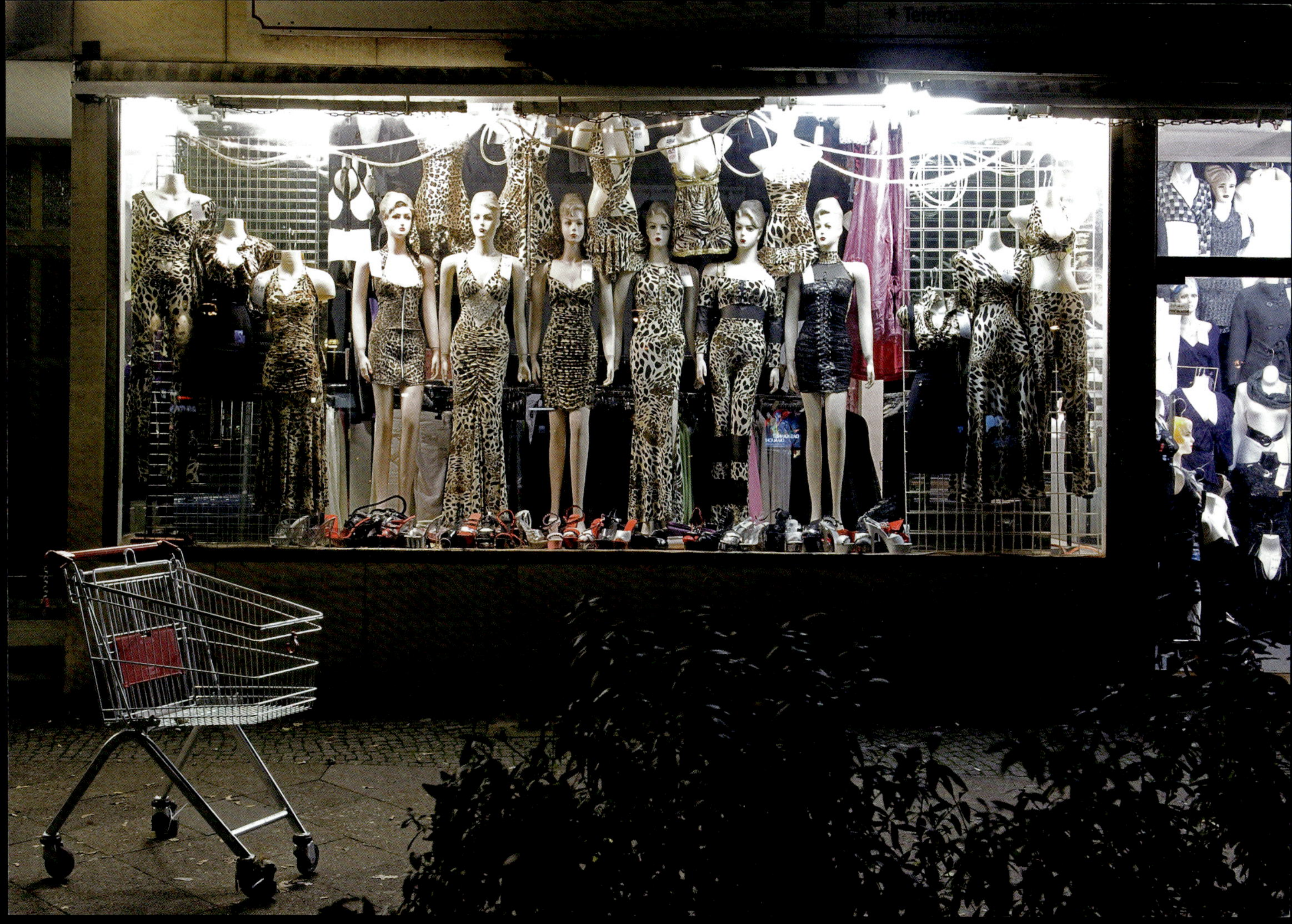

**DAS SPIEL IST AUS, DIE FUSSBALLFANS HABEN DAS AREAL VERLASSEN. EIN KLEINER SCHWARZER PUDEL WARTET ANGEBUNDEN AN EINEM DER GROSSEN PFEILER, ZWISCHEN DENEN DIE RINGE DER OLYMPISCHEN SPIELE AUS DEM JAHR 1936 HÄNGEN.**

*The game is over; the fans have left the arena. A small black poodle waits outside where it is leashed to one of the large pillars between which the rings from the 1936 Olympic Games hang.*

**11** Olympiastadion
*Olympischer Platz 3 . Berlin-Charlottenburg*

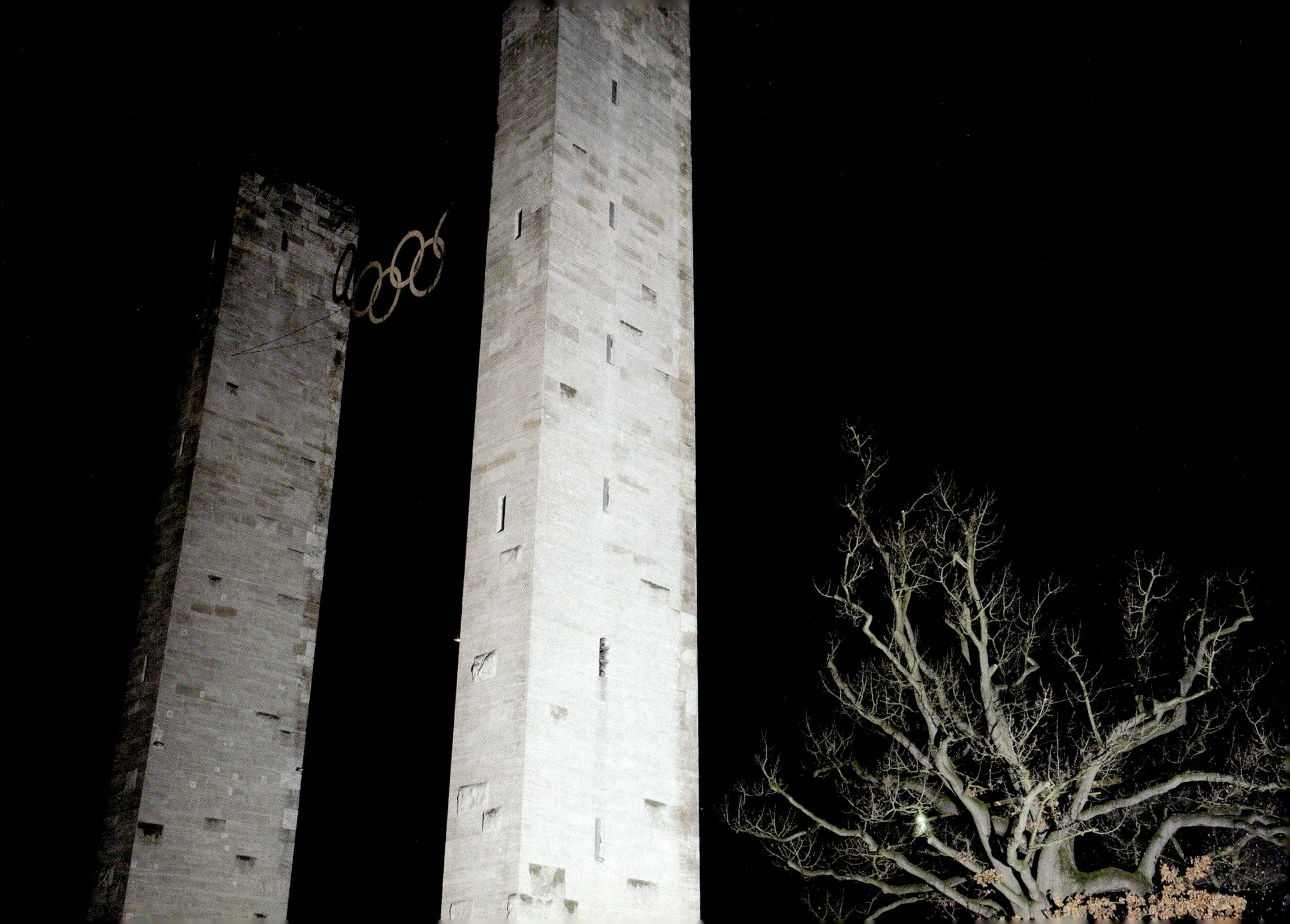

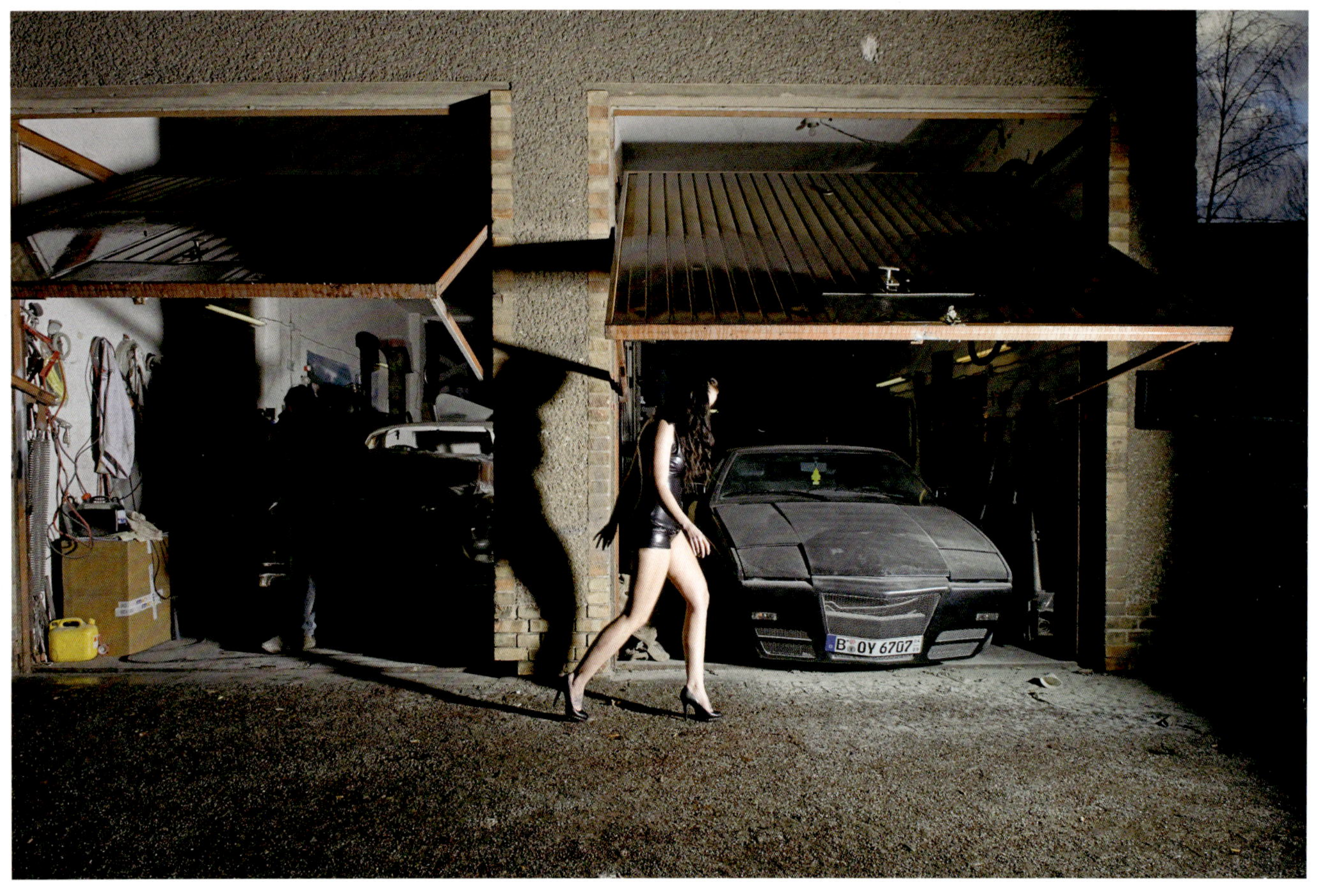

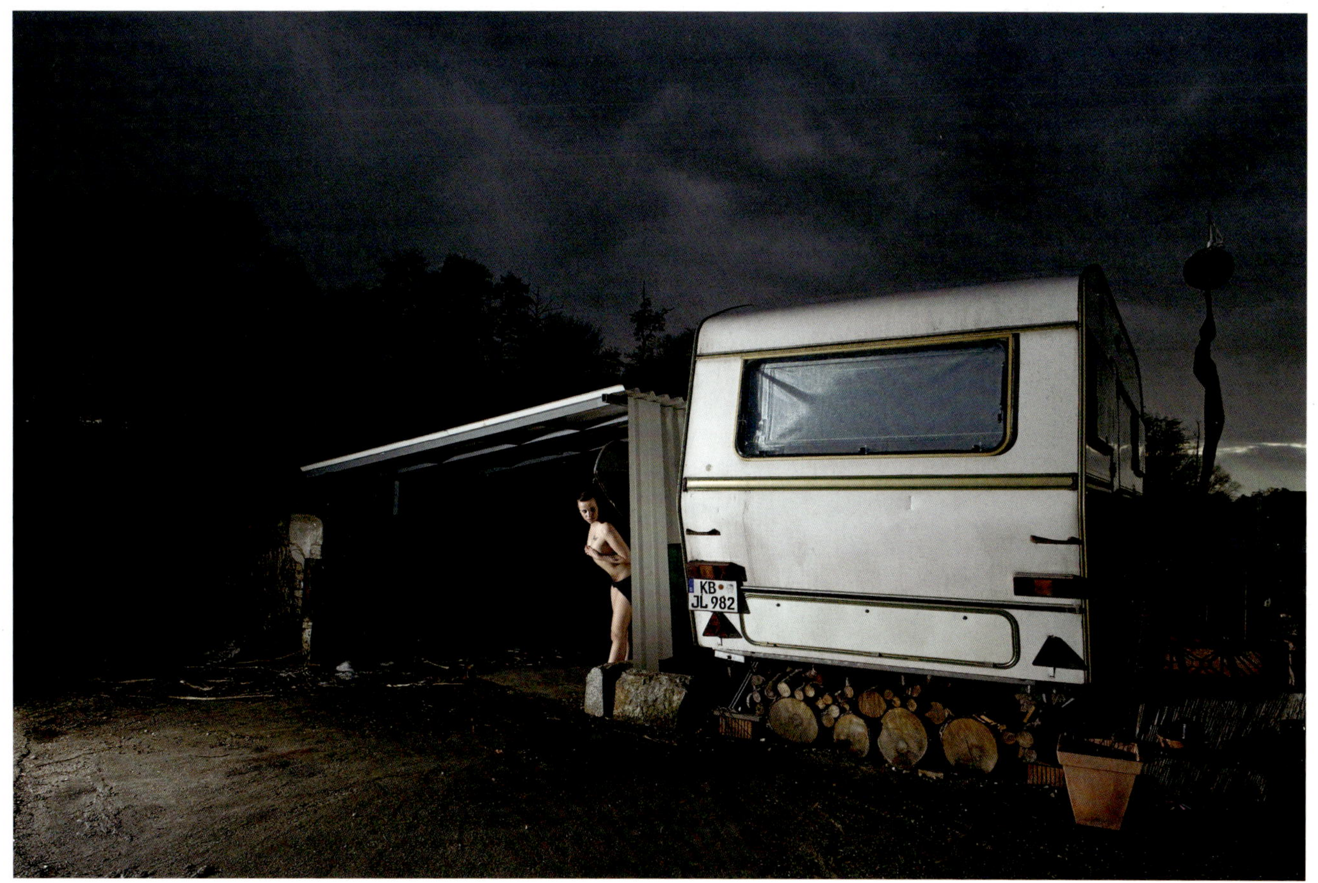

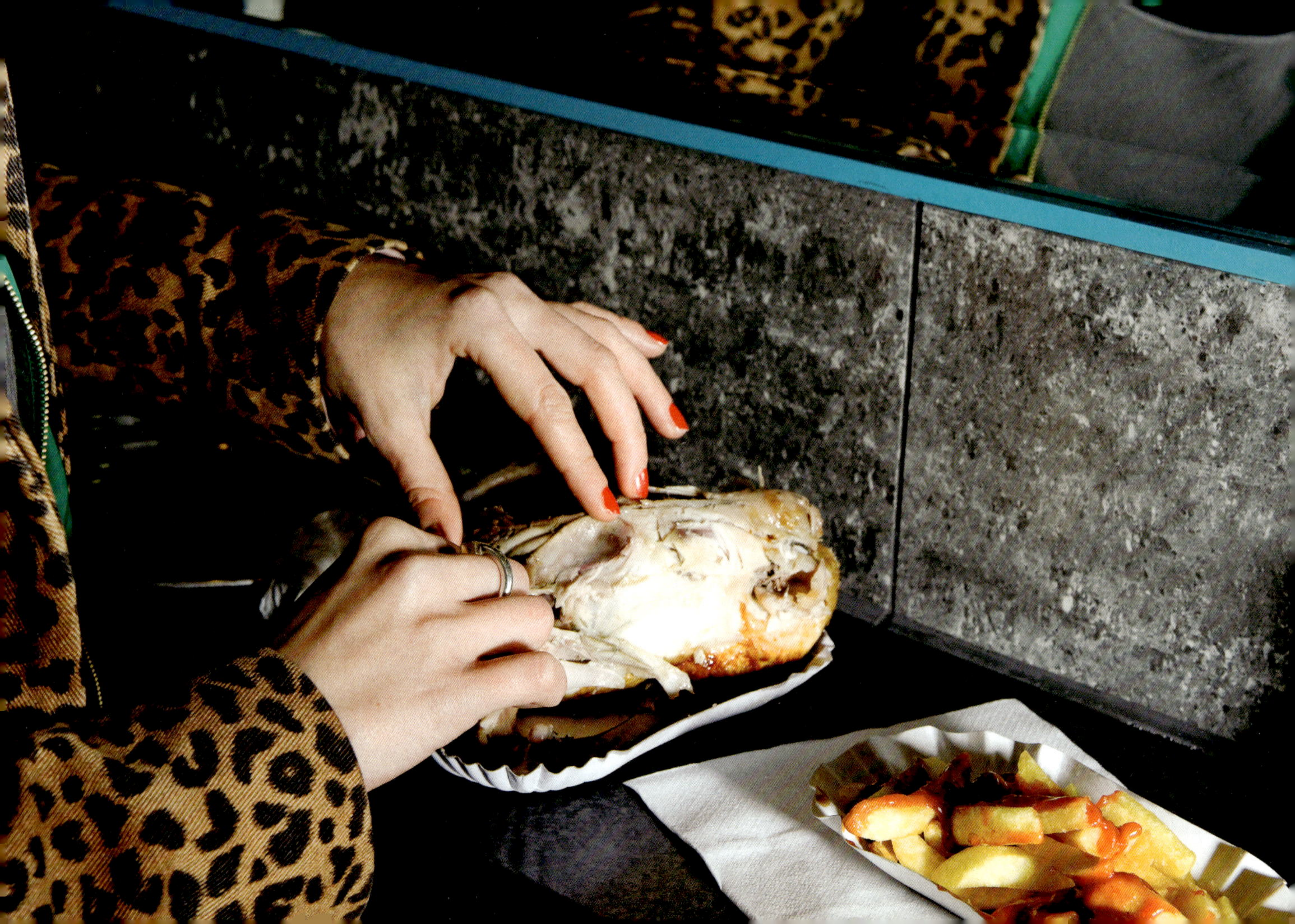

FRIEDRICHSHAIN:
ZWEIRAUMWOHNUNG, ZUCKERBÄCKERSTIL,
ELEKTRO-TRASH DER DDR

# FRIEDRICHSHAIN: ZWEIRAUMWOHNUNG, ZUCKERBÄCKERSTIL, ELEKTRO-TRASH DER DDR

## Friedrichshain:
## Two-room apartment, gingerbread style, East German electronic trash

Kneipenviertel und ehemalige Besetzerszene, Freilichtbühne im Volkspark, Dartshow in der O$_2$ World, Gentrifizierungsprozesse und urbane Lässigkeit am Boxhagener Platz, Hundekot und wild Plakatieren, die Schwimmhalle im SEZ, Friedhof der März-gefallenen und Frankfurter Tor.

*Bar district and former home of the squatter scene, open-air theater in the Volkspark, dart show in the O$_2$ World, gentrification processes and urban nonchalance on Boxhagener Platz, dog shit and flyposting, the swimming pool at the Sports and Recreation Center, the Cemetery for the Victims of the March 1848 Revolution and Frankfurter Tor.*

# KARNICKEL IM JAGDREVIER
## Rabbits in the hunting ground



Die hell leuchtenden Bürotürme des Potsdamer Platzes werfen ihr Licht durch die kahlen Bäume des angrenzenden dunklen Tiergartens. Die frische Schneedecke ist von Kaninchenspuren durchzogen. Das Rascheln des gefrorenen Laubes verrät, wer die wirklichen Herrscher des Parks sind, deren Population im Laufe der Jahre dramatisch anstieg. Ein großer Dobermann hat Witterung aufgenommen und setzt zur Verfolgung eines flüchtenden Karnickels an. Die Pfiffe des Herrchens finden kein Gehör. Die Hatz verliert sich im Gebüsch, aus dem der Hund mit schneebedecktem Kopf bellend zurückkehrt. Im Rosengarten inmitten des Parks erinnern bronzene Hirschskulpturen an Zeiten, in denen der preußische Adel auf Treibjagd ging.

*The brightly illuminated office towers on Potsdamer Platz cast their light through the leafless trees of the adjacent dark Tiergarten. The fresh blanket of snow is covered with rabbit tracks. The rustling of the frozen leaves betray who the real rulers of the park are and whose population has grown dramatically over the years. A large Doberman has gotten wind of a fleeing rabbit and sets off in pursuit. His master's whistles land on deaf ears. The chase ends up in the shrubbery from which the dog emerges, yelping with a snow-covered head. Bronze statues of stags in the rose garden at the center of the park recall the days when the Prussian nobility still took part in the hunt.*

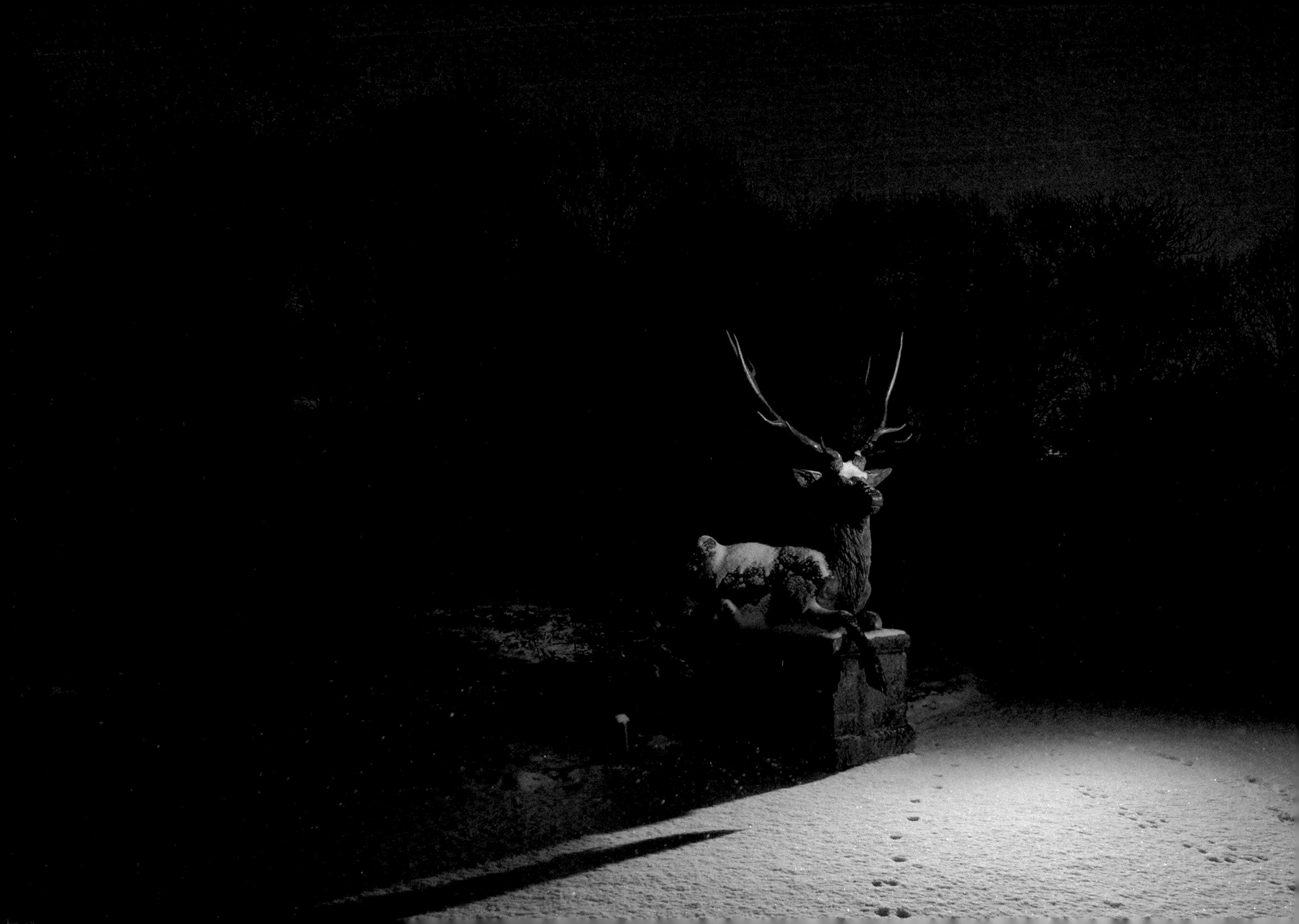

# NARKOSE, TUPFER, LUFTALARM
## *Anesthesia, swabs, air-raid alarm*

**13** **Operationsbunker**
*Teichstraße . Berlin-Reinickendorf*

Das kalte Licht der großen Lampe erhellt den grün gekachelten Raum, in dem einst Verwundete auf dem OP-Tisch behandelt wurden. Selbst während eines Luftangriffs bestand die Möglichkeit, in den gas- und bombensicheren Räumen zu operieren. Durch einen unterirdischen Verbindungsgang mit dem damaligen Humboldt-Krankenhaus gelangte man direkt in den Bunker. Im Vorraum hängt noch immer der weiße Arztkittel neben dem Medizinschrank, gefüllt mit braunen Arzneiflaschen, Mullbinden und Spritzen. Im Nebenraum erinnern große zylinderförmige Behälter zur Desinfektion des Bestecks an das Geschehen von damals. Der Kasten am Ausgang mit der roten Aufschrift »Luftschutz Hausapotheke« lässt erahnen: Reinickendorf war für den Ernstfall gerüstet.

*The cold light of the large lamps illuminates the green-tiled room where the wounded were once treated on the operating table. It was even possible to operate in the gas- and bomb-proof rooms during air raids. The bunker could be accessed from the former Humboldt Hospital through an underground corridor. The white doctor's coat still hangs next to the medicine cabinet filled with brown medicine bottles, gauze bandages, and syringes. A large cylinder-shaped container to disinfect the operating equipment recalls the occurrences of those times. The box at the exit inscribed "Air Raid Medicine Chest" in red letters allows one the conjecture that Reinickendorf was prepared for the worst-case scenario.*

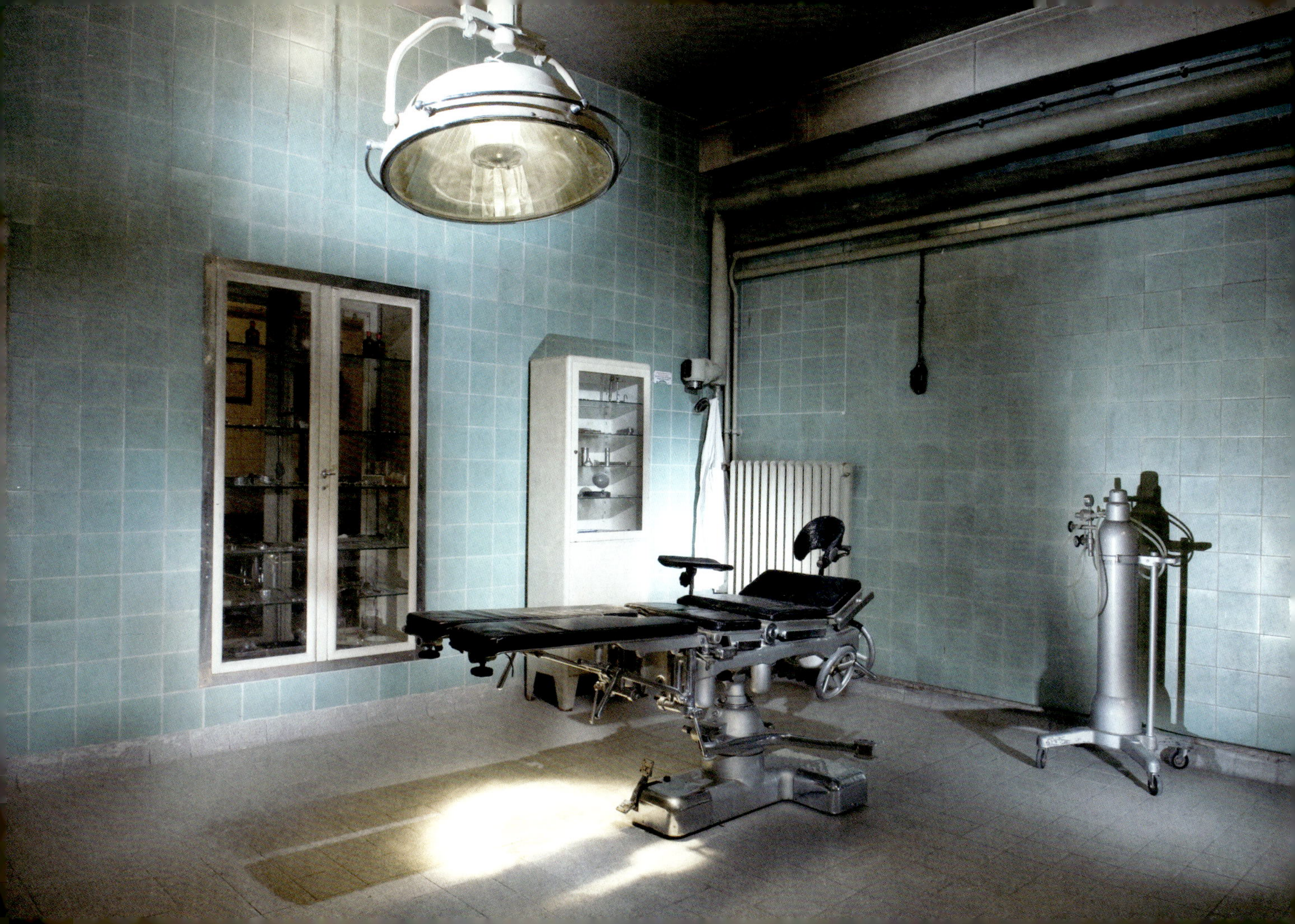

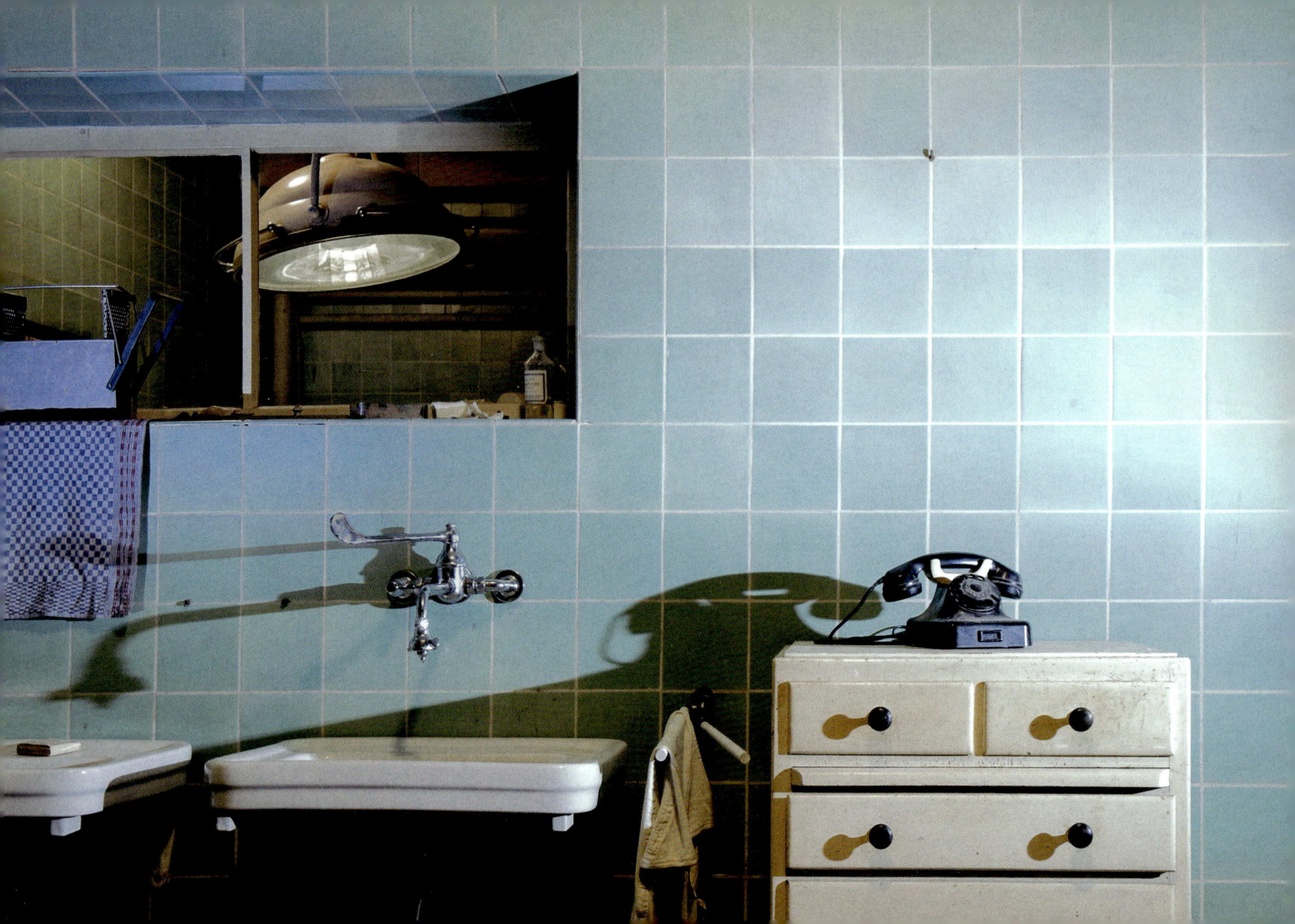

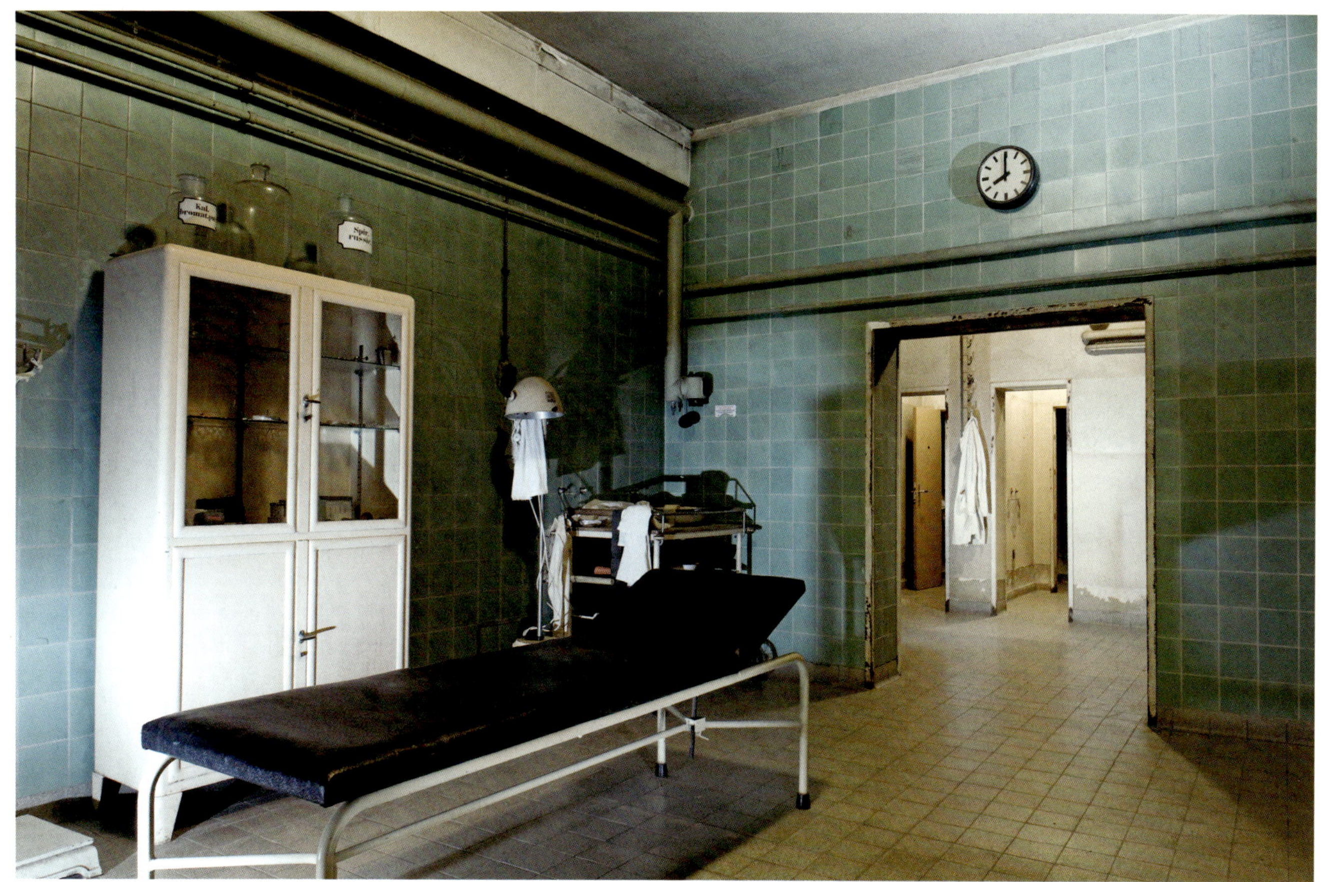
Kal.
bromat.
Spir.
russ.

# PAILLETTEN UND TUTU
## Sequins and tutus



»Noch fünf Minuten bis Showbeginn«, tönt es aus den Lautsprechern. In der Maske sitzt eine Gruppe Tänzerinnen auf großen Schminksesseln. Ein Mädchen klebt sich vor einem Spiegel ihre falschen Wimpern an. Im Stauraum hinter der Bühne geht eine Tänzerin im weißen Bodysuit mit Paillettenaufsätzen noch einmal trippelnd die Tanzschritte ihres bevorstehenden Auftritts durch. Die Show beginnt. Neonröhren tauchen den Backstage-Bereich in blaues Licht. Plötzlich öffnet sich die Bühnentür und zwölf Revuetänzerinnen mit Federkopfschmuck und Engelsflügeln hüpfen kreischend und schnellen Schritts zurück in ihre Umkleiden. Aus dem Saal erklingt gedämpft der tosende Applaus.

*"Five minutes till show time," resonates from the loudspeakers. A group of dancers sit on large adjustable chairs in the make-up room. One of the girls pastes on her false eyelashes in front of a mirror. One of the dancers wearing a sequined white bodysuit trippingly goes through the steps of her next number. The show begins. Neon tubes submerge the backstage area in blue light. The stage door suddenly opens and twelve chorus girls wearing feathered headdresses and angel wings stridently jump with quick steps back to their dressing room. The muffled sound of thunderous applause resounds from the hall.*

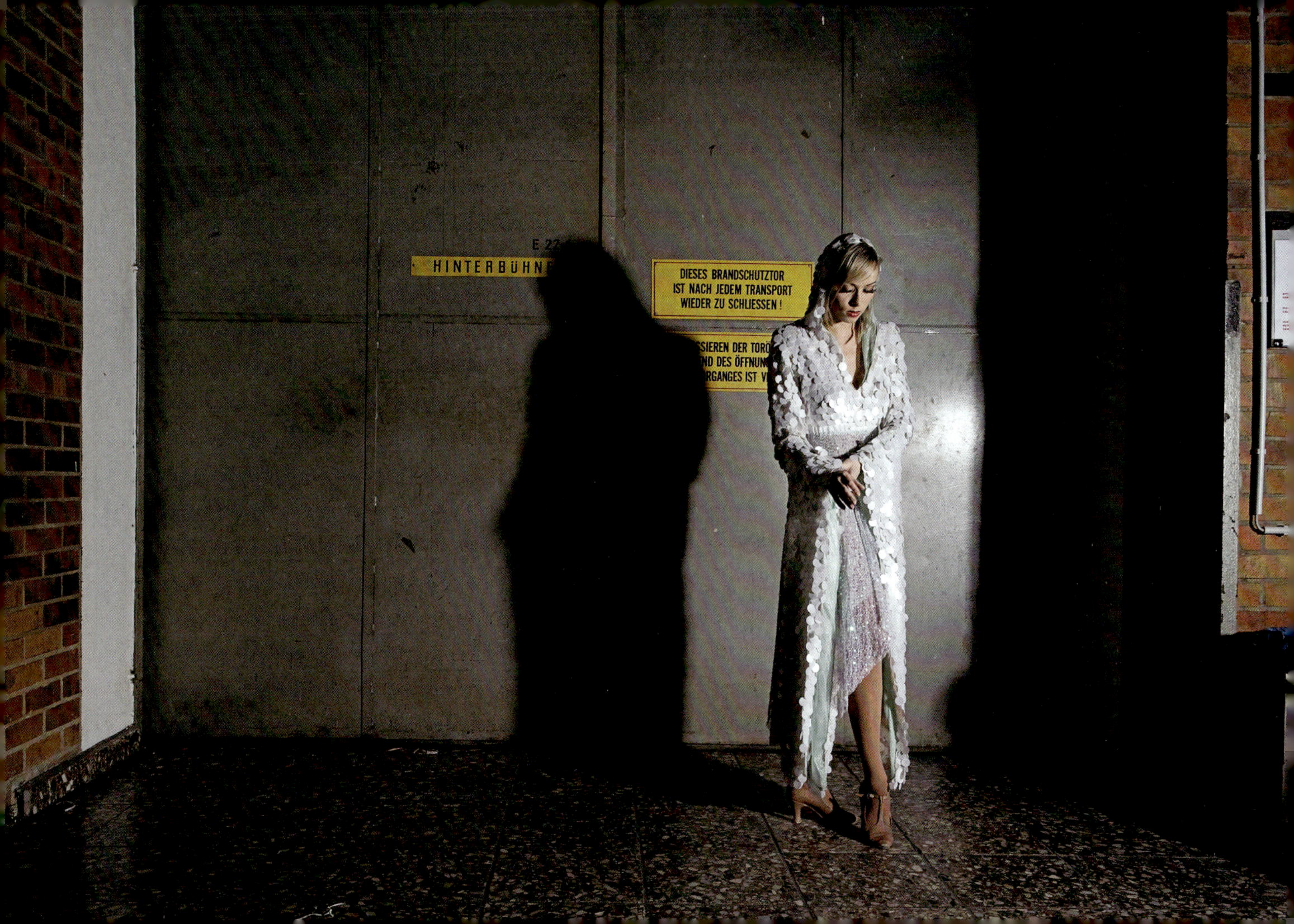
E. 22
HINTERBÜHNE
DIESES BRANDSCHUTZTOR
IST NACH JEDEM TRANSPORT
WIEDER ZU SCHLIESSEN !

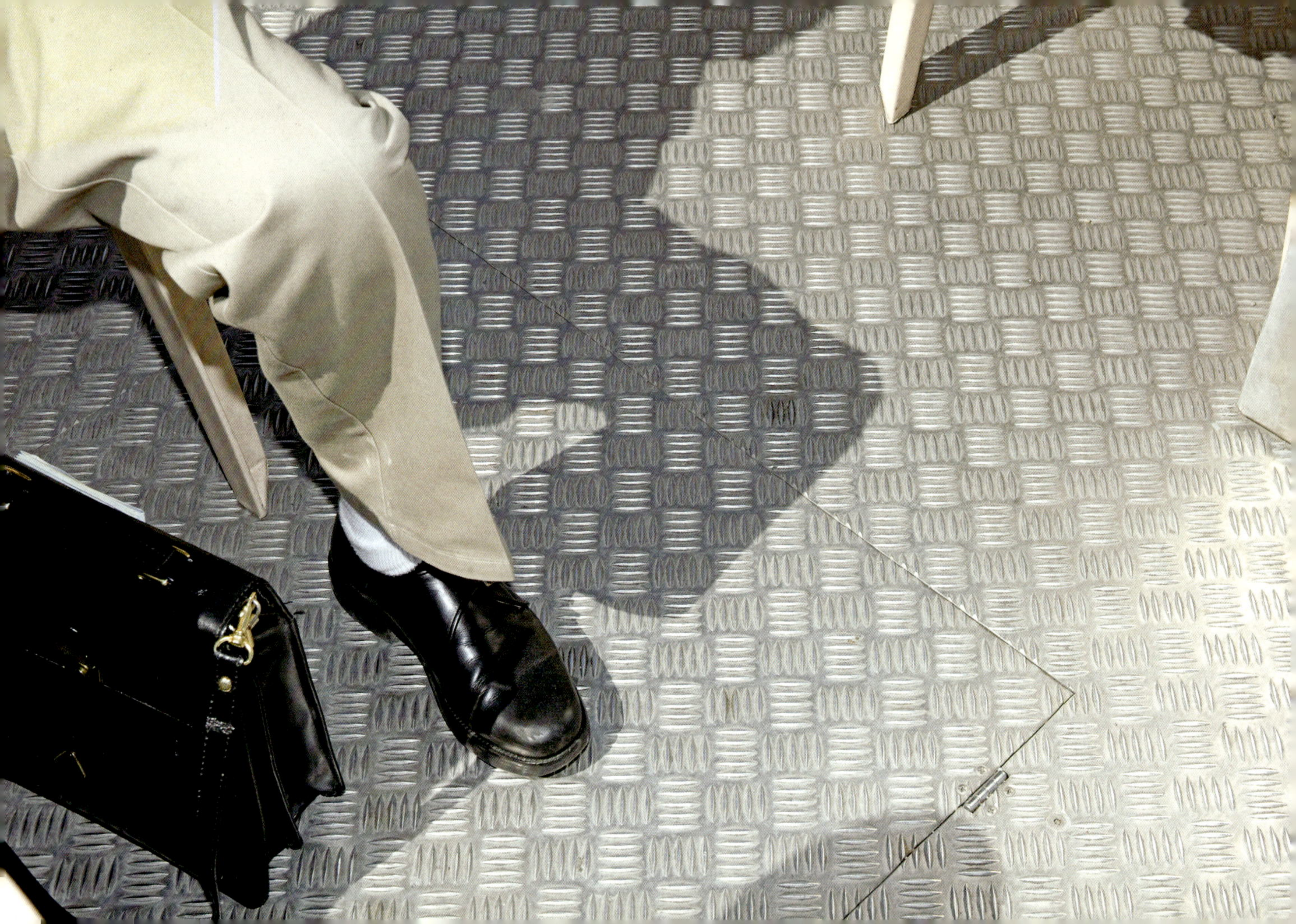

**AUF DEM OBERDECK EINES AUSFLUGSDAMPFERS SITZT EIN HAMBURGER KEGELVEREIN AUF BEIGEFARBENEN PLASTIKSTÜHLEN. UNTER DECK WIRD DERWEIL DIE KÄSESAHNETORTE DES CLUBS GLÜCK POTSDAM ANGESCHNITTEN.** ▬▬▬

*Members of a ninepins league from Hamburg sit on beige-colored plastic chairs on the upper deck of an excursion boat. Below deck, the Club Glück from Potsdam is cutting their cheese cake.*

**15** **Stern und Kreisschifffahrt**
*Station Pergamonmuseum . Berlin-Mitte*

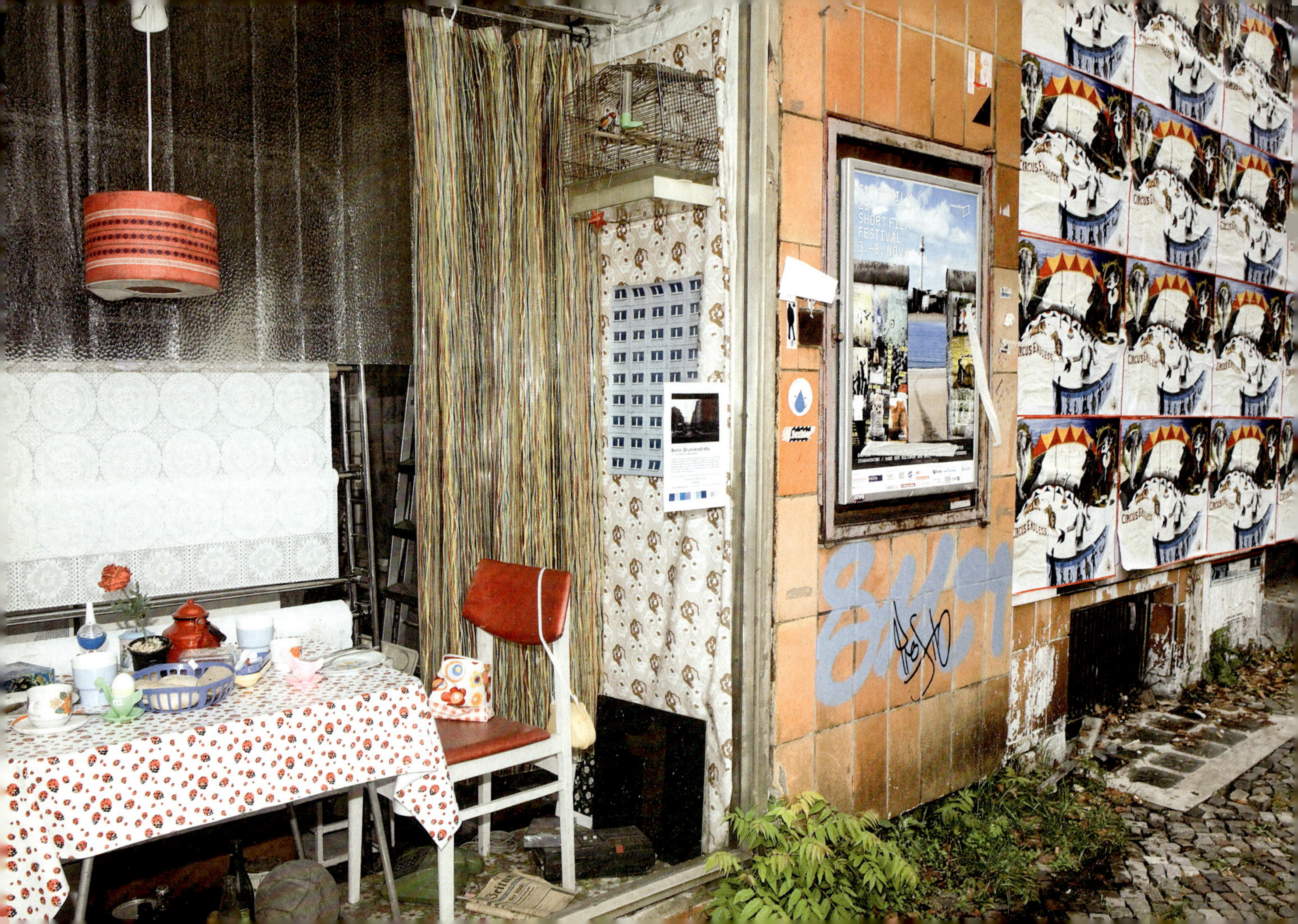

SHORT FILM
FESTIVAL
3.-8. NOV

# DER KUNDE GREIFT NACH ORNAMENTO BIANCO, EINEM WEISSEN DUSCHVORHANG MIT CREMEFARBENEN RANKEN. IM SCHAUFENSTER WARTET DAS MODELL PALMENSTRAND AUF EINEN ABNEHMER.

*The customer reaches for Ornamento Bianco, a white shower curtain with cream-colored tendrils. In the shop window, the Palm Beach model waits for a taker.*

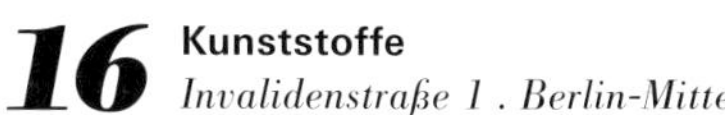

**16** **Kunststoffe**
*Invalidenstraße 1 . Berlin-Mitte*

# SCHWOFEN IM SPIEGELSAAL

## Bopping in the Hall of Mirrors

**17** **Clärchens Ballhaus**
*Auguststr. 24 . Berlin-Mitte*

Die Stimmen von Elvis und Udo Jürgens dringen aus Berlins ältestem Tanzlokal. Am Eingang springt Günter Schmidtke, ältester Garderobier der Stadt und ehemals begabter Boxer, über den Tresen und nimmt Mantel und Jacke mit »Berliner Schnauze« entgegen. Im Saal nebenan schwingen rüstige Ost-Rentner, Schlipsträger und Berliner Girlies das Tanzbein auf dem Parkett – einsame Herzen auf der Suche nach dem Glück. Hier tanzt die Hauptstadt. Lange Tische und altmodische Vorhänge säumen den Saal, die Gäste essen Berliner Bulette und wähnen sich in den 1920er-Jahren. Im Spiegelsaal darüber, in dem tagsüber noch aufgestuhlt war und und nur die Sonnenstrahlen tanzten, spielt eine quirlige Gipsy-Band. Der Lärmpegel erreicht seinen Höhepunkt.

*The voices of Elvis and Udo Jürgens emerge from Berlin's oldest dance hall. Günter Schmidtke, the city's oldest checkroom attendant and a former talented boxer, jumps over the counter at the entrance and takes coats and jackets with a portion of "Berlin lip." In the adjacent hall, sprightly East Berlin pensioners, assorted suits, and Berlin girlies shake a leg on the dance floor; lonely-hearts in pursuit of happiness. The capital dances here. Long tables and old-fashioned curtains line the halls; the guests eat Berlin meatballs and imagine they are back in the Roaring Twenties. An exuberant gipsy band plays in the Hall of Mirrors on the floor above; rows of chairs stood there during the day and only rays of sunshine danced about. The noise level reaches its zenith.*

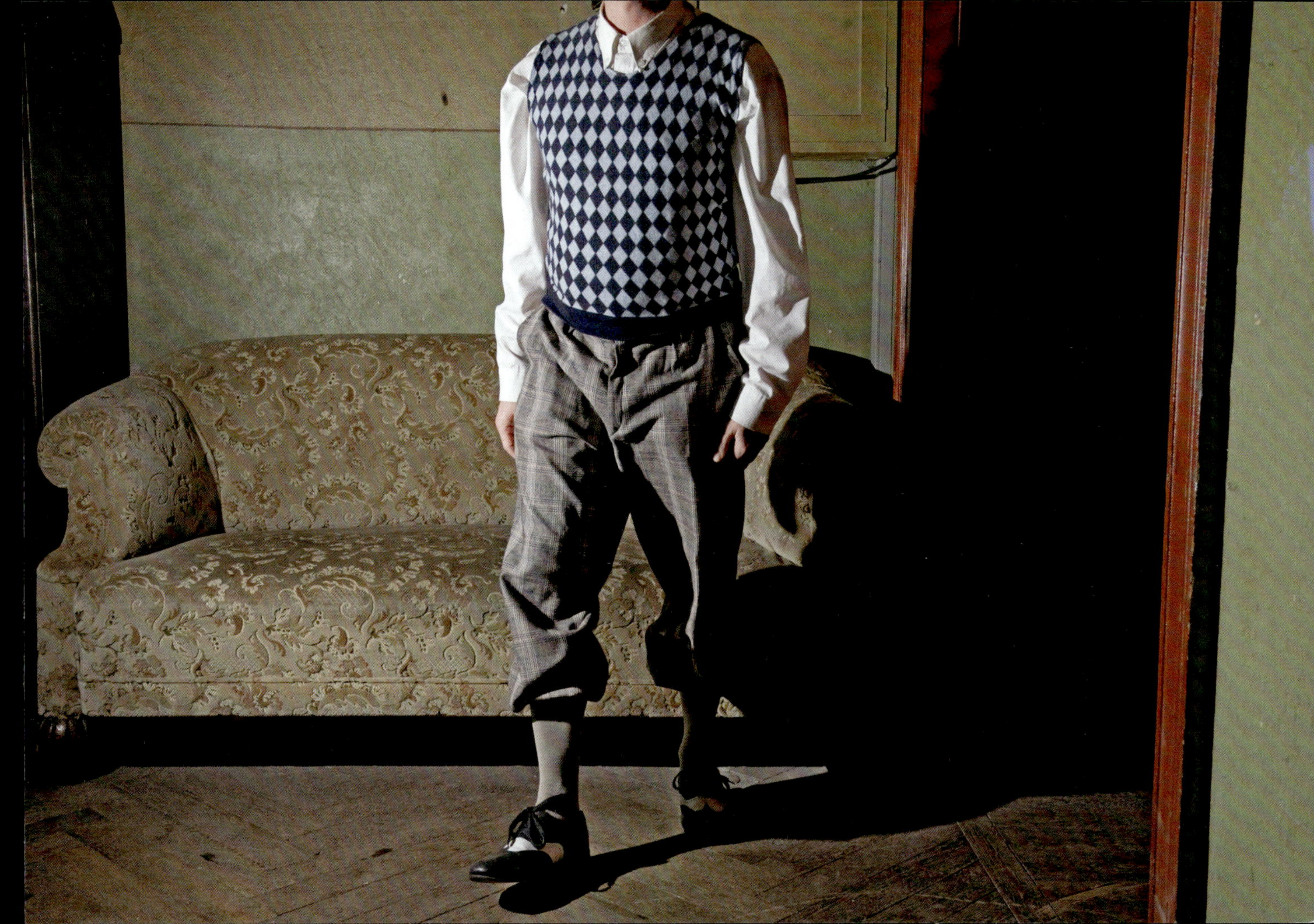

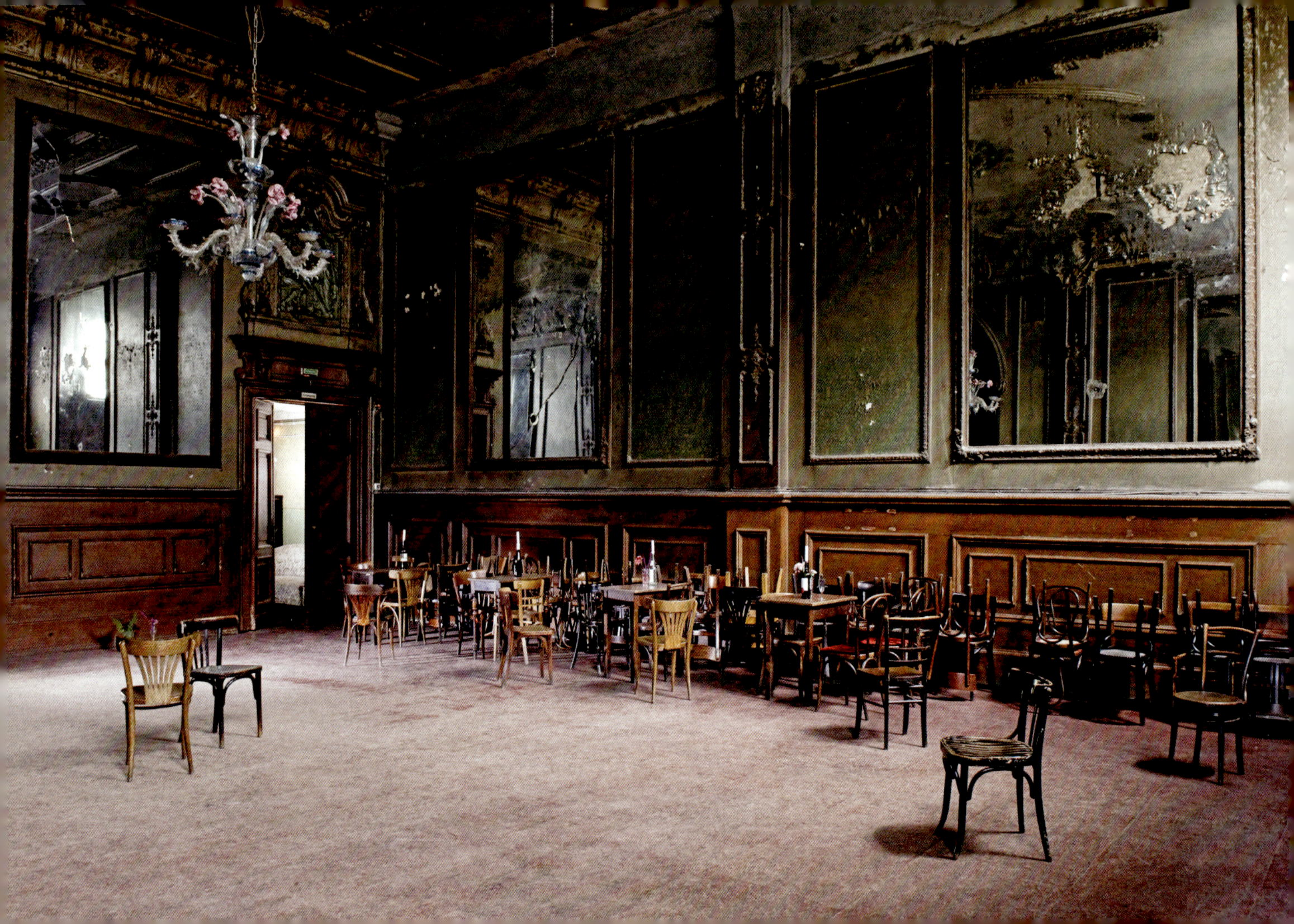

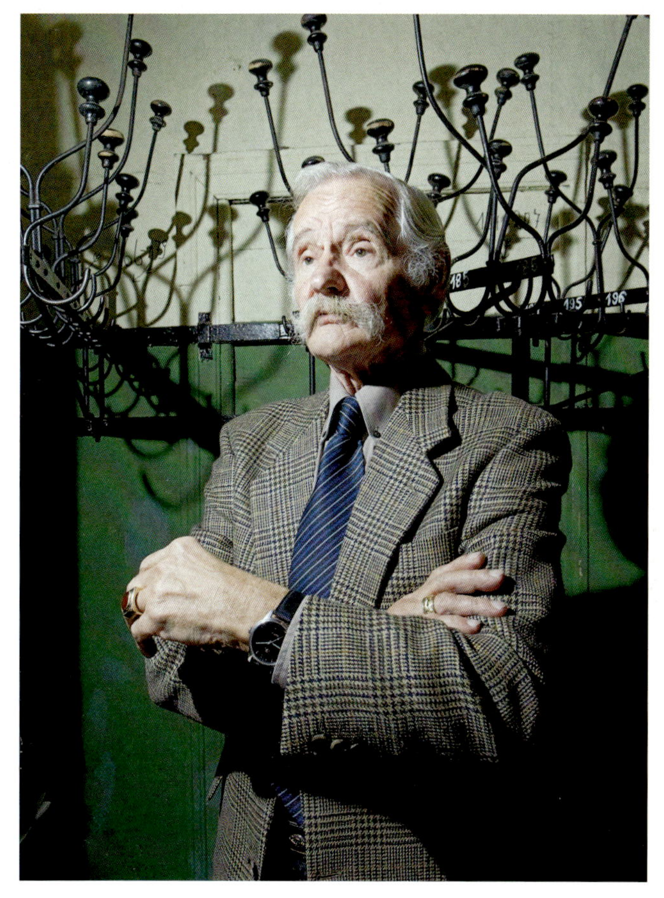

## ▬▬▬ DAMALS SCHAUTEN PARTEIFUNKTIONÄRE AUS IHREM WOHNZIMMER VERSCHÄMT RÜBER IN DEN WESTEN. HEUTE BLINKT KAPITALISTISCHE PROPAGANDA VON DEN DÄCHERN.

*Party officials used to look bashfully from their living rooms windows across to the West. Capitalist propaganda now blinks from the roofs.*

**18** **Bebauung an der Leipziger Straße**
*Leipziger Straße . Berlin-Mitte*

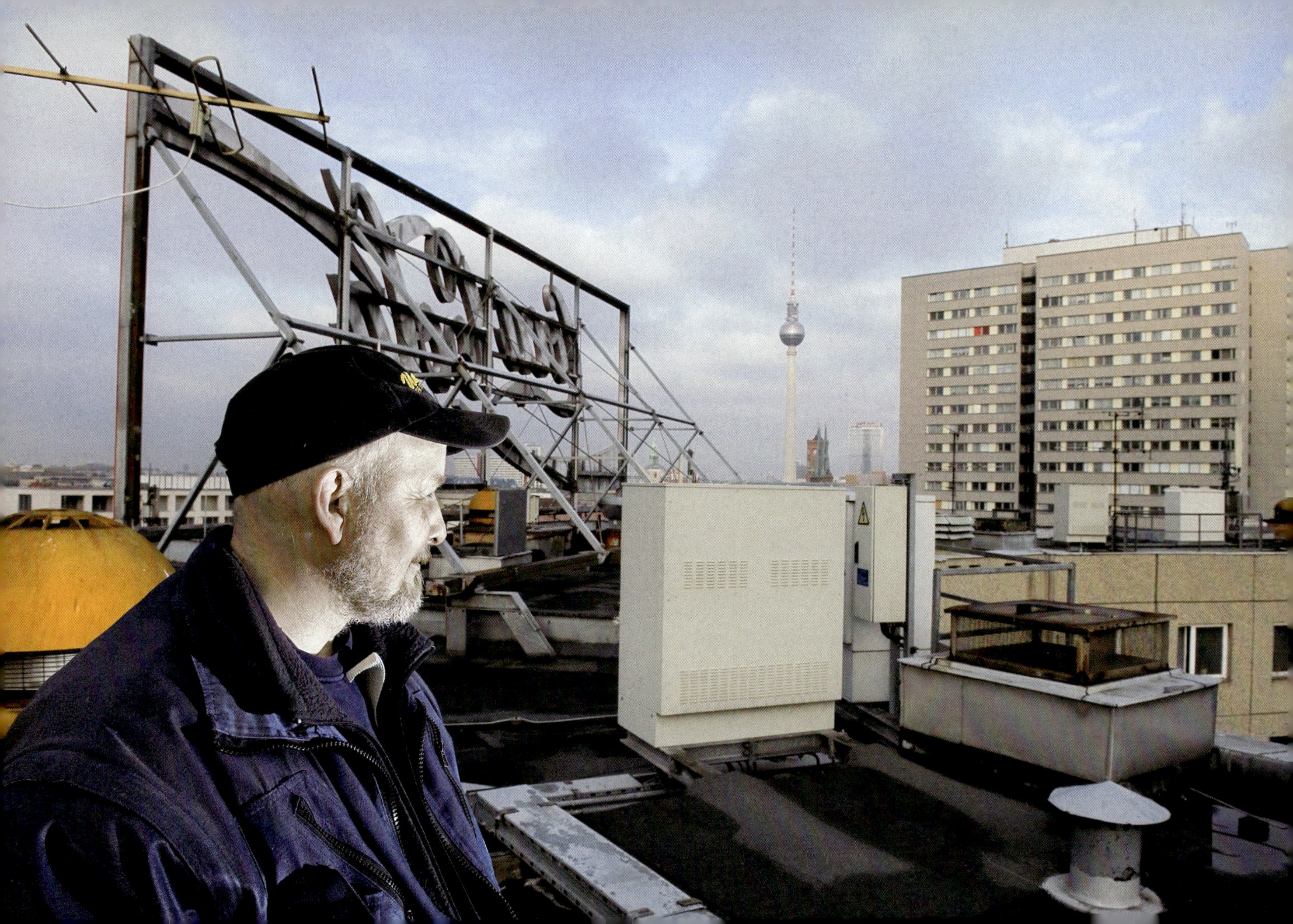

# ██ DIE WAHL FÄLLT AUF NR. 86, 84 UND 25: DSCHINGIS-KHAN, CHINESISCHE BAUERNHOCHZEIT UND HUHN AUF DEM SCHEITERHAUFEN.

*The winners are numbers 86, 84, and 25:*
*Genghis Khan, Chinese Village Wedding, and fried*
*chicken with special hot sauce.*

**19** **Restaurant Himmelspagode**
*Oranienburger Straße 3 . Hohen Neuendorf*

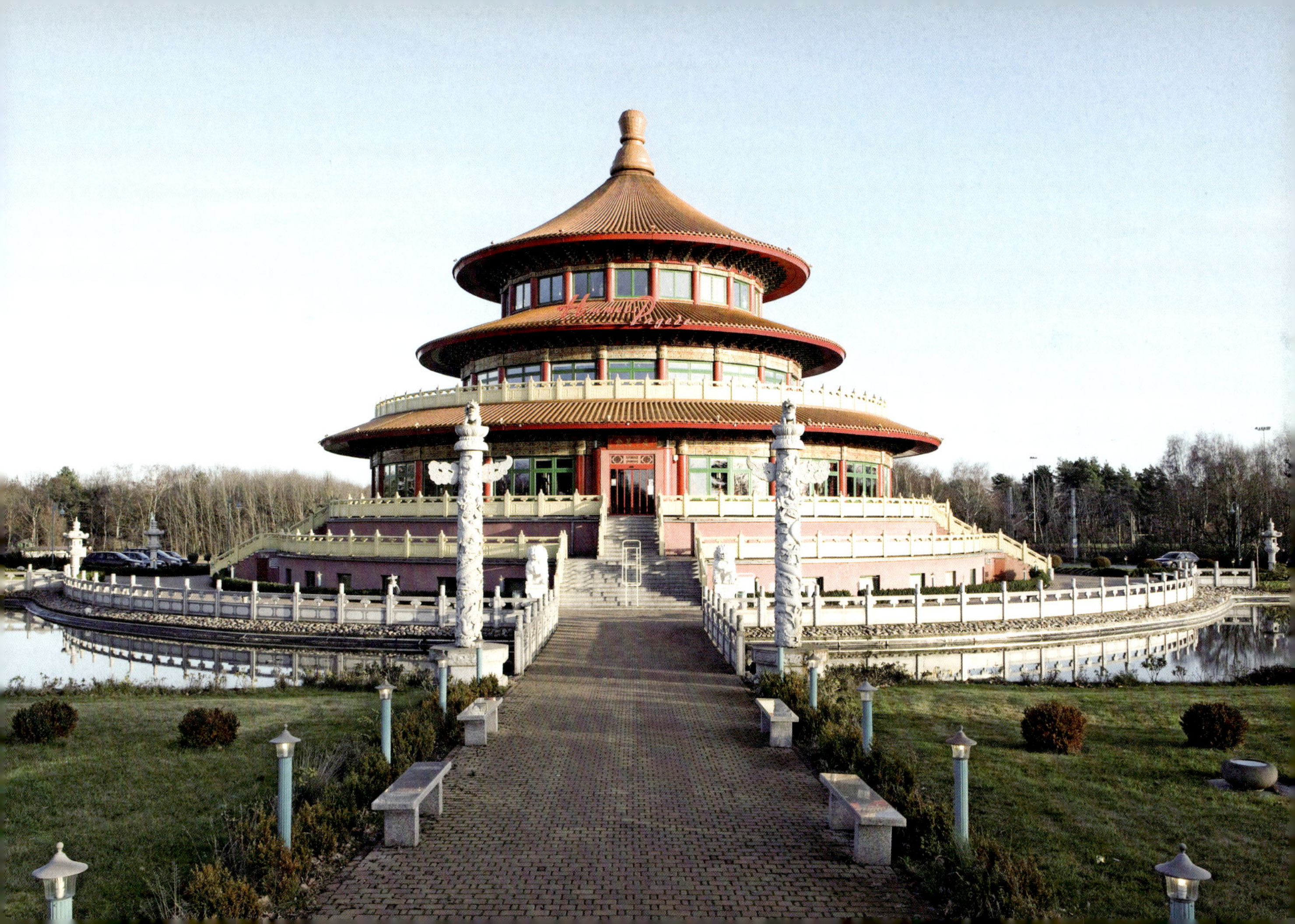

**DIE SCHRITTE DES STUDENTEN, DER EINEN GEWALTIGEN SUBWOOVER SCHLEPPT, HALLEN DURCH DAS STILLGELEGTE BAD. DIE VORBEREITUNGEN ZU EINER VERNISSAGE AM ABEND SIND FAST ABGESCHLOSSEN.**

The student's steps echo across the abandoned baths; he is schlepping an enormous subwoofer. The preparations for the preview in the evening are almost completed.

**20** **Stadtbad Wedding**
*Gerichtstraße 65–69 . Berlin-Wedding*

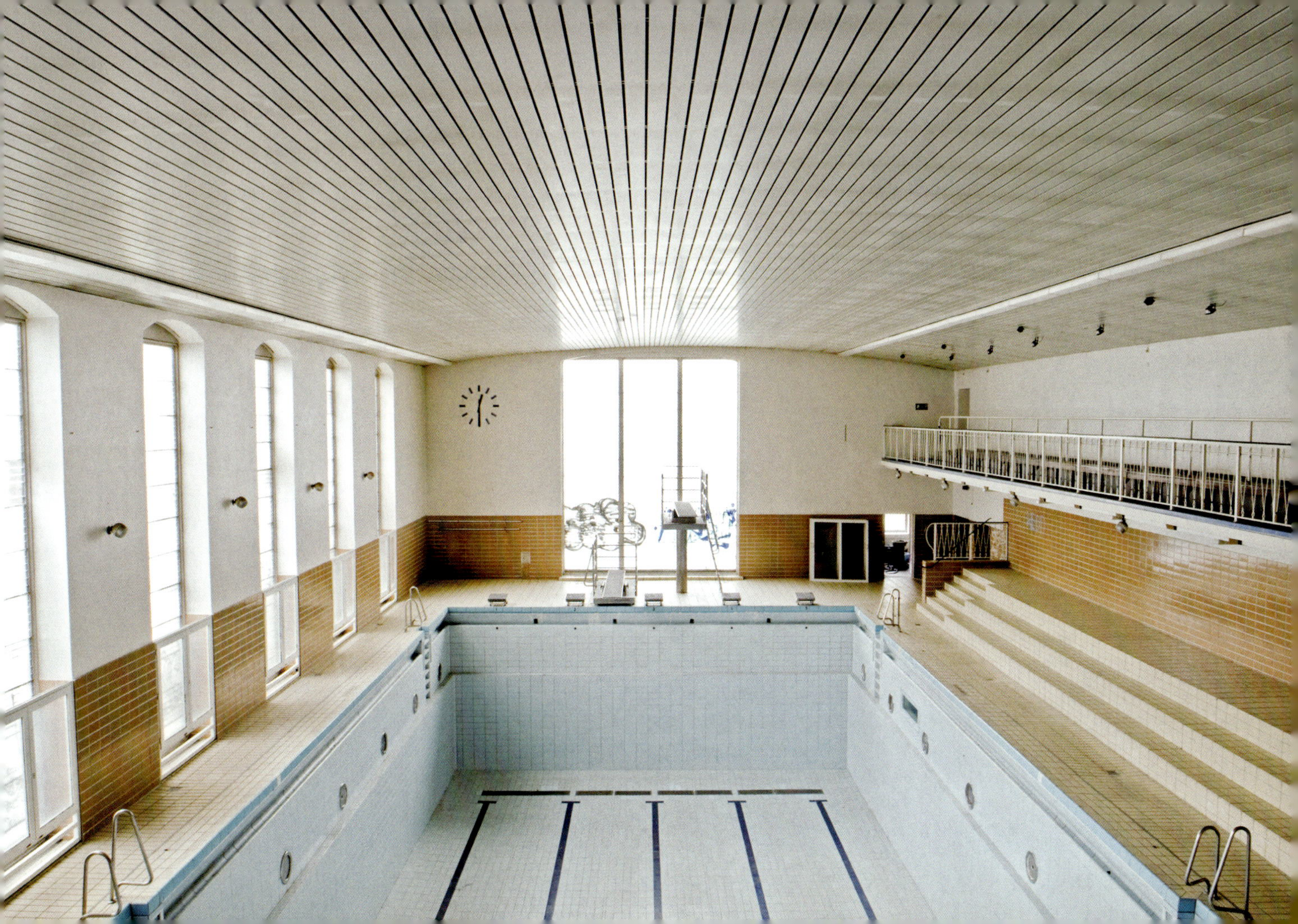

# DIE ALTE DAME DES RADAUS
## The old lady of raising Cain

**21** **Kunsthaus Tacheles**
*Oranienburger Straße 54–56a . Berlin-Mitte*

»It might be from Ex-GDR!«, ruft ein mit Kamerahandy bewaffneter Australier seiner Gattin zu und verschwindet knipsend im Eingang der seit 1990 besetzten Kunstruine Tacheles, die 1908 als Teil eines »Passage-Kaufhauses« errichtet wurde. Das Auge auf das Display gerichtet, steigt der Mann zwischen graffitiübersäten Wänden die Treppe hinauf. Vorbei an Künstlerateliers zieht es ihn nach oben. Seine Begleiterin, eine blasse, hoch aufgeschossene Frau im gestreiften Sommerkleid, inspiziert derweil das Areal hinter dem Gebäude. Scheinbar chaotisch reihen sich Skulpturen aus Metall und Holz aneinander, im Café Zapata nebenan lauscht man kubanischer Musik. Wenig später verlässt das Pärchen das Areal um 150 Fotos reicher mit dem Kommentar: »So arty, this place.«

*"It's like from the old GDR!" an Aussie armed with a mobilephone camera calls out to his wife and disappears into the entrance of the Tacheles Art Ruin which was originally built in 1908 as part of a "passage department store" and has been occupied by squatters since 1990. With his eye firmly fixed on the display, the man climbs up the stairs between graffiti-studded walls. Past the artists' studios, he makes a beeline for the top. In the meanwhile, his companion, a tall pale woman wearing a striped summer dress, is inspecting the area behind the building. Sculptures made out of metal and wood stand about in seemingly chaotic rows and people are listening to the strains of Cuban music in the adjoining Café Zapata. The couple, richer by 150 photographs, departs the area a short while later with the commentary: "So arty, this place."*

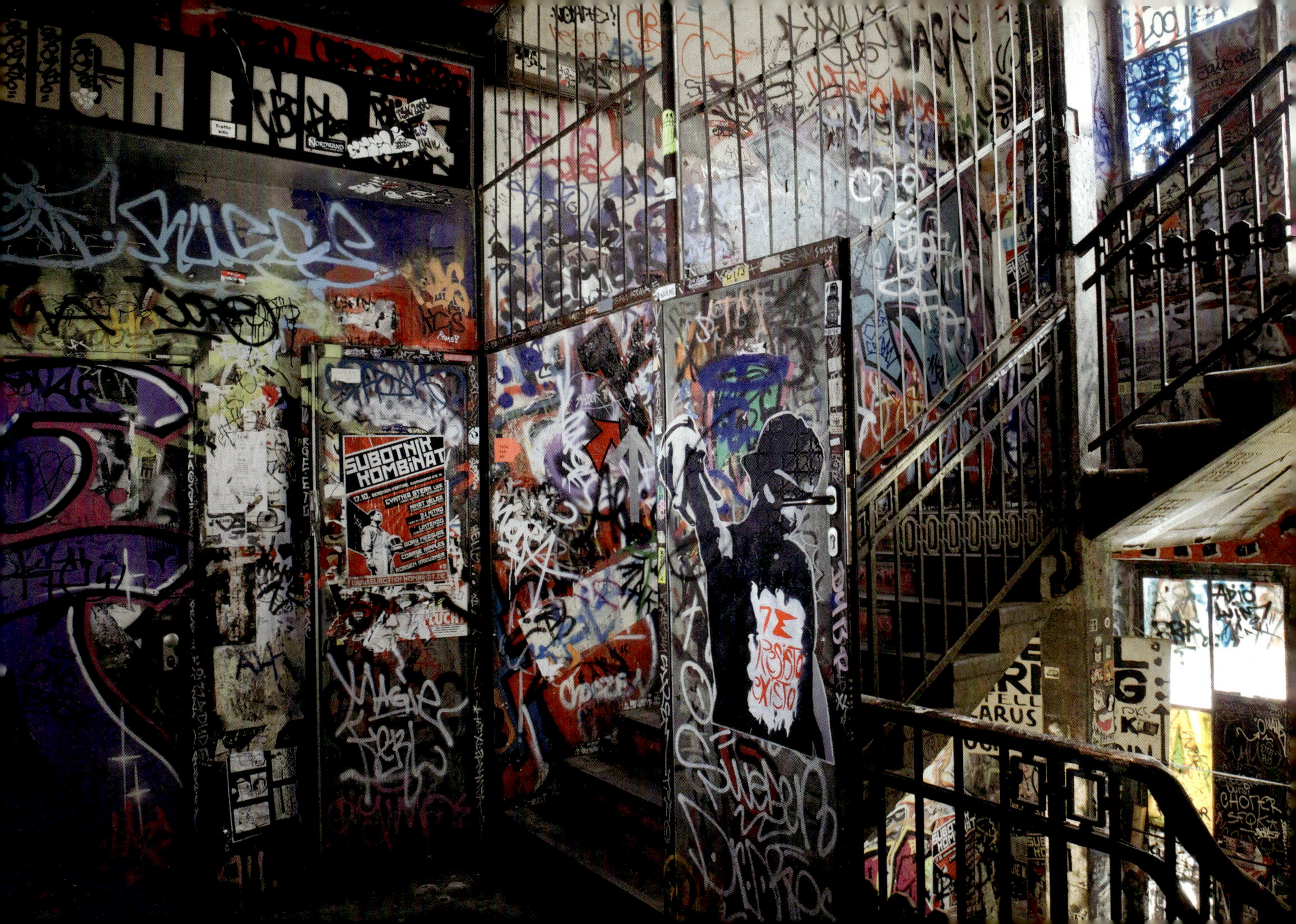

# BERLINER EDELPUFF
## *High-class brothel, Berlin style*



Die hauseigene Stretchlimousine hält vor der Berliner Stadtvilla nahe dem Olympiastadion. Ein Mann und zwei Damen betreten nach einer erotischen Stadtfahrt das Haus. Die Tür öffnet sich, und man lässt sich auf den schweren Ledersofas im Loungebereich nieder. An der Bar wartet man auf Kunden der Bootsmesse. Hinter einer Tür plätschert es dahin. Im hauseigenen Pool verlustiert sich ein Pärchen bei tropischen Temperaturen. Die VIP-Suite gleich nebenan, die über einen separaten Zugang verfügt, ist unbesetzt. Am Eingang führt eine Treppe hoch in den ersten Stock mit sieben weiteren Gemächern. In Zimmer Nr. 4 wird der Whirlpool eingelassen, auf Ölgemälden an den Wänden rekeln sich lasziv Gespielinnen.

*The in-house stretch limousine stops in front of the urban Berlin villa near the Olympic Stadium. A man and two women enter the house after an erotic drive around town. The doors opens and one of the ladies of the house sits herself down on one of the heavy leather sofas in the lounge area. Another is waiting at the bar for customers from the boat fair. Water is being splashed about behind a door. A couple is amusing itself at tropical temperatures in the in-house swimming pool. The now empty VIP suite next door features its own separate entrance. A staircase leads from the entrance up to the first floor with seven further rooms. Water is being filled into the whirlpool in room number four; playmates loll about lasciviously in oil paintings on the walls.*

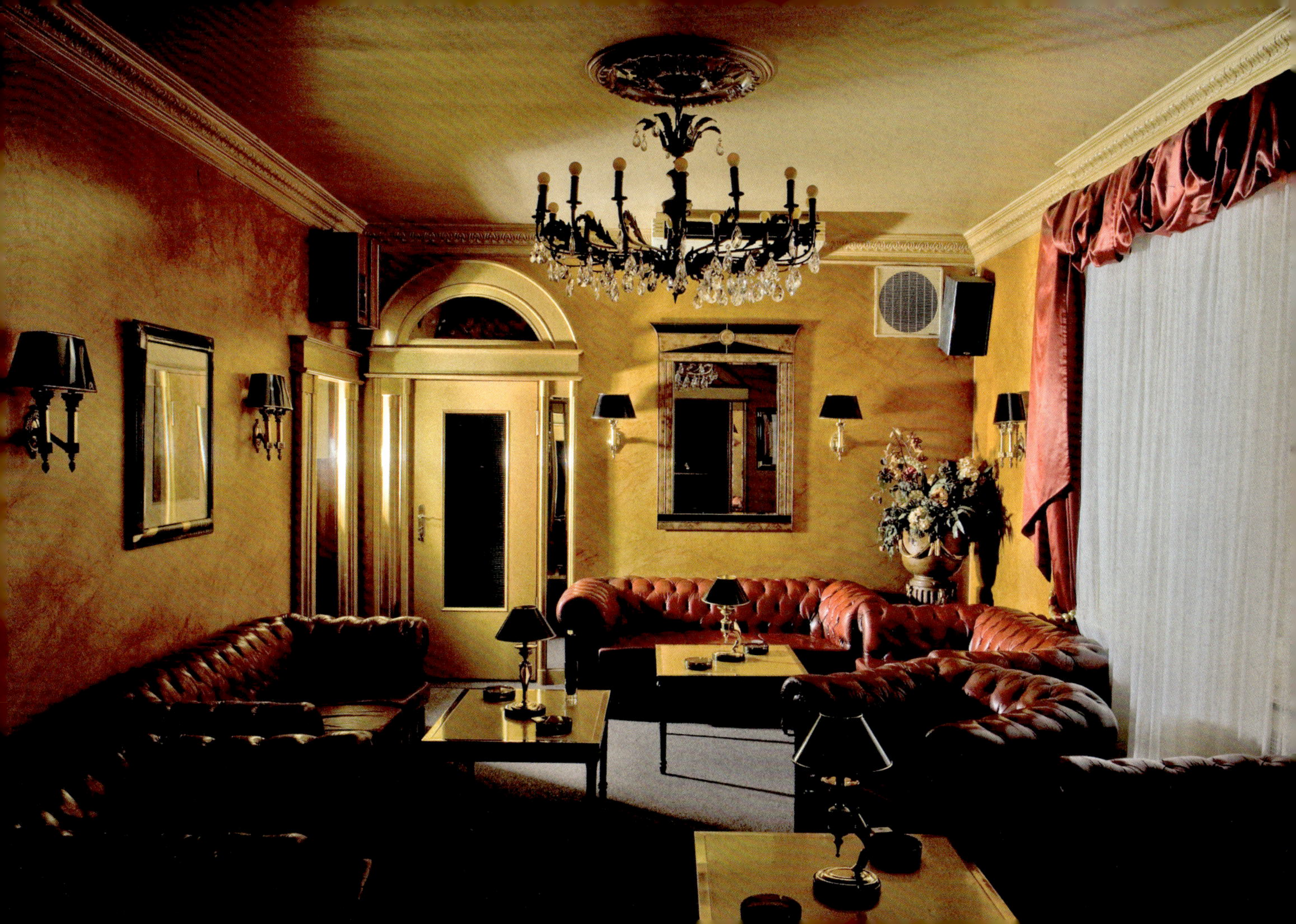

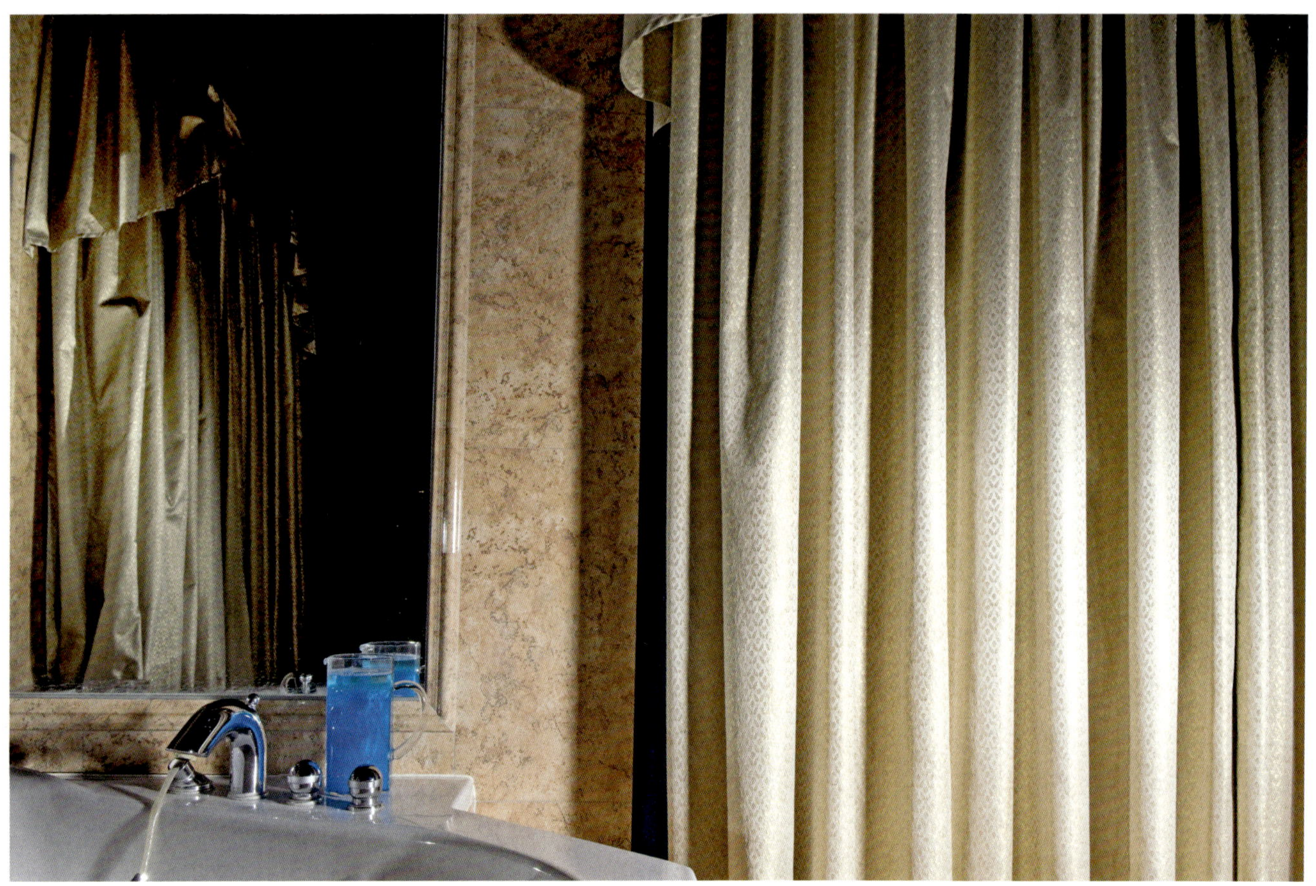

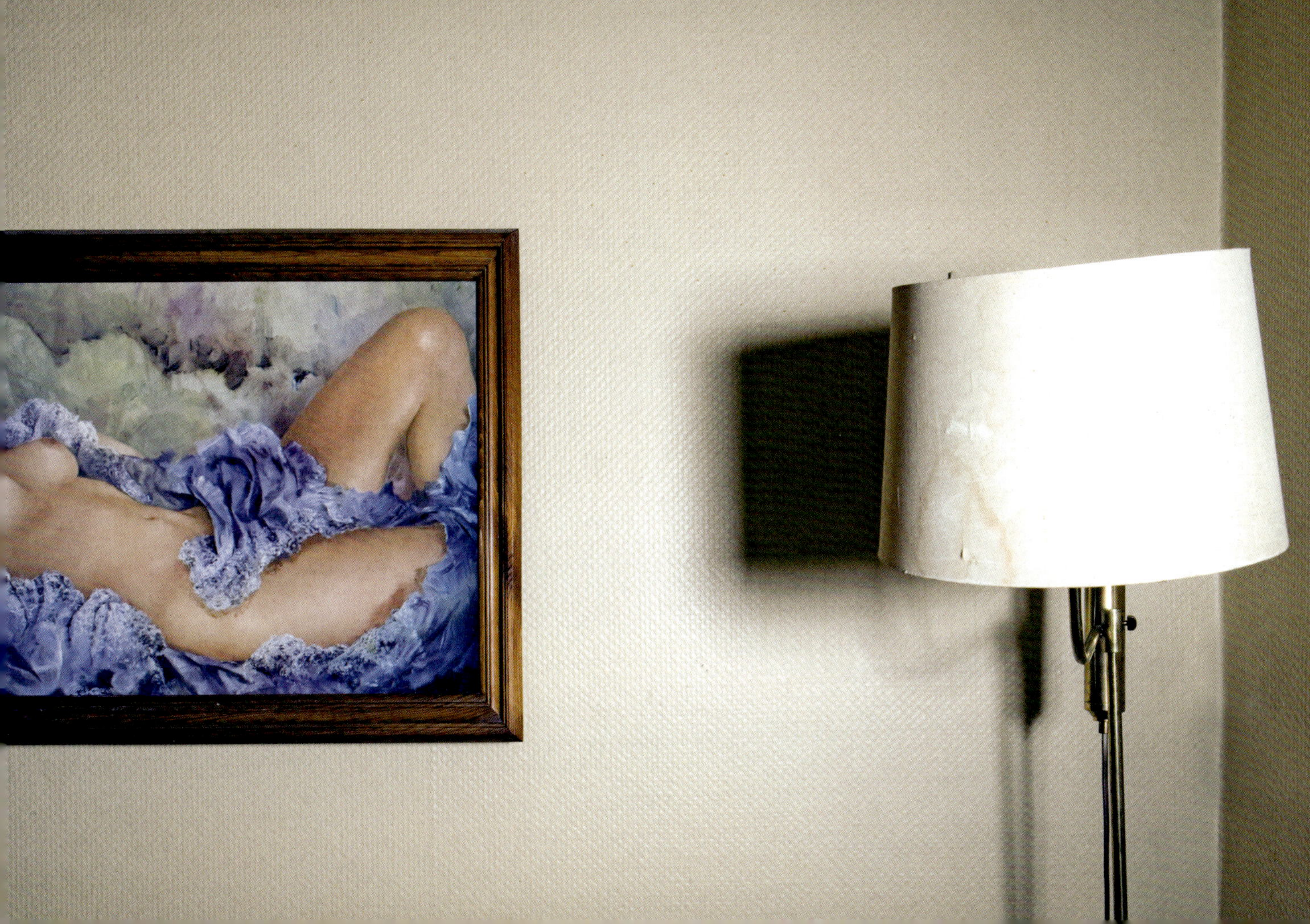

# LIMOUSINENSERVICE, MARMORDAMPFSAUNA, TANTRA, MASSAGEN MIT HAPPY END

*Limousine service, marble steam room, tantra, massage with a happy end*

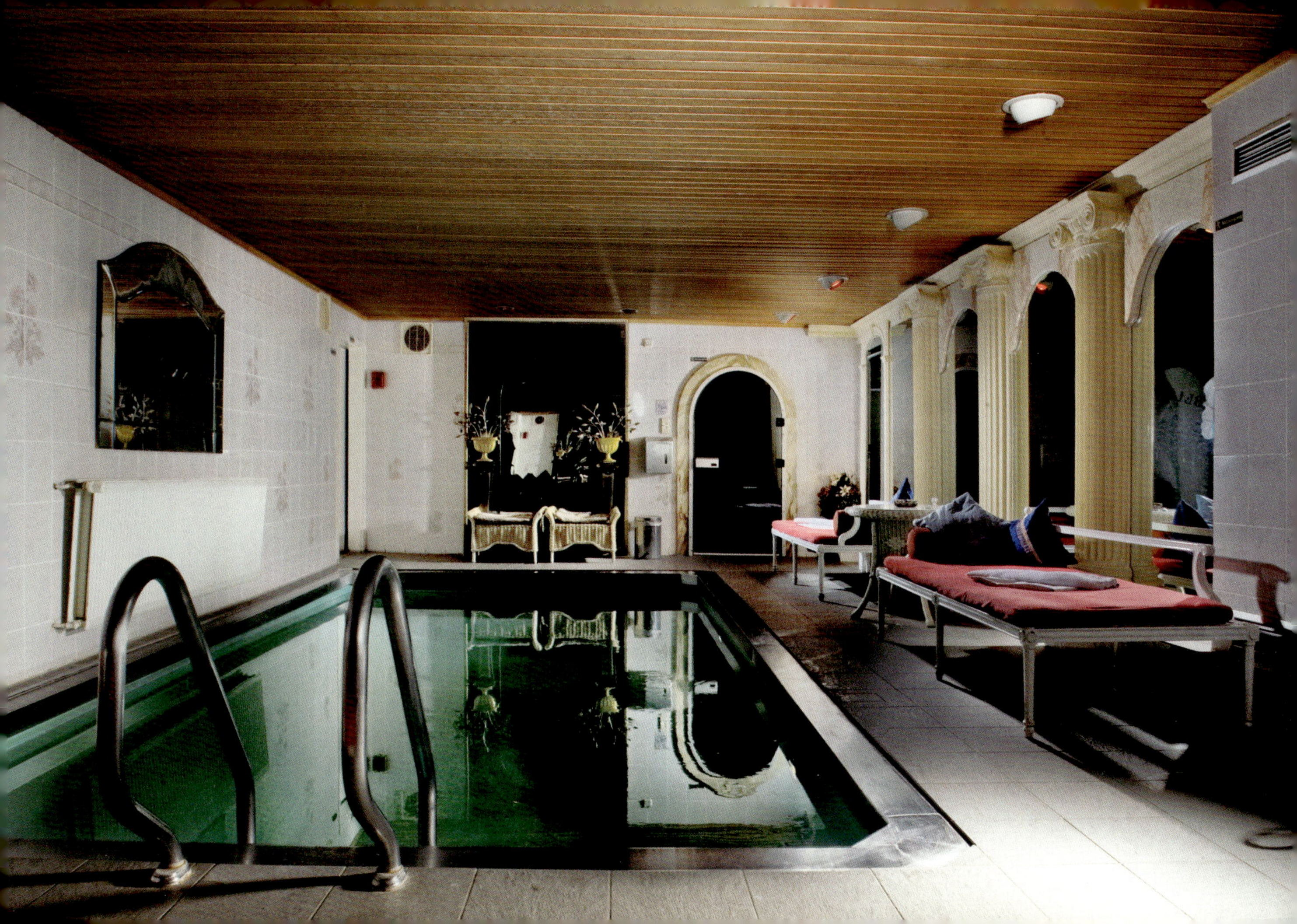

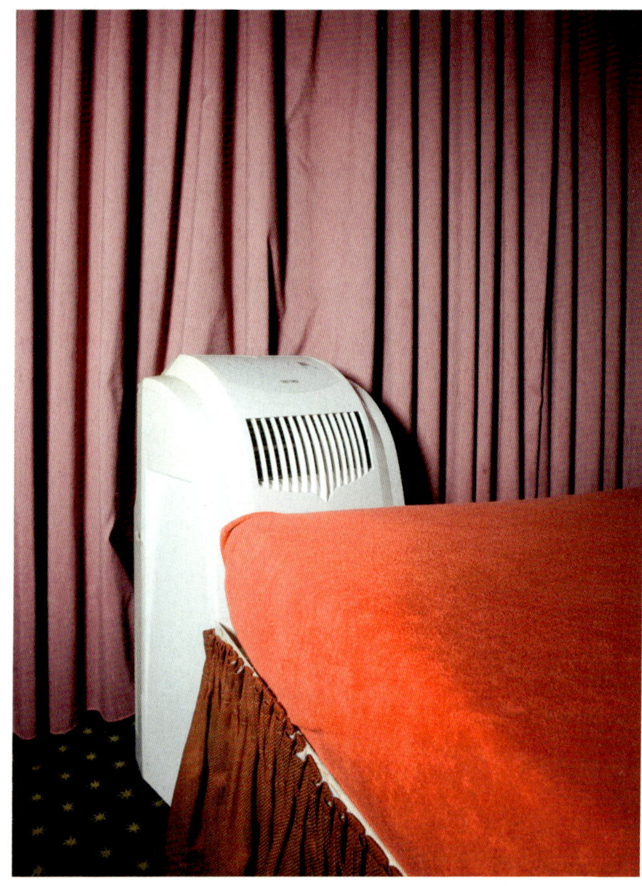

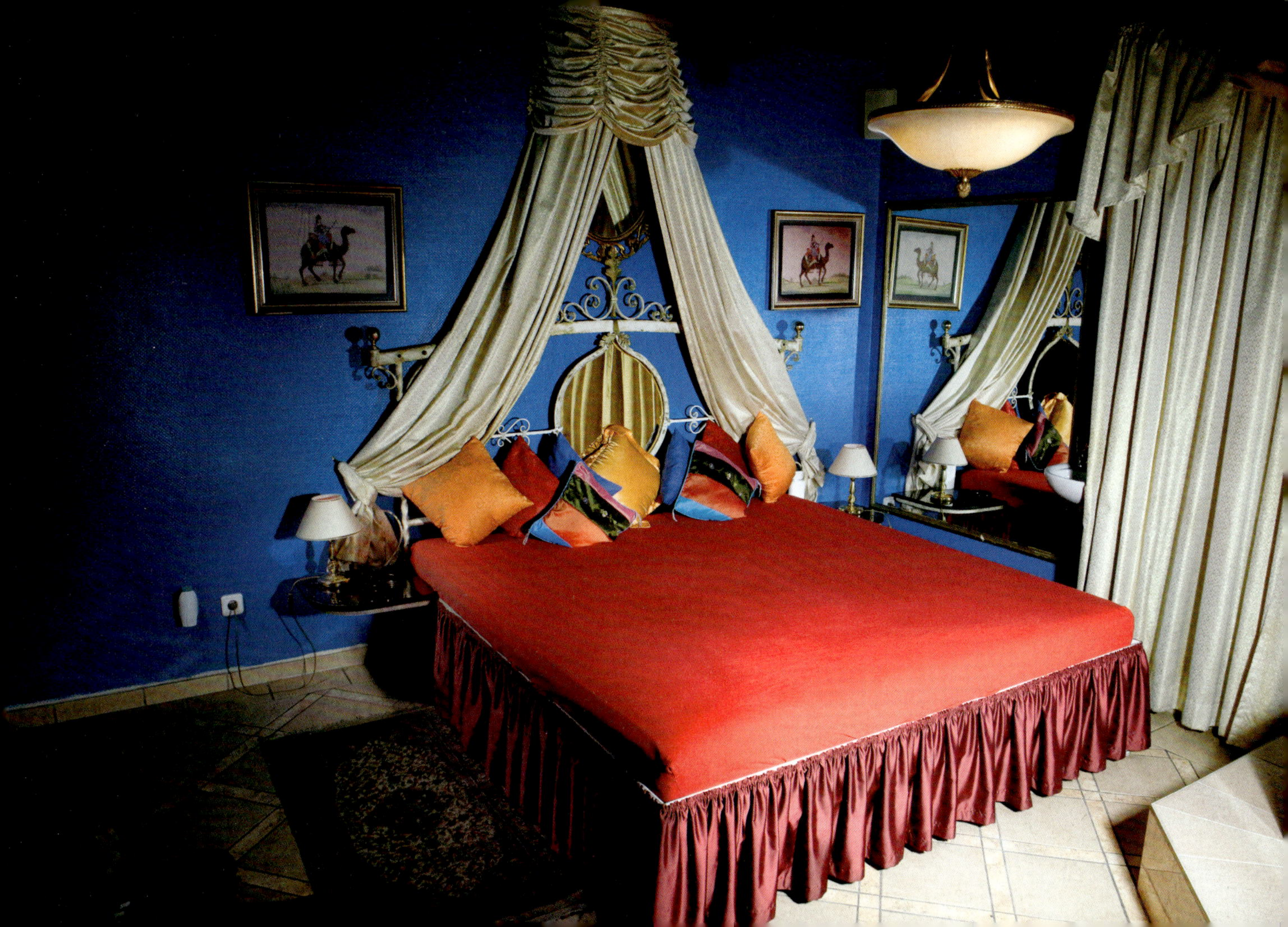

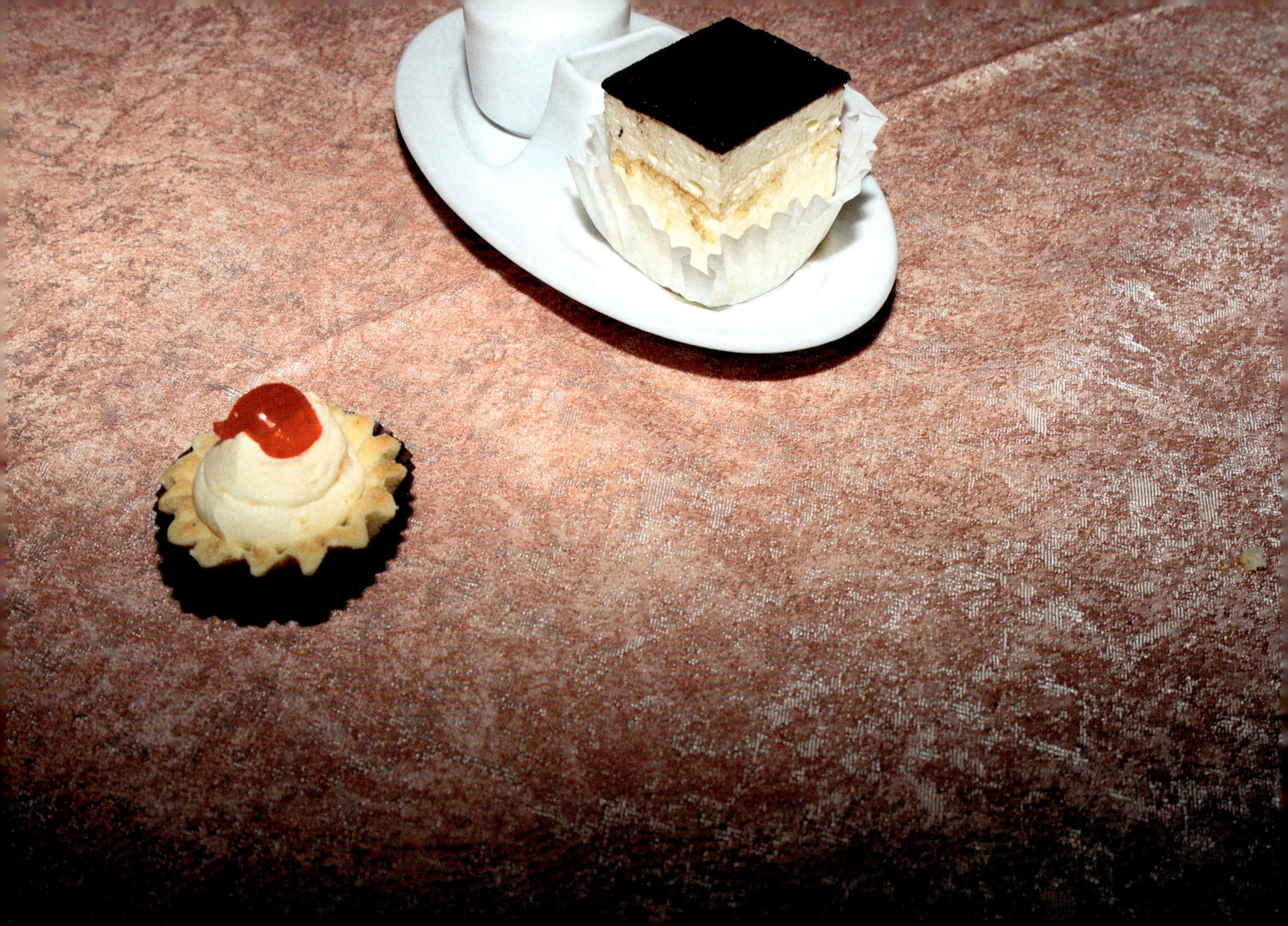

# ZEHLENDORF: PREUSSISCHE BOHEME UND VILLENCHIC

## Zehlendorf:
## Prussian bohemia and chic villas

Autoputz in der Villenkolonie, Loggia Alexandra auf dem Böttcherberg, preußische Erbengemeinschaften, beheizte Pools in Gartenhäusern, Studentenpartys am Schlachtensee, fröhlich ablegen am Wannseesteg, Hochfinanz im Großstadtrausch.

*Washing the car in the colony of villas, Loggia Alexandra on Böttcherberg, Prussian communities of heirs, heated swimming pools in summer houses, student parties at Schlachtensee, cheerfully departing the Wannsee jetty, high finance in urban jungle fever.*

# 203 METER IN 40 SEKUNDEN, 2 UMDREHUNGEN PRO STUNDE

## 203 meters in 40 seconds, 2 rotations per hour

**23** Fernsehturm am Alexanderplatz
*Panoramastraße 1a . Berlin-Mitte*

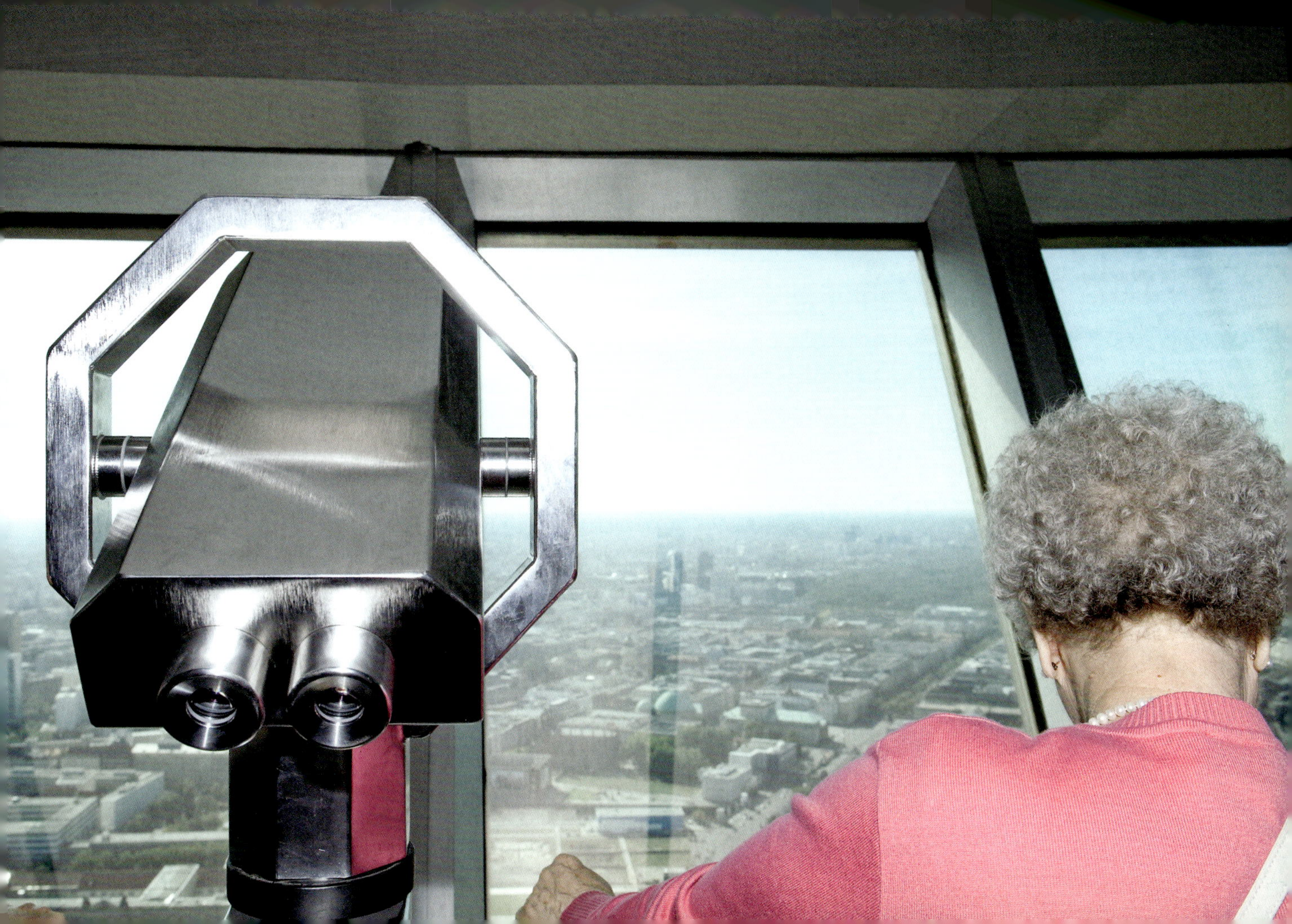

██████ **ÜBER DEN DÄCHERN BERLINS: ZU DEN BÄSSEN DER PLAYBACKEINSPIELUNG LÄSST EINE SÄNGERIN IM GELBEN OUTFIT IHRE HÜFTEN KREISEN. EIN LAUTES »CUT« BEENDET DIE SZENE. DAS MUSIKVIDEO IST IM KASTEN.**

*Overlooking Berlin's roofs: A singer dressed in a yellow outfit swings her hips to the bass beats of the playback recording. The scene is ended with the loud call "cut!" The music clip is in the can.*

**24** **Haus des Berliner Verlags**
*Karl-Liebknecht-Straße 29 . Berlin-Mitte*

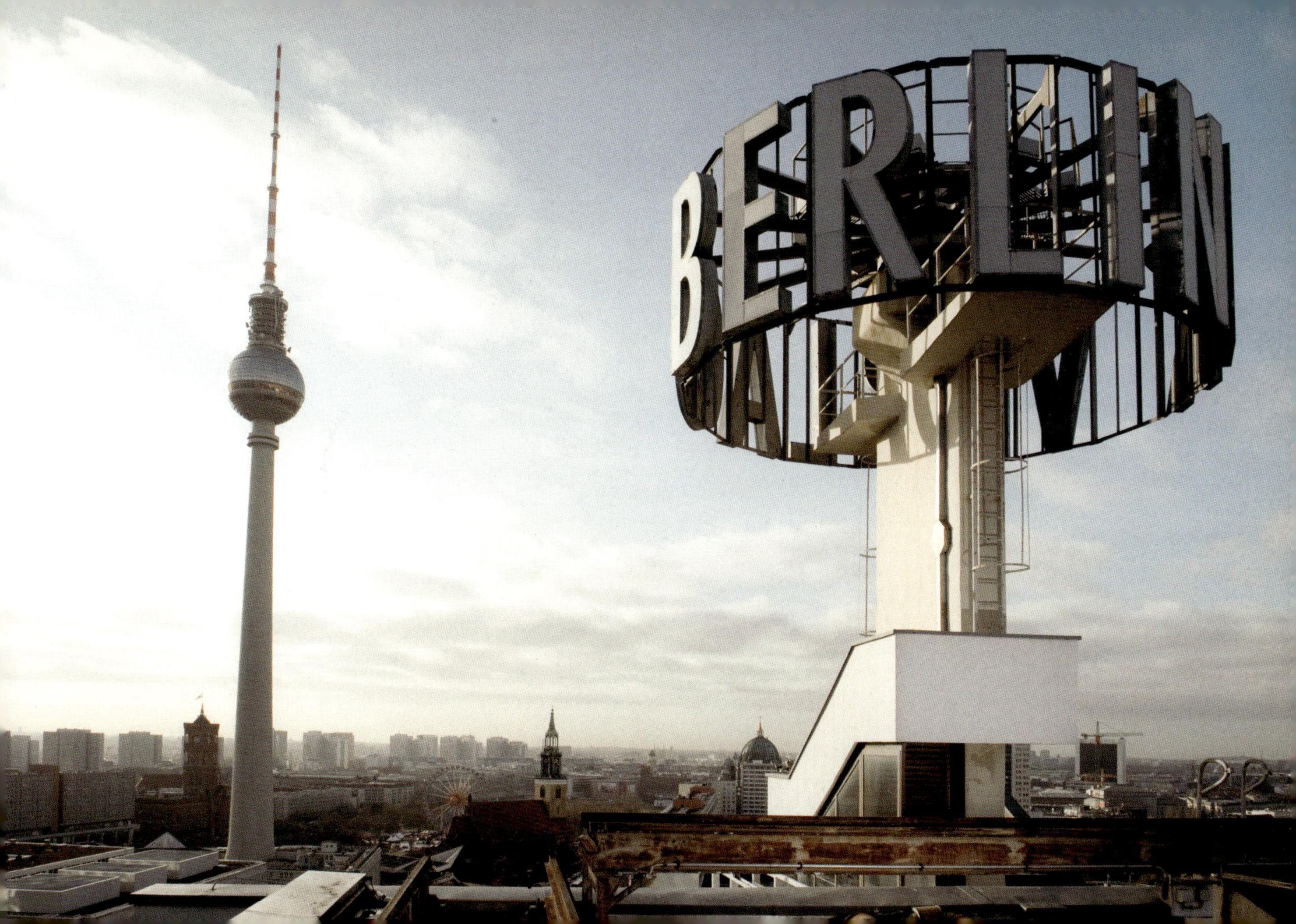
BERLIN

# GEWEIHT DER LIEBE UND DEM SCHMERZ

## Dedicated to love and pain

**25** **Club Avalon**
*Zitadellenweg 20e . Berlin-Spandau*

Der Geruch von Gummi durchzieht einen mit schwarzem Latex ausgekleideten Raum. Das an der Wand bereithängende Sortiment lässt kaum Wünsche offen. Latexkleider, Handschuhe, Strümpfe und Masken (von der Gasmaske bis zum Schweinekopf) sind frisch gereinigt. Choräle erklingen aus dem Studio nebenan. Ein Stahlkäfig mit Sitzbank bietet dort seine Dienste an. Eine Tür weiter geht es härter zu: Liebhaber von elektrischen Schlägen kommen hier auf ihre Kosten. Man darf in einem eisernen Stuhl mit Lederriemen und Halsmanschette Platz nehmen. Plötzlich erfüllt das Geräusch klackernder Stiefelabsätze den Korridor. Eine der »Ladies« empfängt den ersten Patienten, der Weg führt direkt in die Klinik – ein Notfall.

*The smell of rubber pervades a room lined with black latex. The assortment of items hanging at the ready on the walls has something for everyone. Latex dresses, gloves, stockings, and masks (ranging from gasmask to a pig's head) have been freshly cleaned. Chorals reverberate from the adjoining studio. A steel cage with a bench offers its services there. The approach is a bit harder one door down: Lovers of electrical blows get their money's worth here. You can take a seat in an iron chair with leather straps and a neck brace. The corridor is suddenly filled with the sound of clattering high-heel boots. One of the "ladies" receives the first patient; the paths leads right to the clinic—an emergency.*

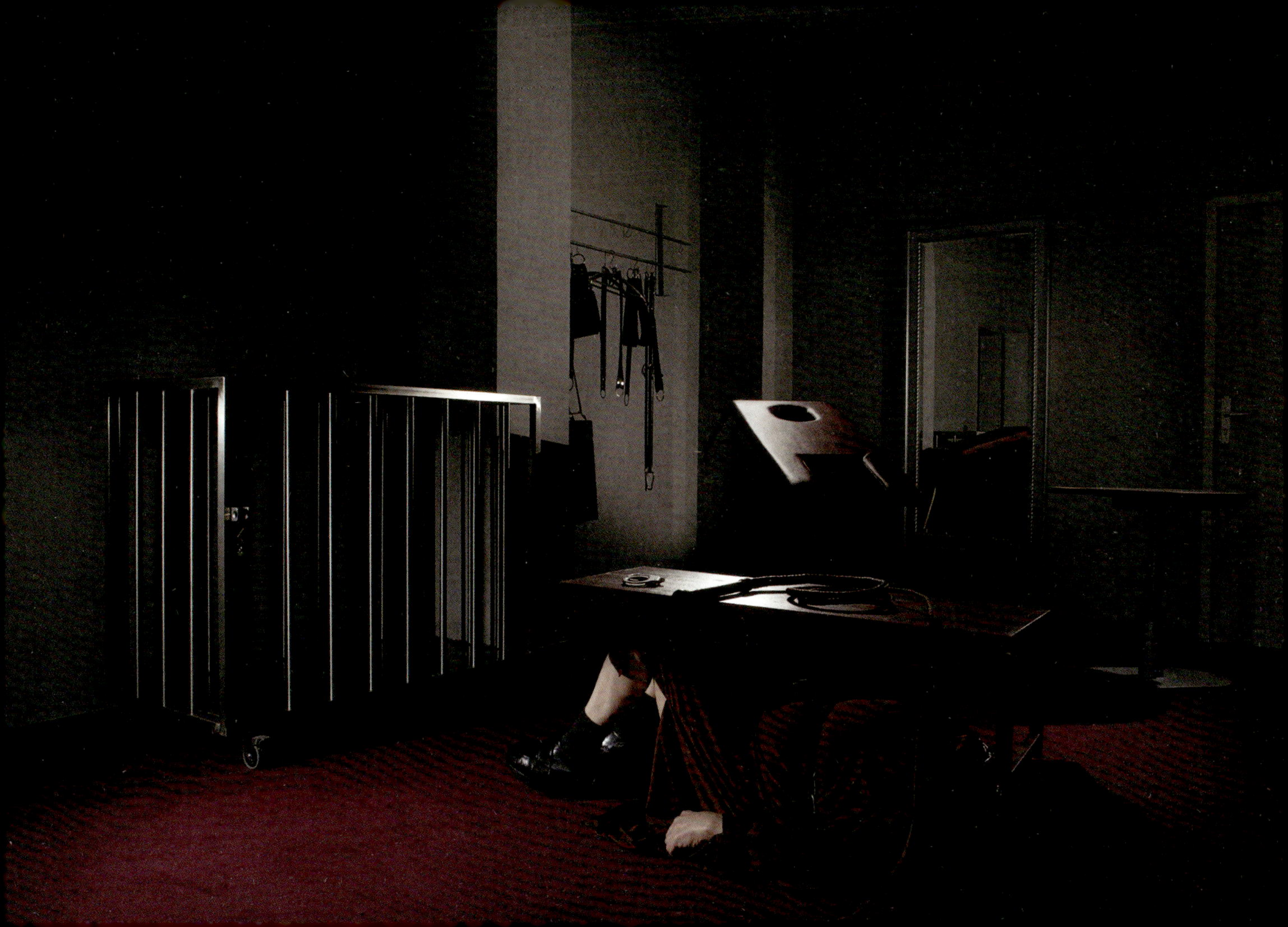

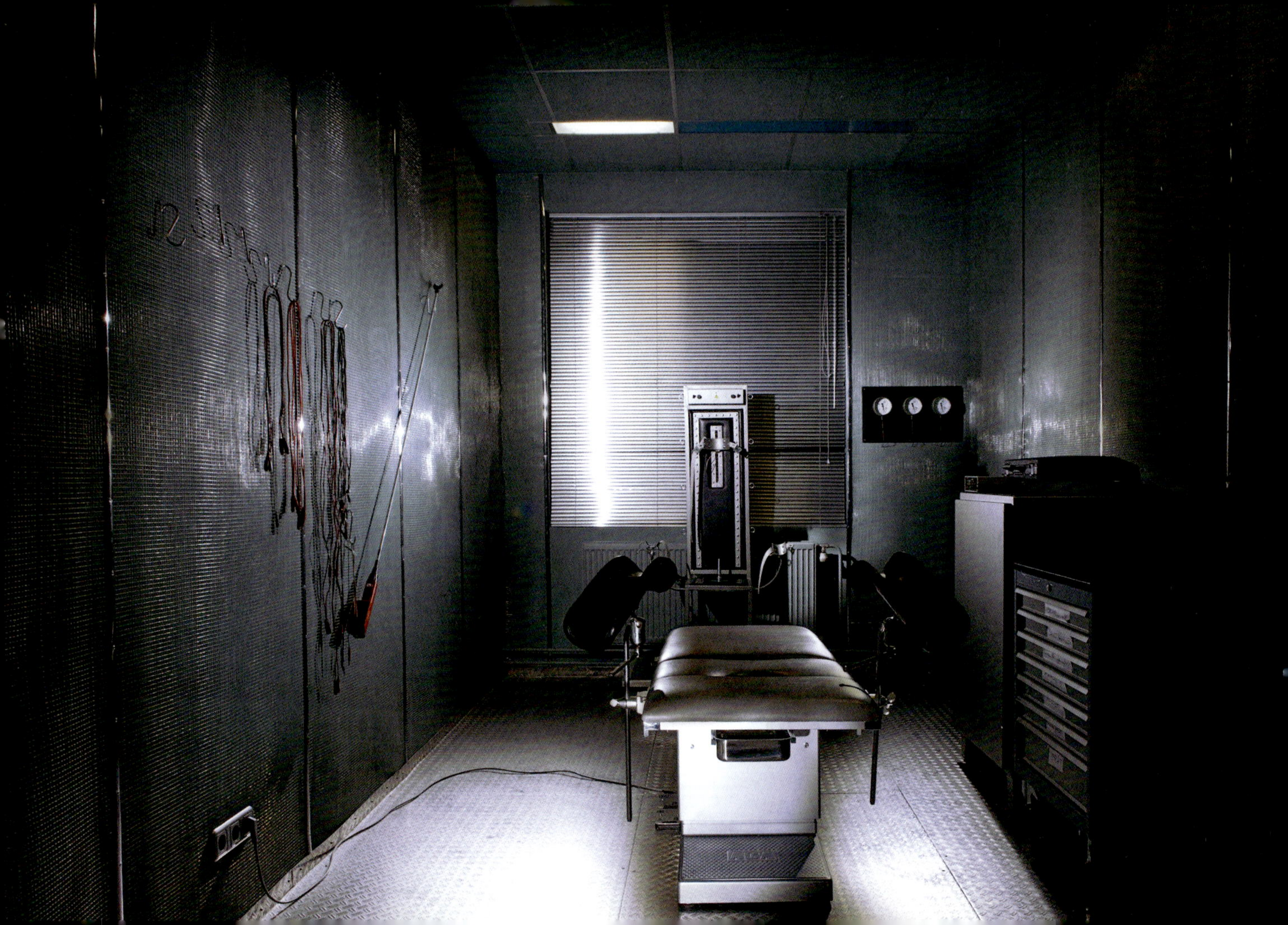

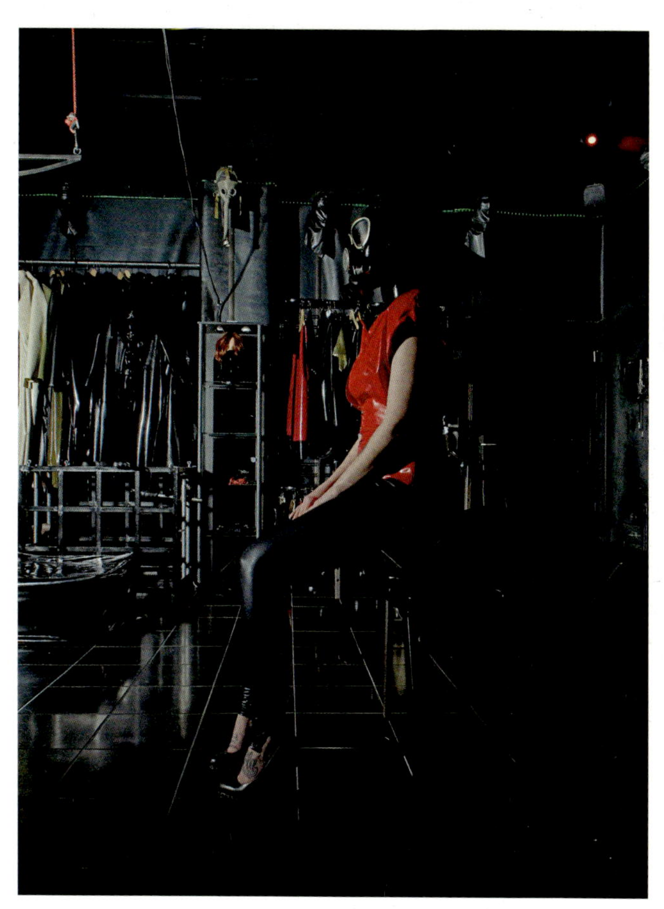

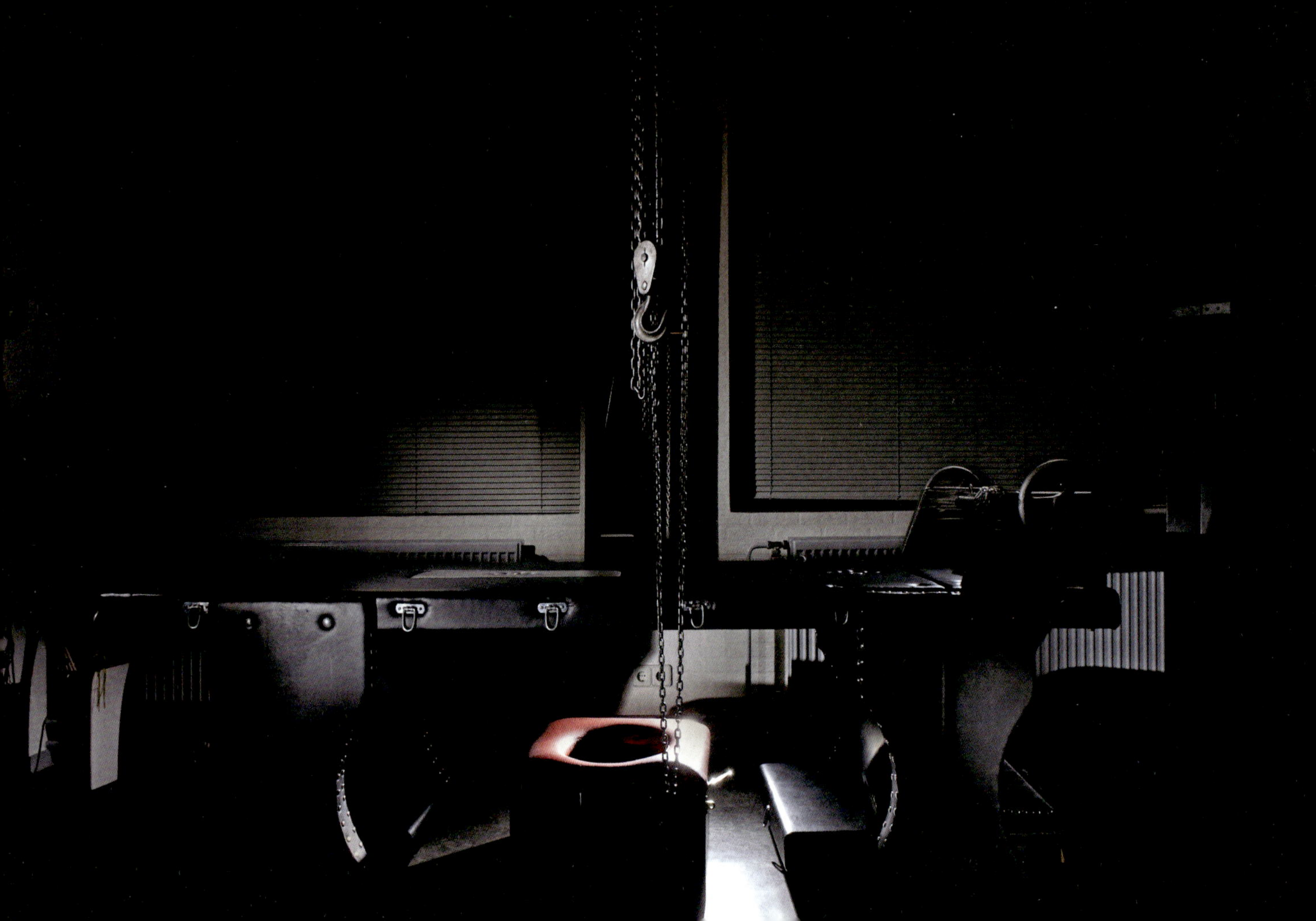

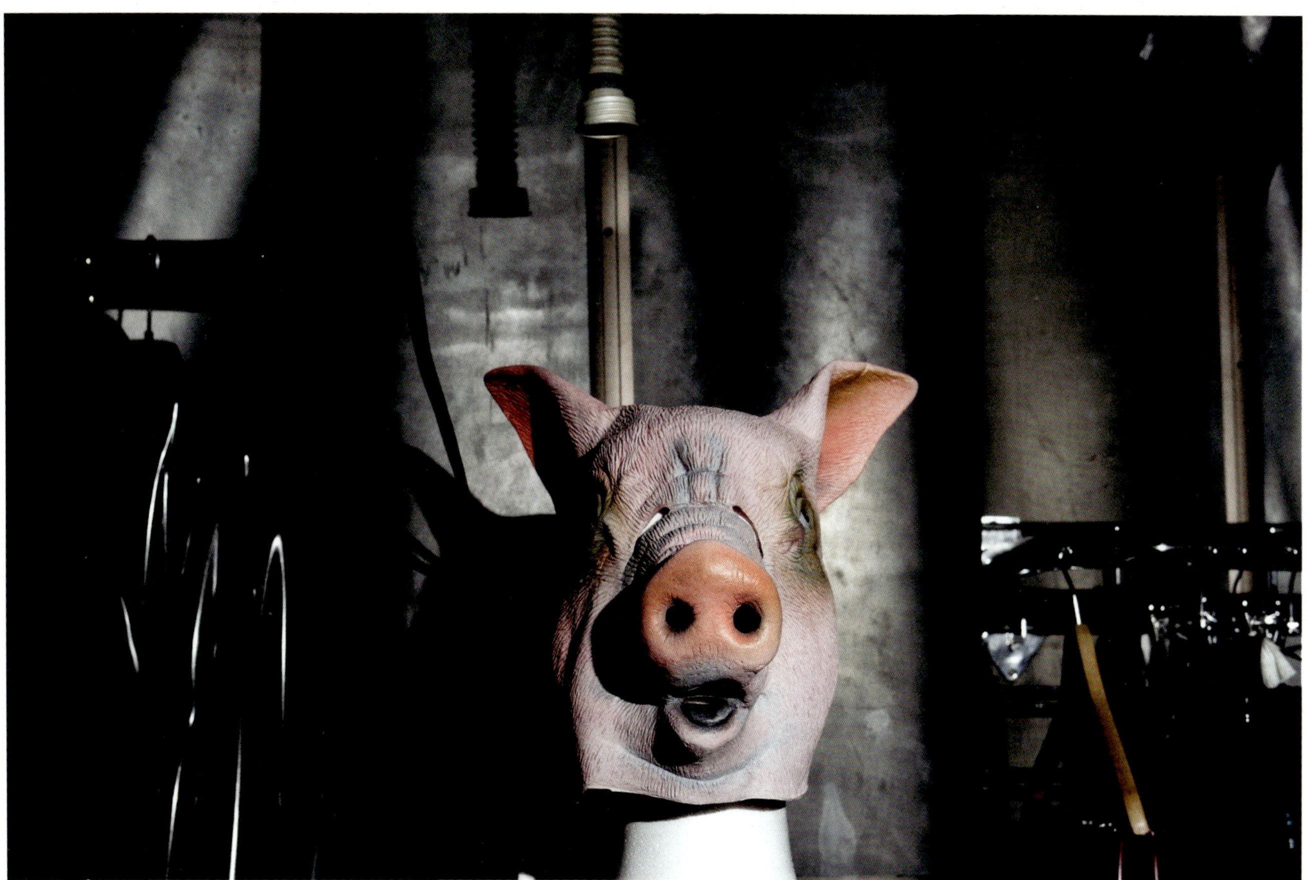

# DER WEDDING: GASSI ZWISCHEN SPIELBANK UND TEXTILDISCOUNT

## Wedding: Walking the dog between casino and discount clothing stores

Pilsatorbier zum Schleuderpreis, nächtliche Straßenfeste und Bauchtänze, Rabattaktionen beim Juwelier, Kopftuchmode im Textildiscounter, Männerrunden in Sportclubs, nächtliche Ampelrennen, Gemüsestände anatolischer Supermärkte und Eckkneipen mit Altberliner Charme, reges Treiben am Leopoldplatz.

*Cut-rate Pilsator Beer, nocturnal block parties and belly dancing, discount sales at the jeweler's, headscarf fashion at the discount clothing store, circles of men in the sport clubs, nighttime traffic-light races, vegetable stands at the Anatolian supermarkets and corner bars with Old Berlin charm, the madding crowd on Leopoldplatz.*

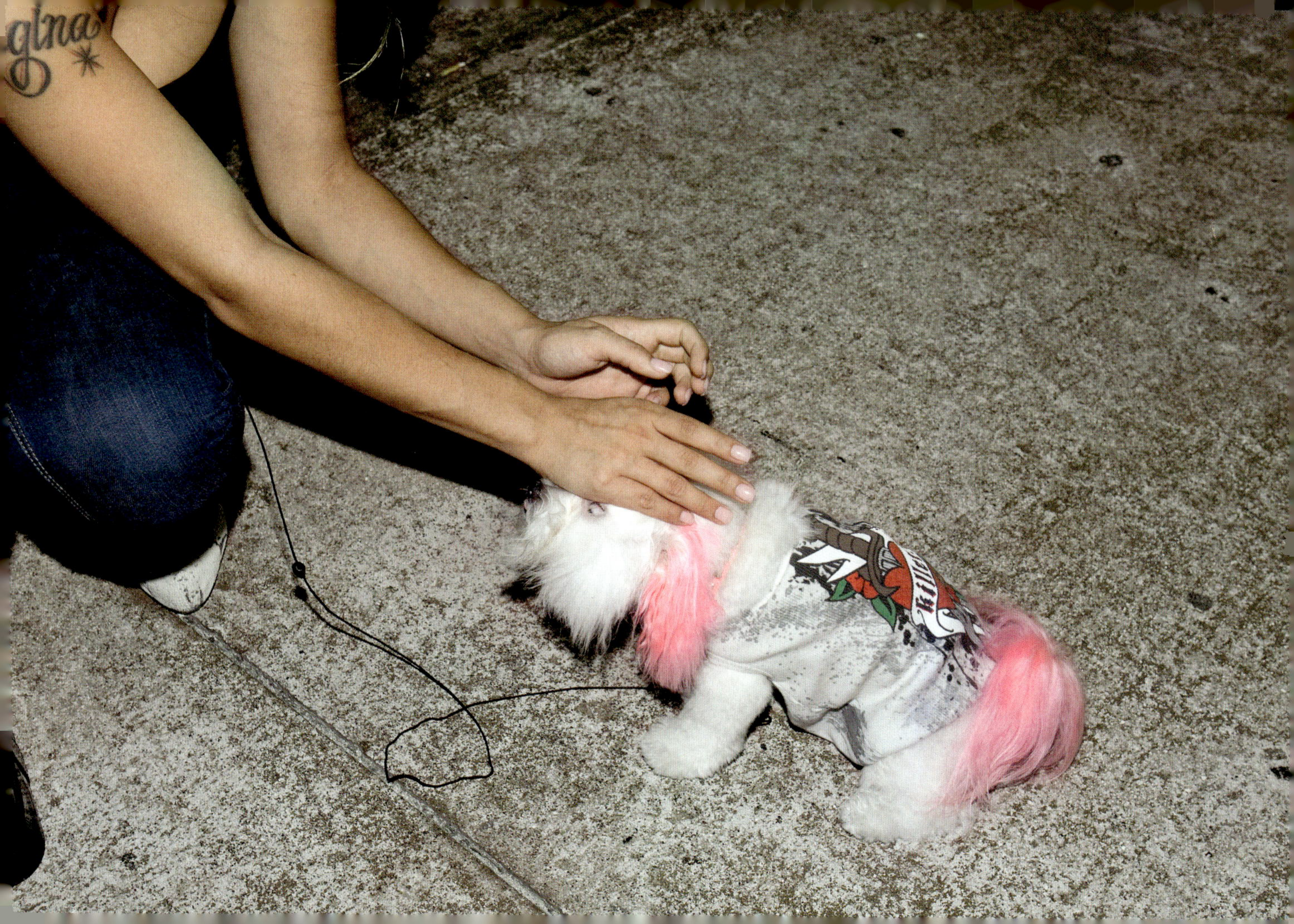

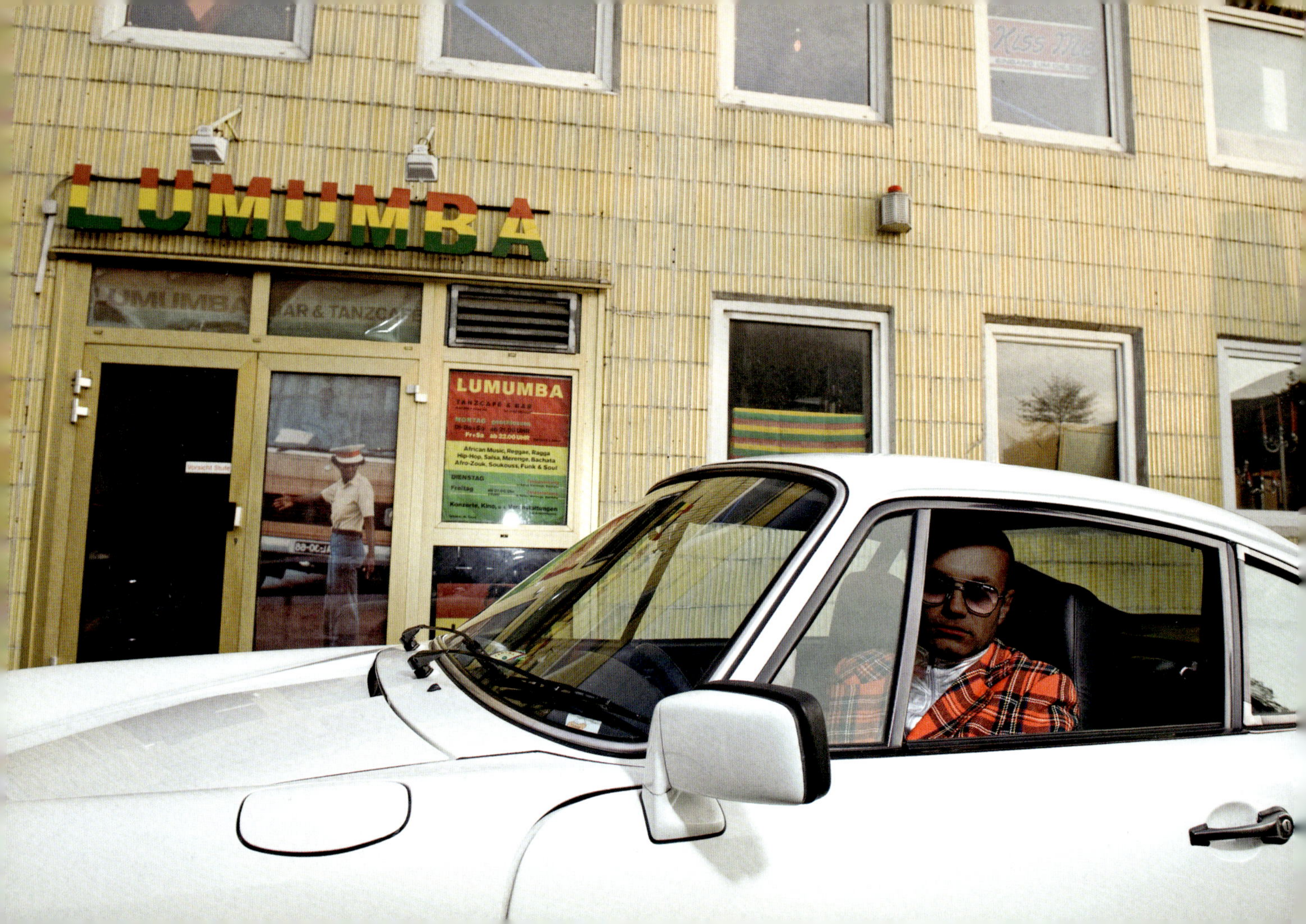

LUMUMBA
LUMUMBA BAR & TANZCAFÉ
LUMUMBA
TANZCAFÉ & BAR
MONTAG
Di–Do + Sa ab 21.00 Uhr
Fr+Sa ab 22.00 Uhr
African Music, Reggae, Ragga
Hip-Hop, Salsa, Merenge, Bachata
Afro-Zouk, Soukouss, Funk & Soul
DIENSTAG
Freitag
Konzerte, Kino, u. Veranstaltungen
Vorsicht Stufe
Kiss Me

**■■■■■■ AUS DEN BOXEN IM LUMUMBA DRÖHNT AFRO-ZOUK UND SOUKOUS. IM ERSTEN STOCK SCHMINKEN SICH AFRIKANISCHE SCHÖNHEITEN. VOR DEM EINGANG WARTET MAN MIT LAUFENDEM MOTOR AUF SEINE ANGEBETETE.**

*Afro Zouk and Soukous boom from the loudspeakers in the Lumumba. African beauties are making themselves up on the first floor. One waits for one's inamorata in front of the entrance with the motor running.*

**26** **Café Lumumba**
*Karl-Marx-Allee 35 . Berlin-Mitte*

**■ PREMIERE IM KINO INTERNATIONAL. BUNTE GÄSTE, DARUNTER SELBST ERNANNTE AVANTGARDISTEN, BLICKEN AUF DIE STRASSE, WO SICH TAXIFAHRER NEBEN DEM GROSSEN SOZIALISTISCHEN WANDFRIES DES GEBÄUDES POSTIERT HABEN.**

*Premiere in Kino International. The colorful guests, including some self-proclaimed members of the avant-garde, look off to the street where taxi drivers are posted next to the building's large socialist wall frieze.*

**27** Kino International
*Karl-Marx-Allee 33 . Berlin-Mitte*

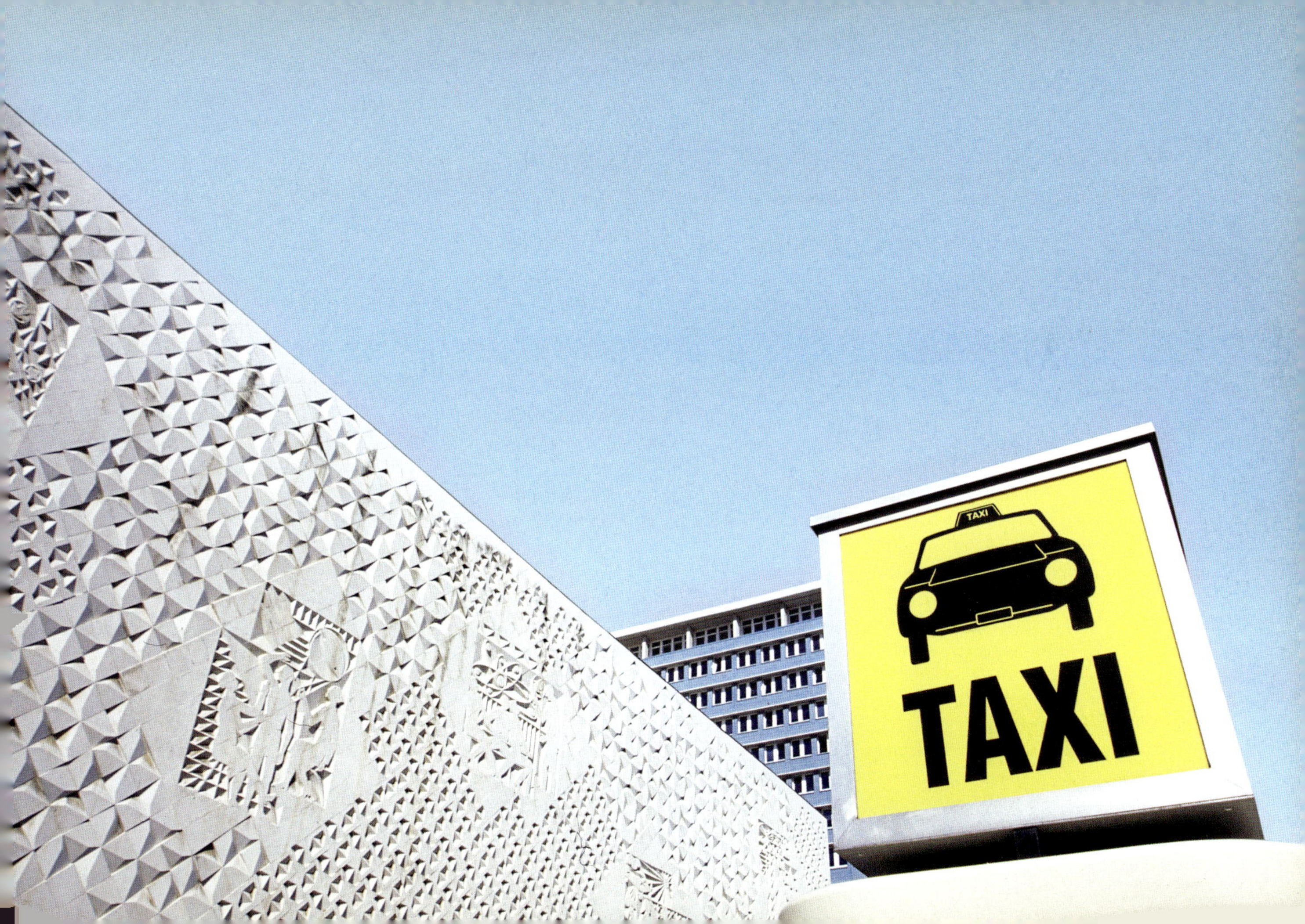
TAXI
TAXI

# ERICH MIELKES ZIMMERPFLANZE

## *Erich Mielke's house plant*

**28** **Stasimuseum Berlin**
*Ruschestraße 103 . Berlin-Lichtenberg*

Im dritten Stock des Plattenbaus ziehen Besucher ihre Runden durch die musealen Gänge der ehemaligen Zentrale für Staatssicherheit der DDR. Eine Schulklasse inspiziert das einstige Arbeitszimmer des Leiters Erich Mielke. Die offene Tür eines Tresors an der Wand offenbart Leere. Aus einem Aktenvernichter am Fuße des Chefsessels quellen geschredderte Dokumente. Im Nebenzimmer verharrt ein Tontechniker bewundernd vor einer der Telefonanlagen, die direkten Kontakt zum Kreml boten, und blickt hinauf zum Transistorradio. Dort kleben noch Markierungen der ehemaligen verbotenen westdeutschen Radiofrequenzen. Der Staat ist tot, die ausgeprägte Flora der ehemaligen Zentrale – Dutzende von Topfpflanzen – lebt weiter.

*On the third floor of the prefabricated building, the visitors make their rounds through the museum-like corridors of the former headquarters of the East German Ministry for State Security. A group of school children inspect the office of its old head, Erich Mielke. The opened door of a wall safe reveals emptiness. Documents swell from the file shredder at the foot of the executive chair. In an adjacent room, a sound technician stands frozen in amazement in front of one of the telephone systems that offered contact to the Kremlin and looks up to the transistor radio. Markings indicating the frequencies of formerly prohibited West German radio stations are still pasted on the radio. The state is dead, the distinctive flora of the former headquarters, dozens of potted plants, lives on.*

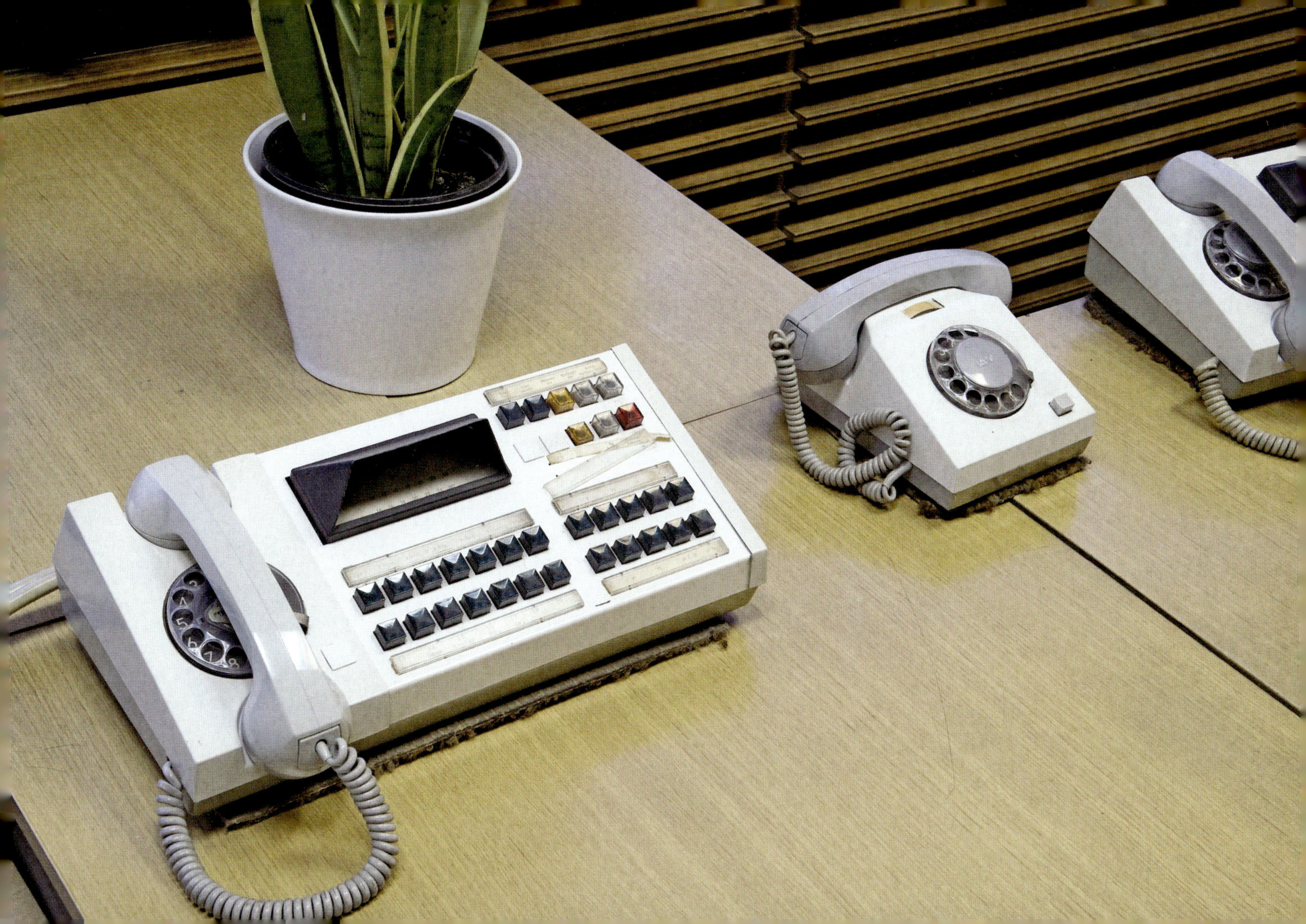

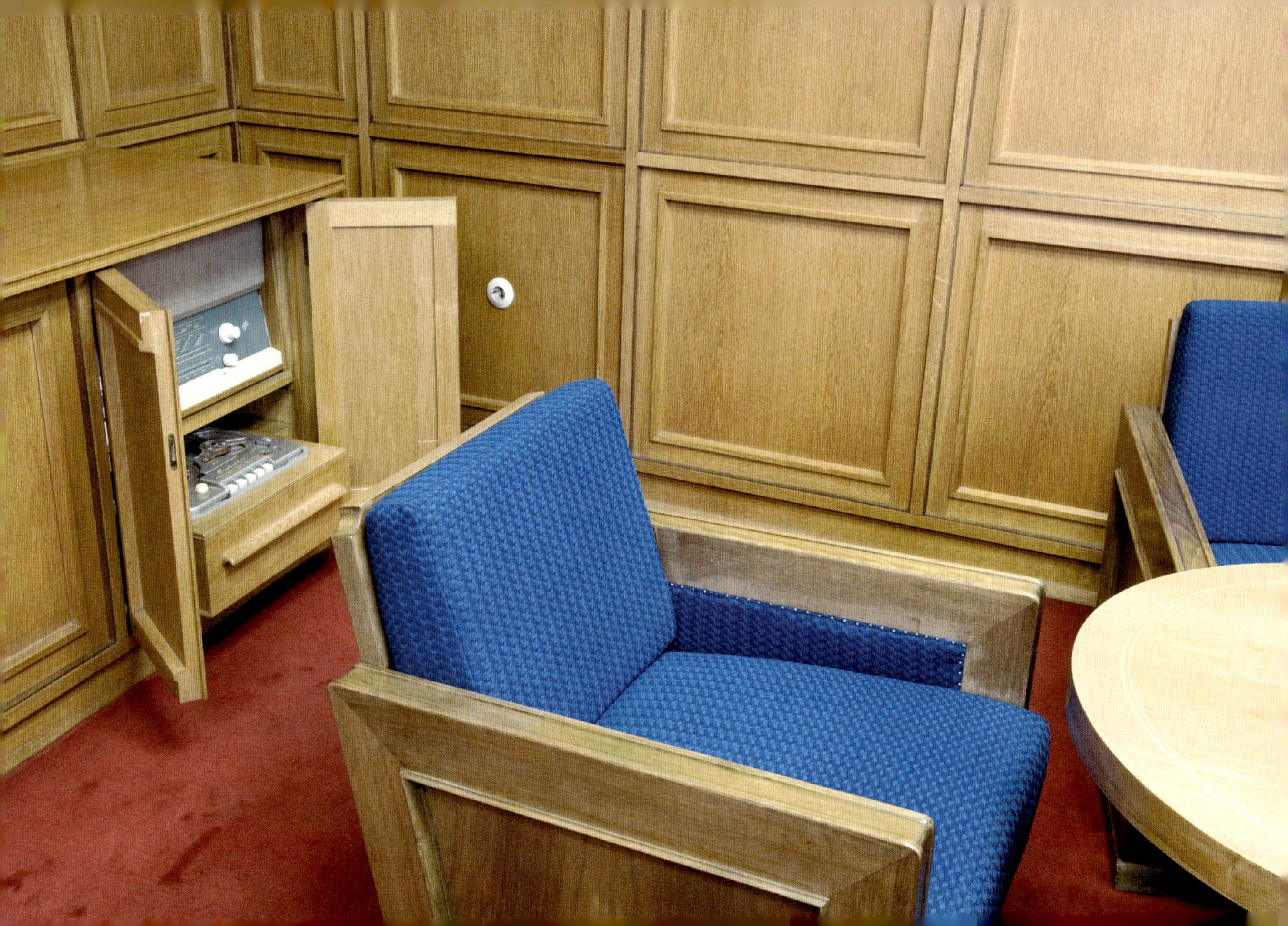

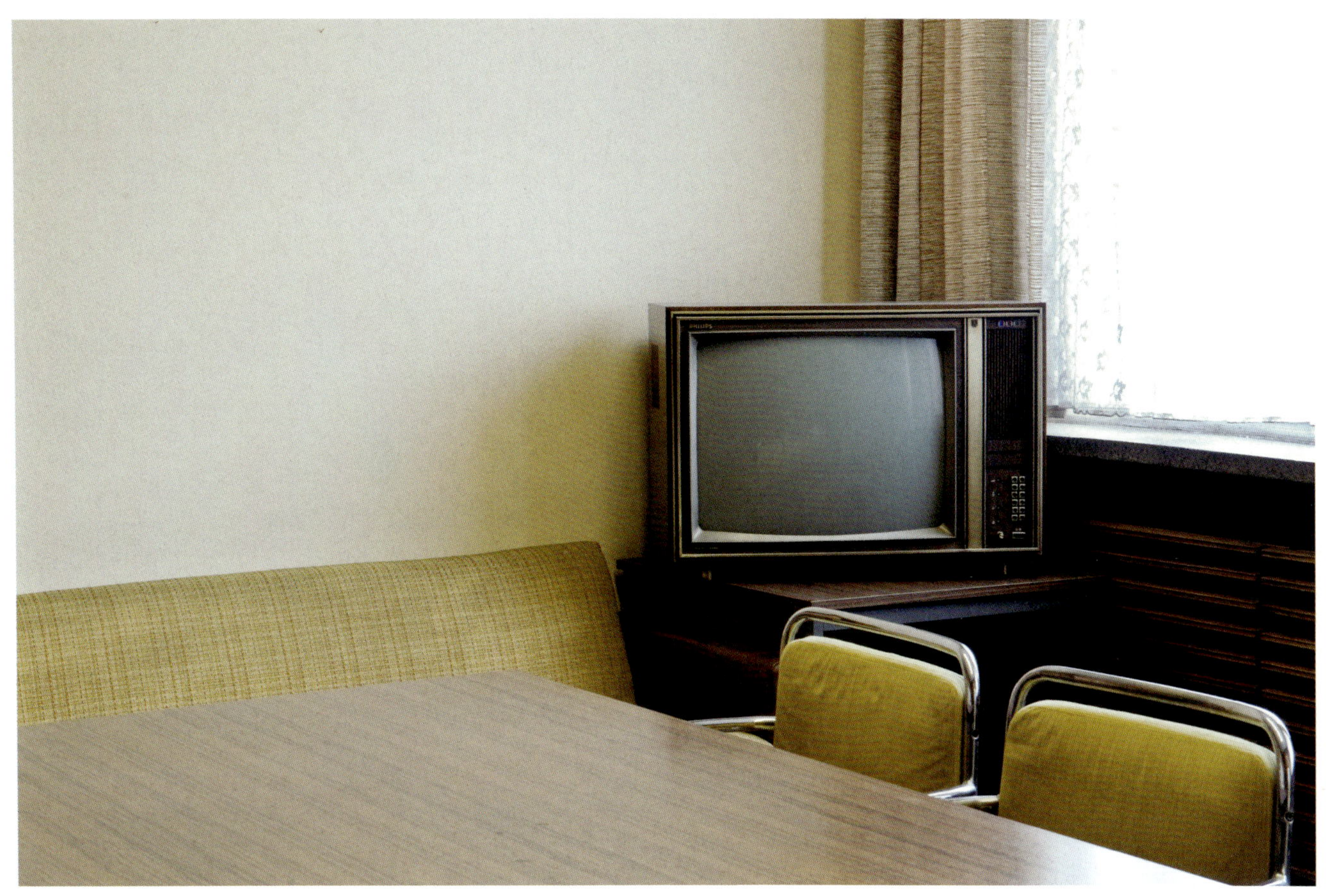

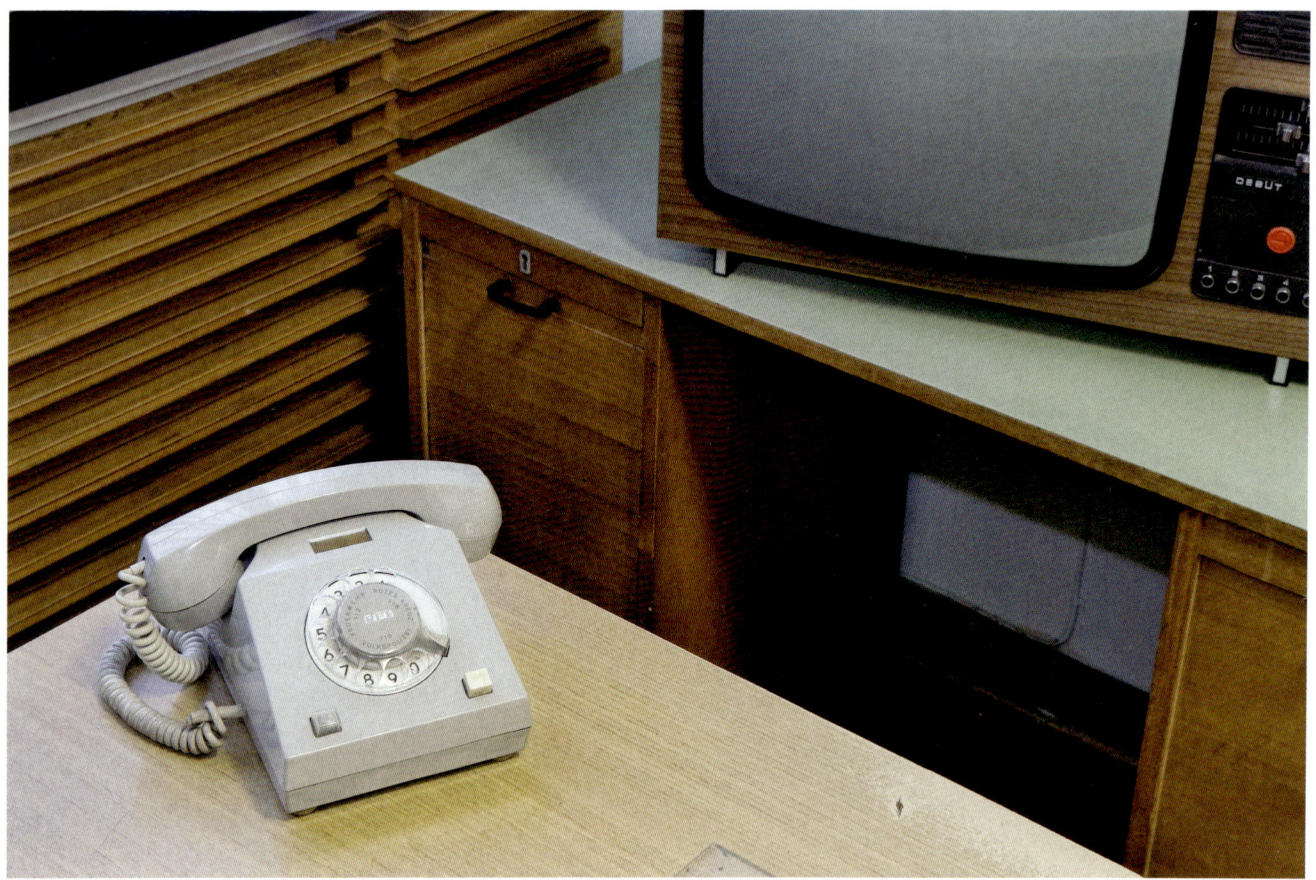

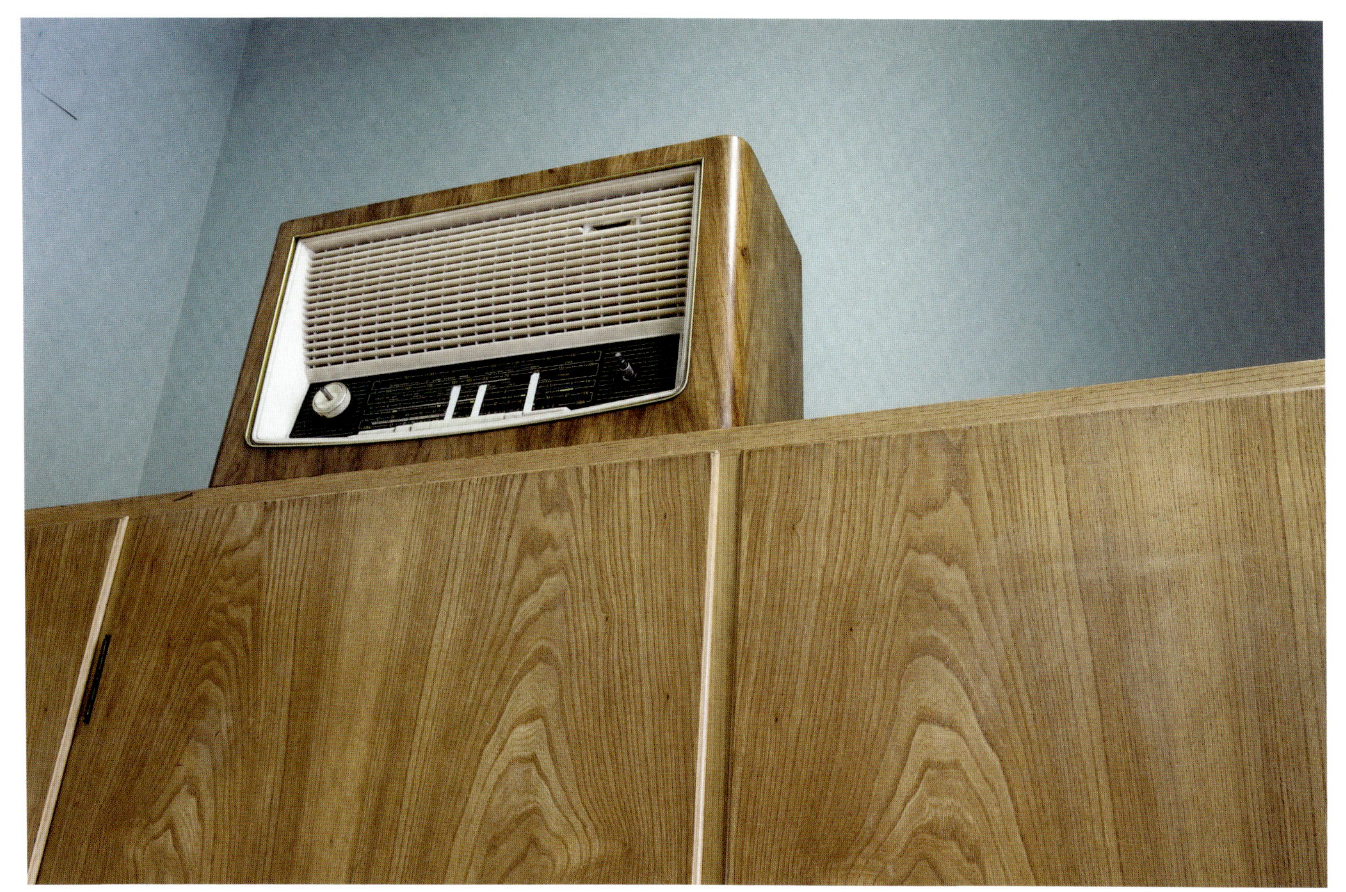

# DEUTSCHER TIMES SQUARE
## German Times Square

**29** **Potsdamer Platz**
*Berlin-Tiergarten*

Hell leuchtet die amerikanisch anmutende Skyline des Potsdamer Platzes vor dem nächtlichen Himmel. Vor dem Ritz Carlton Hotel fährt eine Limousine vor, ein Mann mit Borsalino auf dem Kopf steigt aus und betritt flotten Schritts die im Art-déco-Stil gehaltene Hotellobby. Eine Gruppe Geschäftsmänner verlässt mit Schnaps angefüllt eine der aufgebauten Almhütten gegenüber und versucht ein Taxi herbeizurufen. Die auf einem wackligen Klappfahrrad vorbeiradelnde Studentin runzelt die Stirn und biegt in Richtung Kreuzberg ab. Vereinzelt tauchen Gestalten, meist Touristen, zwischen den Häuserfluchten auf. Gegen Mitternacht ist das Areal wie leergefegt. Berliner Nächte finden woanders statt.

*The seemingly American skyline of Potsdamer Platz is brightly lit against the nocturnal sky. A limousine drives up to the Ritz Carlton Hotel. A man wearing a fedora gets out and walks sprightly through the Art Deco hotel lobby. A group of schnapsfilled business men leave one of the alpine cabins constructed on the other side and try to hail a cab. A student riding past on a rickety folding bicycle furrows his brows and makes a turn in the direction of Kreuzberg. Various figures, usually tourists, turn up one at a time on the cavernous streets. The area is empty around midnight. Berlin nights take place somewhere else.*

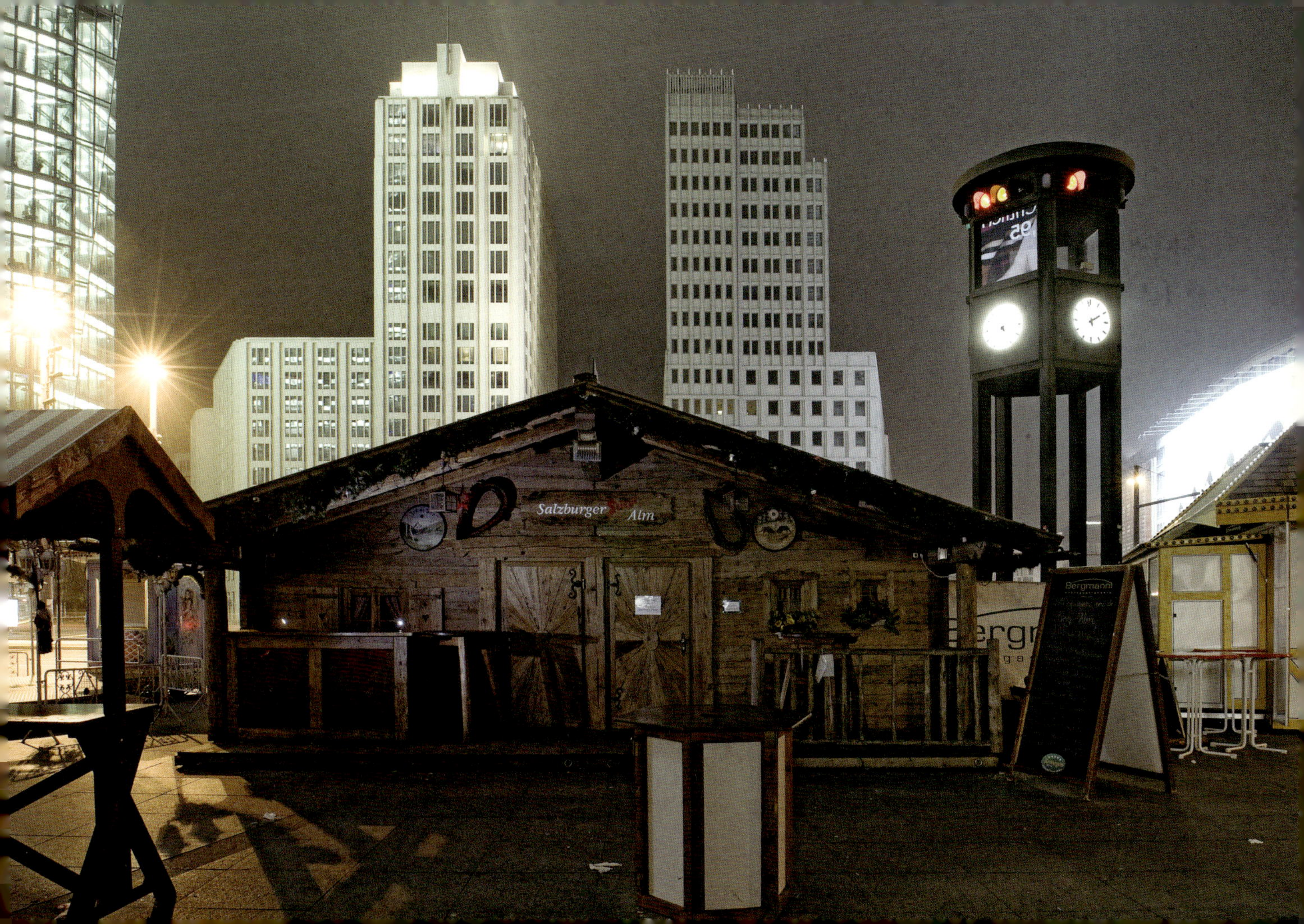

Salzburger Alm
Bergmann

Equipped with a map, the old man blazes his trail through the back streets. And then salvation … The object of his desire stands before him: one of the few still-existing East German watchtowers.

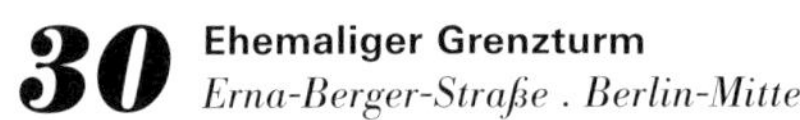

**30** **Ehemaliger Grenzturm**
*Erna-Berger-Straße . Berlin-Mitte*

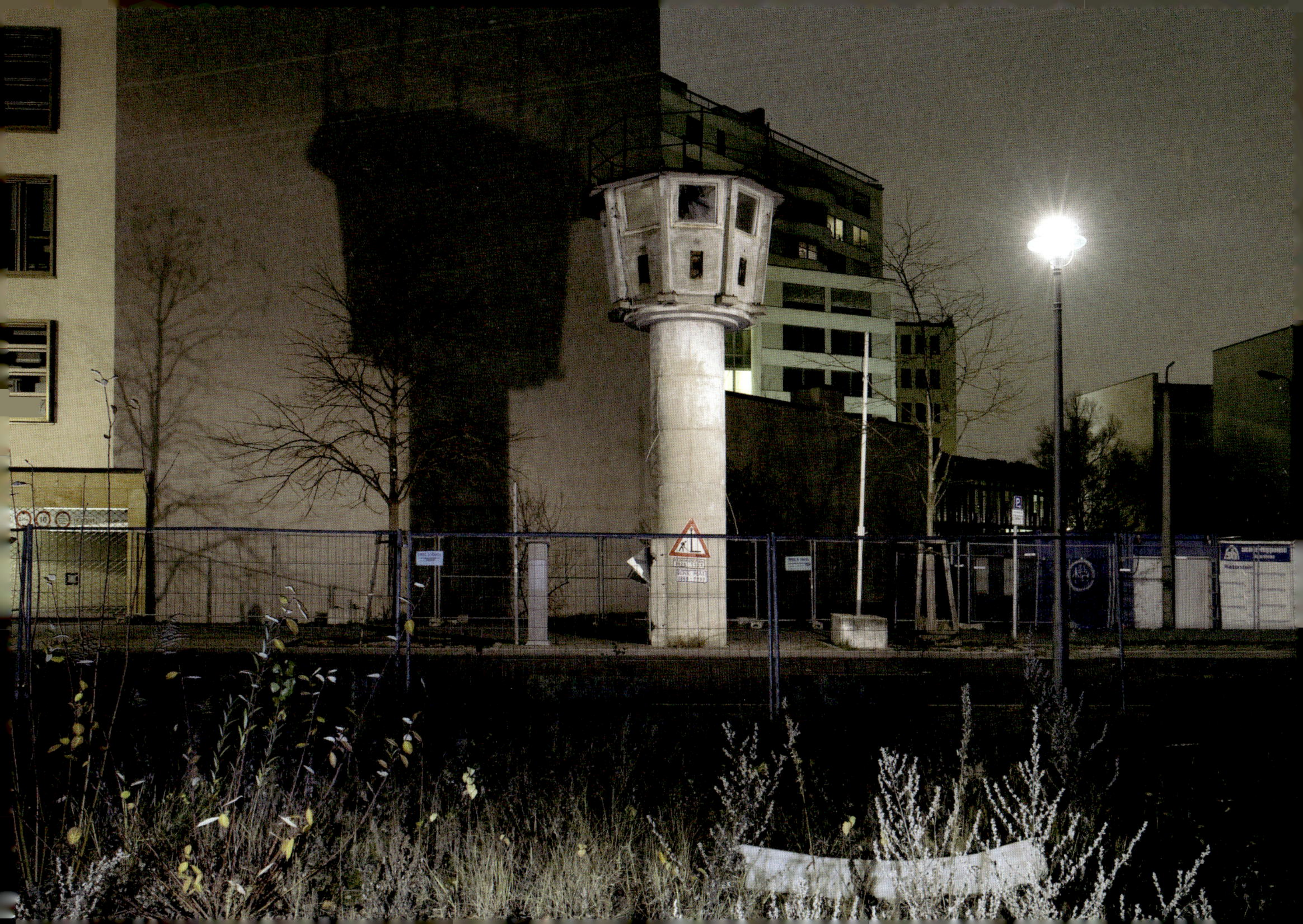

**■ HEKTISCHES TREIBEN NACH MESSESCHLUSS IM ICC. GESCHÄFTSLEUTE FÜLLEN DEN U-BAHNHOF. EIN MANN IM DUNKELBLAUEN ZWEIREIHER UND MIT JACHTPROSPEKTEN UNTER DEM ARM EILT IN RICHTUNG BAHNSTEIG.**

*Hustle and bustle after the trade fair at the ICC.*
*Business people fill up the subway station. A man wearing a dark*
*blue double-breasted suit and with yacht brochures under his*
*arm hurries off towards the platform.*

**31** **Messe Berlin**
*Messedamm 22 . Berlin-Charlottenburg*

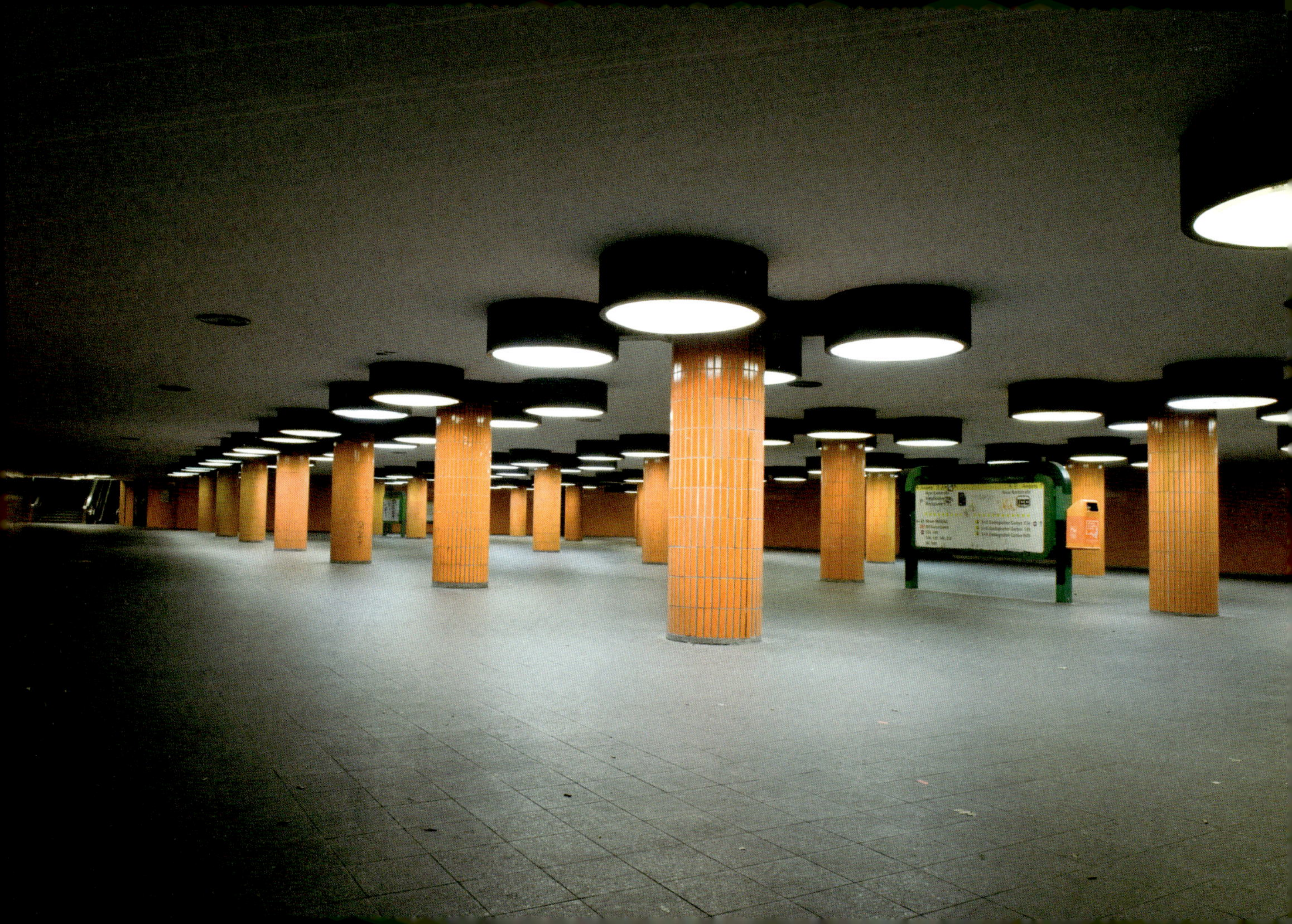

# STUTEN AM STUTTI
## *Sluts on Stutti*



Plateau Pumps mit schillernd blauen Plastiksohlen gleiten an der verchromten Stange hinab. Der schlanke Körper einer langbeinigen Schönheit rekelt sich auf dem Catwalk. Die fünf Besucher der Tabledance-Bar, die Junggesellenabschied feiern, werfen den Animierdamen gierige Blicke zu. Einer legt seinen Arm um die Taille der gelb gekleideten Bedienung. Draußen vor der Tür versucht Hure Elvira mit einem überlegten Griff in Gürtelhöhe einen der flanierenden jungen Männer in die Bar hineinzuziehen. Der aber hat die Billigshops nebenan und einen Waffenladen im Auge und widersteht der Versuchung. In einem angrenzenden Restaurant spielen sich zur selben Zeit andere Szenen ab. Medienleute, Lebenskünstler und Schauspieler sitzen dort bei Linguine mit Scampi.

*Plateau pumps with glitzy blue plastic soles slide along the chromed pole. The slender body of a long-legged beauty lolls down down the catwalk. The five visitors at the table-dance bar celebrating a stag party cop a voracious look at the hostesses. One of them winds his arm around the waist of the waitress dressed in yellow. Outside, at the entrance, the whore Elvira tries to rope in one of the young men strolling past the bar with a deliberate belt-level grasp. But he is more attracted by the neighboring discount stores as well as the gun store and thus resists temptation. Different scenes are playing out at the same time in an adjoining restaurant. Media figures, connoisseurs of the art of living, and actors sit there over plates of linguine with prawns.*

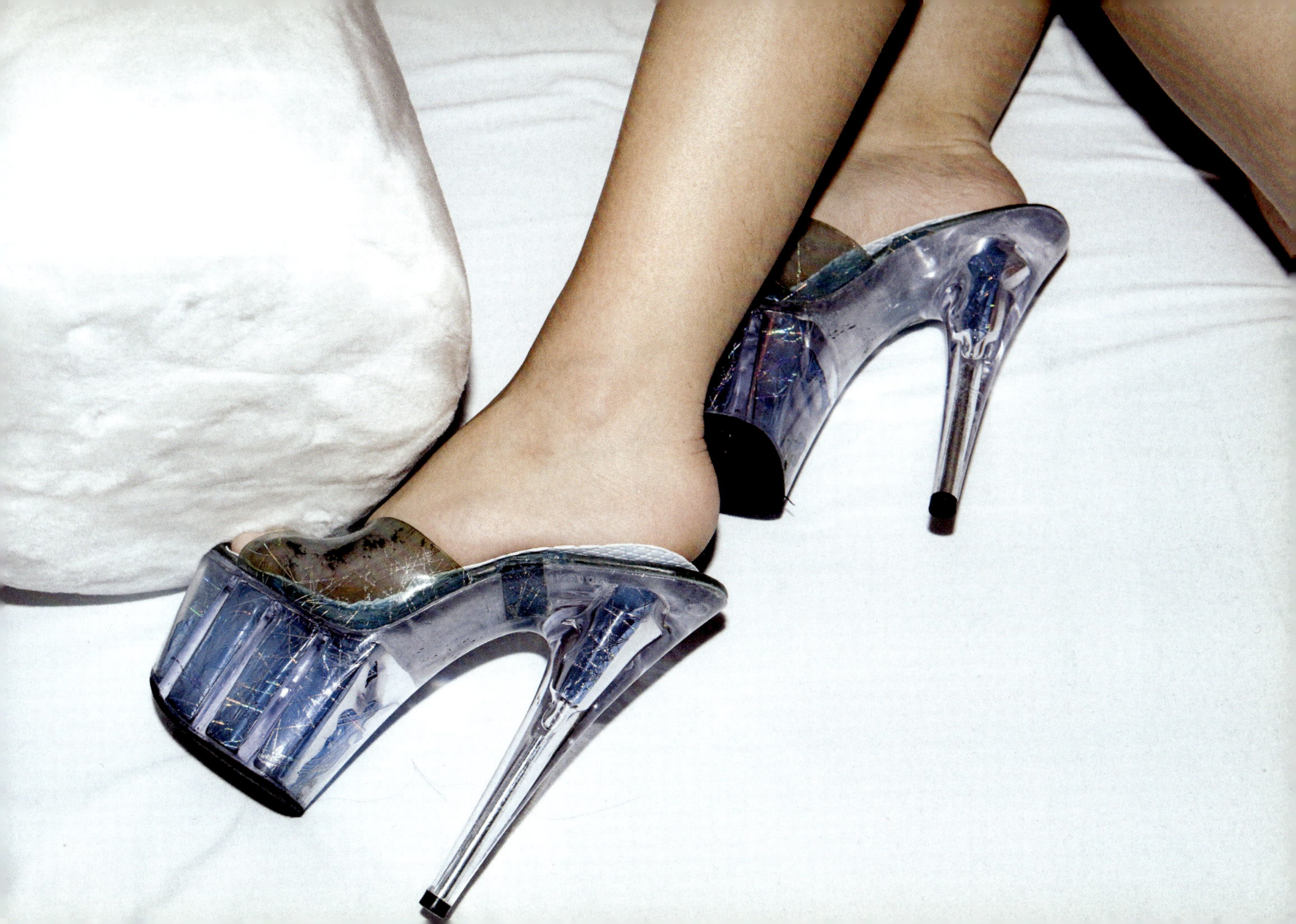

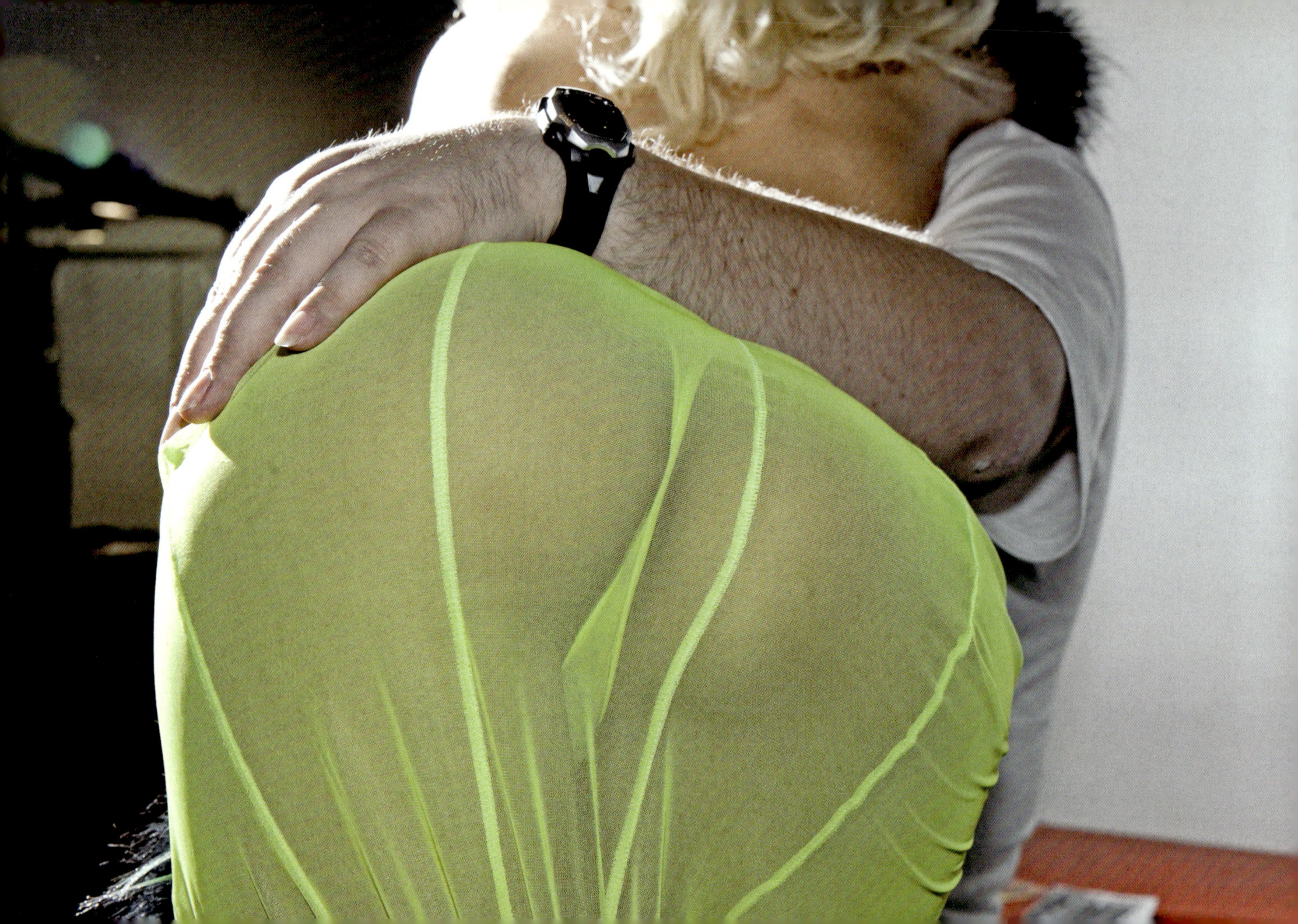

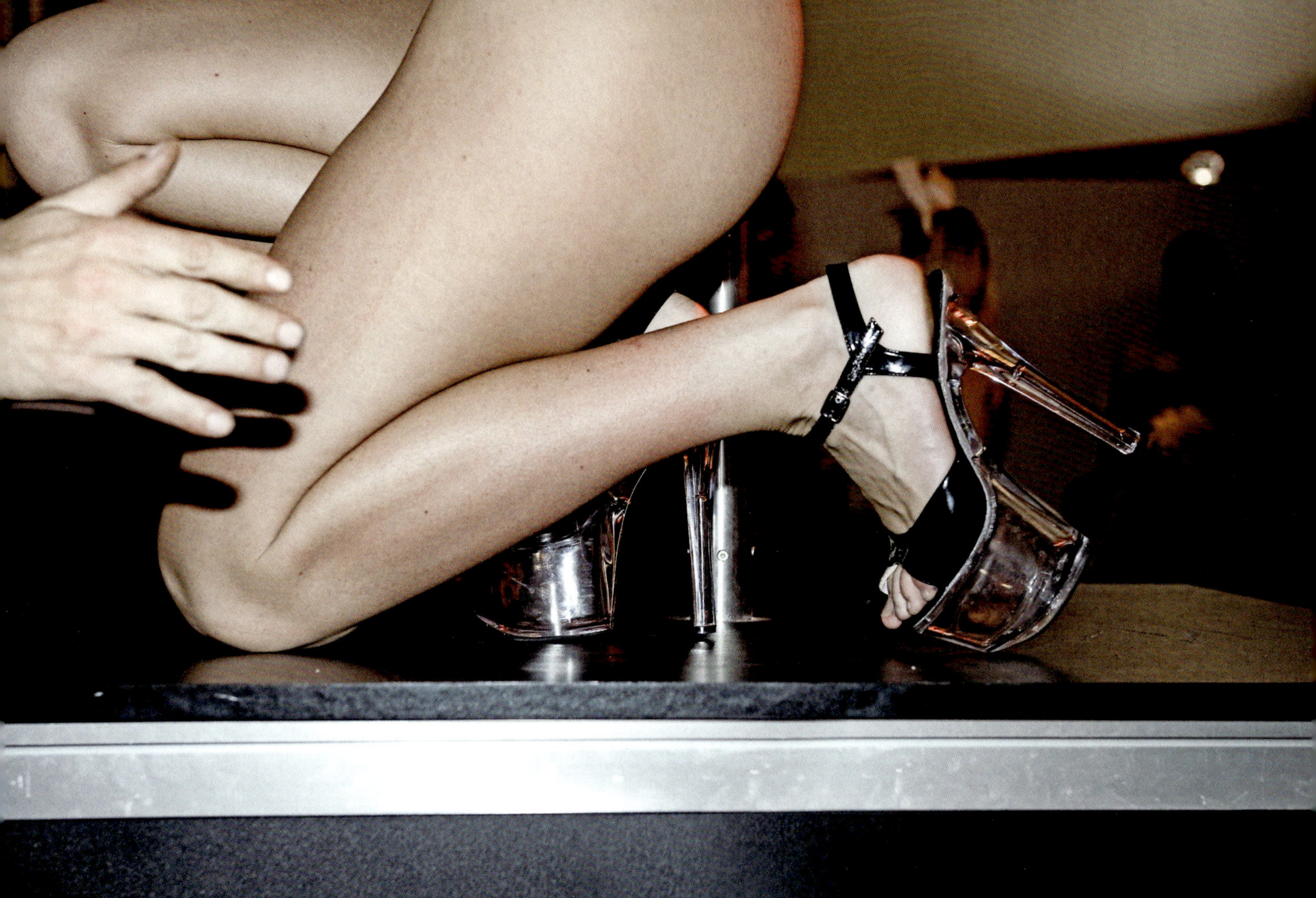

## Spandau:

## citadel, sluice, and colonists

Spandauer Forst und Birkenwäldchen, Senioren auf dem Wochenmarkt, FKK am Grimnitzsee, Tretboote auf der Havel, »Berliner Schnauze« in der Bierschenke, Andacht in der St. Nikolai-Kirche, Komödie auf der Freilichtbühne, Barbecue in der Kolonie Alpenveilchen, Haselhorst und Juliusturm, Softeis in den Arkaden.

*Spandau Forest and birch woods, senior citizens at the farmers' market, nude bathing at Lake Grimnitz, paddleboats on the Havel river, some "Berlin lip" at the alehouse, a prayer meeting in the Church of St. Nicholas, a comedy at the open-air theater, a barbecue in the Cyclamen Colony, Haselhorst and Juliusturm, soft ice cream at the Arkaden.*

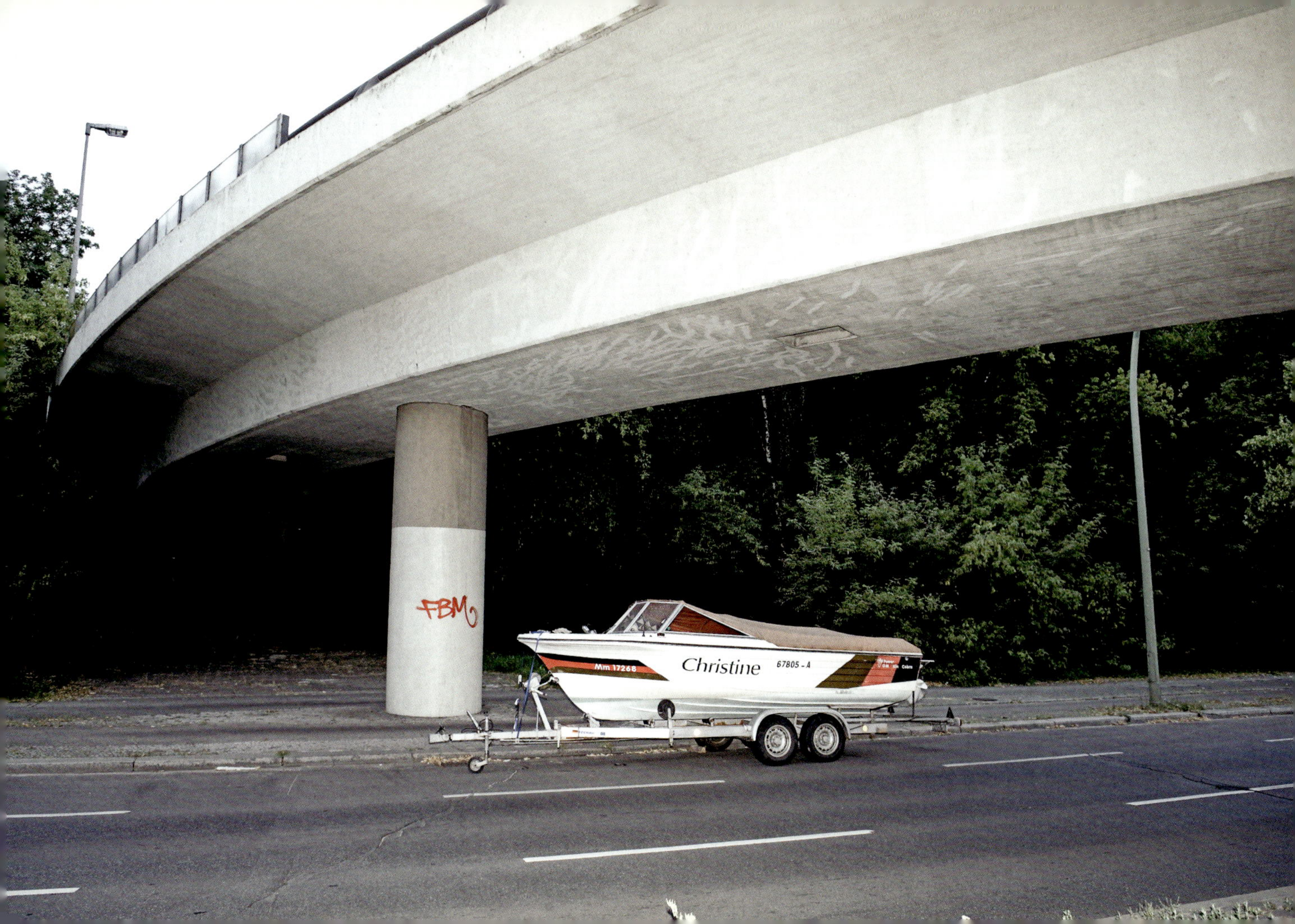
FBM
Christine
Mm 17268
67805 - A

# PROJEKT ECHELON
## Echelon Project

**33** **Ehemalige US-Radarstation**
*Teufelsberg . Berlin Charlottenburg*

Die ehemalige US-Radarstation aus den Zeiten des Kalten Krieges steht verlassen auf der Spitze des Teufelsberges. Die weitläufige Ruine stemmt sich dem pfeifenden Wind entgegen. Kugelförmige Aufsätze auf Dach und Türmen – früher Abhöranlagen – leuchten weiß. Fetzen der Abdeckung peitschen umher. Der Weg führt ins Innere des Komplexes. Hinter einem der Eingänge verbergen sich zerstörte Büroräume und ehemals abhörsichere Bereiche. Im Hauptgebäude führt der Weg durch einen Treppenschacht hinauf auf eine Aussichtsplattform. Zwei der gewaltigen »Abhörkugeln« liegen dort wie überdimensionale Golfbälle. Der Blick reicht weit, auf dem benachbarten Berg lassen Familien ihre Drachen steigen.

*The former American radar station dating from the Cold War era stands deserted on the peak of Teufelsberg. The expansive ruin braces itself against the howling wind. Spherical attachments on the roof and the towers, old listening devices, glow white. Tattered shreds of their old casings flap about. The path leads to the interior of the complex. Demolished offices and formerly bug-proof areas are hidden behind one of the entrances. In the main building, the path leads up through a stairwell to an observation deck. Two of the monumental "listening spheres" lie there like over-sized golf balls. The view goes on for miles; families are flying their kites on the adjacent hill.*

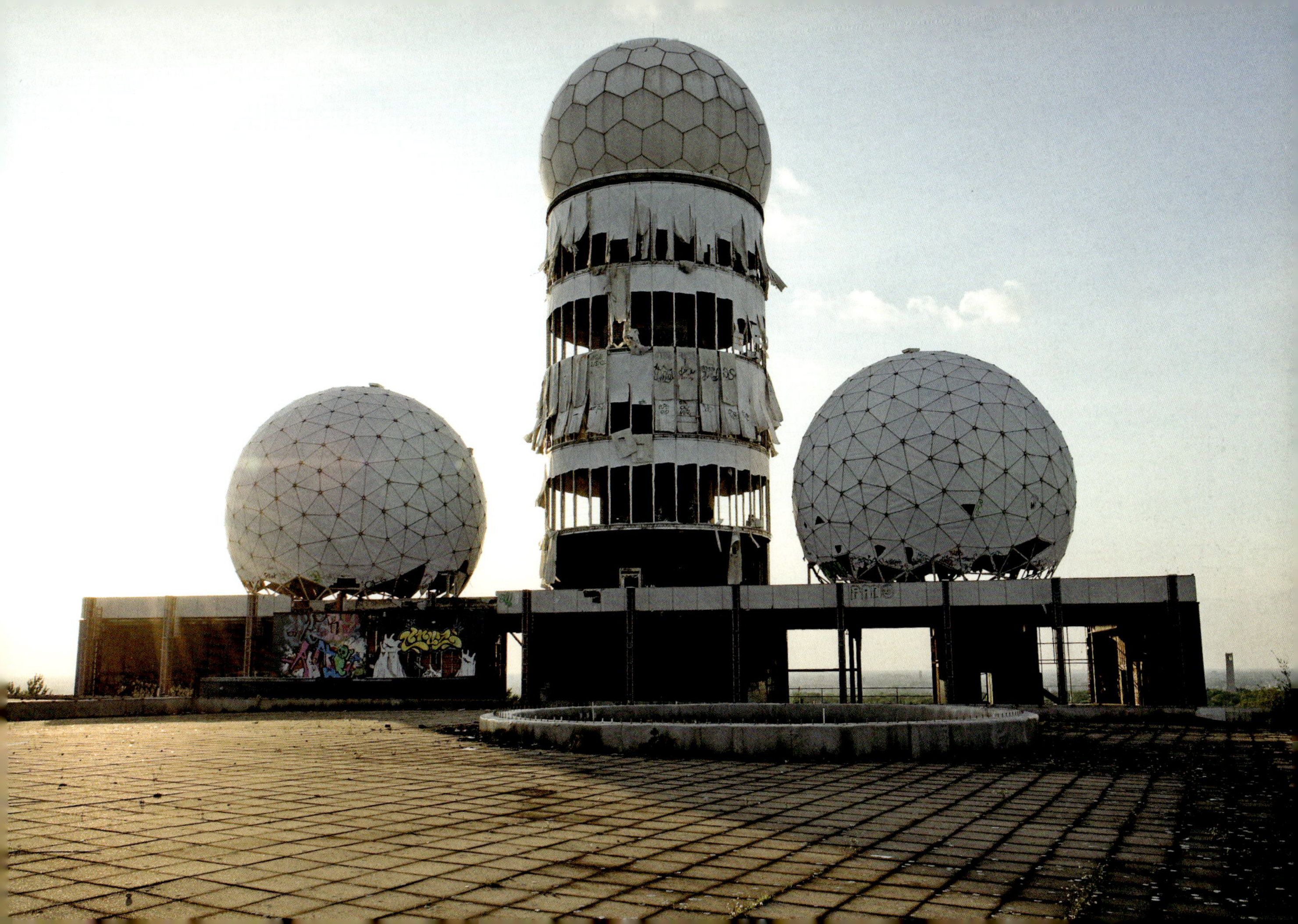

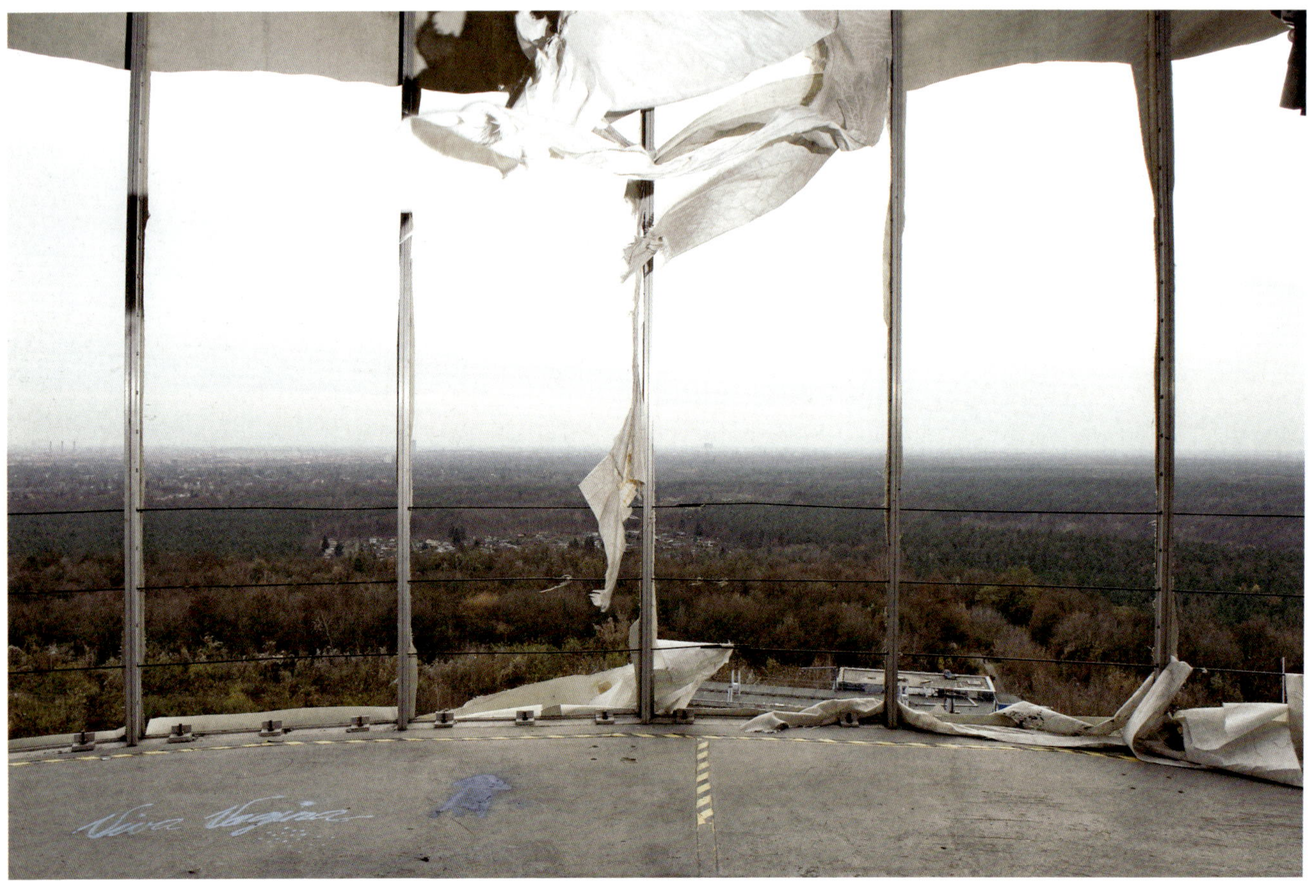

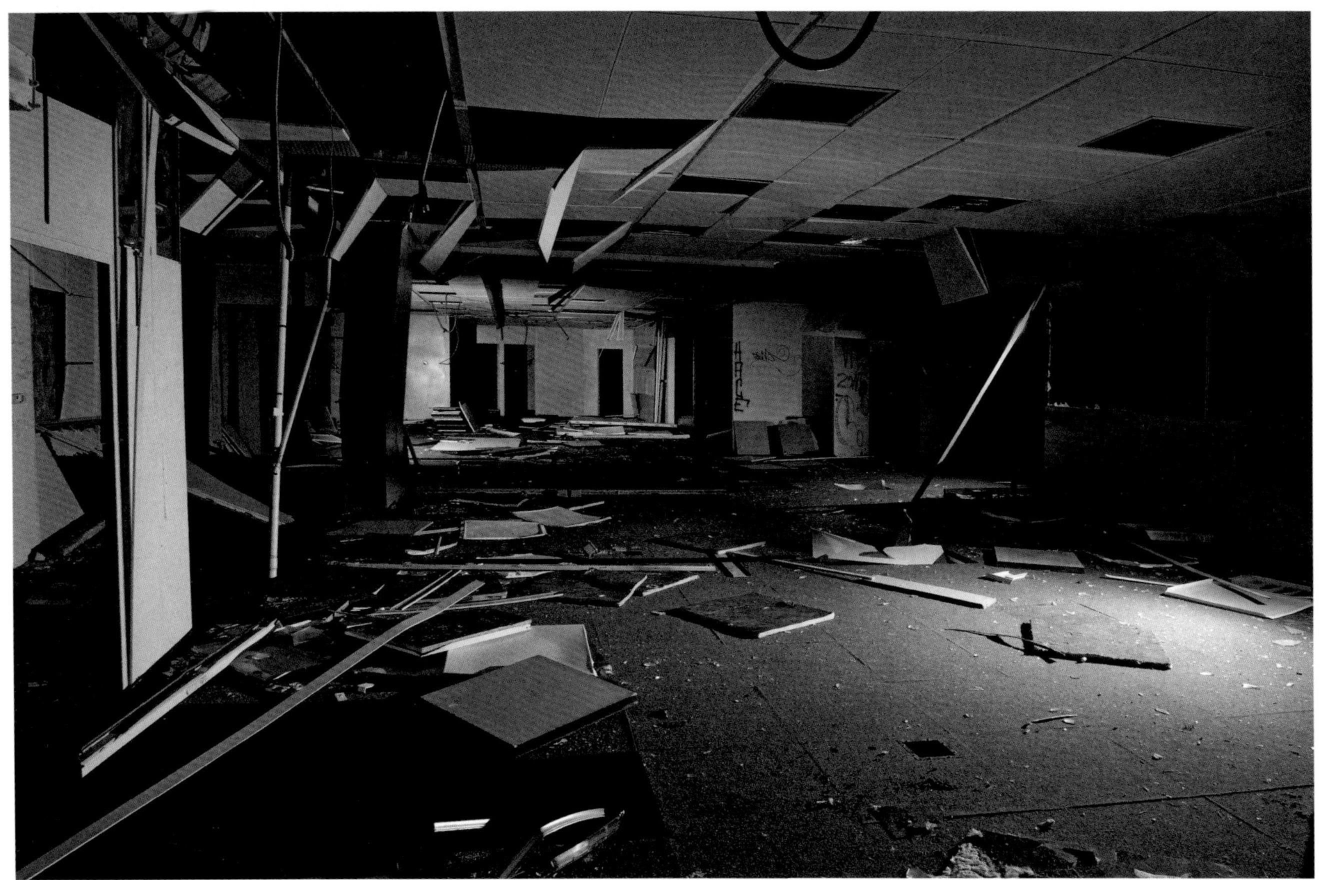

# DIE TURBINEN DREHEN SICH NICHT MEHR

## The turbines no longer spin

**34** **Flughafen Tempelhof**
*Platz der Luftbrücke 5 . Berlin-Tempelhof*

Auf dem Vorfeld erklingt die stramme Marschmusik des sich in korrekter Formation bewegenden Musikcorps. Ein Besucher wippt mit seiner braunen Sandale den Takt mit und beißt genüsslich in einen Pfannkuchen. Mit einem Abschiedstusch wird das Ende des Flughafenbetriebs zelebriert. Die untergehende Sonne wirft ihr Licht auf den gigantischen, geschichtsträchtigen Komplex und dessen Hangars mit den grünen Toren. Noch einmal salutiert ein ordenbehangener Offizier in Richtung Vorfeld, Tränen fließen. Eine angereiste Amerikanerin posiert hastig vor einem Rosinenbomber für ein letztes Foto zu zweit. Leise ertönt der Ruf des Muezzins aus der benachbarten Sehitlik Moschee.

*The brisk march music of a music corps moving in a correct formation resounds on the maneuvering area. A visitor keeps time with his brown sandal and takes obvious pleasure in biting into a pancake. The end of the airport operations is celebrated with a final fanfare. The setting sun casts its light on the gigantic, historical complex and its hangars with their green gates. An officer with a chest full of medals salutes one last time in the direction of the maneuvering area; tears flow. An American visitor hastily poses in front of a "raisin bomber" for a last picture of the two of them. The call of the muezzin from the neighboring Sehitlik mosque resounds softly.*

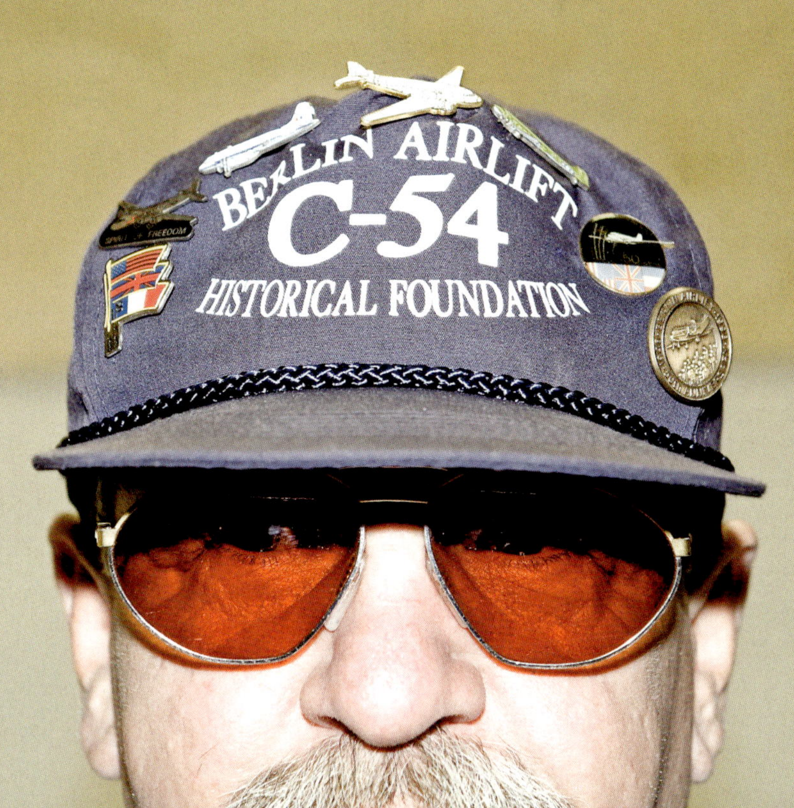
BERLIN AIRLIFT
C-54
HISTORICAL FOUNDATION
SPIRIT + FREEDOM

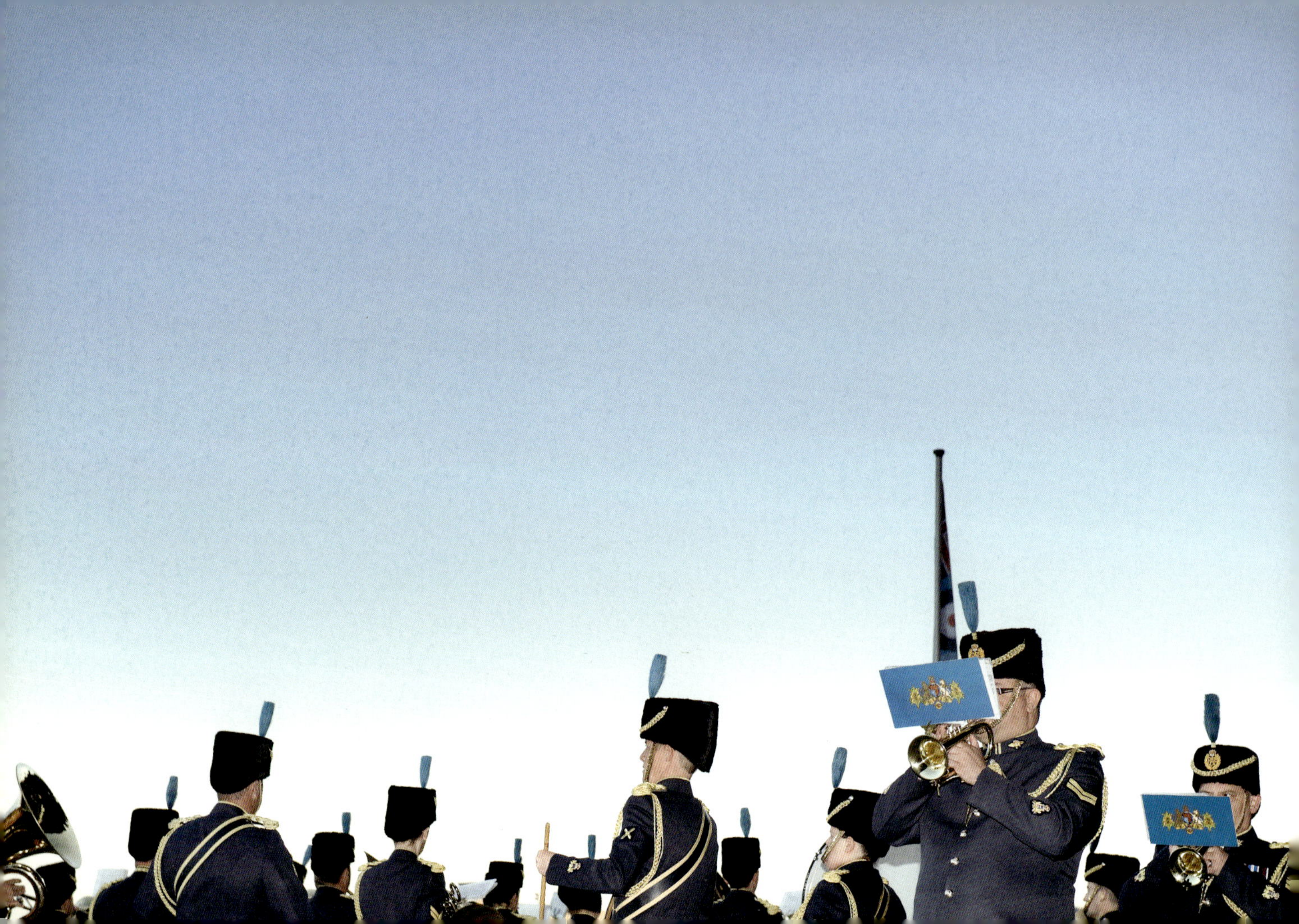

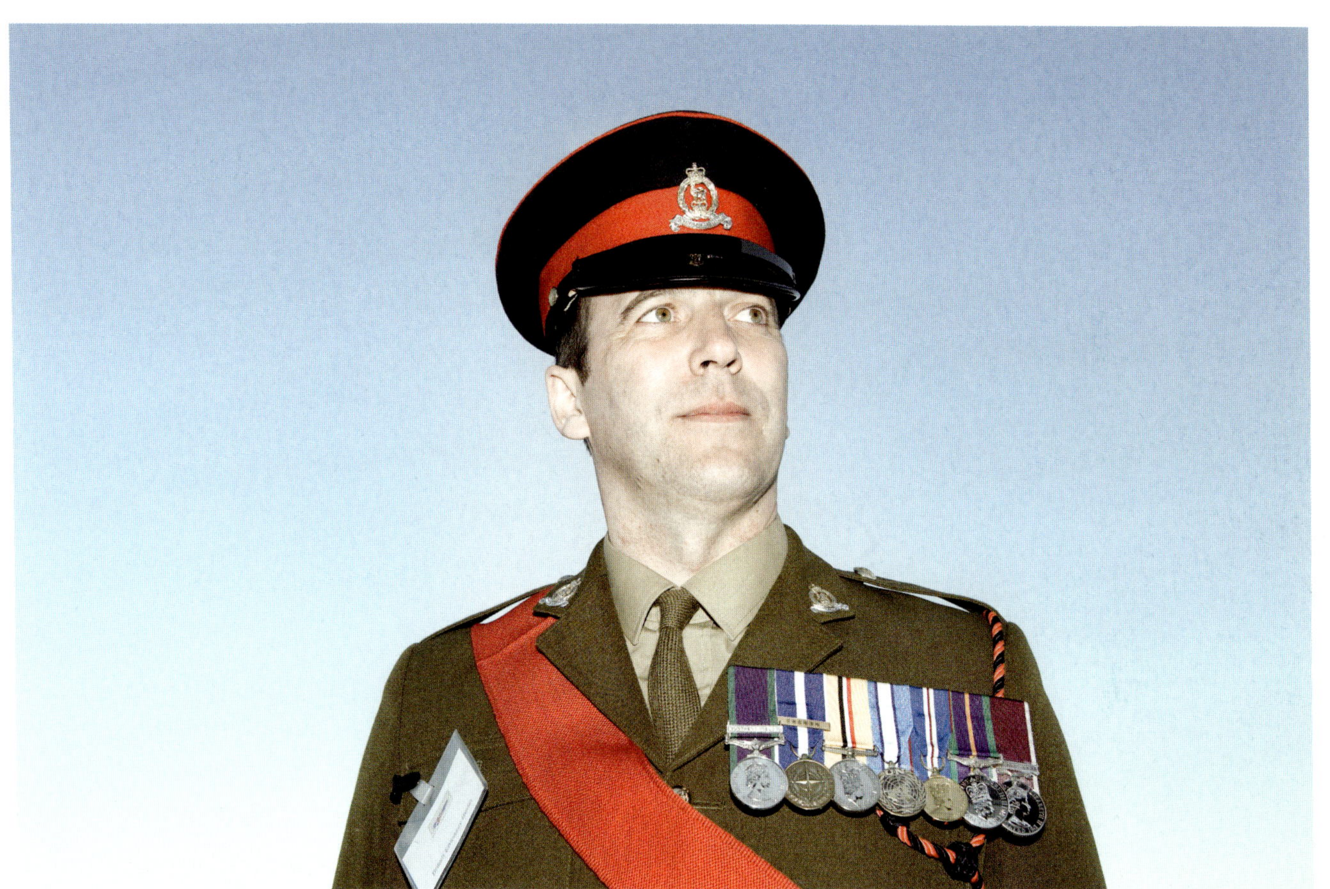

**DIE BERLINER TRABRENNGEMEINDE: MAN WETTET AUF DIE STUTE LANCELOT UND FAHRER ROLF HAFVENSTRÖM IM ARTHUR-KNAUER-RENNEN 'NEN ZEHNER. DER DUFT VON GEGRILLTEN RIPPCHEN WEHT UM DIE NASE.**

*The Berlin trotting community: You bet a ten-spot on the mare Lancelot and jockey Rolf Hafvenström in the Arthur Knauer Race. The smell of barbecued spareribs wafts around your nose.*

**35** Trabrennbahn Karlshorst
*Treskowallee 129 . Berlin-Karlshorst*

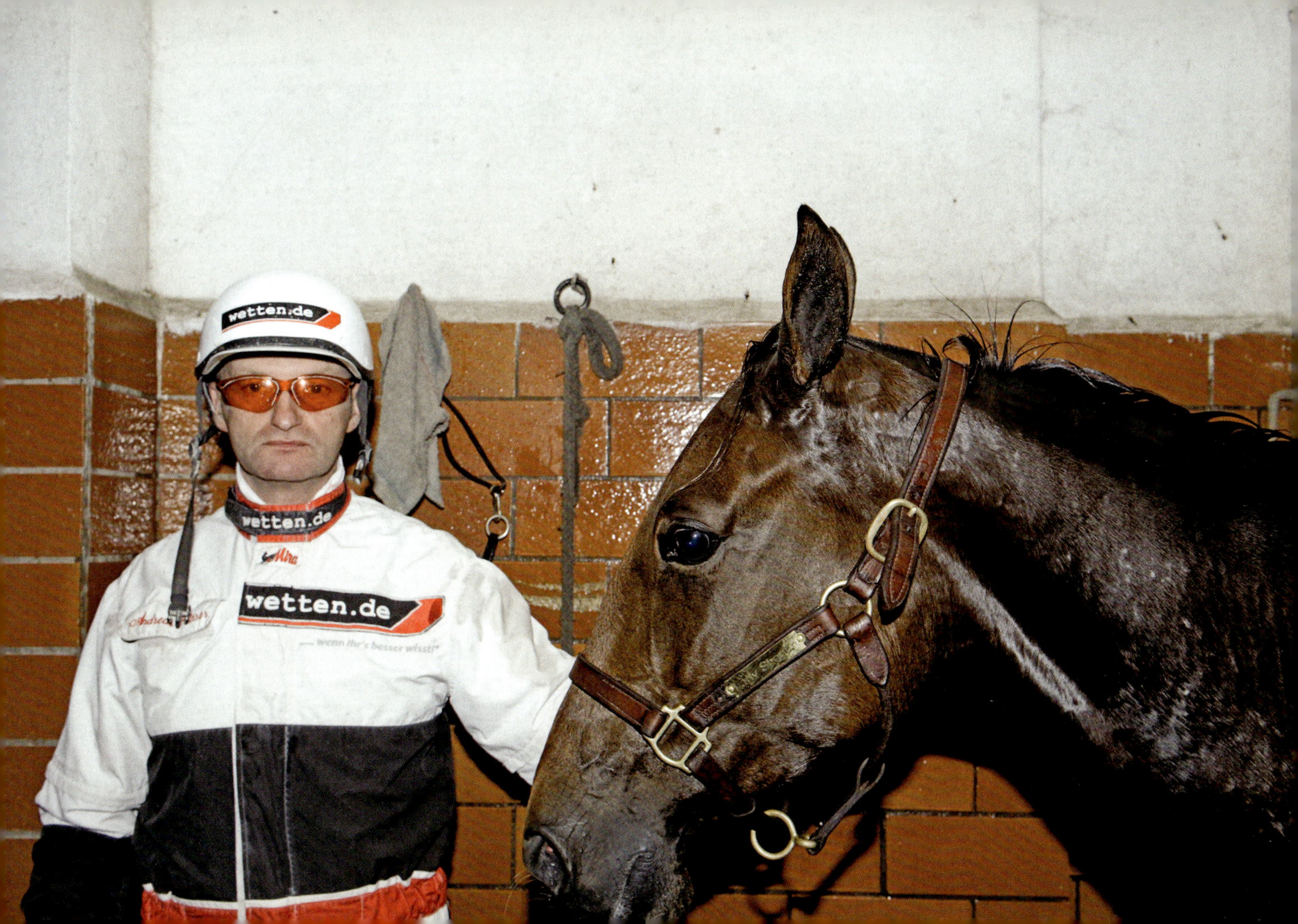

wetten.de
wetten.de
wetten.de
— wenn Ihr's besser wisst!®

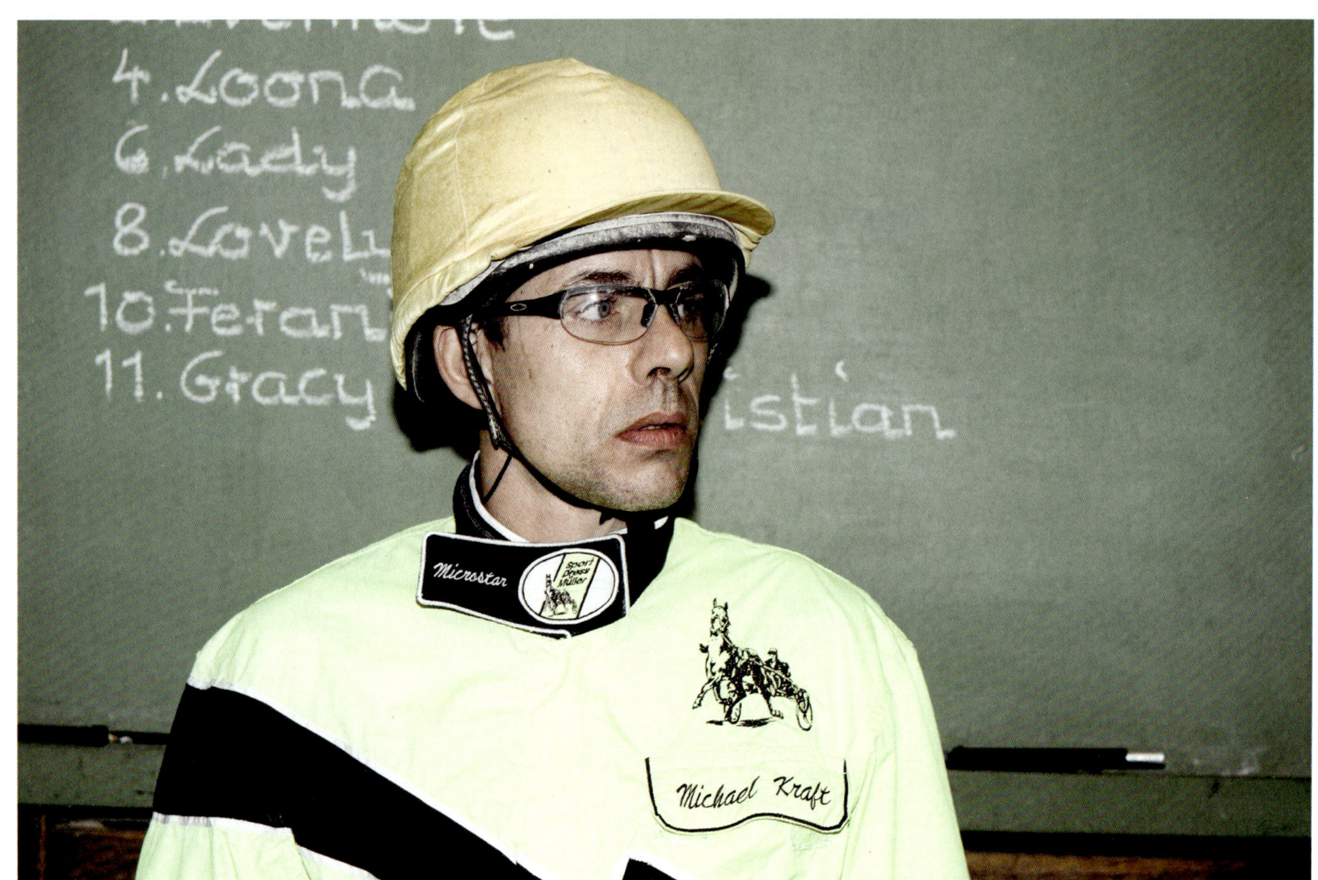

4. Loona
6. Lady
8. Loveli
10. Ferari
11. Gracy
istian
Microstar
Michael Kraft

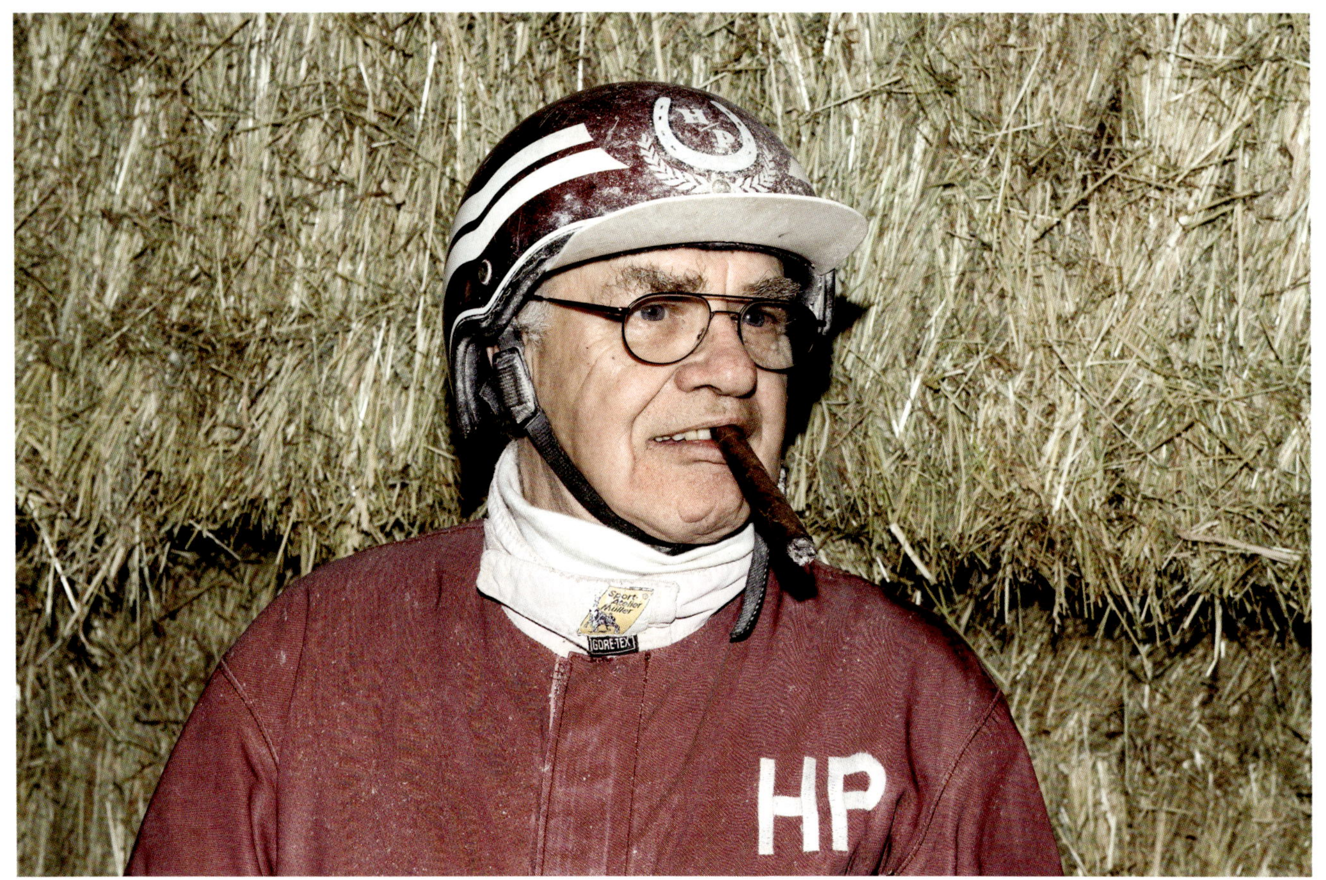

# VON MÄGDEN UND KNECHTEN
## *Of maids and menials*

**36** **Equipage**
*Nostitzstraße 30 . Berlin-Kreuzberg*

Der Rittmeister persönlich begrüßt die eintreffenden Gäste
in seinem Gestüt in einem Kreuzberger Kellergewölbe. Aus der
Umkleide tritt eine blonde Frau in schwarzem Latex-Catsuit.
An der mit Bruchstücken von alten Grabsteinen verzierten Bar,
sitzt ein Mittdreißiger im dunklen Smoking und blickt an die
Werkzeugwand. Diverse Utensilien von der klassischen Gerte
bis hin zur Peitsche des Zorro sind griffbereit. Im gegenüberliegenden Separee hängt neben einem mit Latexmatratze be-
stückten Bett ein überdimensionaler Käfig aus Stahl. Der Vogel
ist ausgeflogen. Dafür hat ein Pärchen dort Platz genommen
und versucht sich über die Rollenverteilung zu einigen. Die Stal-
lungen im Nebenraum warten noch auf ihren Einsatz.

*The cavalry captain personally greets the guests arriving at his
stud farm in a vaulted Kreuzberg cellar. A blond woman attired in
a black latex cat suit emerges from the dressing room. A fellow in
his mid-thirties wearing a dark tux sits at the bar decorated with
fragments of old tombstones and glances at the wall covered with
various instruments. Utensils ranging from the classic riding crop
to Zorro's whip are ready to hand. An oversized steel cage hangs
next to a bed fitted with a latex mattress in the private room across
the way. The bird has flown the coop. But a couple has taken
its place and is trying to agree about the allocation of their roles.
The stables in the adjacent room are still waiting to be used.*

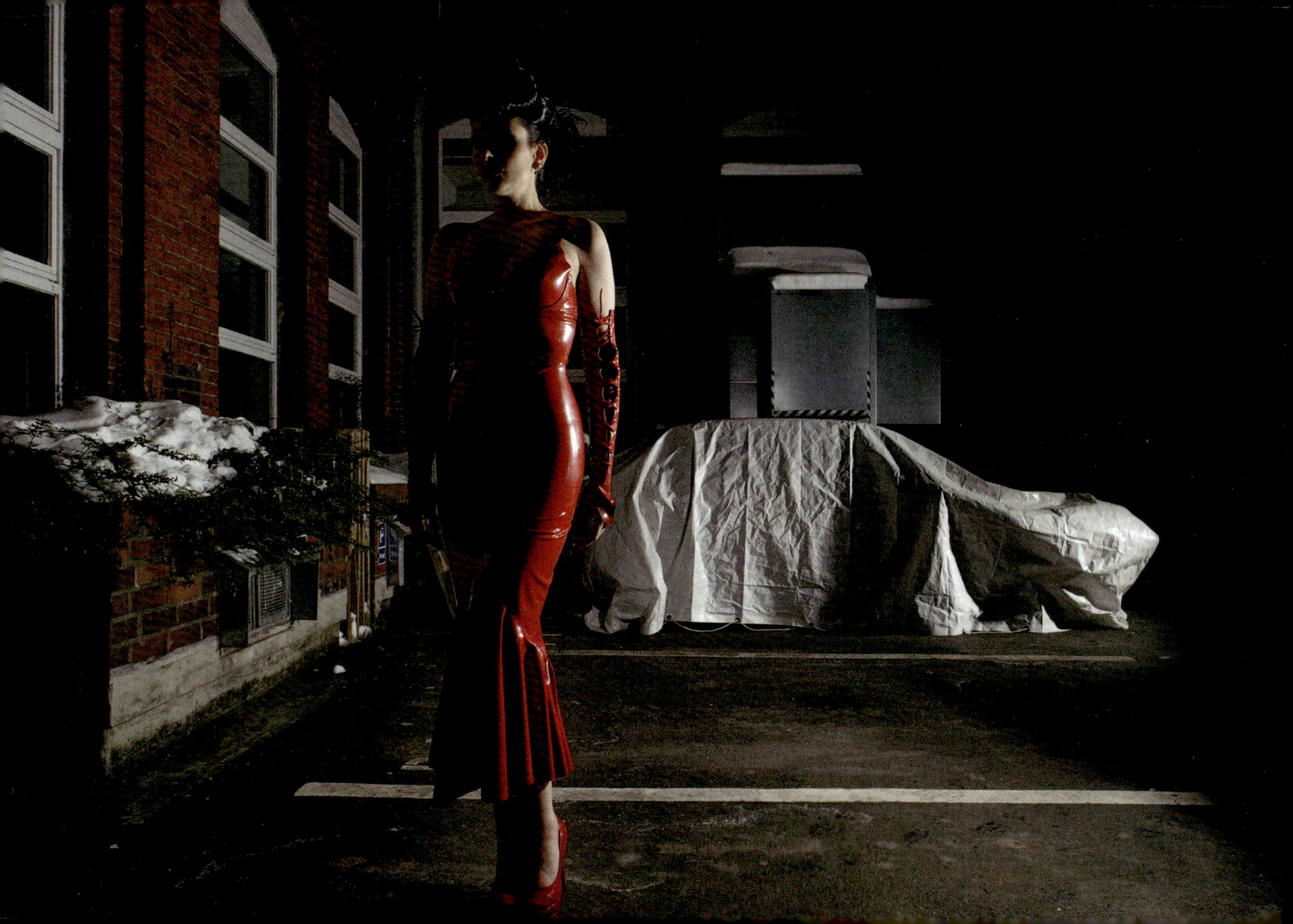

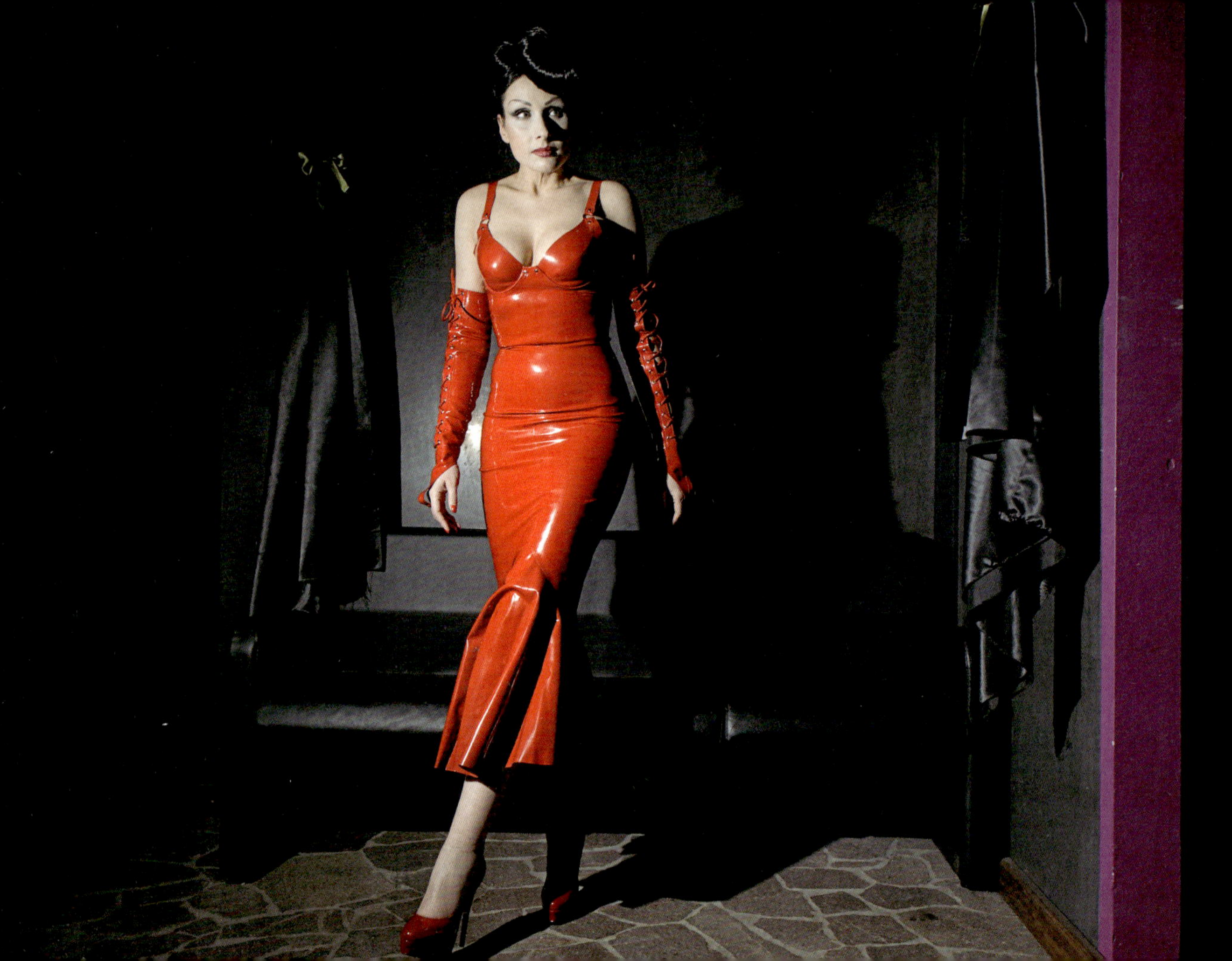

# FESTGEZURRT AN DER LEINE, BETRITT DER UNTERGEBENE DEN ZWINGER. SANFTE SCHLÄGE HALLEN DURCH DEN RAUM.

*Firmly leashed, the underling enters the kennel. Muffled blows resound through the room.*

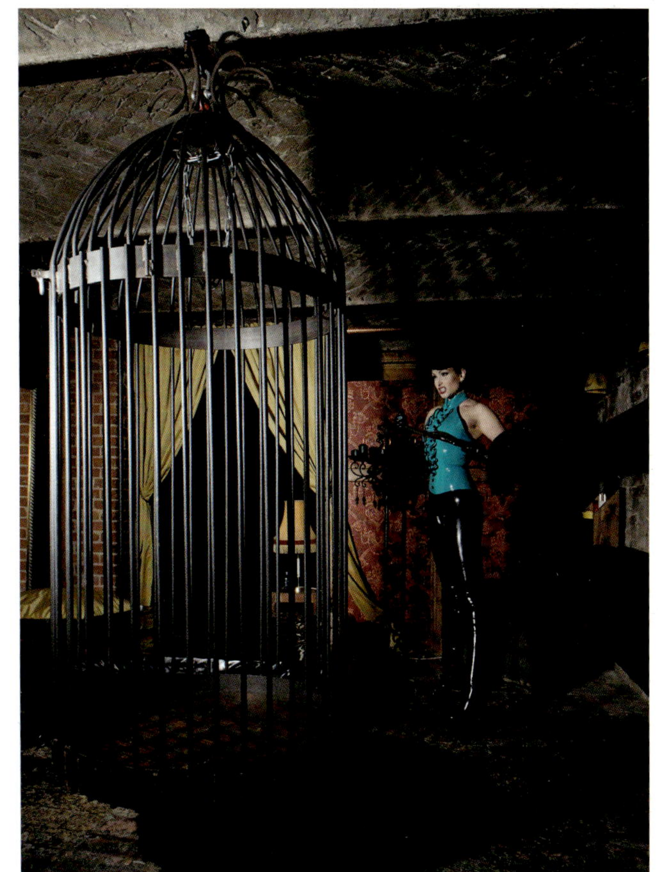

# HEISSE HUFE IN DER KREISBAHN

## Hot hooves at the racetrack

**37** Berliner Trabrenn-Verein e. V.
*Mariendorfer Damm 222 . Berlin-Mariendorf*

Schwere Rauschschwaden hängen zwischen den Monitoren, die die Trabrennen live übertragen. Mancher greift vor dem Start noch hastig zum Büffet. Unter den eingefleischten Wettpäpsten hält sich das Gerücht, Bahn 9 mache diesmal das Rennen. Wettscheine werden mit zitternden Händen ausgefüllt. In der Stallung weist eine Tafel mit der Aufschrift »Vorsicht bissig« auf die angespannten Nerven von Reiter und Pferd hin. Die staubige Bahn wird noch einmal bewässert, und der Startschuss fällt. Eine Frau mit großem Sonnenhut und im rosa Kostüm nimmt auf der Besucherterrasse Platz, den Blick auf die herannahenden Pferde gerichtet. Hans Nidermann auf Jacky führt in der dritten Außenbahn mit formidablem Vorsprung.

*Heavy clouds of smoke hang between the monitors broadcasting the harness race live. Some hastily rush over to the buffet before the start. There is a rumor among the die-hard bet experts that track 9 will win this one. Betting slips are filled out with trembling fingers. A sign in the stables reading "Caution! Snappy!" indicates how jumpy jockey and horse are. The dusty track is hosed down one more time and the starting gun sounds. A woman wearing a large sun hat and a pink-colored jacket and skirt takes her place in the viewing stand and focuses her attention on the approaching horses. Hans Nidermann on Jacky takes a formidable lead on the third outer track.*

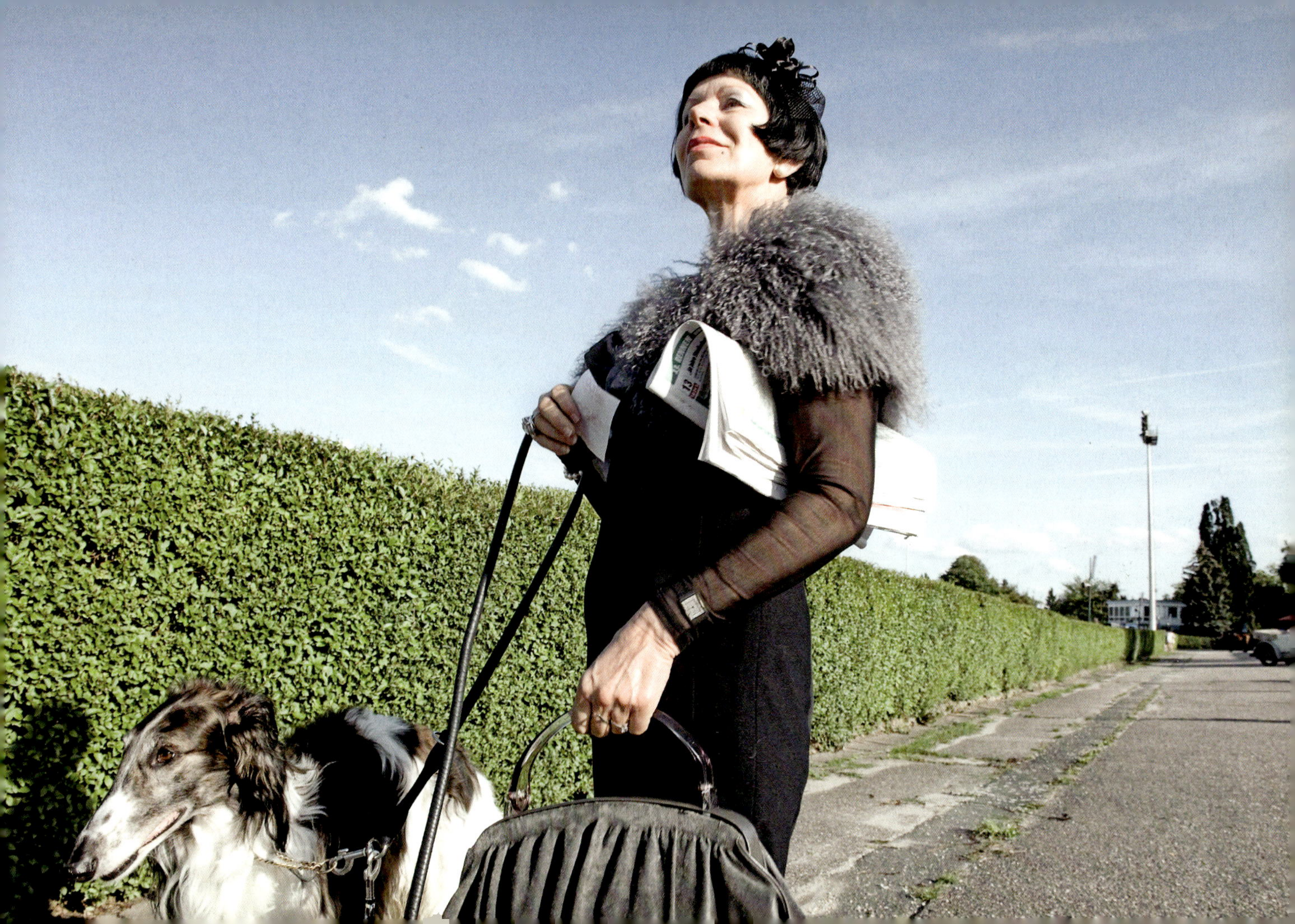

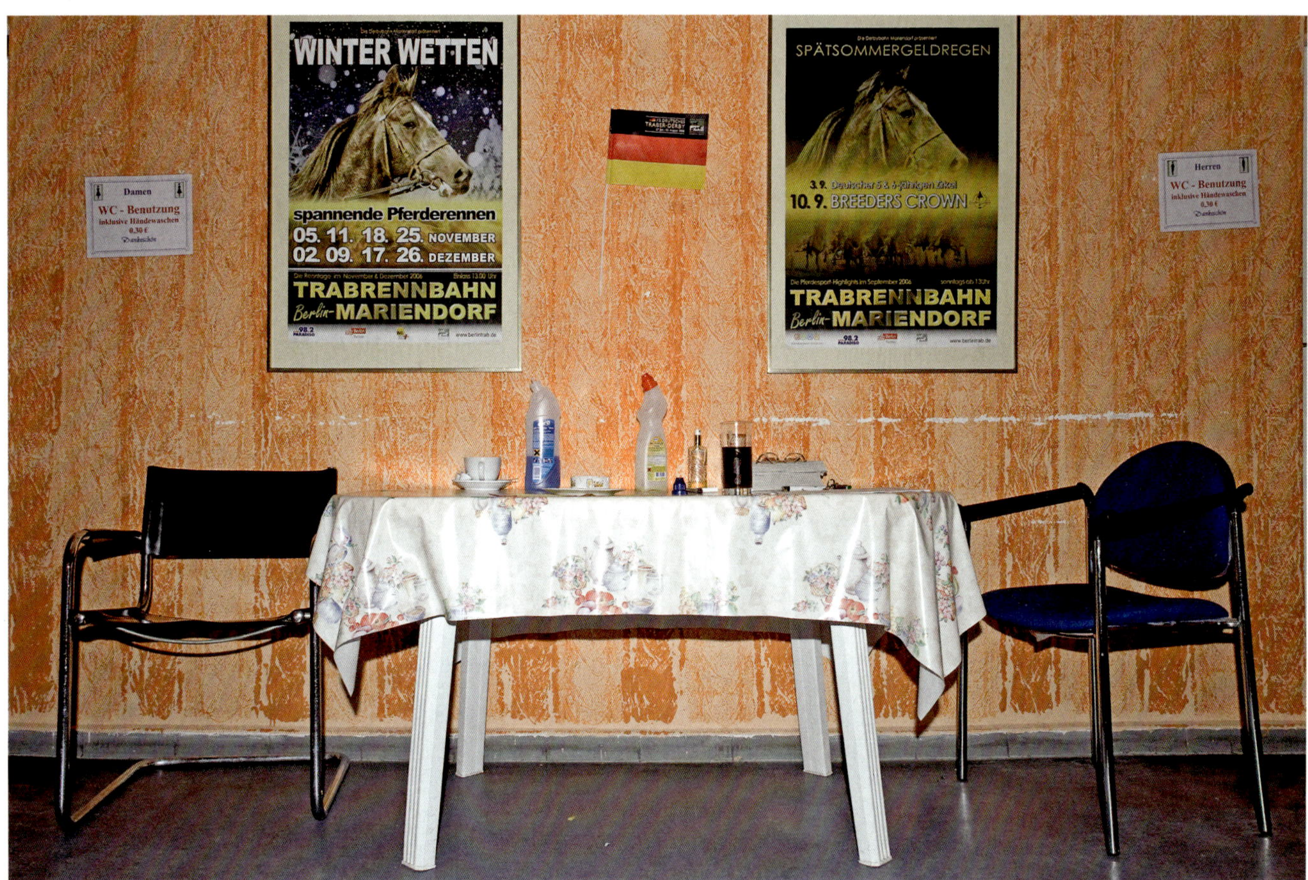
Damen
WC - Benutzung
inklusive Händewaschen
0,30 €
Dankeschön
WINTER WETTEN
spannende Pferderennen
05. 11. 18. 25. NOVEMBER
02. 09. 17. 26. DEZEMBER
TRABRENNBAHN
Berlin-MARIENDORF
98.2
PARADISO
SPÄTSOMMERGELDREGEN
3.9.
10.9. BREEDERS CROWN
TRABRENNBAHN
Berlin-MARIENDORF
98.2
PARADISO
Herren
WC - Benutzung
inklusive Händewaschen
0,30 €
Dankeschön

S Rennen
15
15
15
Rennen 15

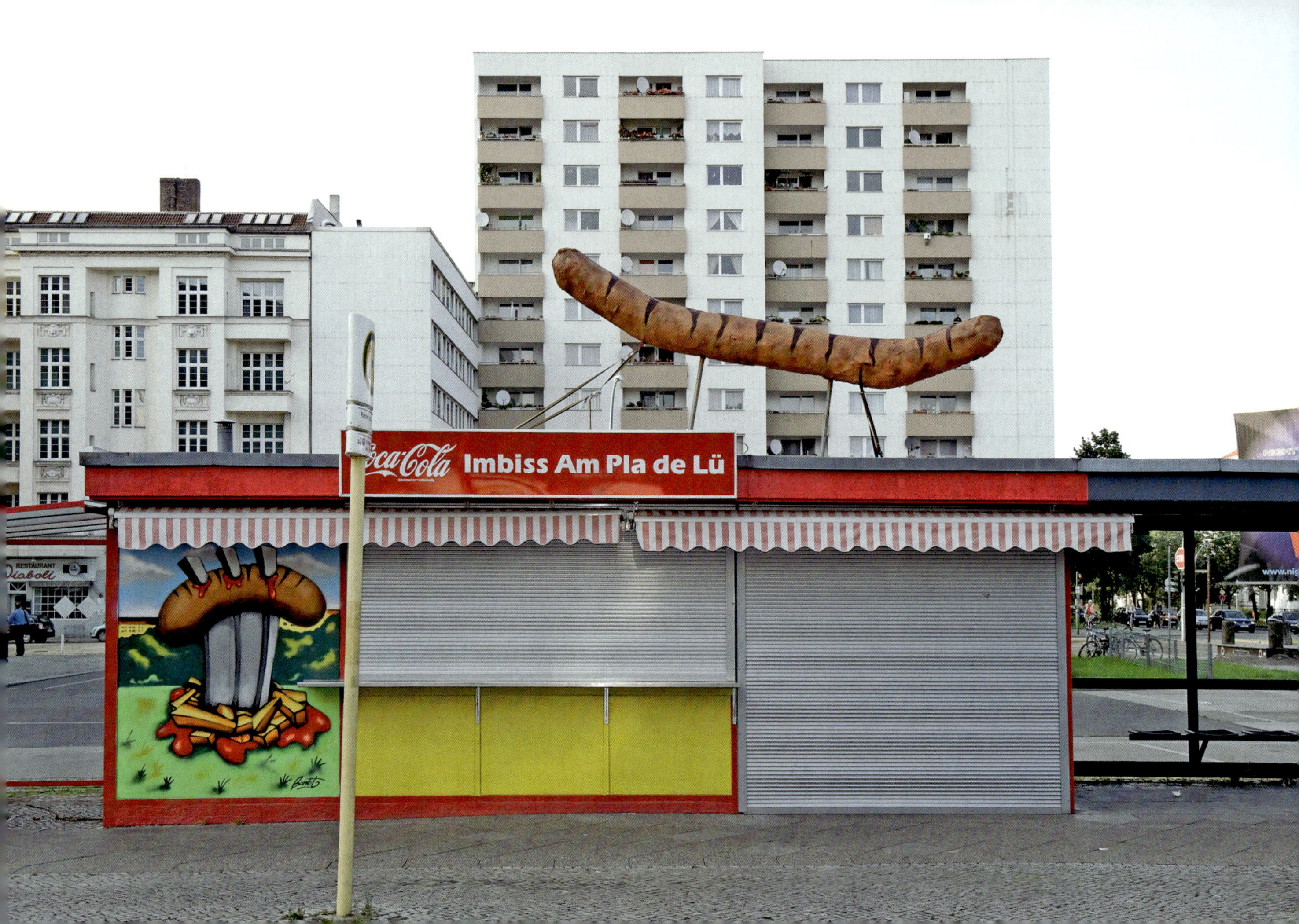

Coca-Cola
Imbiss Am Pla de Lü
RESTAURANT
Diaboli
www.nig

**DER IMBISSBETREIBER NIMMT SEINE LETZTEN BULETTEN VOM GRILL UND VERSCHLIESST DAS HÄUSCHEN — FEIERABEND. SEINE CURRYWURST RAGT SIEBEN TAGE DIE WOCHE IN DEN BERLINER HIMMEL.**

*The snack-bar operator takes the last burgers off the grill and closes up the booth—quitting time. His curry sausage juts into the Berlin sky seven days a week.*

**38** Imbiss am Pla de Lü
*Platz der Luftbrücke . Berlin-Tempelhof*

# SCHÖNEBERG: BEAMTENSCHICK UND ALT-68ER, WOCHENMARKT UND GAY-LABYRINTH

## Schöneberg: chic officialdom and the vets '68, farmers' market and gay labyrinth

Zugezogene vor dem Mauerfall, Pallasseum und der Knopfladen Fichu, Club Goya und Ü30-Party, das Museum der unerhörten Dinge, Schöneberger Regenmantelsammler, Café Einstein und Straßenstrich, Billardspiel und Dartomat, Motzstraßenfest und Pommesbuden in Regenbogenfarben, Sommerbad am Insulaner.

*Newcomers before the Fall of the Wall, Pallasseum and the Fichu button store, Club Goya and over 30s party, the Museum der unerhörten Dinge, Schöneberg raincoat collectors, Café Einstein and street-walkers' patch, billiards and dart-o-mat, Motzstraße Street Festival and rainbow-colored french-fries stands, summer swimming pool at the Insulaner.*

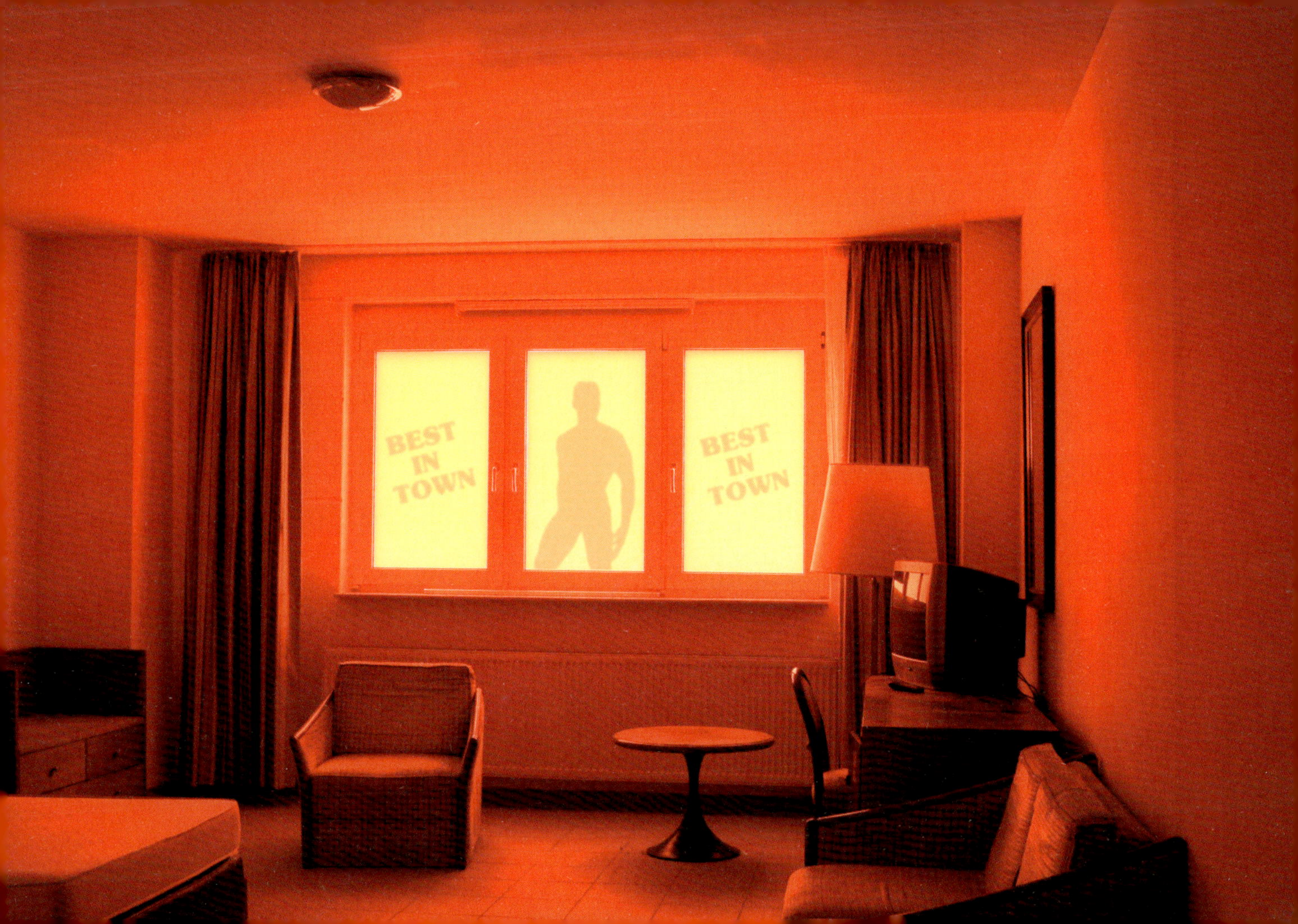

BEST
IN
TOWN
BEST
IN
TOWN

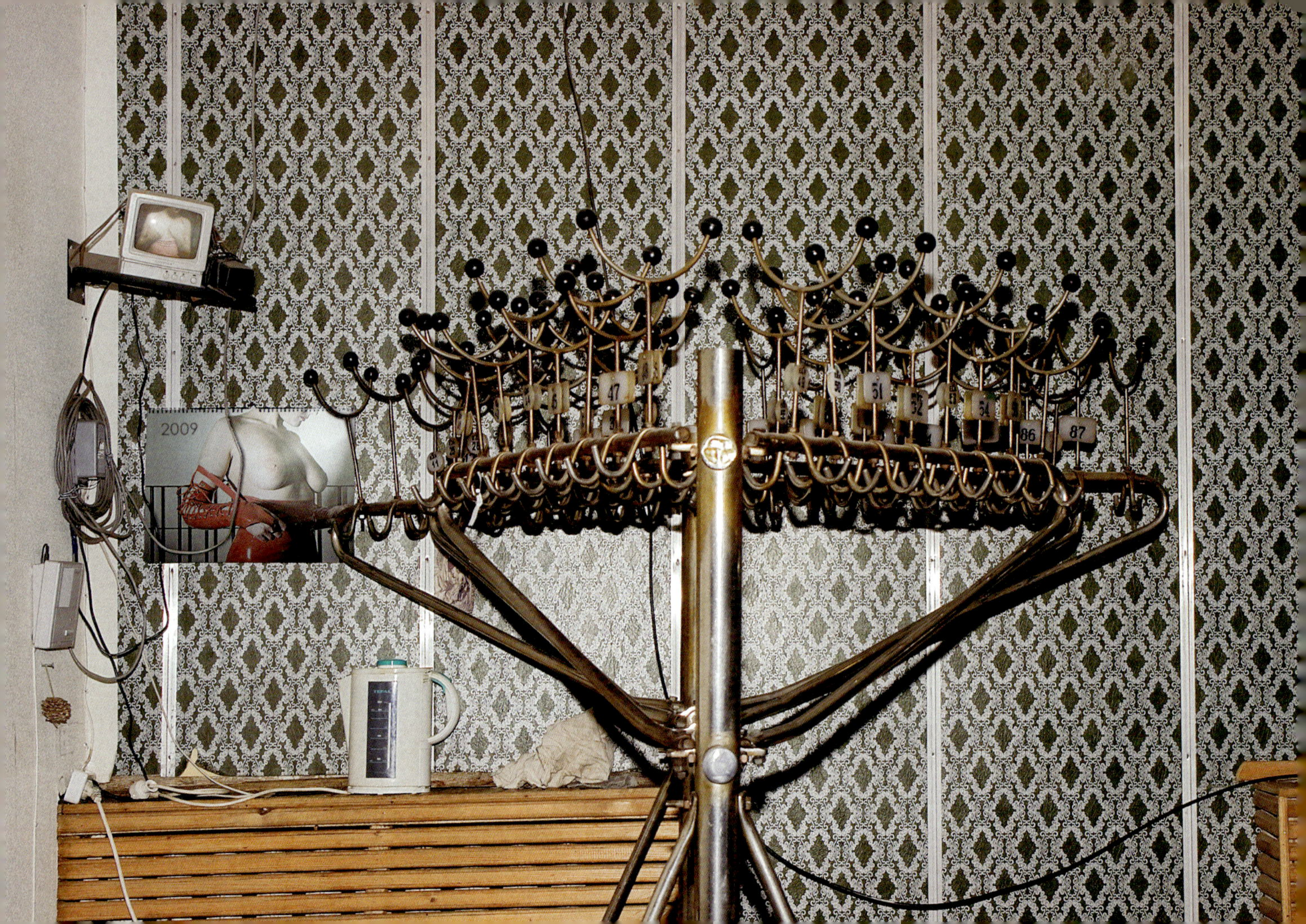

2009

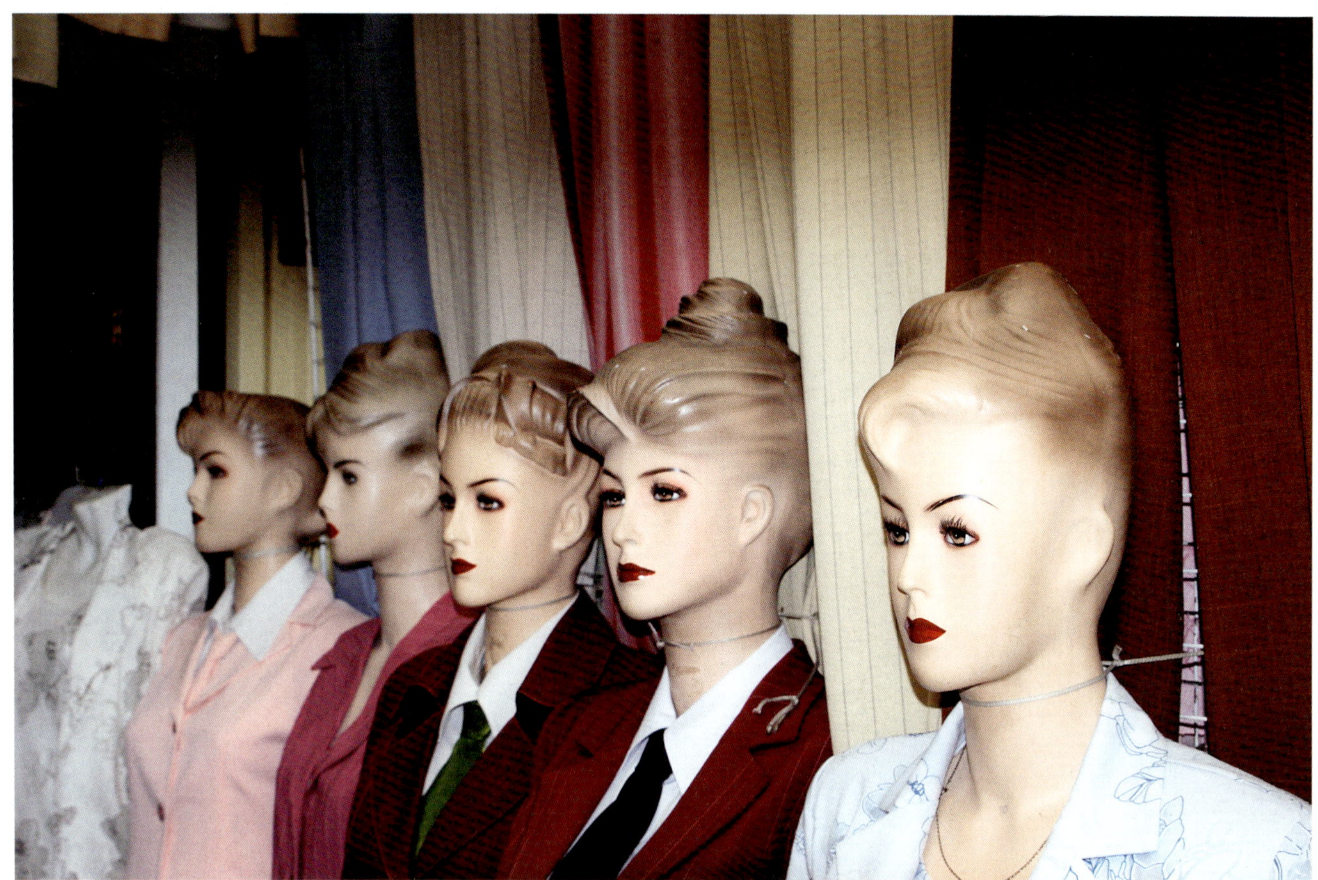

# SEEKÜHE UND GEBIRGSANLAGEN
## Sea cows and mountain ranges

**39** **Tierpark Berlin**
*Am Tierpark 125 . Berlin-Lichtenberg*

Salatköpfe schwimmen an der Oberfläche des riesigen Wasserbeckens. Vor der Aquariumscheibe steht eine Frau im Skianzug. Gespannt schauen sie und ihr Windhund durch das dicke Panzerglas, das im Licht der Strahler grün leuchtet. Eine große Seekuh schwebt mit einem Salatkopf im Maul aus dem Nichts hervor. Im gegenüberliegenden Gehege zerlegt Elefantenbulle Mambo unter lautem Knacken einen Tannenbaum. Im Alfred-Brehm-Haus ist Fütterungszeit. Wie eine Theaterbühne mit felsiger Kulisse präsentiert sich die Tiger- und Löwenanlage, deren Bewohner unter lautem Brüllen ihrem Hunger Ausdruck verleihen. Unruhig tänzelt die Salzkatze im Gehege über trockenes Geäst. Der Jaguar nagt schon am Knochen.

*Heads of salad swim about the surface of the gigantic water basin. A woman wearing a ski suit stands in front of the aquarium glass. She and her greyhound look excitedly through the thick armored glass that has a greenish hue in the shine of the spotlights. A large sea cow appears from nowhere, emerging with a head of salad in its mouth. In the compound on the other side, bull elephant Mambo takes a fir tree apart amidst loud crackling sounds. It's feeding time in Alfred Brehm House. The enclosure for the lions and tigers looks like a theatrical stage with mountain scenery and its inhabitants give voice to their hunger with loud bellows. The Geoffroy's cat dances about anxiously on dried branches in its cage. The jaguar is already gnawing on a bone.*

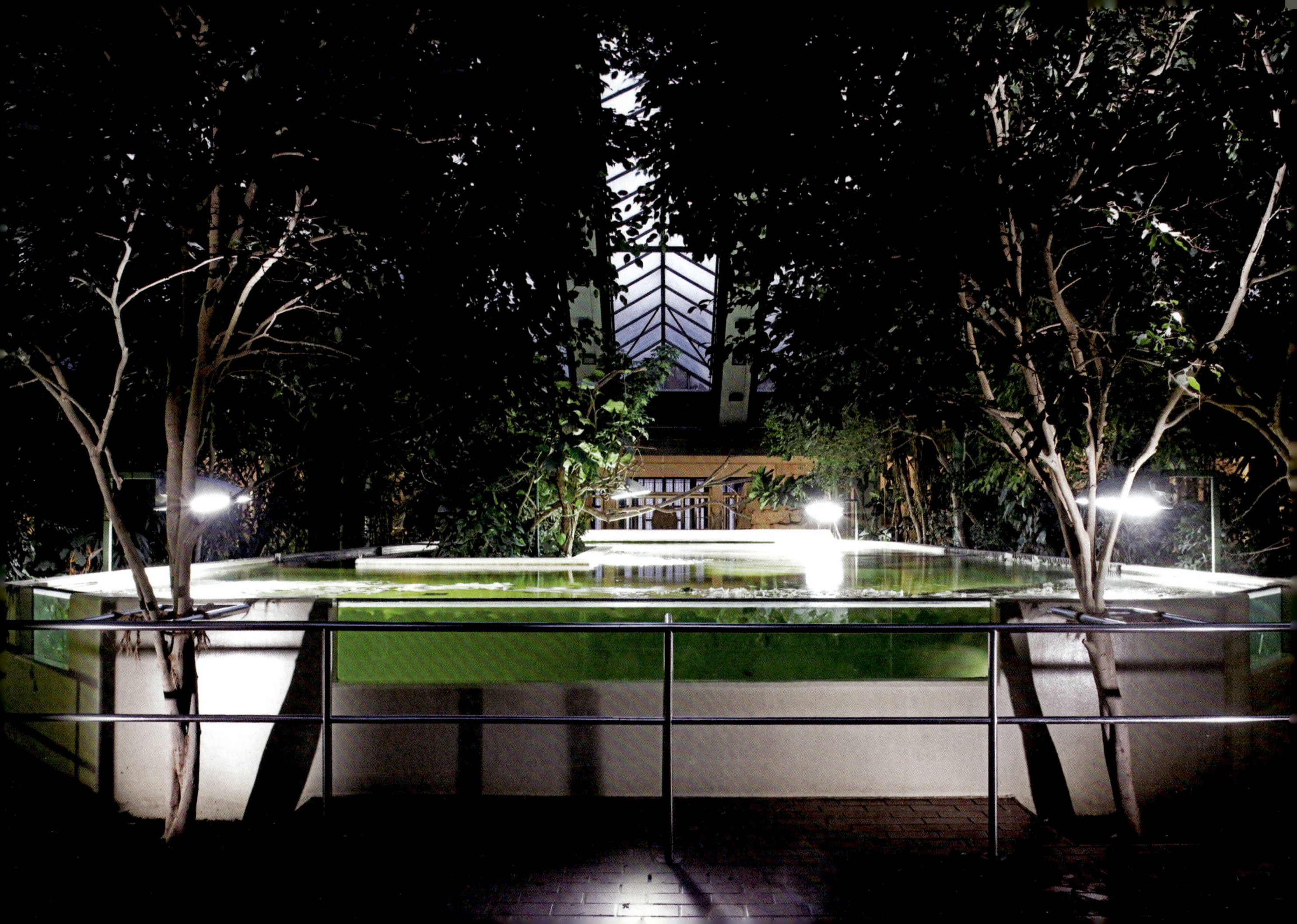

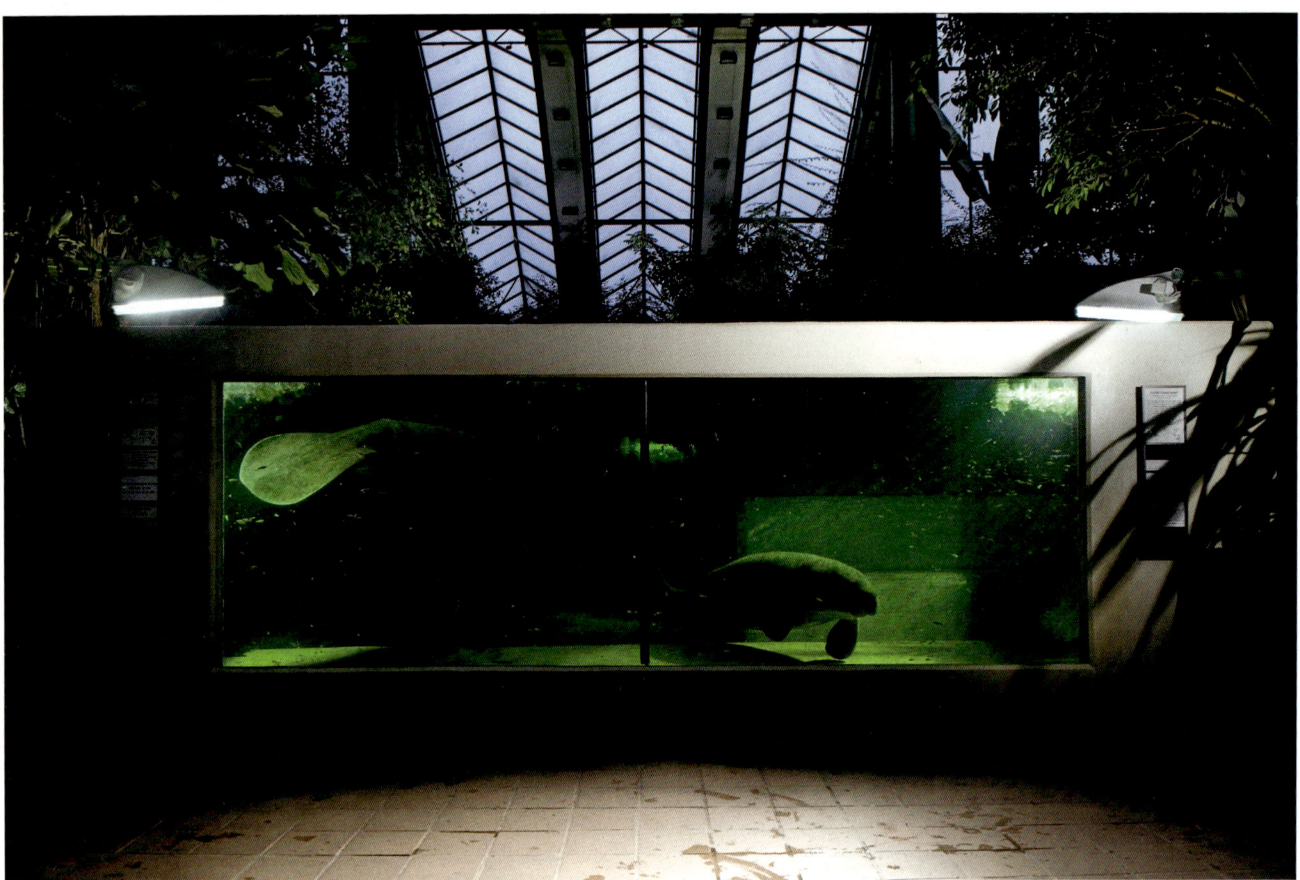

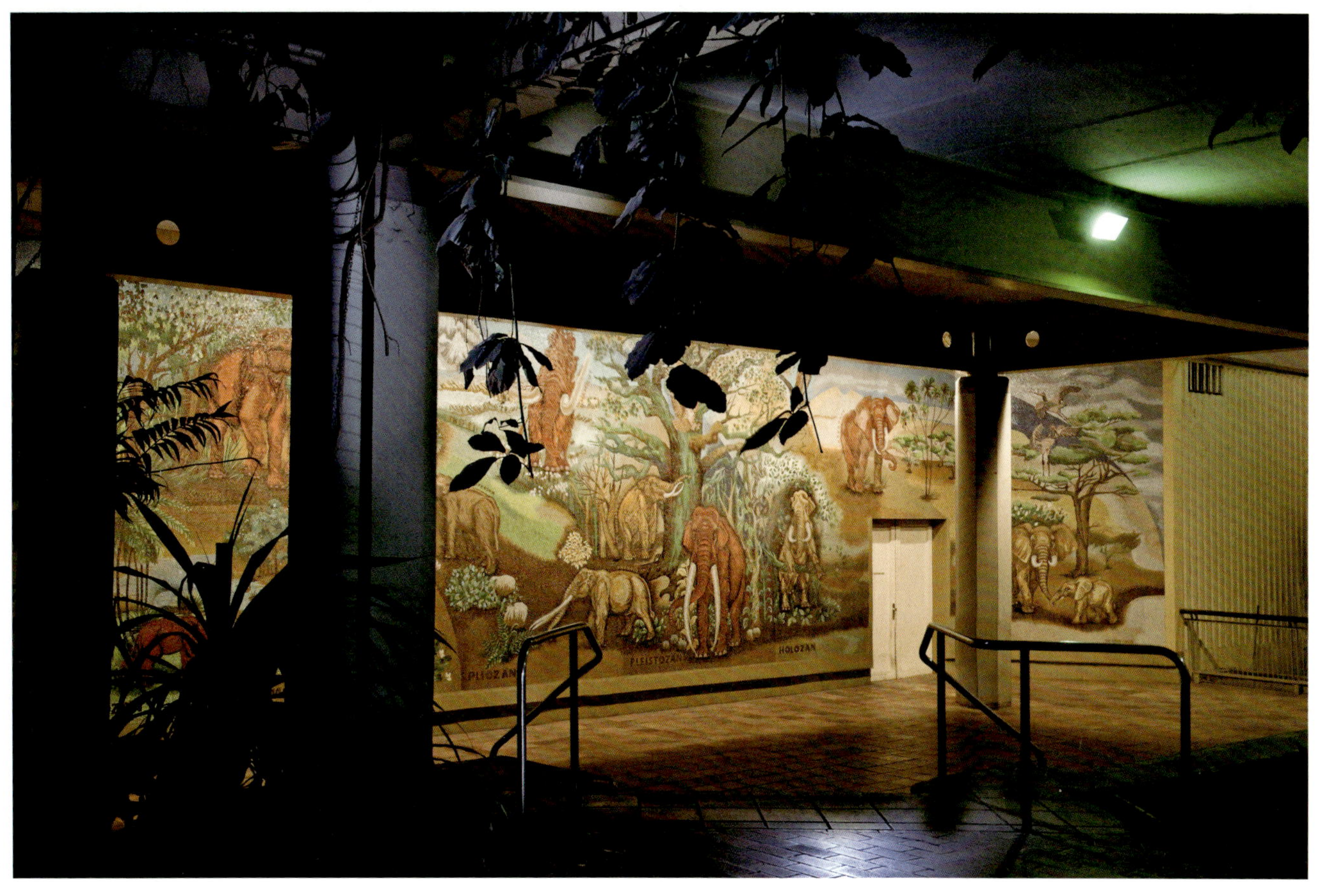
PLIOZÄN
PLEISTOZÄN
HOLOZÄN

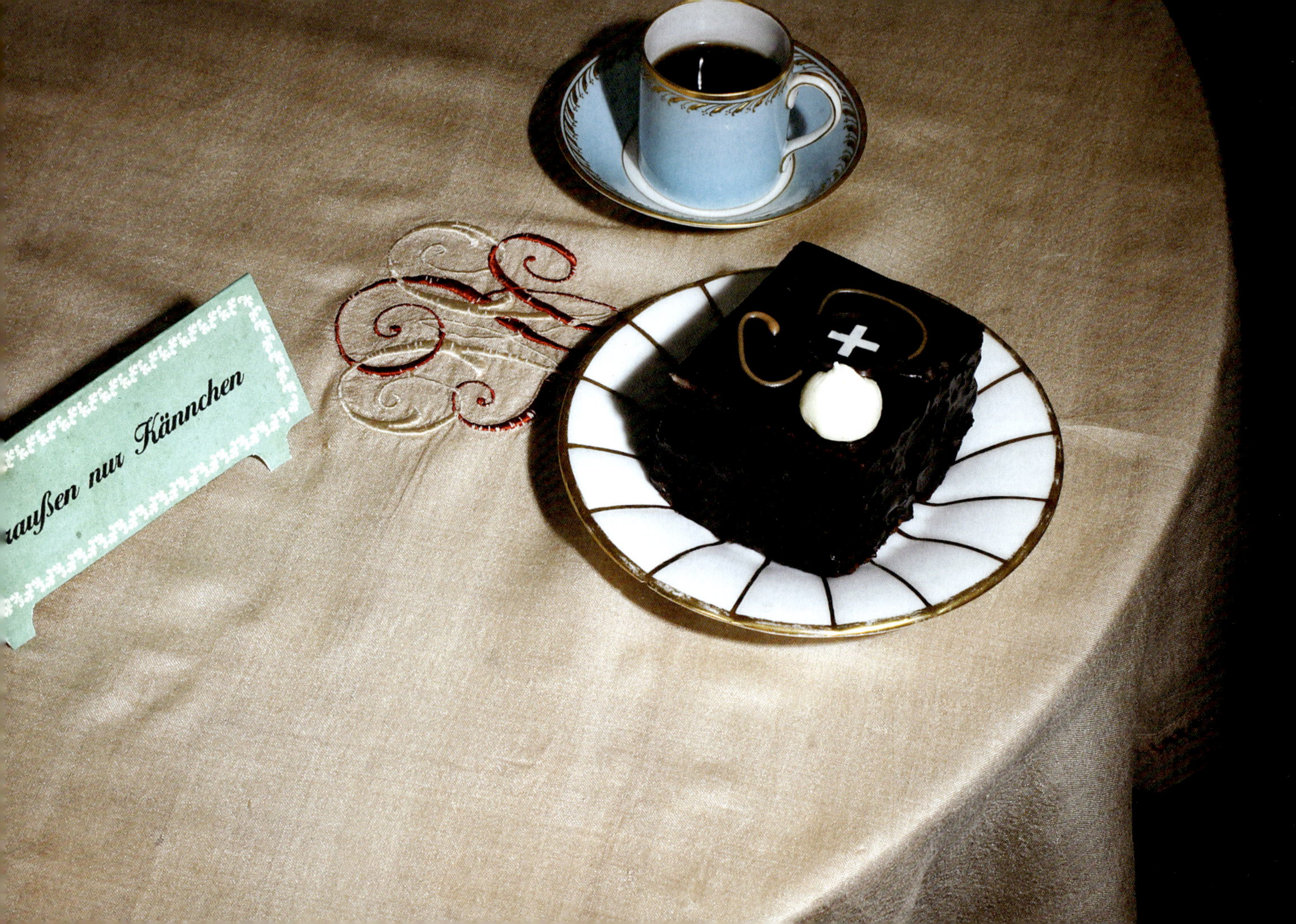
raußen nur Kännchen

Joggen auf dem Trimm-dich-Pfad, Fassbrause im Waldlokal Schwarzer Eber, Treibjagd und Halali im Berliner Forst, Barockvilla und Gartenteich, Hofeinfahrten mit venezianischen Marmorstatuen, Goldfischbassin und Stacheldraht, Hecken-schnitt und Sonntagsritt, Überwachungskameras am Gartentor.

*Jogging on the keep-fit trail, soft drinks at the Schwarzer Eber restaurant in the forest, hunting party and death halloo in the Berlin Forest, Baroque villa and garden pond, courtyard entrances with Venetian marble statues, goldfish basin and barbwire, cut hedges and a Sunday ride, observation cameras on the garden gate.*

# BOARDING IM HAUS EDEN
## *Boarding in Eden House*



Der vollbesetzte Aufzug erreicht den zehnten Stock des Hauses Eden. Die Tür öffnet sich, und die Gäste wähnen sich zurückversetzt in die Zeit der 1960er-Jahre. Funk erklingt schon im Flur der Lounge, die damals ein beliebter Treffpunkt für Piloten und Stewardessen der Pan American Airways war. Eine Veranstaltung russischer Geschäftsleute ist in vollem Gange, eine blonde Ukrainerin steigt mit einem Martiniglas bewaffnet über den Kopf eines am Boden liegenden ausgestopften Grizzlybären. Ihr Mann im Nadelstreifenanzug genießt derweil löffelweise Kaviar an der Bar. Von einer kleinen Terrasse aus fällt der Blick in den Zoologischen Garten. Die Geräusche der vorbeiführenden Straße vermischen sich mit dem Schnattern von Flamingos.

*The packed elevator reaches the tenth floor of Eden House. The door opens and the guests feel that they have been transported back to the nineteen-sixties. Radio music can already be heard in the hallway of the lounge that used to be a popular meeting place for Pan Am pilots and stewardesses. An event for Russian business people is in full swing; armed with a martini glass, a blond Ukrainian climbs over the head of a stuffed grizzly bear spread out on the floor. For his part, her husband wearing a pinstriped suit has been enjoying spoon after spoon of caviar at the bar. One can look over to the Zoological Garden from a small terrace. Passing street sounds mix in with the cackling of the flamingos.*

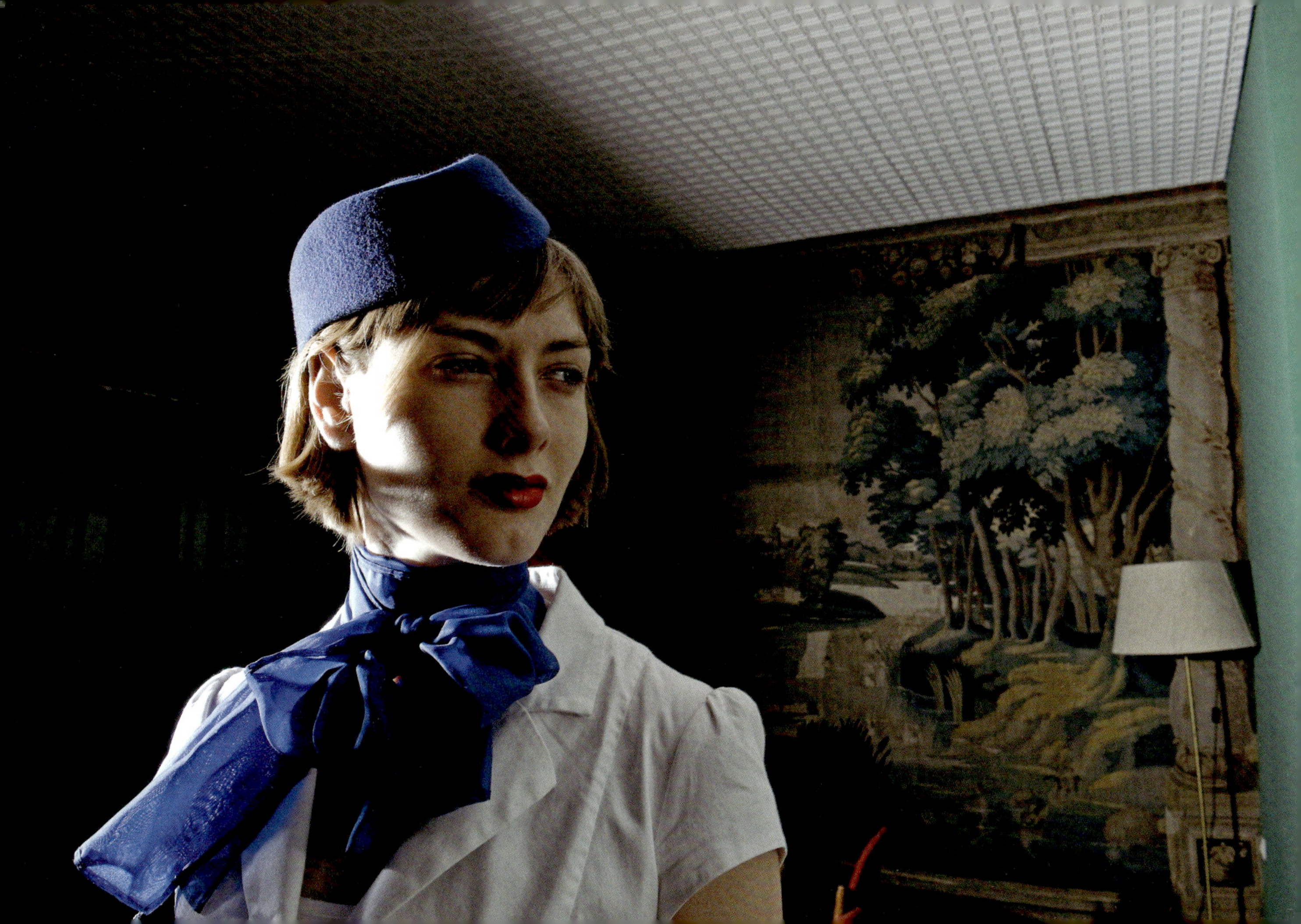

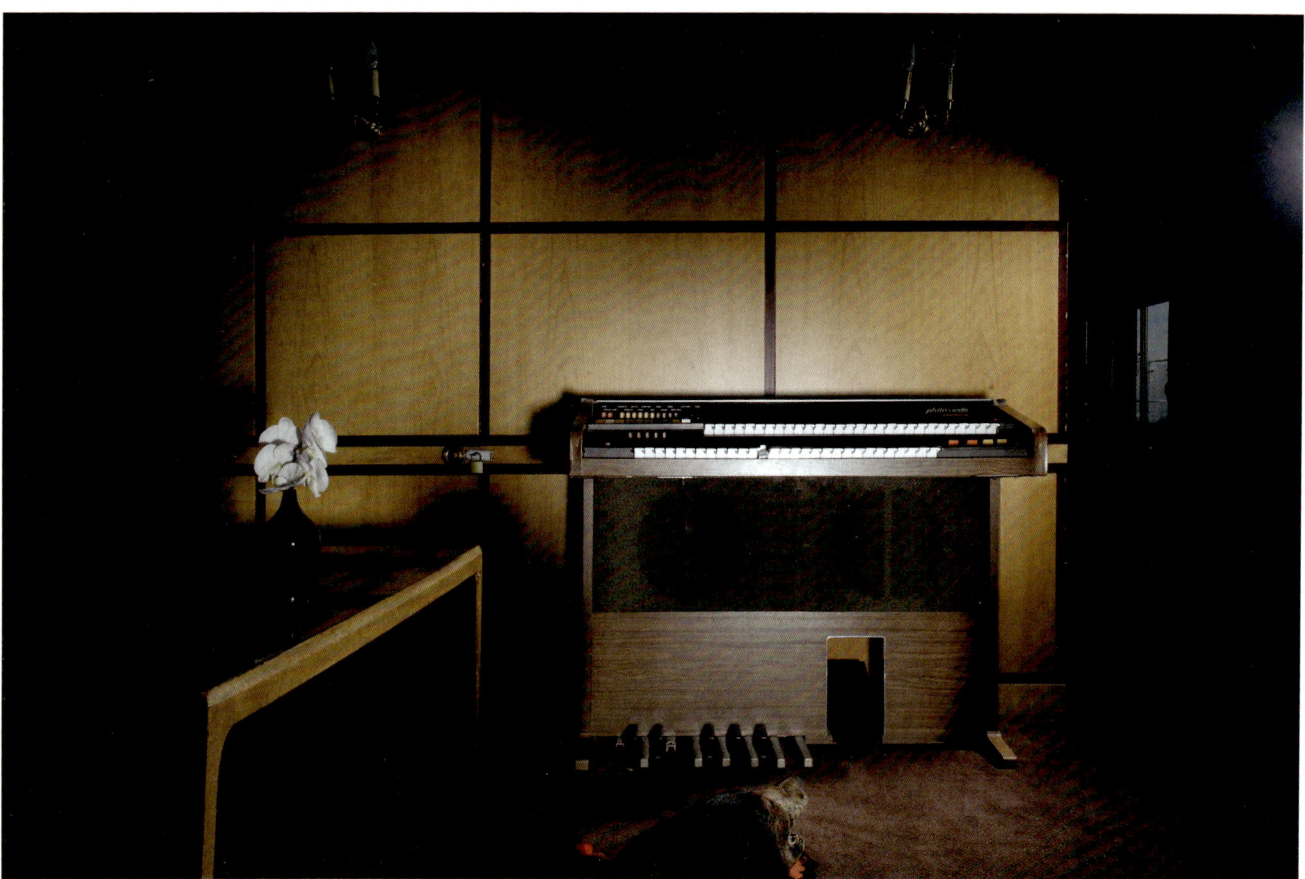

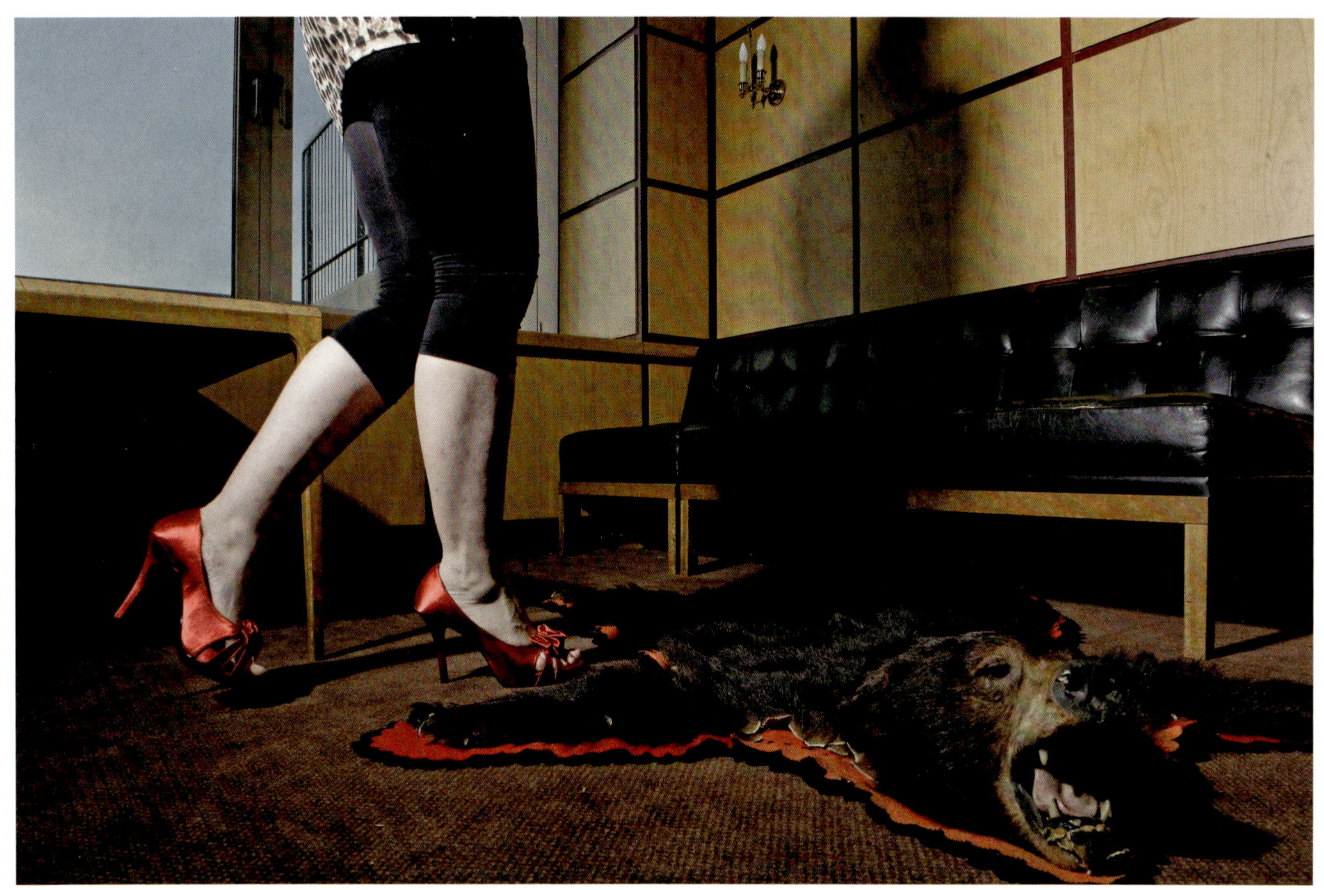

**ÜBER EINEN GEHEIMEN VIP-ZUGANG MISCHT MAN SICH UNTER DIE GÄSTE. AUF DEM GEGENÜBERLIEGENDEN DACH STEIGEN BADE-GÄSTE NACKT IN DIE HEISSEN THERMEN DES EUROPA-CENTERS.**

One mixes with the guests via a secret VIP entrance. On the roof across the way, naked bathing guests submerge in the hot thermal bath at the Europa Center.

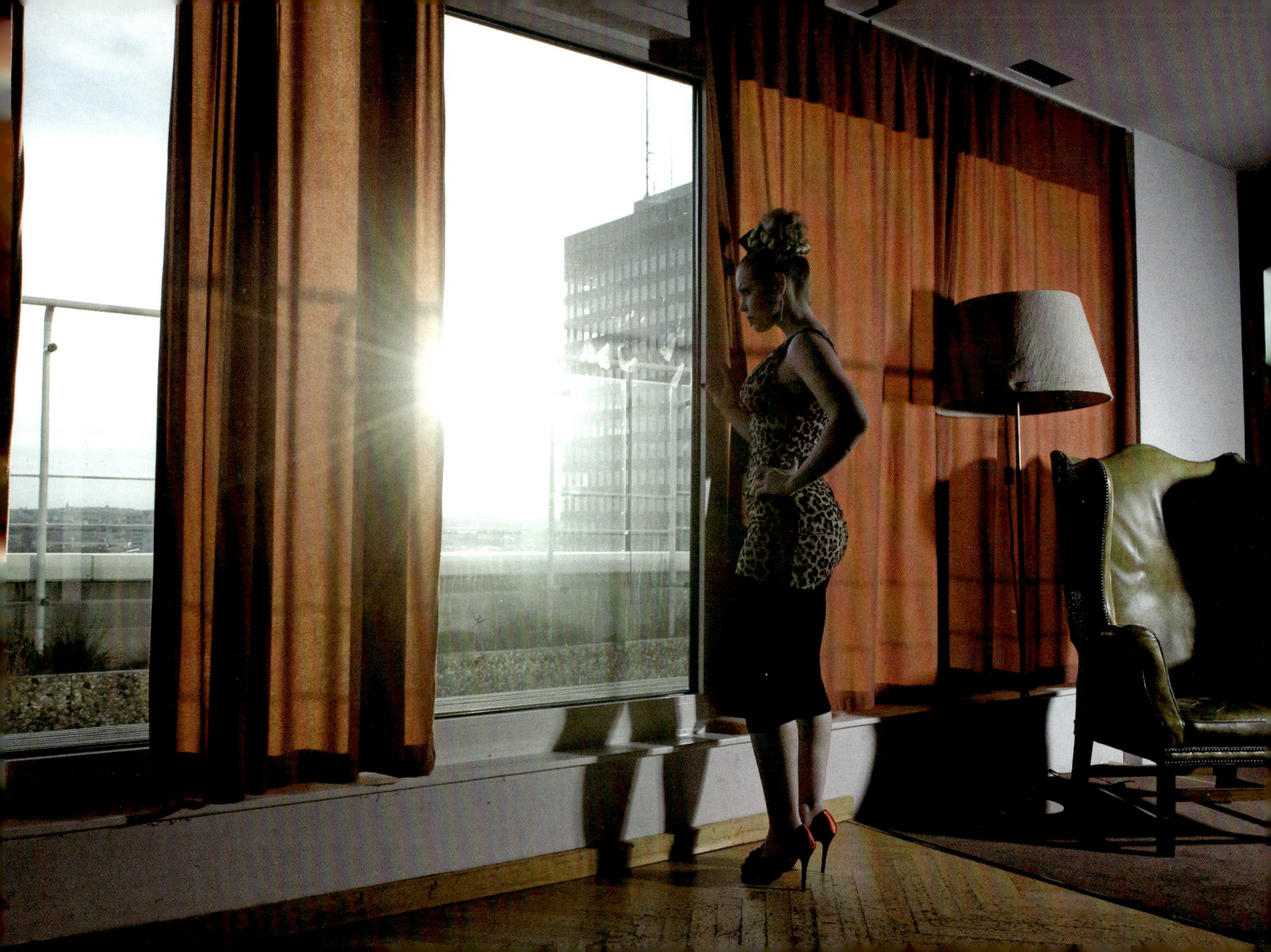

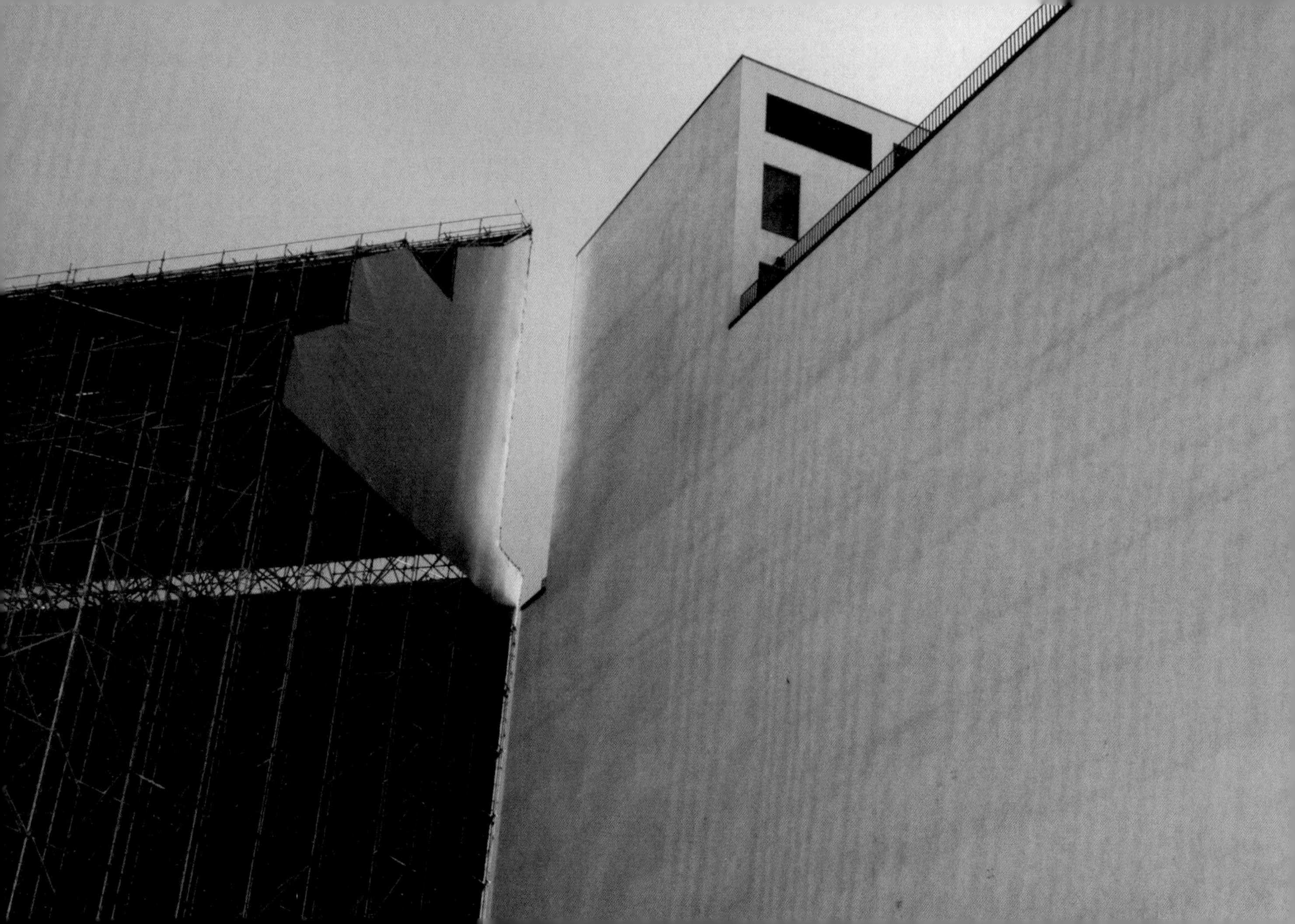

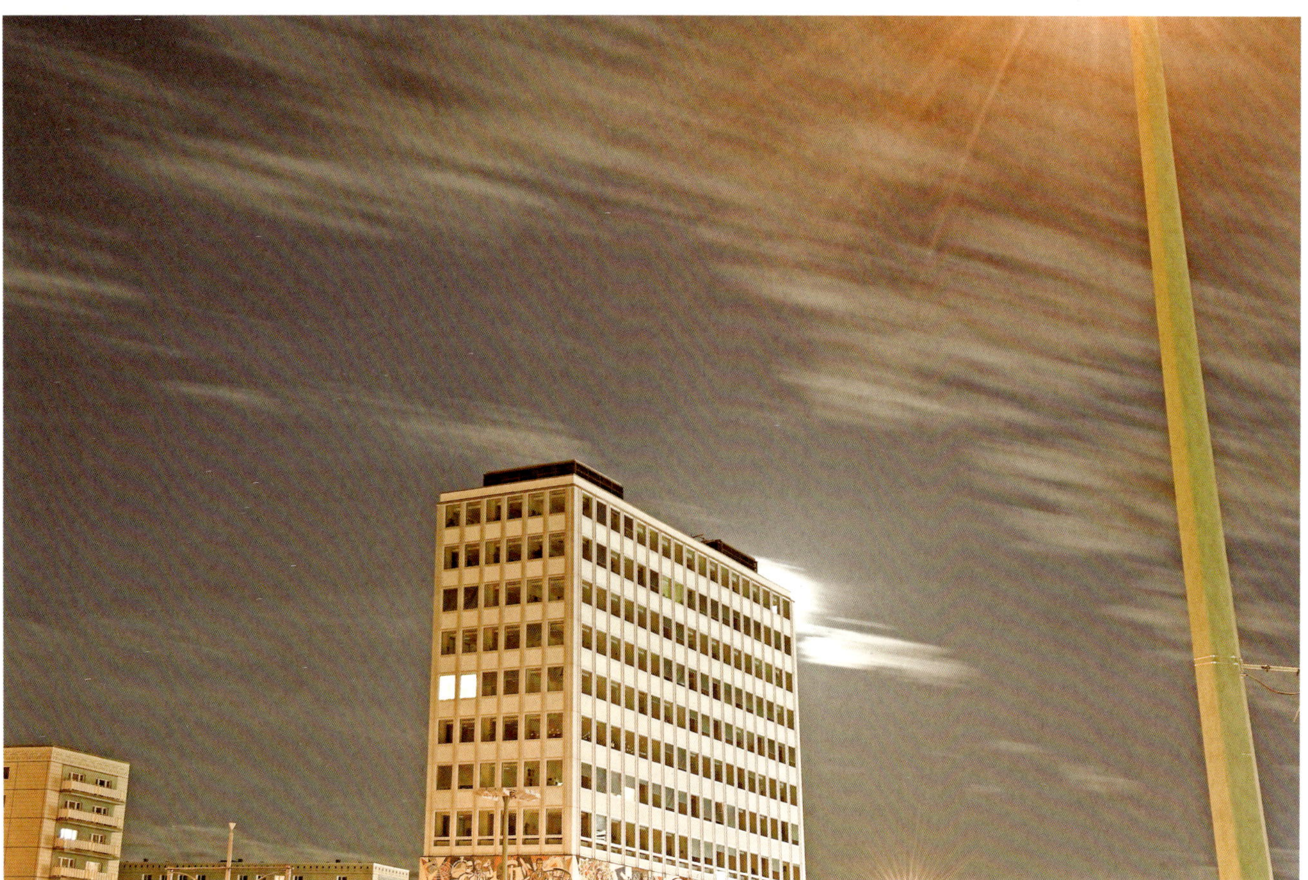

# NEVERLAND IM PLÄNTERWALD

## Neverland in Plänterwald

**41** **Spreepark Plänterwald**
*Kiehnwerderallee 1–3 . Berlin-Treptow*

Alarm! Eindringlinge im Bereich der Wildwasserbahn. Sofort rückt ein Wachteam in den Spreepark aus. Bewaffnet mit Hund und Taschenlampe, werden fünf neugierige Jugendliche im Tunnel der Achterbahn Mega-Loop ausfindig gemacht und gestellt. Danach fällt der Freizeitpark inmitten des Plänterwaldes wieder in seinen verwunschenen Schlaf. Dicht gedrängt stehen Schwanenboote unter Holzbalustraden, Gestrüpp überwuchert das wie ein UFO anmutende 3D-Kino. Gleich daneben fällt der Blick auf den Wohnwagen des einstigen Parkbesitzers. Im Saloon der ehemaligen Westernstadt sind schon vor Jahren alle Lichter ausgegangen. Zu Ostzeiten zog der Santa-Fe-Express noch seine Runden, und Nina Hagen sprang über die Showbühne.

*Alarm! Intruders in the vicinity of the white-water ride. A search party immediately sets off for Spreepark. Armed with a dog and a flashlight, five curious adolescents are spotted and cornered in the tunnel of the Mega Loop rollercoaster. The amusement park right in the middle of Plänterwald than falls back into its enchanted sleep. Swan boats are packed close together under wooden balustrades; the 3-D movie house that looks more like a UFO is covered with briars. Right next to it, you can see the trailer of the park's ex-owner. The lights went out in the saloon of the former Western city years ago. Back in the days of East Germany, the Santa Fe Express still made its rounds and Nina Hagen dashed about the stage.*

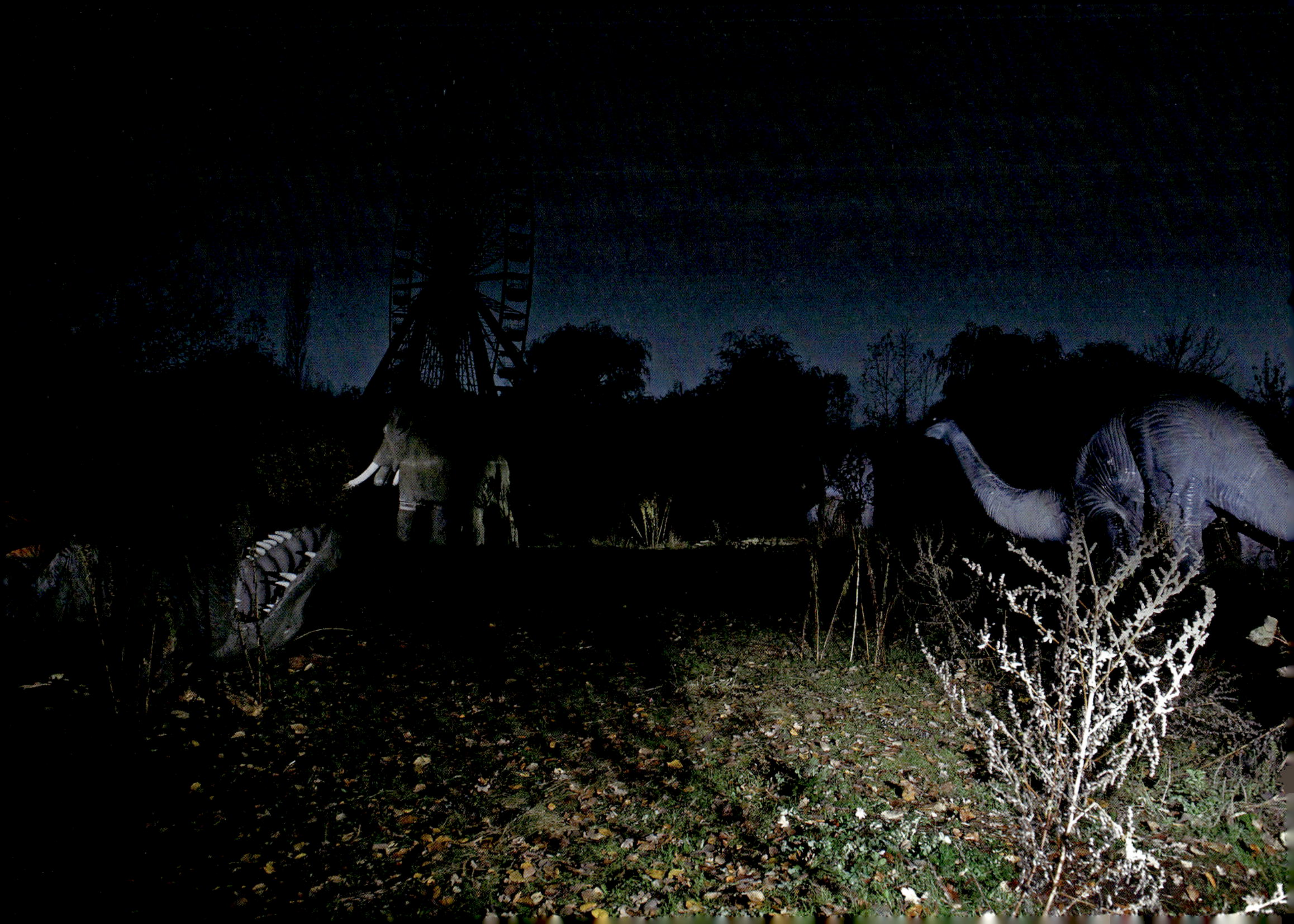

**DER WILD RIVER IST AUSGETROCKNET. LAUB FÜLLT DAS BETT DER EINSTIGEN WILDWASSERBAHN. IM TRÜBEN TÜMPEL HAT DAS QUAKEN DER FRÖSCHE BEGONNEN.** ▬

*The Wild River is dry. The bed of the one-time white-water ride is filled with leaves. The frogs in the pond have begun croaking.*

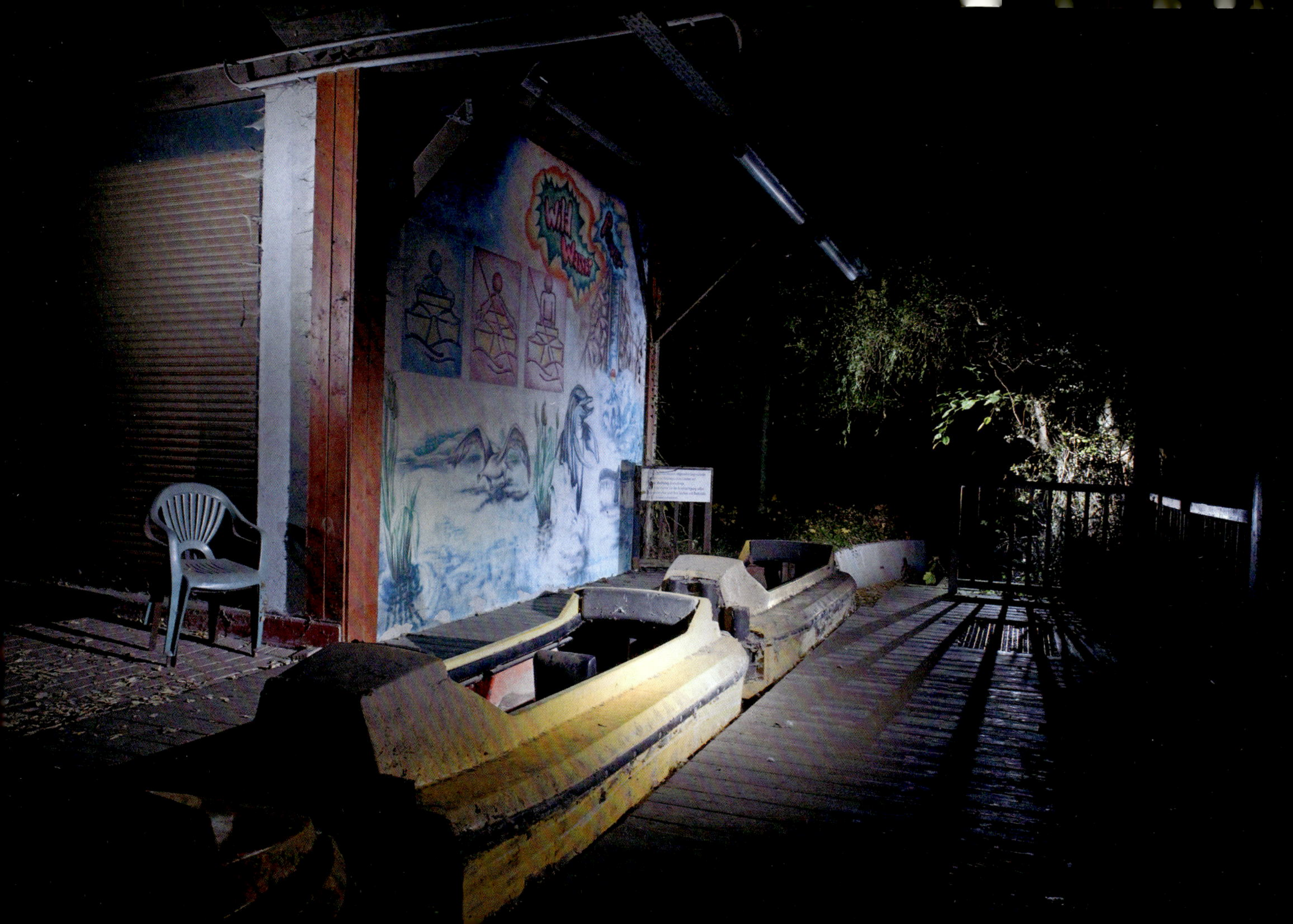

Willkommen

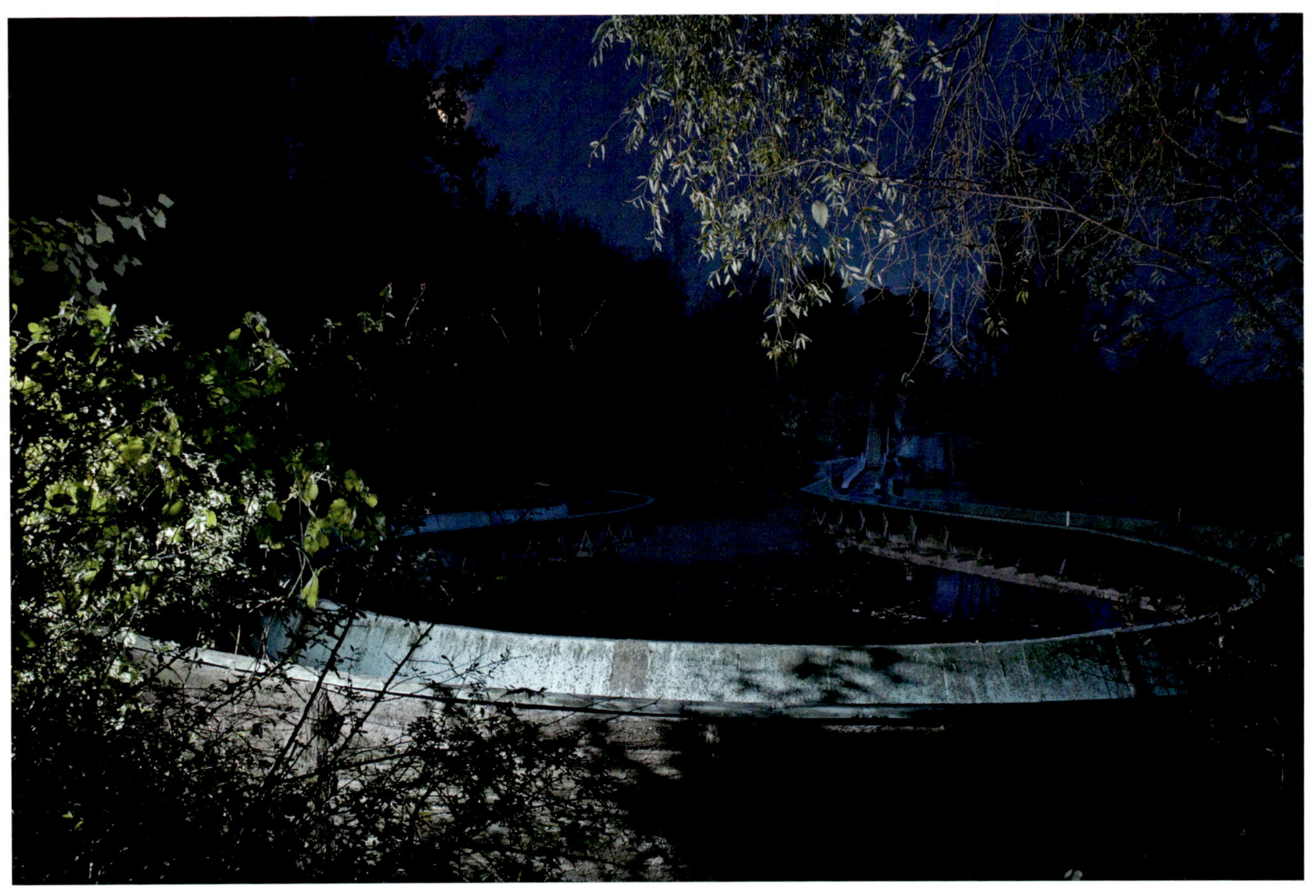

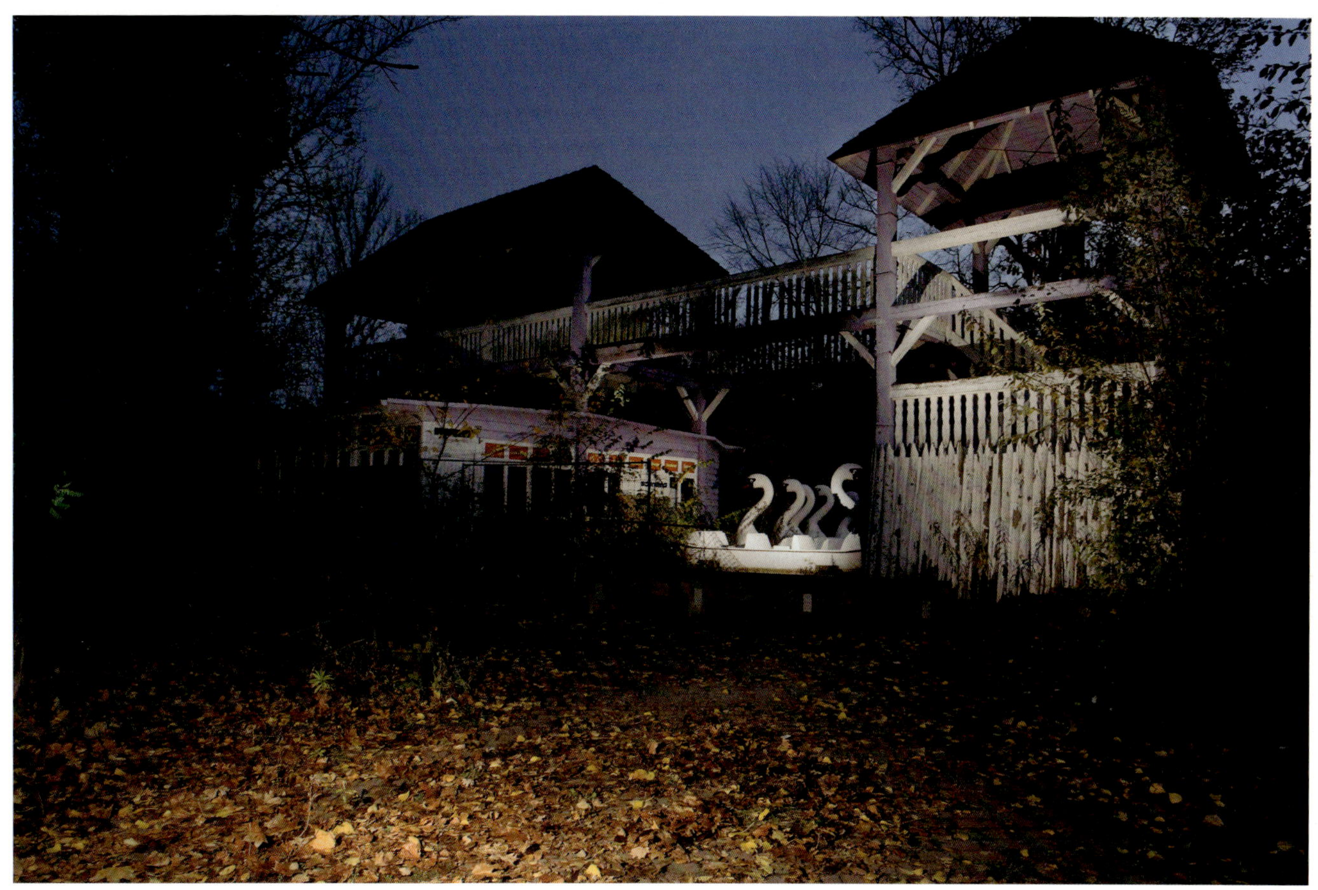

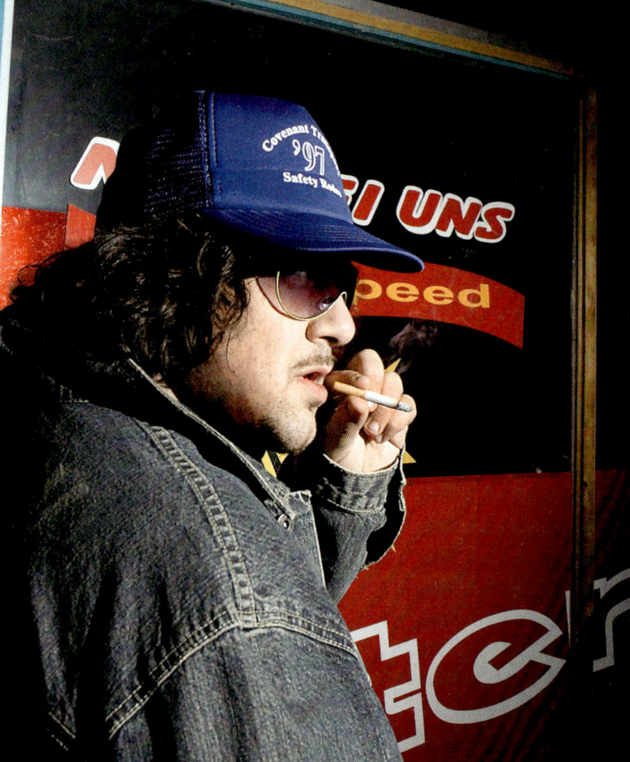

Telefonieren Sie
bis zu 70%
günstiger als mit
herkömmlichen
Tarifen !
Uygun fiyatla
efon Görüsmesi
e varan
mden
anin !
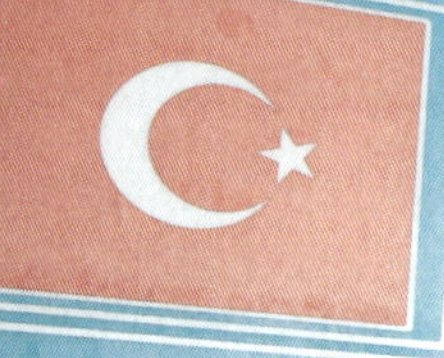
Covenant Tr
'97
Safety Ro
EI UNS
peed

# KREUZBERG: TÜRKISCHER TEE, STUDENTEN-WGs, INTERNETCAFÉS

## Kreuzberg:

## Turkish tea, shared student apartments, Internet cafés

Kleinkunst im Hinterhof, Shawarma und Iskender Kebab, Swingertreiben im Zwanglos I und II, Feierabendbier im Holsteneck, Razzia in der Hasenheide, Designbüros in Metzgereien, Sambatanz und Kulturkarneval, autarkes Leben in den Wagenburgen, Sommerfrische am Maybachufer.

*Cabaret in the back courtyard, shawarma and Iskender kebap, swingers do their thing at Zwanglos I and II, a beer at quitting time at the Holsteneck, crackdown in the Hasenheide, design studios in meat markets, samba dancing and culture carnival, self-sufficient living in the circled wagon trains, summer retreat on Maybachufer.*

# PAPAS PARTYKELLER

## *Dad's basement party room*



Hinter Butzenscheiben im Erdgeschoss flackert eine Felllampe. Ein Kiezbewohner mit Schirmmütze betritt die Bar und preist seine Ware auf einer umgebauten Holzschublade an – türkische Abzeichen und Uhren der Marke Bronex. Plattencover der vergangenen Jahrzehnte und grelle Tapeten zieren den Raum. Der Chef persönlich holt eine Langspielplatte aus seinem Sortiment und lässt eine musikalische Perle aus den 1960er-Jahren auf dem Sechs-Watt-Monoplattenspieler anlaufen. Unter zwei Pantoffeln an der Wand sucht ein Pärchen den Rhythmus der knackenden Melodie. Ein runder Tisch mit Blumenplastikdecke vor einer Fototapete mit deutschem Bergpanorama stimmt auf einen nostalgischen Abend ein. Das Gefühl von Heimat macht sich breit.

*A fur-covered lamp flickers behind bull's-eye panes on the ground floor. A local from the neighborhood wearing a visored cap enters the bar and sings the praises of his goods displayed on a converted wooden drawer— Turkish badges and Bronex watches. The room is decorated with LP covers from past decades and otherwise gaudy wall paper. The boss personally takes out a 12-inch record from his collection and places the stylus of a six-watt monaural record player on a musical pearl from the nineteen-sixties. A couple tries out the crackling rhythm beneath two slippers on the wall. A round table with a plastic floral tablecloth in front of photo wallpaper showing the panorama of a German mountain range sets the mood for a nostalgic evening. A sense of homeland is in the air.*

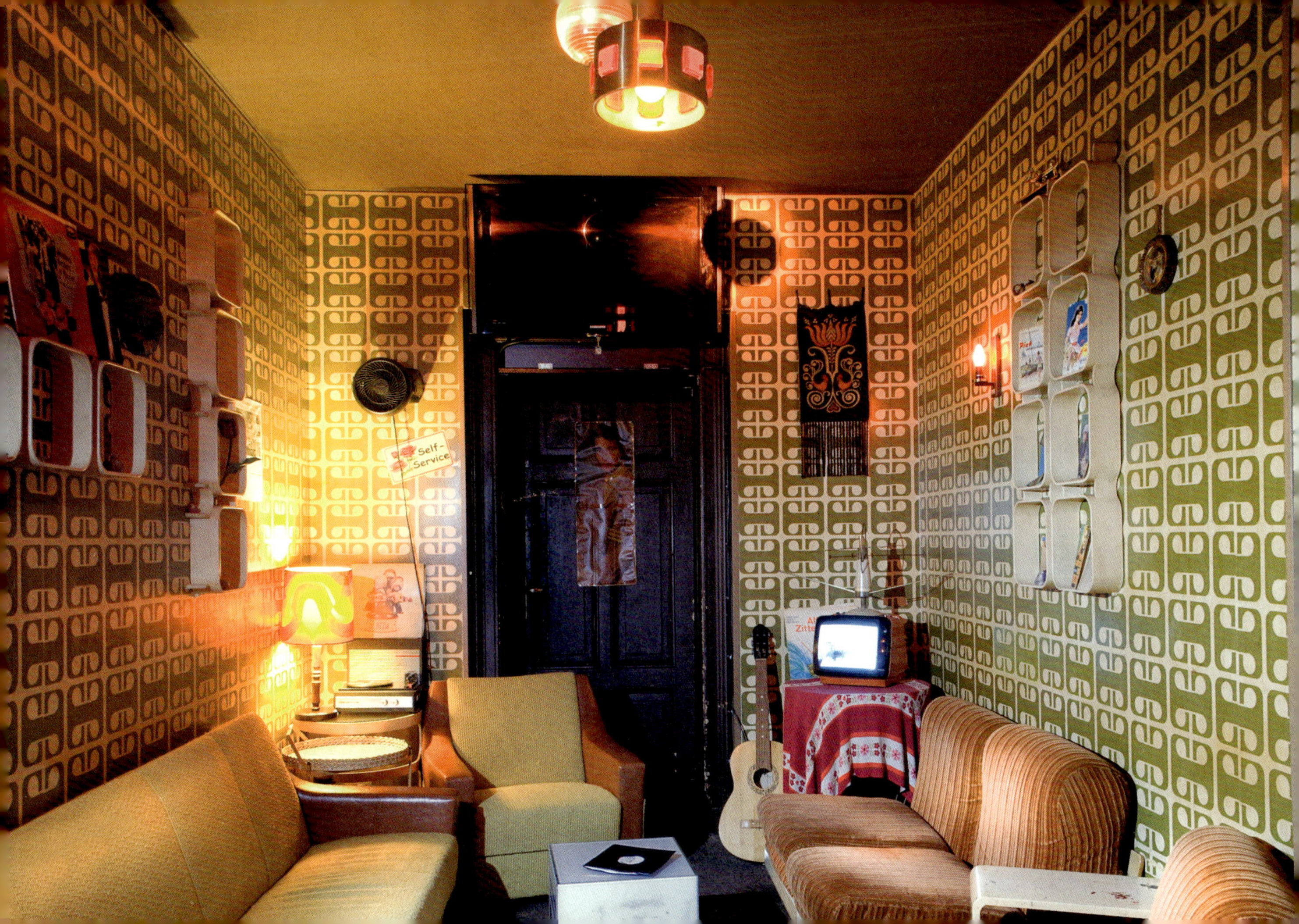
Self-
Service

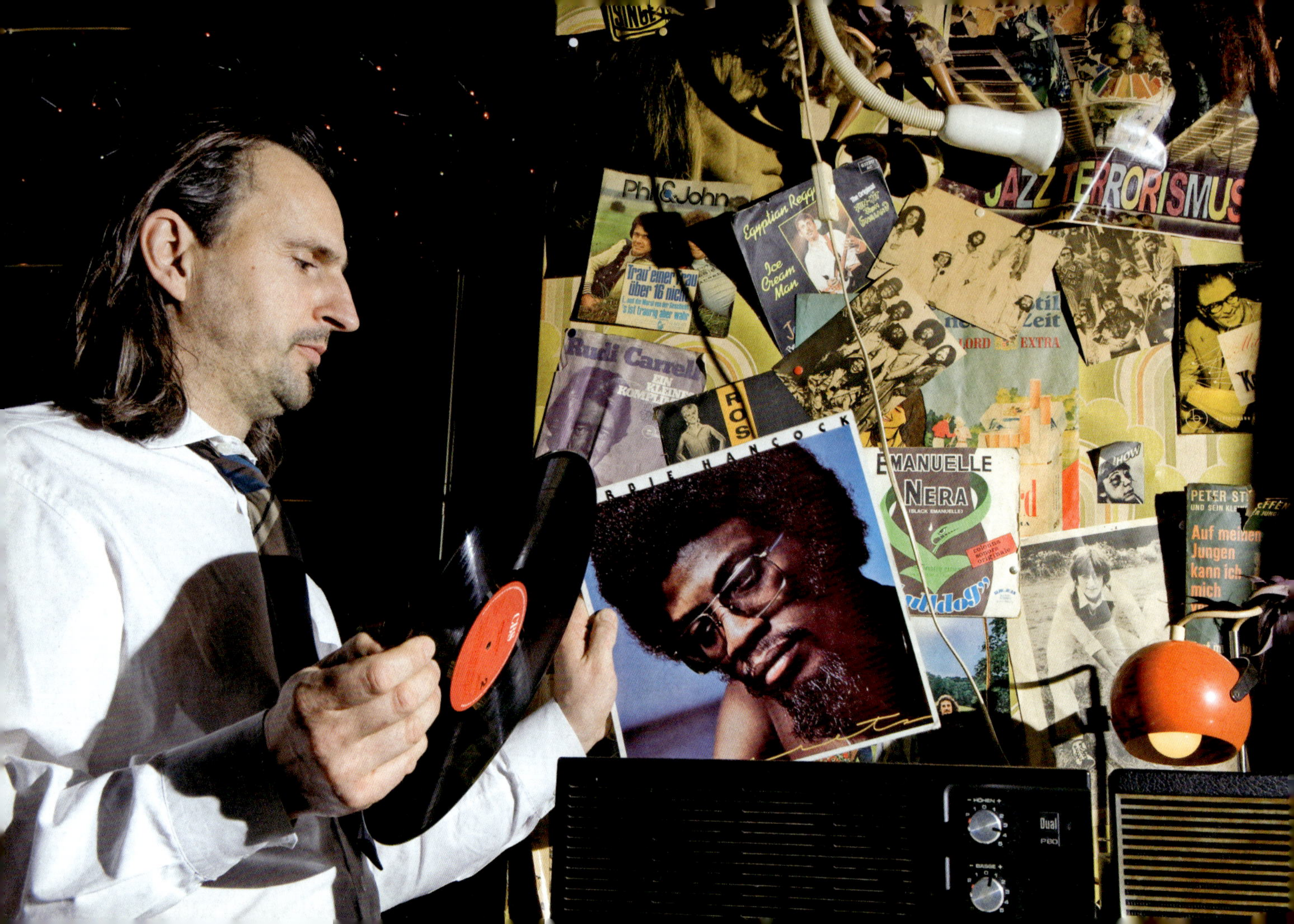

Phil & John
Trau' einer Frau über 16 nicht
Egyptian Reggae
Ice Cream Man
JAZZ TERRORISMUS
Rudi Carrell
EIN KLEINES KOMPLE
HANCOCK
EMANUELLE NERA
(BLACK EMANUELLE)
PETER ST
UND SEIN KLEIN
Auf meinem Jungen kann ich mich
Dual
P80
HÖHEN +
BÄSSE +

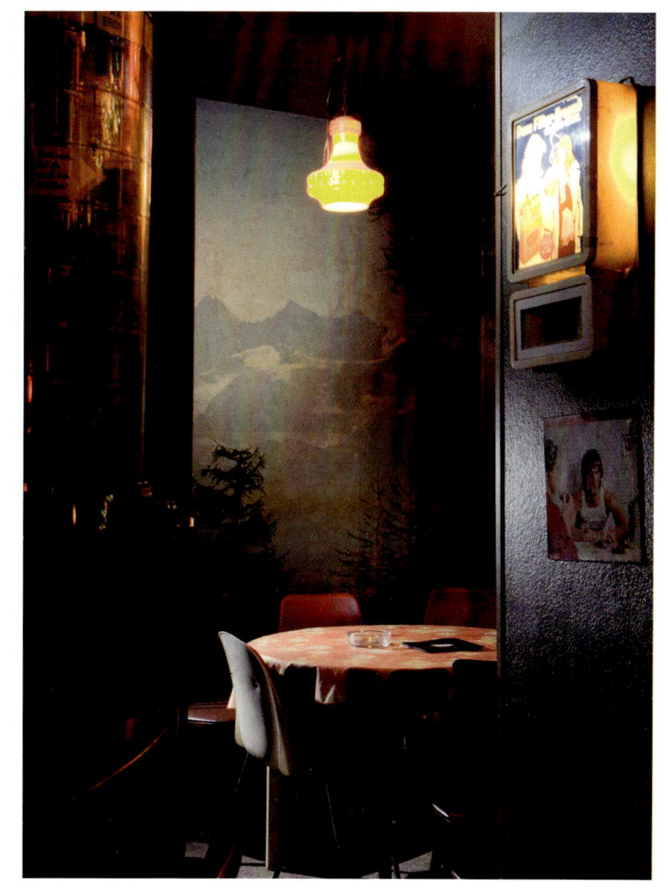

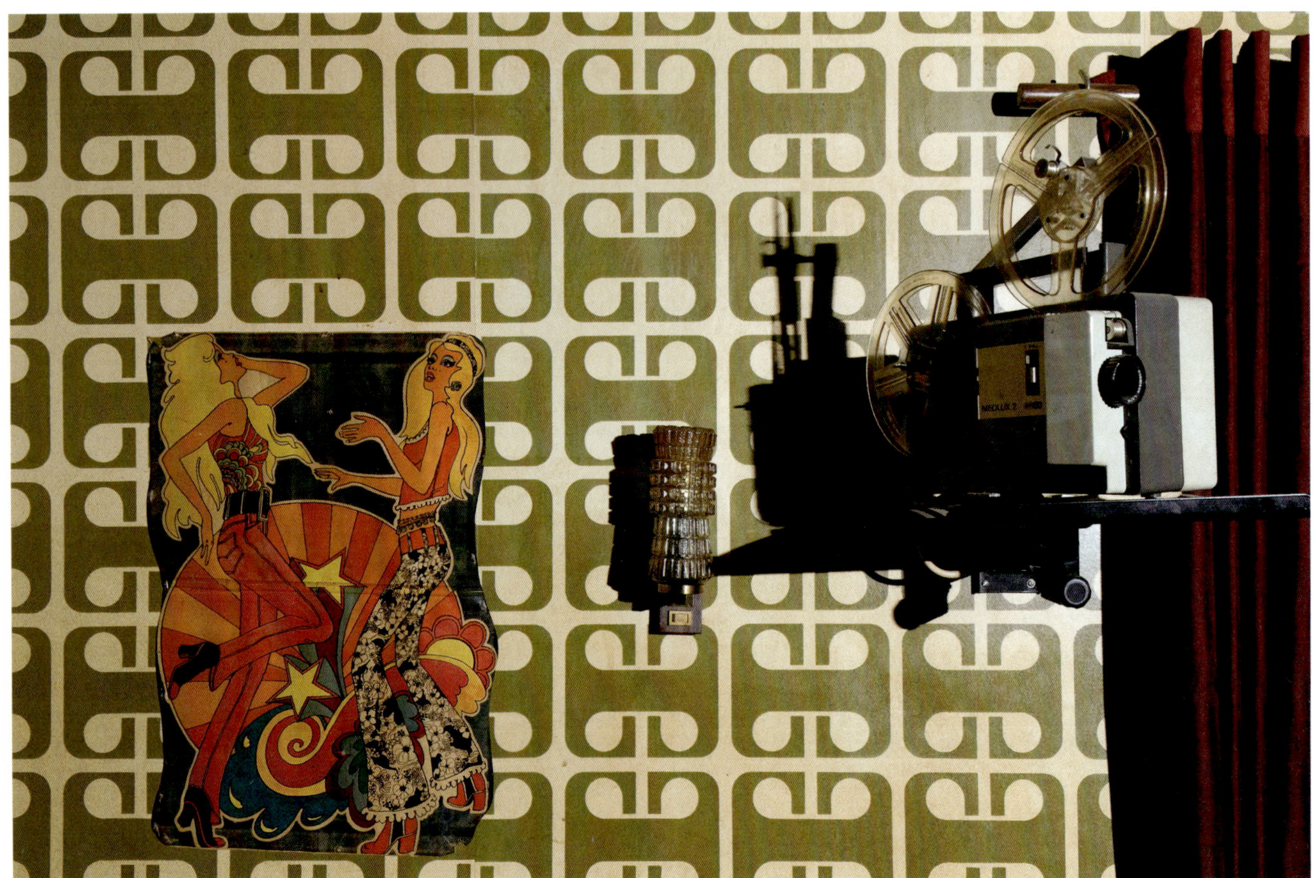

NEOLUX 2

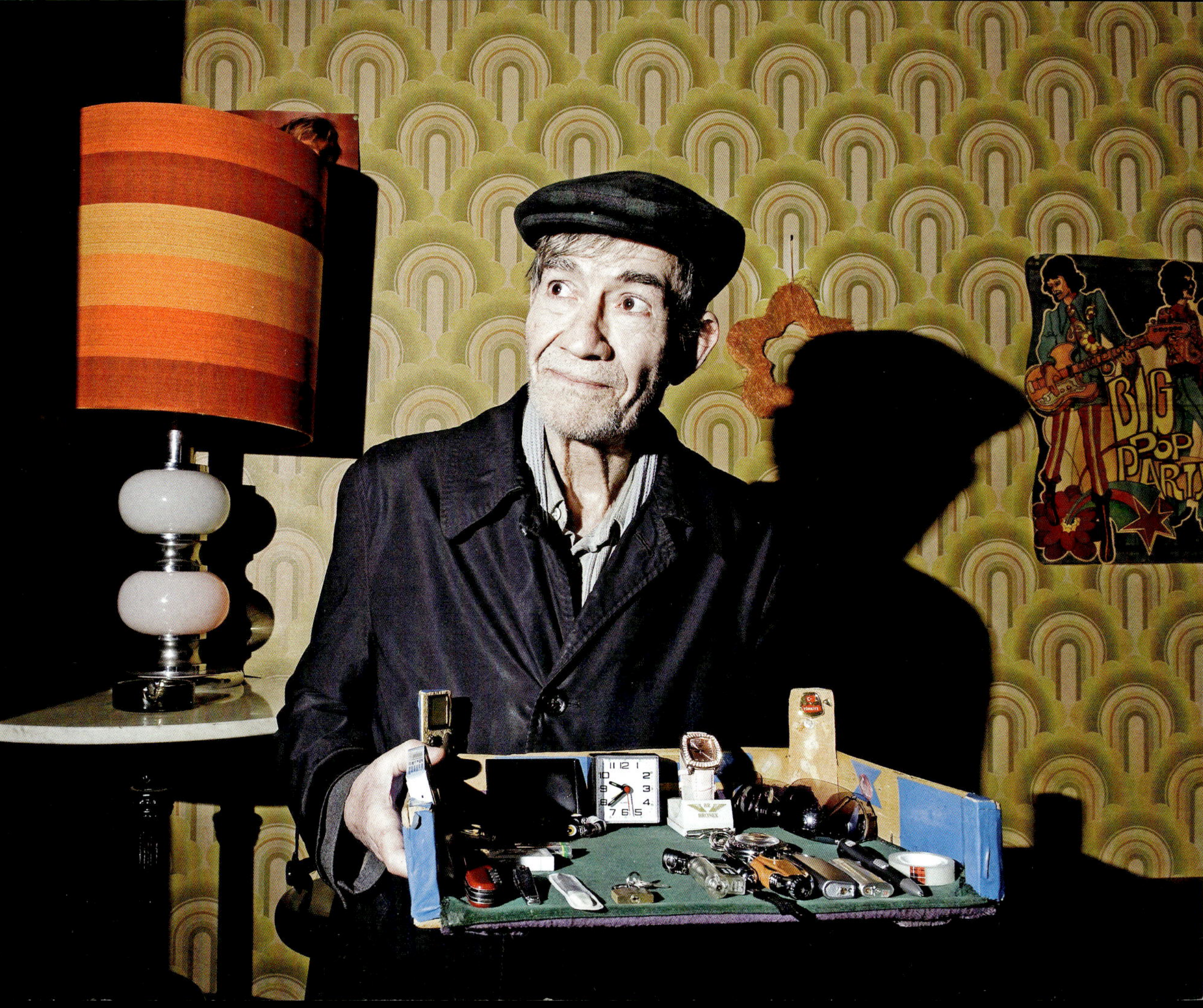
BIG
POP
PARTY

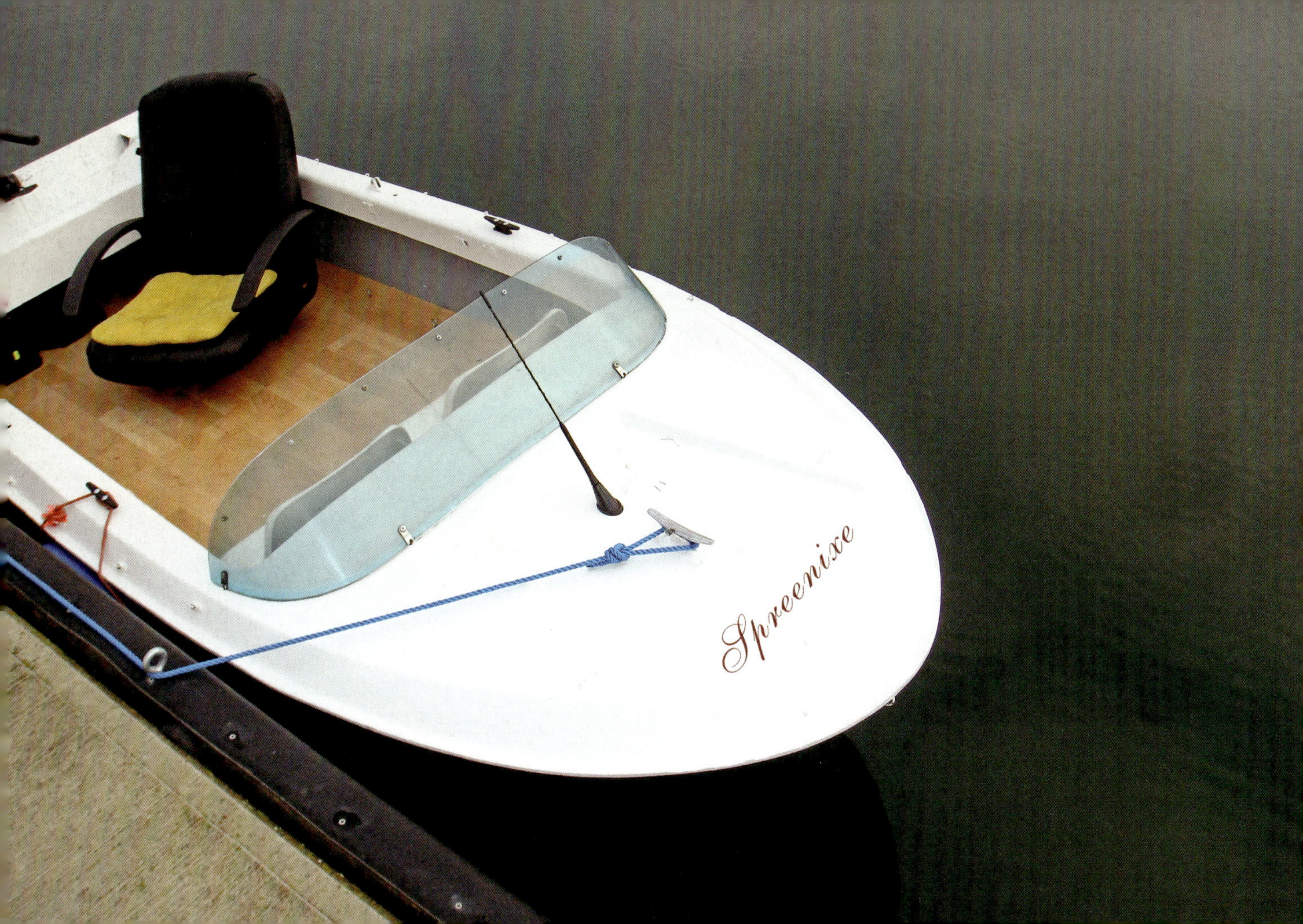
Spreenixe

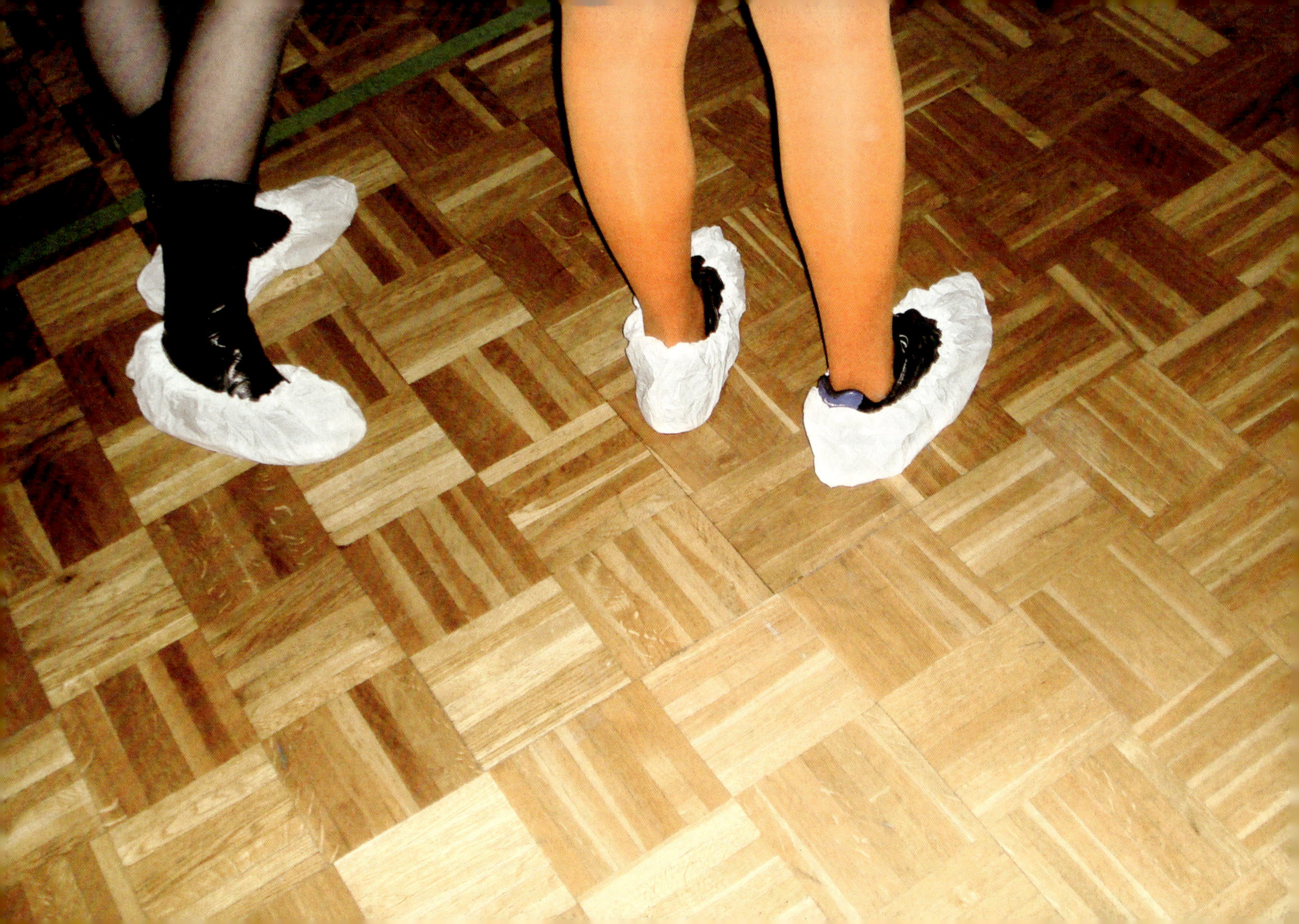

# ARM? BUNT, ABER SEXY!

## Poor? Gaudy, but sexy!

**43** **Nollendorfplatz**
*Berlin-Schöneberg*

Sechs Männer im US-Police-Outfit stürmen über die Straße. Keiner der Passanten blickt sich um, nur ein Tourist wagt einen schüchternen Blick. Die Straßen sind überfüllt, harte Bässe kündigen den herannahenden Menschenzug des Christopher Street Days an. Eine Schaumkanone nimmt die tanzende Masse ins Visier. Weiter südlich Richtung Winterfeldtplatz ist die Stimmung gelassen. In den Cafés tankt ein bunt gemischtes Publikum Sonne und Milchkaffee. Vor der Scheune, einer der zahlreichen schwulen Bars, warten vier starke Männer in schwarzer Montur. Der eine dreht sich um und ruft einer violett gekleideten Dame auf der anderen Straßenseite zu: »Na Tom, auch zum Christopher Street Day unterwegs?«

*Six men wearing American police outfits storm across the street. None of the passers-by take notice; only a solitary tourist risks a bashful glance. The streets are overflowing; hard bass beats proclaim the approaching procession of people on Christopher Street Day. A foam cannon takes aim at the dancing masses. The mood is calm off to the south on Winterfeldtplatz. A ragtag mix of people fills up on sunshine and café au lait. Four strong men in black wait in front of the Scheune, one of the numerous gay bars here in the neighborhood. One of them turns around and calls out to a woman attired in purple on the other side of the street: "Hey Tom, also going to Christopher Street Day?"*

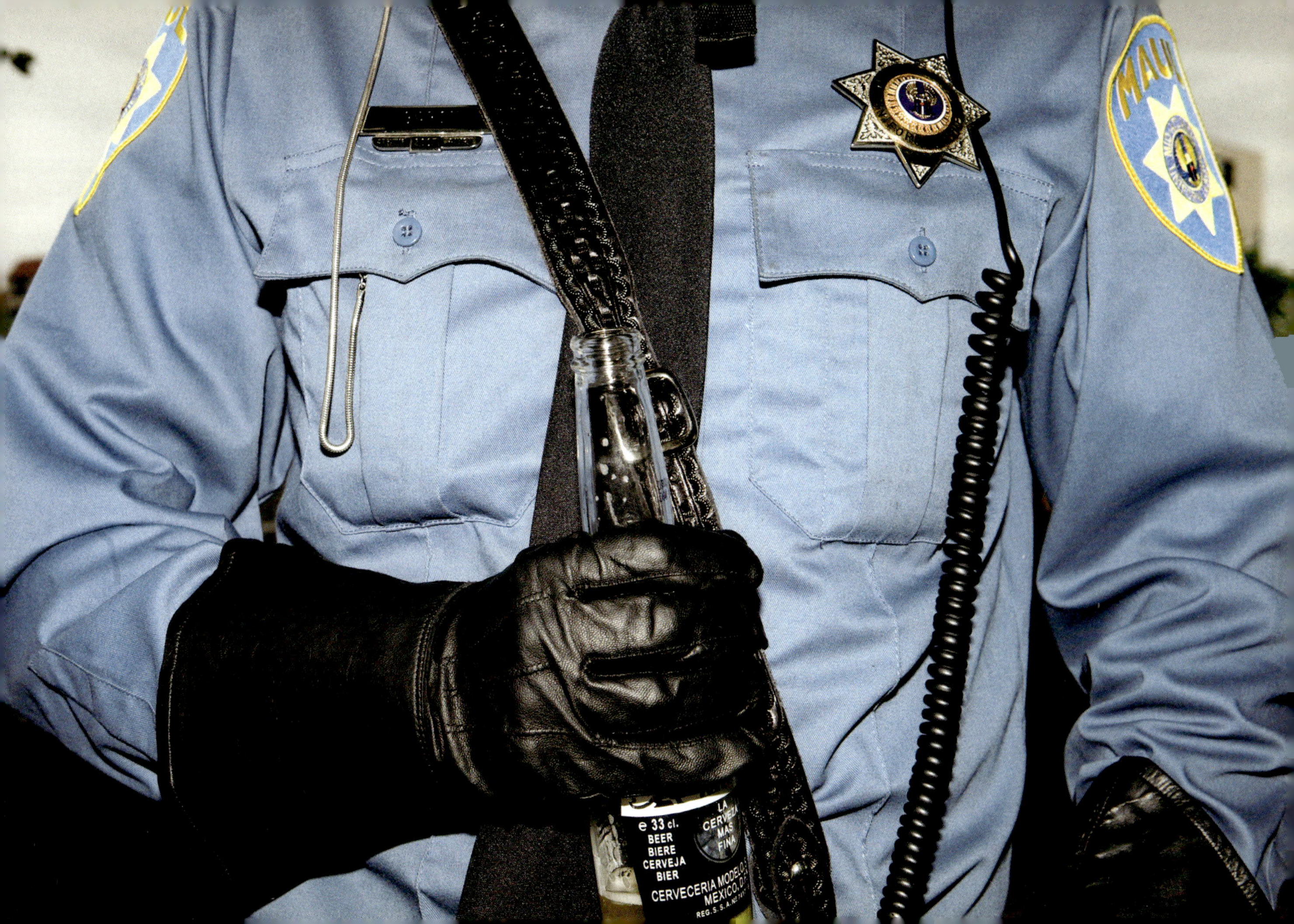
MAL
e 33 cl.
BEER
BIERE
CERVEJA
BIER
LA
CERVEZA
MAS
FINA
CERVECERIA MODELO
MEXICO, D.F.
REG. S. S. A. N°

# »EIN KILO KAVIAR FÜR MEINE FRAU«

## "A kilo of caviar for my wife"



Getrockneter russischer Stör und kaukasisches Rentierfleisch werden in der Auslage des russischen Spezialitätenladens angeboten. Die Stimmung ist gelassen, eine Kundin aus Reinickendorf gibt laut lachend ihre bruchstückhaften Russischkenntnisse preis. Eine Russin beäugt das Gemüsesortiment. Die Blicke des Verkäufers bleiben an den schwarzen Overknee-Stiefeln haften. Ihr Mann steht bei den Kollegen auf der gegenüberliegenden Straßenseite. Aus dem umfangreichen Wodkaregal greift er eine Flasche des Labels Parliament, dazu eine Dose weißen Beluga-Kaviar für 900 Euro. Authentizität strahlt die Deko auf einem der Gefrierschränke aus: ein Samowar und daneben das Bild Lenins.

*Dried Russian sturgeon and Caucasian reindeer meat are offered for sale in the display window of the Russian delicatessen. The mood is unhurried; a woman customer from Reinickendorf loudly betrays her fragmentary knowledge of Russian with a smile. A Russian woman ogles the vegetables. The salesman's glance remains fixed on the black thigh-high boots. Her husband stands in the store on the other side of the street. He reaches for a bottle of Parliament from the well-stocked vodka shelf as well as a can of white Beluga caviar for 900 euros. The decorations exude authenticity on one of the freezers: a samovar and a portrait of Lenin next to it.*

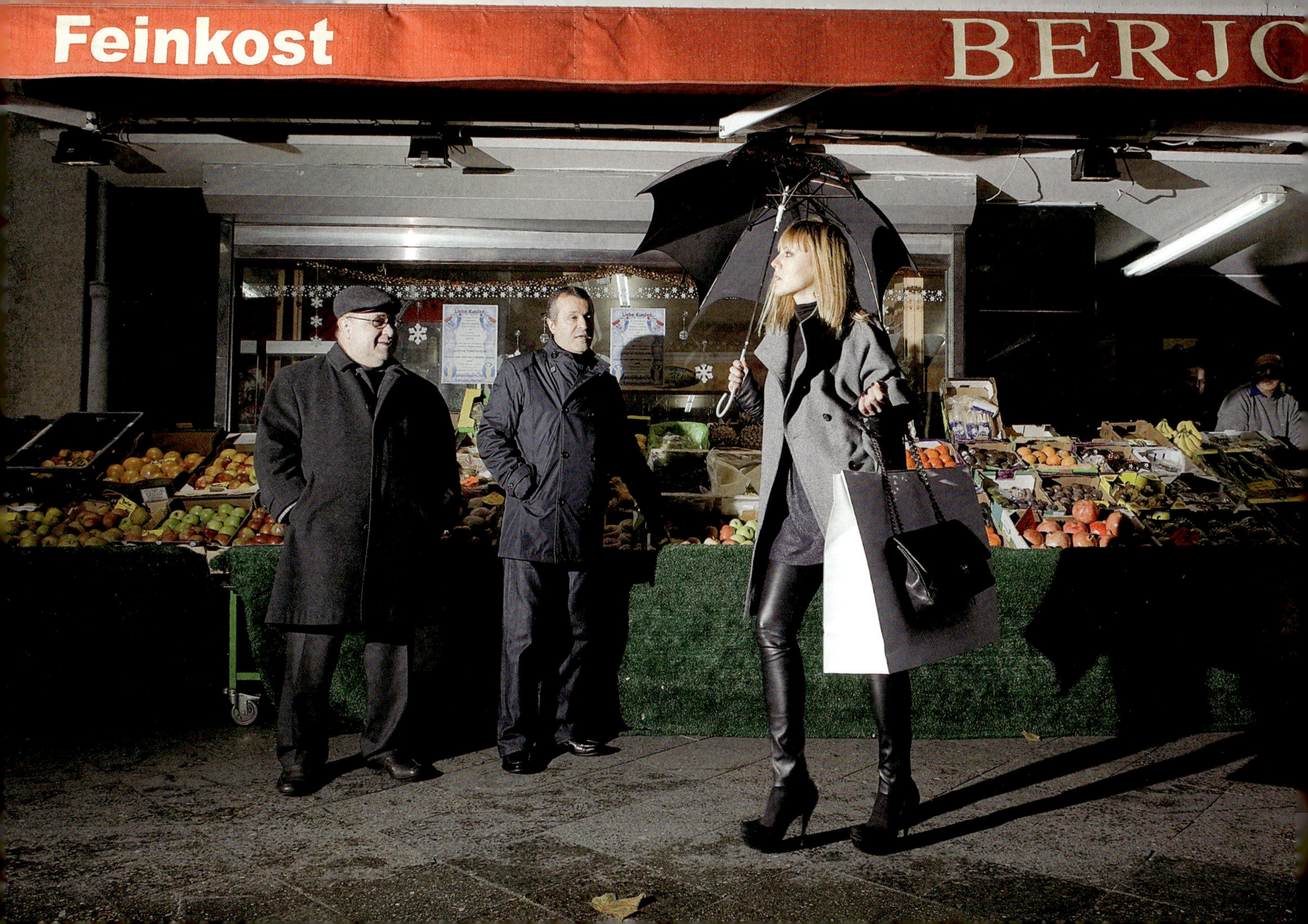

Feinkost
BERJO

# TEMPELHOF:
# WOHNUNGEN MIT ROLLFELDBLICK
# UND HEIZEN AM BERLINER RING


## Tempelhof:

## apartments with a rundway view

## and heating it up

## on Berliner Ring

Soundcheck in der Columbiahalle, Stillstand am Kofferband, Broiler am Pla de Lü, Souvenirs im Fliegerladen, Beziehungskrisen im Waschsalon, Fashionshows in Wartehallen, Flughafenkatakomben mit Bowlingbahn, der Lehnepark mit Wilhelmsteich, Architekturreisen zum Ullsteinhaus.

*Sound check in the Columbiahalle, standstill at the baggage belt, broilers on Pla de Lü, souvenirs in the flight shop, squabbling couples at the laundry, fashion shows in waiting rooms, airport catacombs with bowling lanes, Lehnepark with Wilhelm Pond, architectural trips to Ullsteinhaus.*

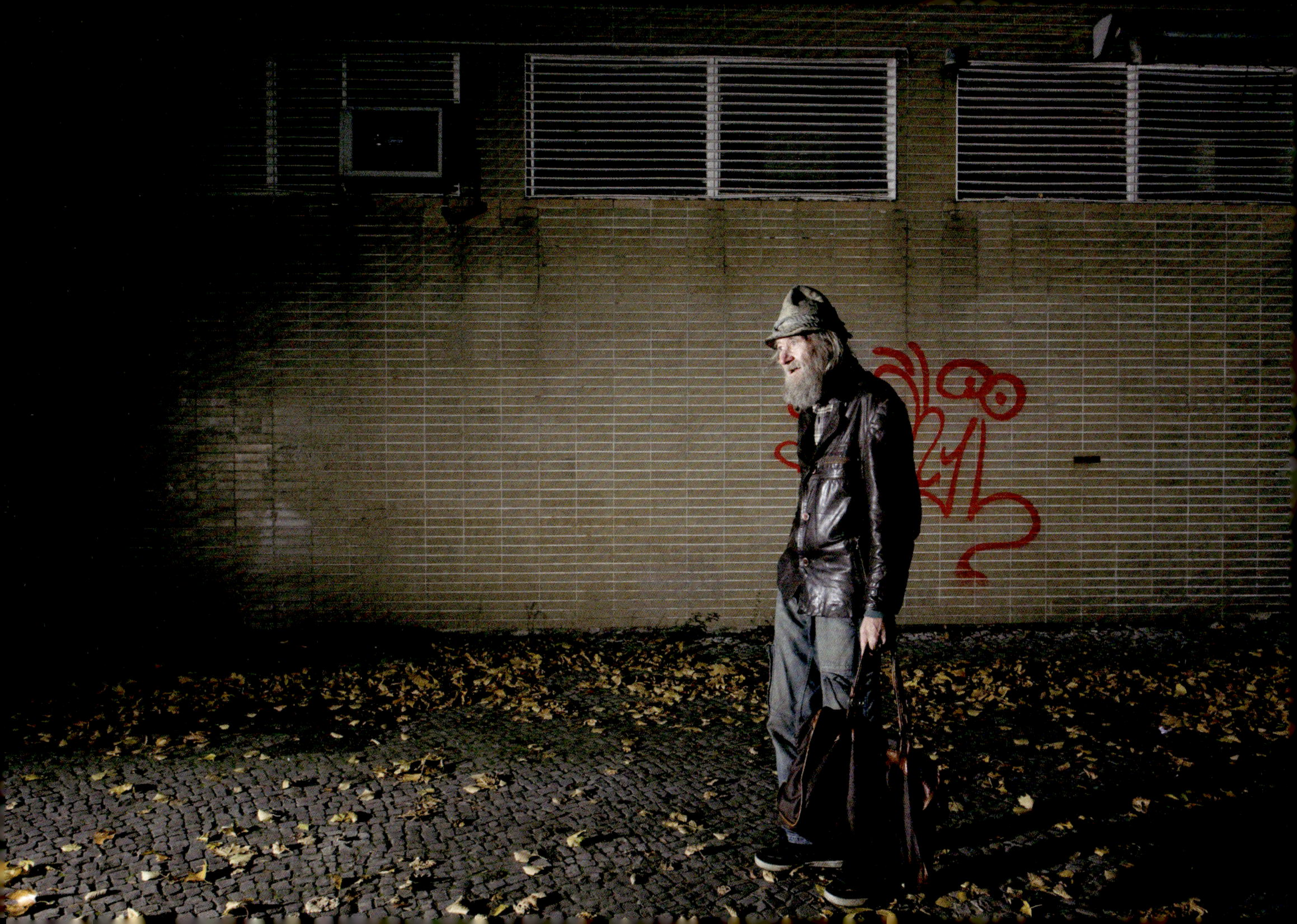

# EIERLIKÖR UND POMERANZENSCHNAPS
## *Advocaat and bitter orange schnaps*

**45** **E & M Leydicke**
*Mansteinstraße 4 . Berlin-Schöneberg*

Durch die gelben Butzenglasfenster dringt verhalten Licht in die Likörfabrik. In einem Holzregal hinter dem Bartresen reihen sich Flaschen mit ausgesuchtem Inhalt aneinander. Preisgekrönte Qualitätserzeugnisse – seit 1922 im hauseigenen Keller gebrannt und dort in großen Holzfässern gelagert. Der Hausherr greift nach der braunen Flasche mit dem Etikett »Schlehenfruchtwein« und gönnt sich ein Gläschen. Die Aufschrift an der Wand »Bist du klug und hast Verdruß, trinke Kakao mit Nuß« verleitet zum Antesten weiterer Geschmacksrichtungen, von Cordial Menoc oder Zitronenlikör. Die Zeiten, als die Siemenswerke noch im großen Stil beliefert wurden, sind vorbei. Damals besiegelte man Verträge mit so manchem Glas Eierlikör.

*Muted light shines into the liqueur distillery through the yellow bull's-eye panes of glass. Bottles with choice contents stand in rows on wooden shelves behind the bar counter. Award-winning high-quality products, distilled since 1922 in the basement and stored there in large wooden casks. The host reaches for a brown bottle with the label "Blackthorn Wine" and indulges himself in a glass. The inscription on the wall "Are you clever and truly vexed, nut-flavored cocoa is what you need next" provides the inspiration to try out a few other tastes like Cordial Menoc or lemon liqueur. The days when the Siemens plant ordered bottles en masse have long passed. Contracts used to be sealed with an advocaat or two.*

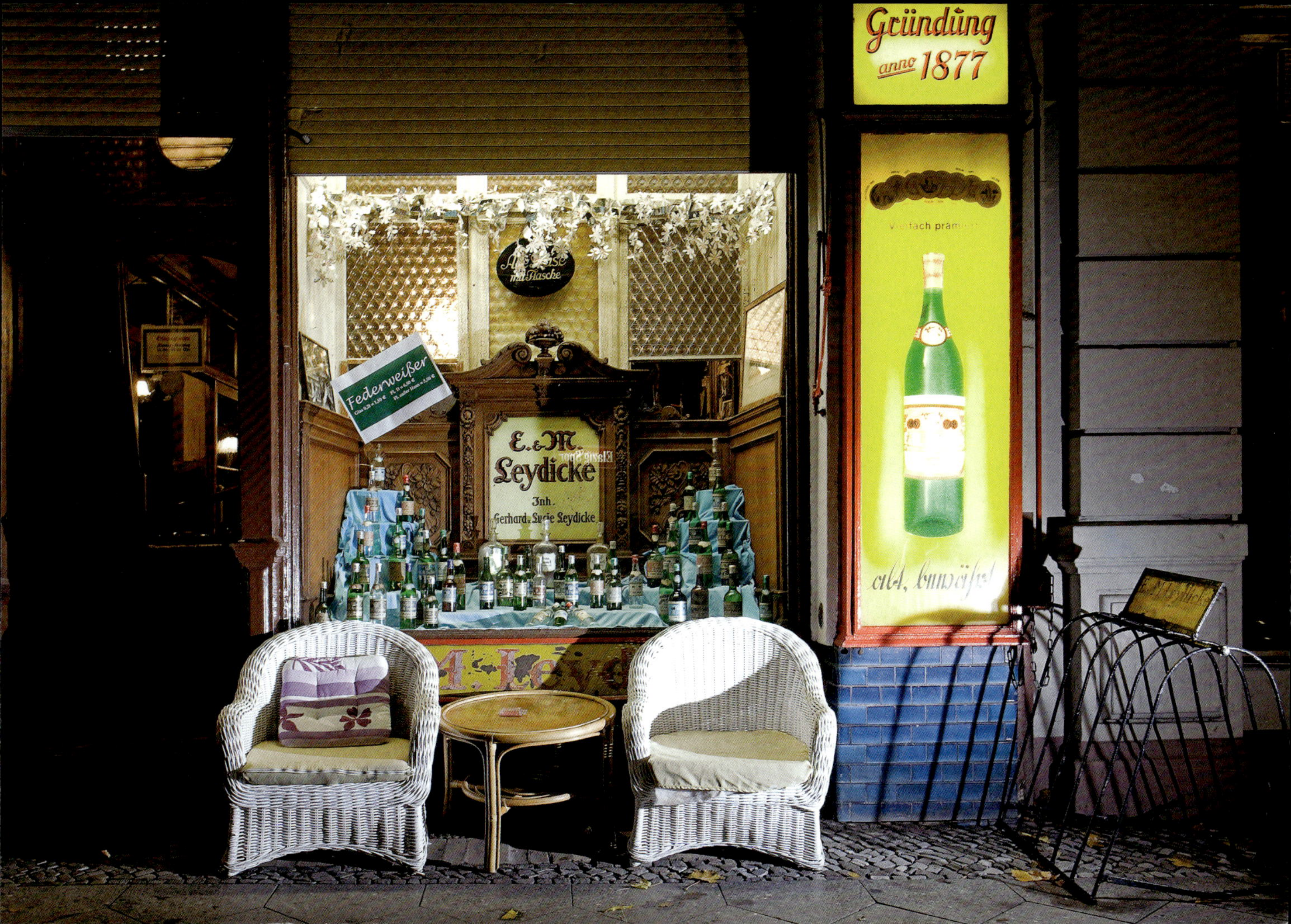

Gründüng
anno 1877
Vielfach prämiert
alt, bewährt
Federweißer
E. & M.
Leydicke
Inh.
Gerhard u. Susie Leydicke

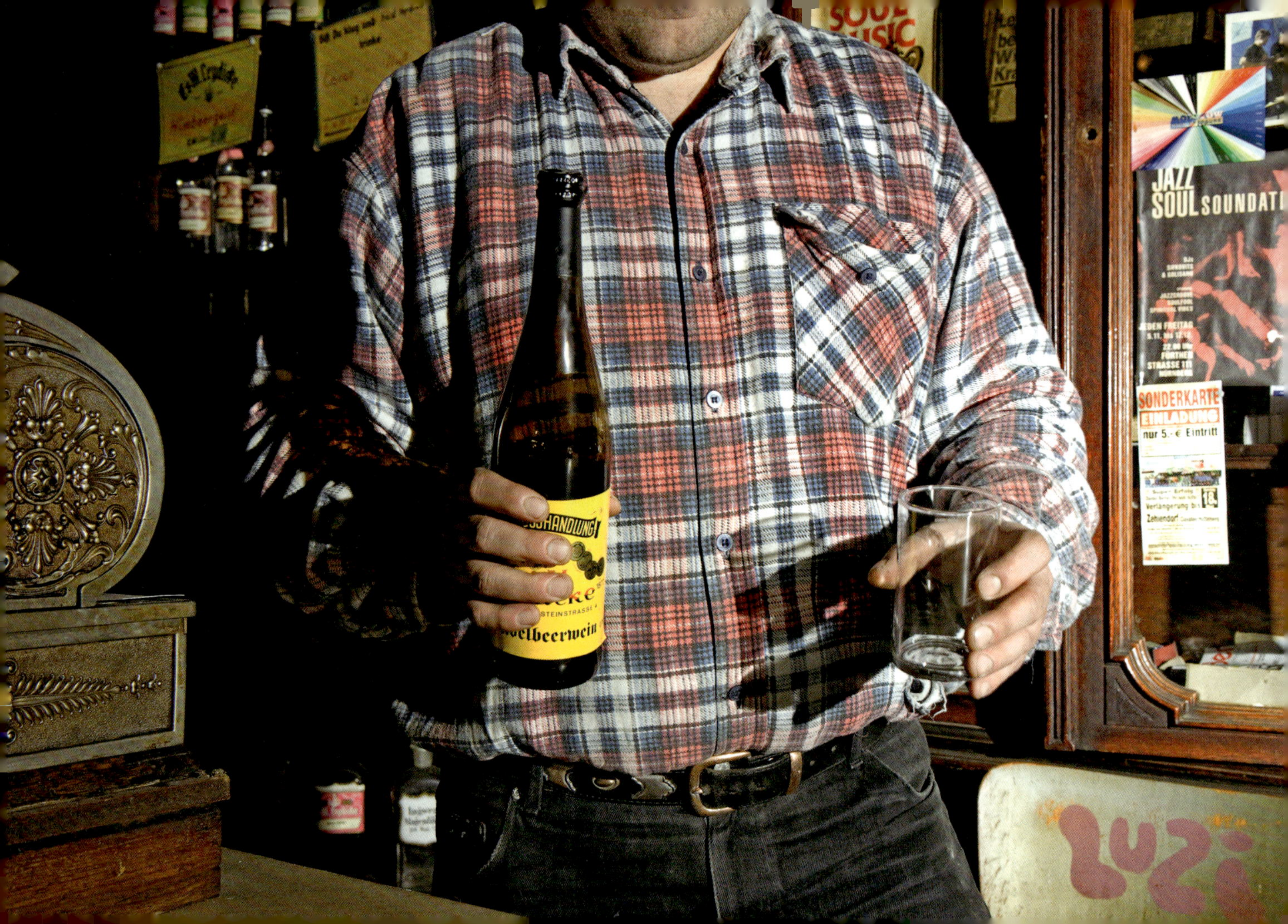

SOUL
MUSIC
JAZZ
SOUL SOUNDATI
JEDEN FREITAG
FÜRTHER
STRASSE
NÜRNBERG
SONDERKARTE
EINLADUNG
nur 5.- € Eintritt
HANDLUNG
Vogelbeerwein
LUZi

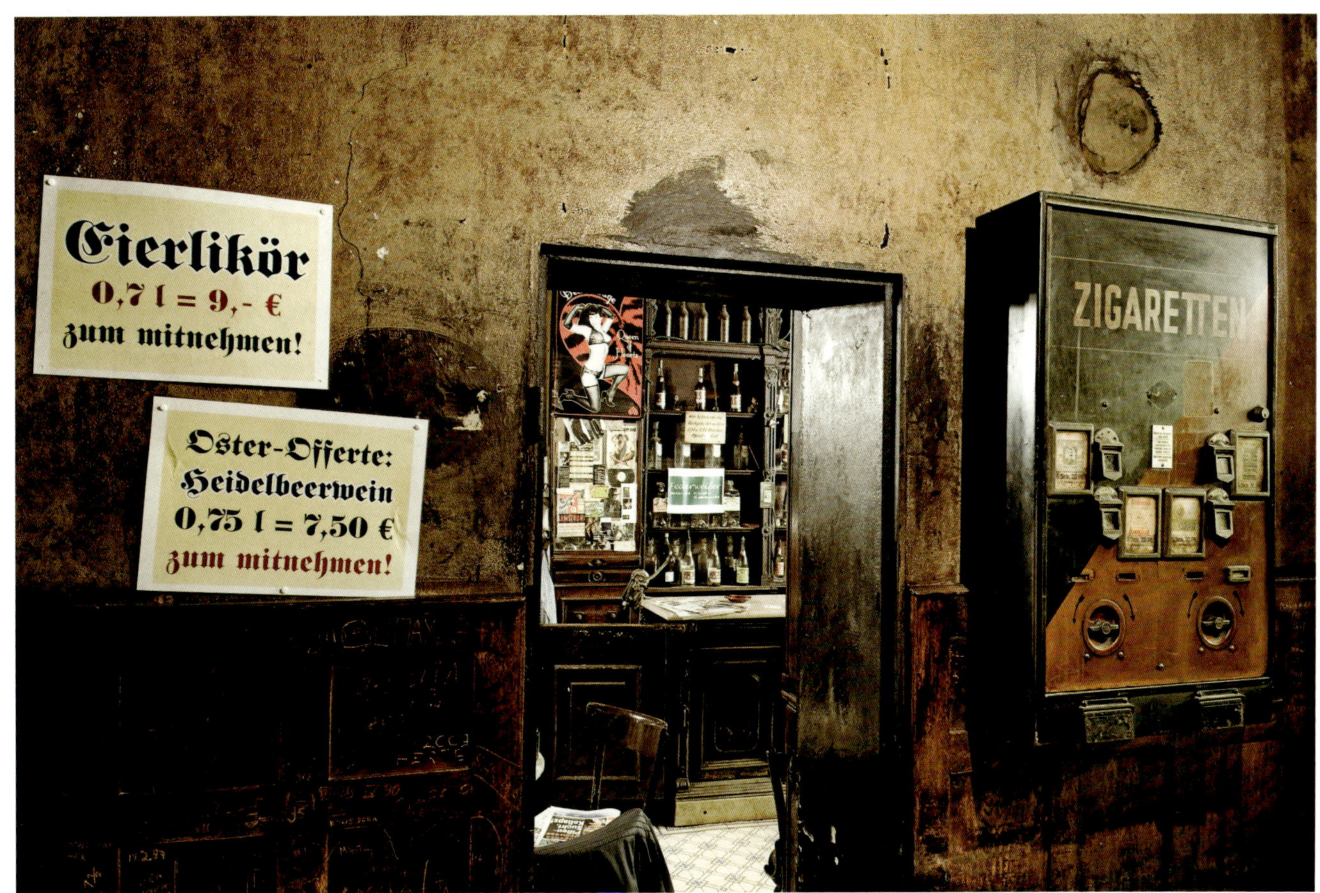
Eierlikör
0,7 l = 9,- €
zum mitnehmen!

Oster-Offerte:
Heidelbeerwein
0,75 l = 7,50 €
zum mitnehmen!

ZIGARETTEN

# ZWEI GRAFFITISPRAYER UND EIN VERLORENER NACHT-SCHWÄRMER TEILEN SICH DIE BRACHFLÄCHE. AM UFER BLICKT SICH EIN ANGLER AUF DER JAGD NACH SPREEBARSCHEN UM: »ROLEX UND KETTCHEN? FRÜHER WAREN DAS BRÄUTE UND PLATTEN.«

*Two graffiti sprayers and a lost nighthawk share the fallow land. A fisherman on the shore looks about in pursuit of Spree perch: "Rolexes and gold chains? It used to be broads and street people."*

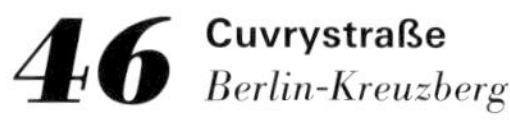

**46** Cuvrystraße
*Berlin-Kreuzberg*

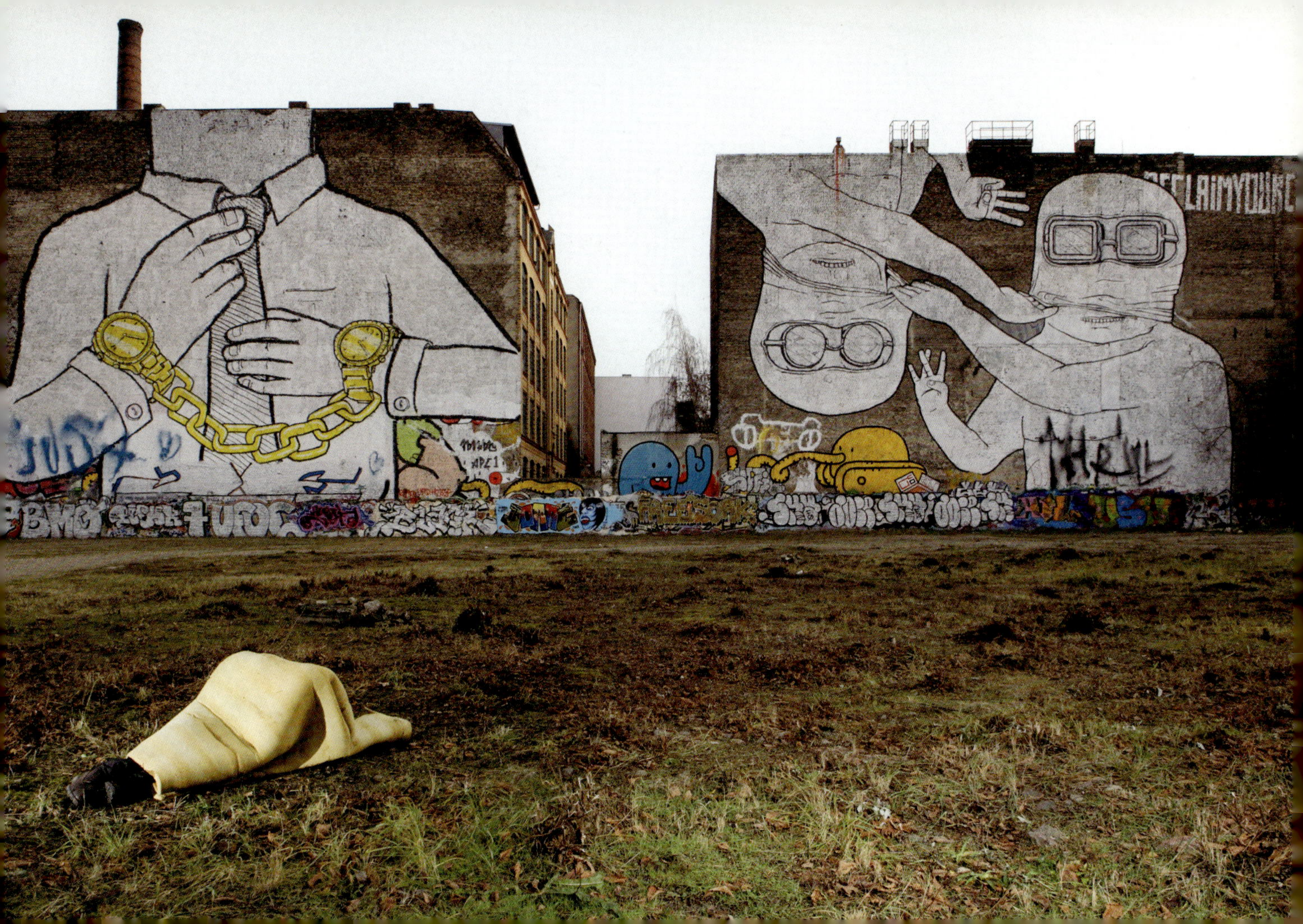
RECLAIMYOURC

# SÜDSEE AN DER GRENZE ZU POLEN

## The South Seas at the Polish border

**47** **Tropical Islands**
*Tropical-Islands-Allee 1 . Krausnick*

Wie ein überdimensionaler Fallschirm überspannt das freischwebende Dach den Südseestrand des Resorts. Dort sind alle Liegen besetzt. Eine Familie mit Schirmchen-Cocktails in den Händen blickt auf das kristallklare Wasser des Schwimmbeckens, in dem eine Dame mit Blumenbadekappe vorüberzieht. Dahinter verspricht der künstliche Horizont 365 Tage blauen Himmel. Auf dem Lehrpfad des größten Indoor-Regenwaldes der Welt fotografieren sich zwei Brandenburger vor dem Vishnu-Saunatempel und wandern zur Kasse des Thai-Hauses Jabarimba. Ein solariumgebräunter, muskulöser Angestellter empfiehlt ihnen dort ein tropisches Barbecue. Ein an einem Seil befestigter Ballon schwebt mit zwei blonden Norwegerinnen in 55 Metern Höhe über der tropischen Urlaubswelt.

*The free-floating roof covers the resort's South Sea beach like an oversized parachute. All the beach chairs are occupied. A family holding cocktails with umbrellas in the hands look across the crystal-clear water of the swimming pool in which a woman wearing a floral bathing cap passes by. In the background, an artificial horizon promises blue skies 365 days a year. Two Brandenburg residents take pictures of each other on the nature trail of the world's largest indoor rainforest in front of the Vishnu Sauna Temple and wander to the check-out at the Jabarimba restaurant in the Thai House. A muscular member of the staff with a fake tan recommends them a tropical barbecue. A balloon attached to a rope hovers with two blond Norwegian women at a height of 55 meters over the tropical vacation world.*

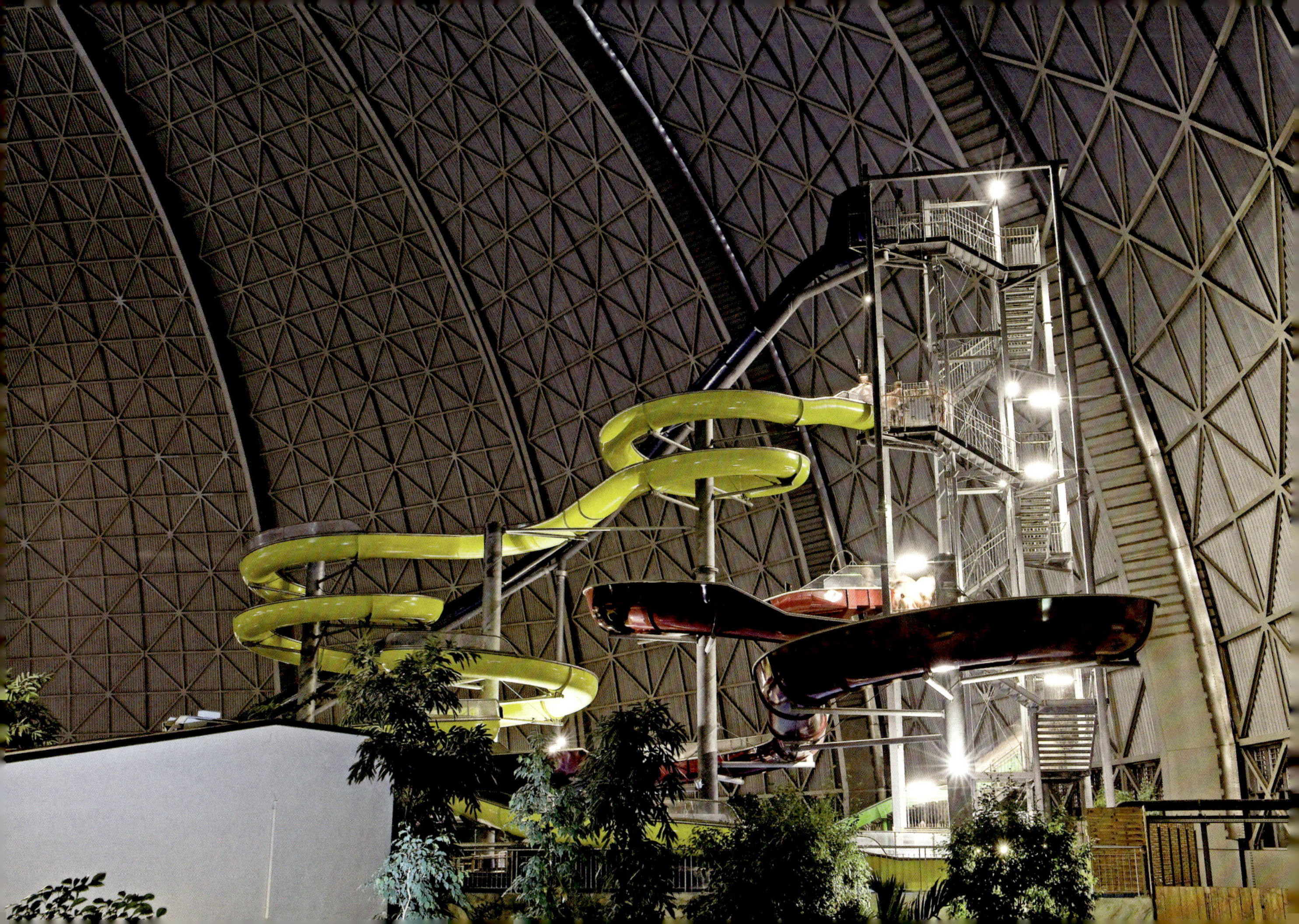

**AM ABEND ERSTRAHLT UNTER DEM HALLENDACH DER GROSSE LAMPENMOND. DAS MOTIV »KARIBIKSTRAND« FÜR DAS EIGENE FAMILIENALBUM RUNDET DEN AUFENTHALT AB.**

*The large lamp moon glows in the evening under the roof of the hall.*
*The "Caribbean Beach" motif for the family photo album rounds up the stay.*

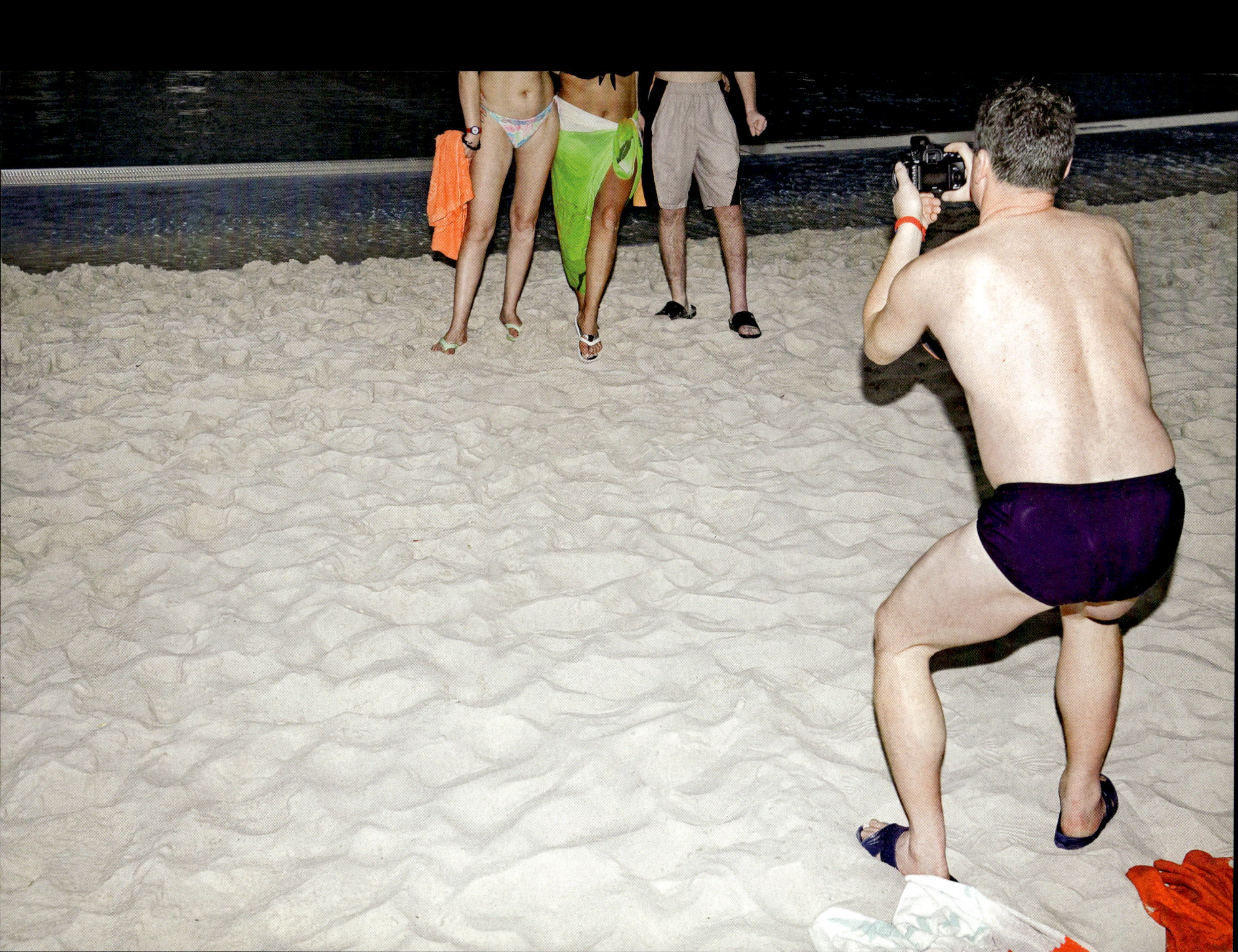

# BERLIN-MITTE: KOKS, KUNST UND KANZLERAMT

## Berlin-Mitte: cocaine, art, and chancellery

Pressetermin im Einstein, Limousinenservice am Adlon, Fashionshows und Spreefahrten, bayerische Touristen auf dem Oberdeck, Sektempfang bei Nofretete, Kulturschock in der Volksbühne, Punkrock in der Diamond Lounge, Blitzlicht und Grill Royal, Vernissagen der Kunstboheme.

*Press conference at Café Einstein, limousine service at the Hotel Adlon, fashion shows and boat trips on the Spree, Bavarian tourists on the upper deck, champagne reception with Nefertiti, culture shock at the Volksbühne, punk rock at the Diamond Lounge, flashbulbs and Grill Royal, bohemian society attends an exhibition preview.*

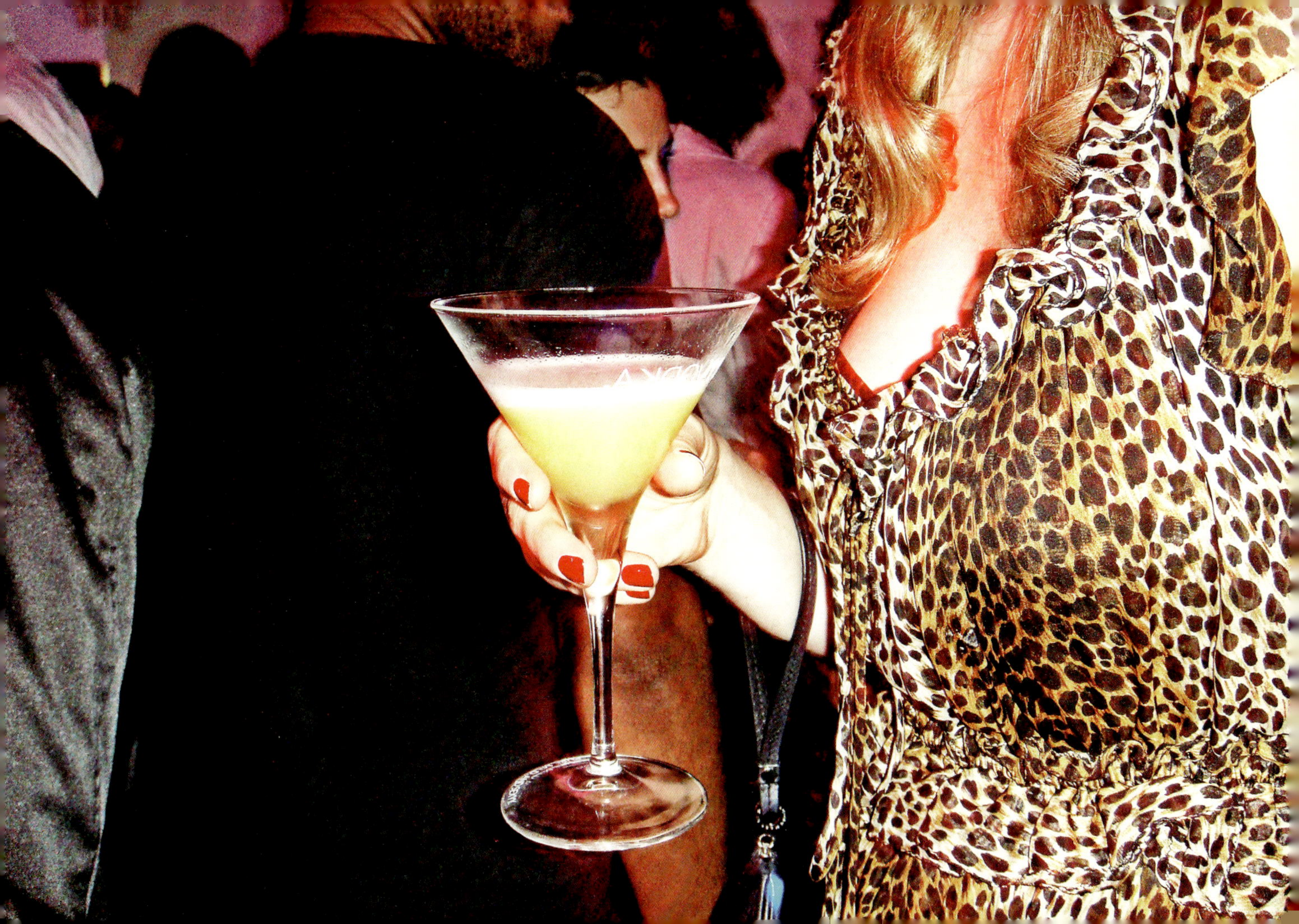

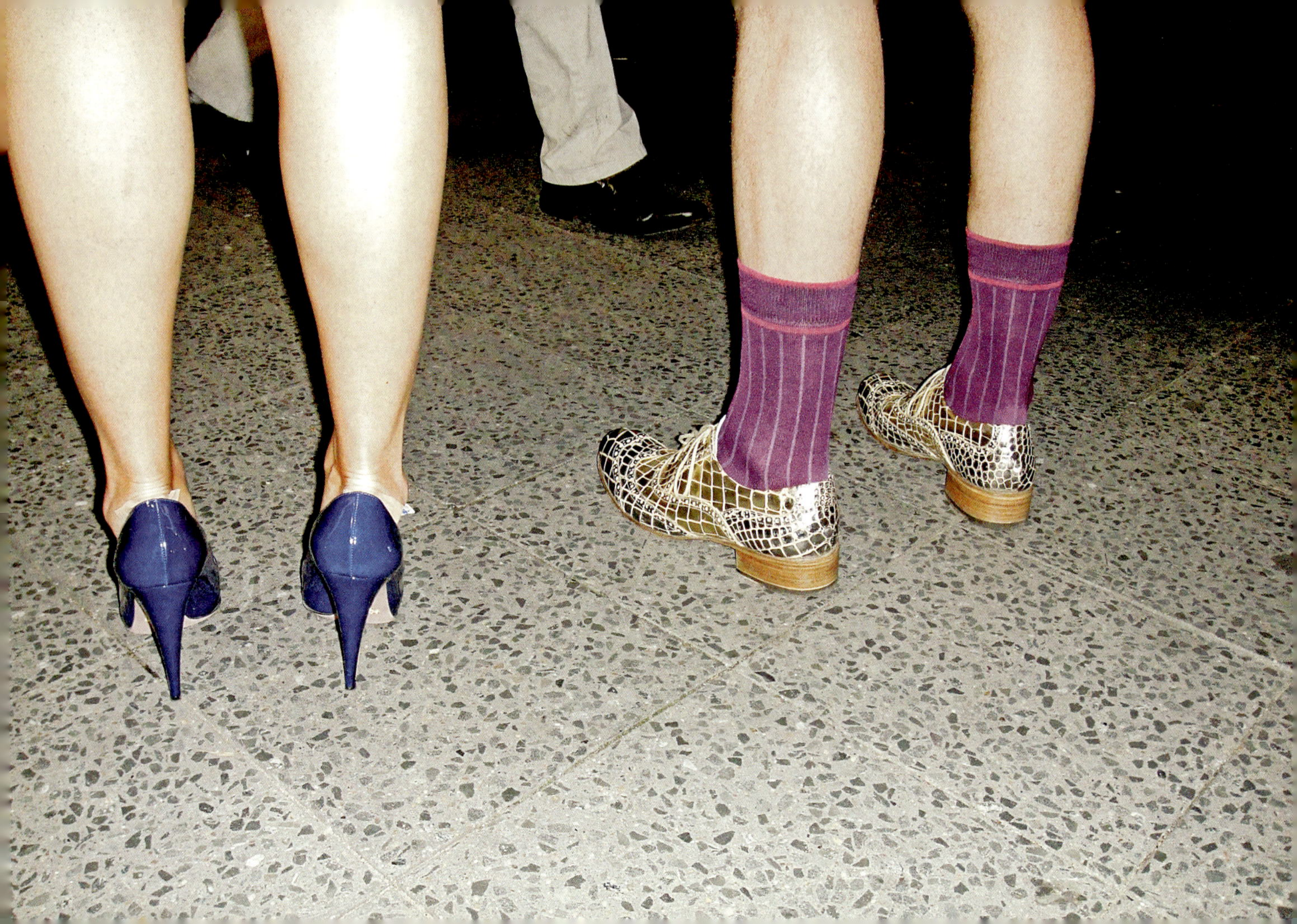

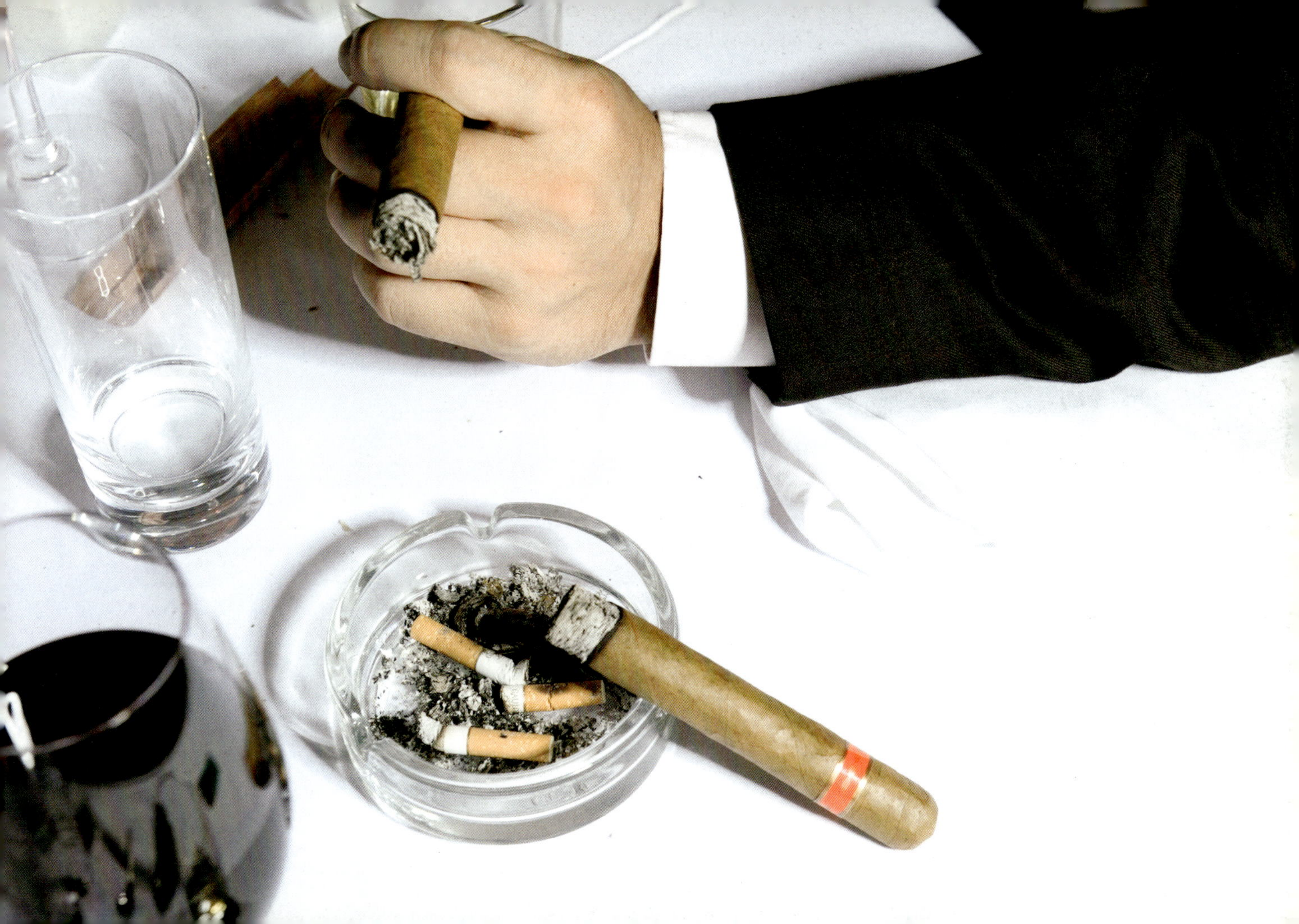

# BUNKERERBSEN ANNO 1978

## Bunker beans anno 1978

**48** **Fichtebunker**
*Fichtestraße 6 . Berlin-Kreuzberg*

Vom Dach eines Hochbunkers und ehemaligen Gasometers blickt ein Junge aus einem der dort erbauten Lofts in die Ferne. Unten öffnet jemand die Zugangstür zum Bauwerk mit den meterdicken Wänden aus dem Jahr 1941. An 240 Räumen – Krankenzimmern, einem intakten U-Boot-Dieselmotor, einem Gefängniszellentrakt und Filteranlagen – führt der Weg vorbei immer weiter hinein. Wandbeschriftungen weisen die Richtung. In einer der Kammern hängen ausgeschnittene Pin-up-Girls aus den 1950er-Jahren, als der Bunker als Obdachlosenasyl diente, an der Wand. Konserven mit Ölsardinen und Brechbohnen erinnern daran, dass das Gemäuer bis 1990 zur Einlagerung von »Senatsreserven« diente.

*A young boy glances out over the horizon from one of the lofts built on the roof of a bunker and a former gasometer. Down below, someone is opening the access door to the structure built in 1941 with meter-thick walls. The path leads past 240 rooms – sick bays, an intact submarine diesel motor, a prison tract, and filtration plants. Lettering on the walls indicates the direction. Cut-out pinups from the nineteen-fifties hang on the walls of one of the cells; they come from the time when the bunker was used as a shelter for homeless people. The cans of sardines in oil and snap beans are reminiscent of the fact that the space was used until 1990 to store the goods stockpiled by the Berlin Senate in case of a second blockade.*

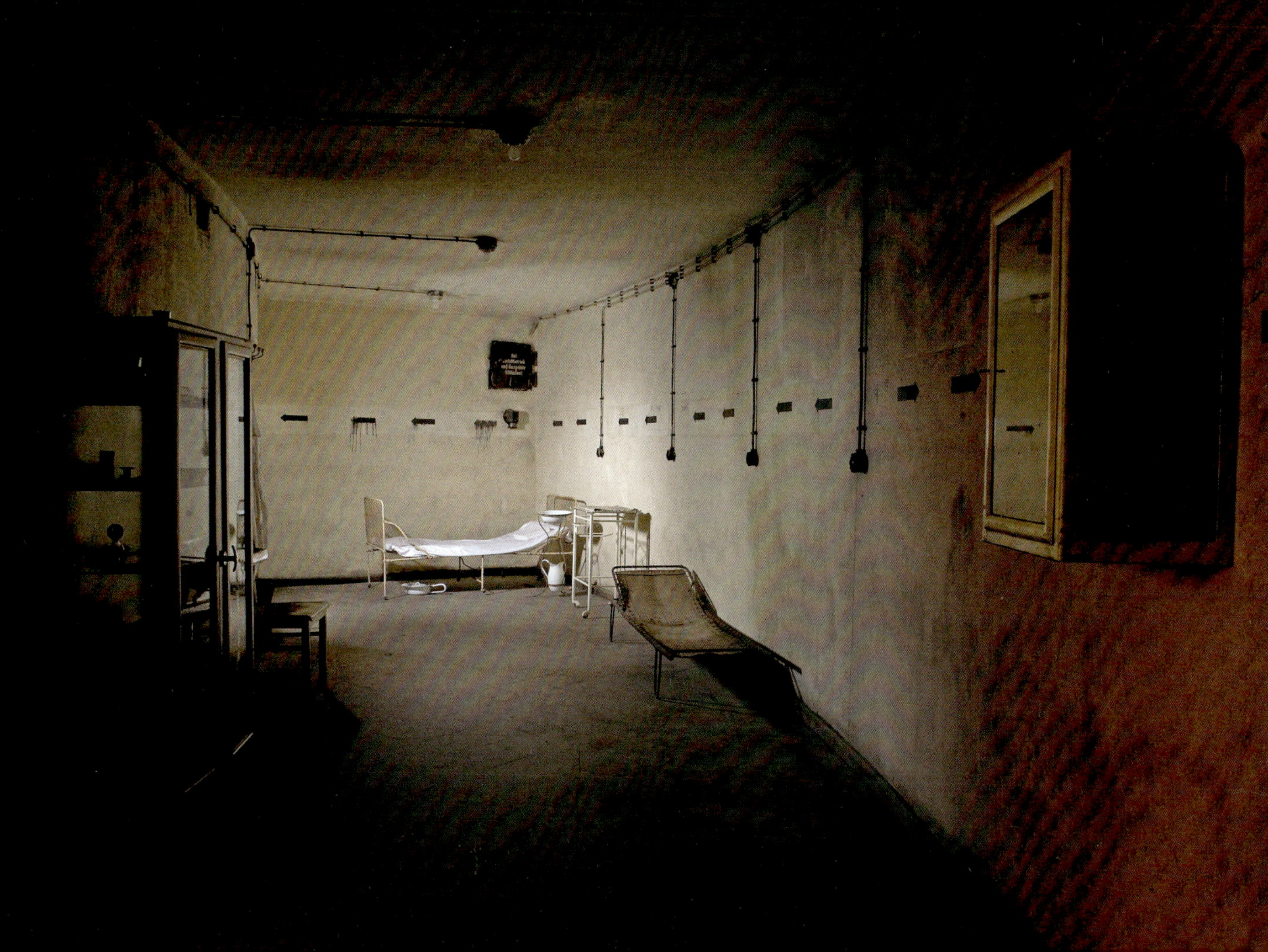

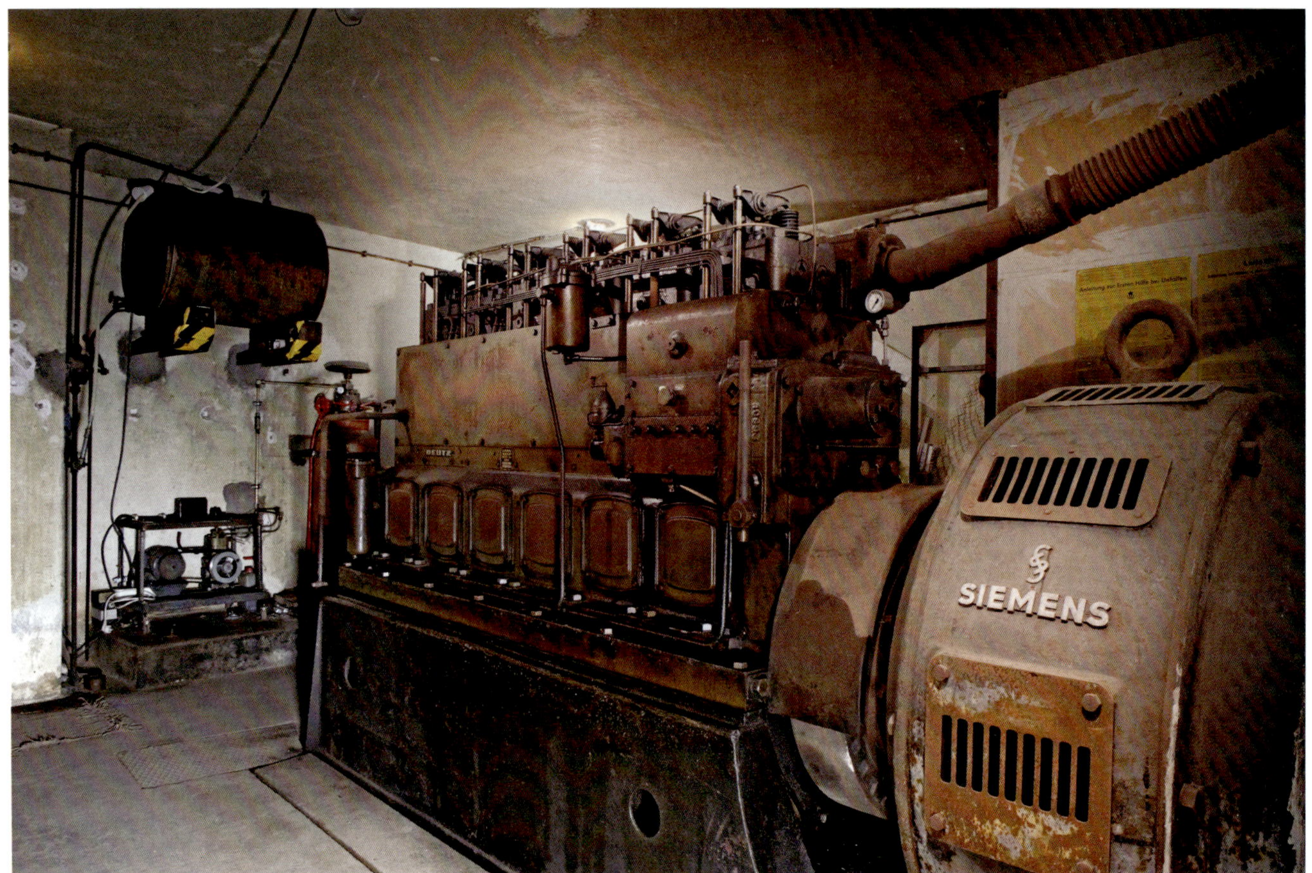

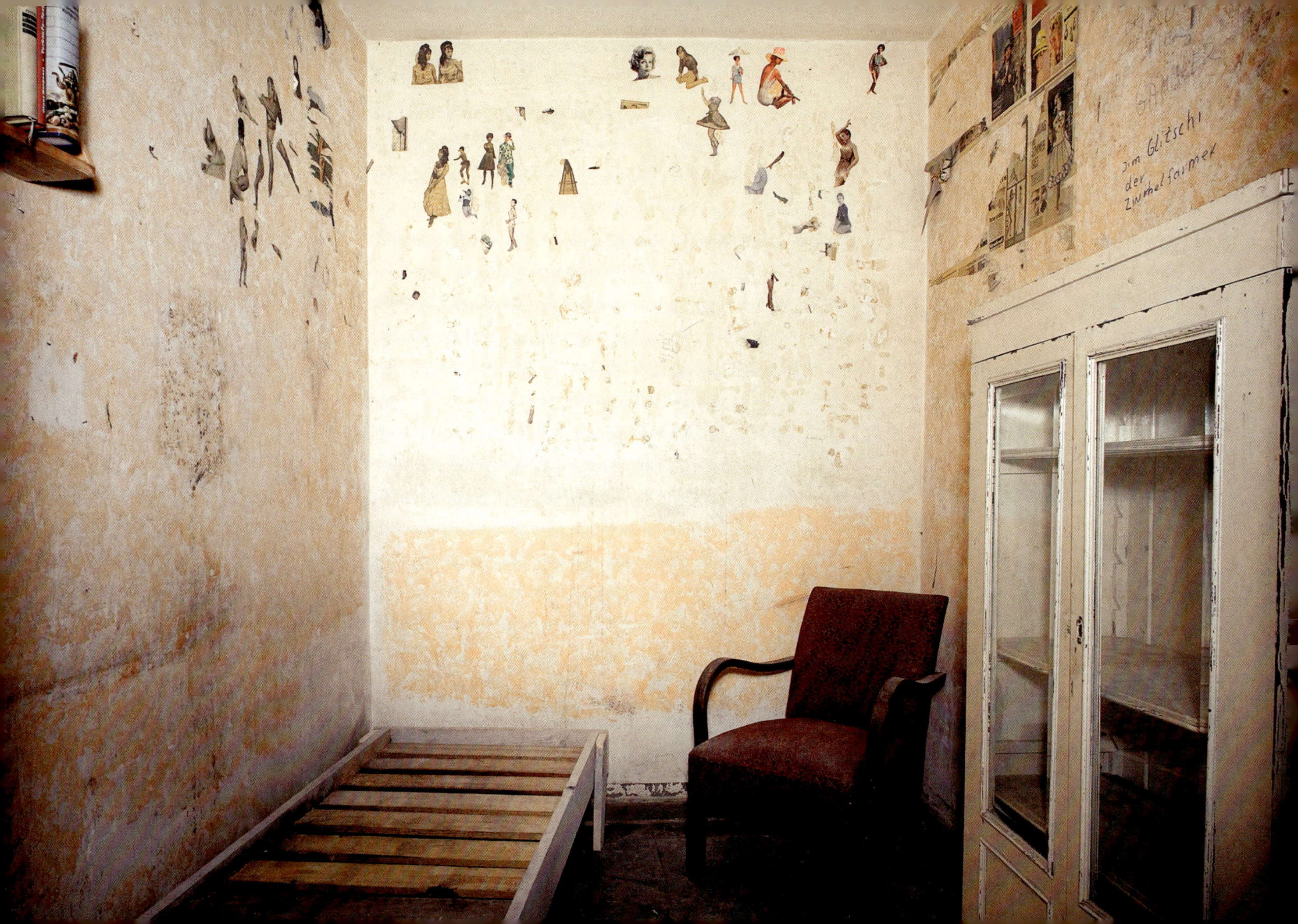
Jim Glitschi
der
Zwiebelfaumer

# NICHT EINE, DIE BERLINER KNEIPE!

## *Not one of, but the Berlin tavern!*

**49 Liesert's Falckensteiner**
*Falckensteinstraße 26 . Berlin-Kreuzberg*

Die liebevoll drapierte Schaufensterdekoration der Lokalität leuchtet in der Nacht. Einer, der im Kiez wohnt, betritt mit seinem Rauhaardackel den von Rauch geschwängerten Tresenraum. An den Wänden stehen stolz aufgereiht Pokale und Urkunden – sie haben ihren Weg selbst bis in die Toiletten gefunden. Die Barrunde blickt sich kurz um und erheitert sich von Neuem an den Kiezneuigkeiten der Wirtin. Liese, die den Laden seit vierzig Jahren betreibt, ruft: »Ich halte die Runde hier bei Laune. Das soll mal einer nachmachen.« Im Raum nebenan geht es gelassener zu. Das wöchentliche Skatspiel neigt sich dem Ende entgegen, als einer sagt: »Charly, weeste wat, ick zieh nochmal om die Häuser.«

*The location's lovingly decorated shop windows are illuminated at night. A local customer enters the smoke-filled bar with his wire-haired dachshund. Rows of trophies and certificates are proudly displayed on the walls, and they have even found their way into the toilets. The drinkers at the bar glance around briefly and then turn their attention back to the barmaid who keeps everyone amused with news from the neighborhood. Liese, who has been running the place for forty years, calls out: "I keep the gang happy here. Let's see someone else do that." Things are a bit calmer in the adjacent room. The weekly game of skat is drawing to a close when one of the players says, "Know what Charlie, I'm gonna hit the streets again."*

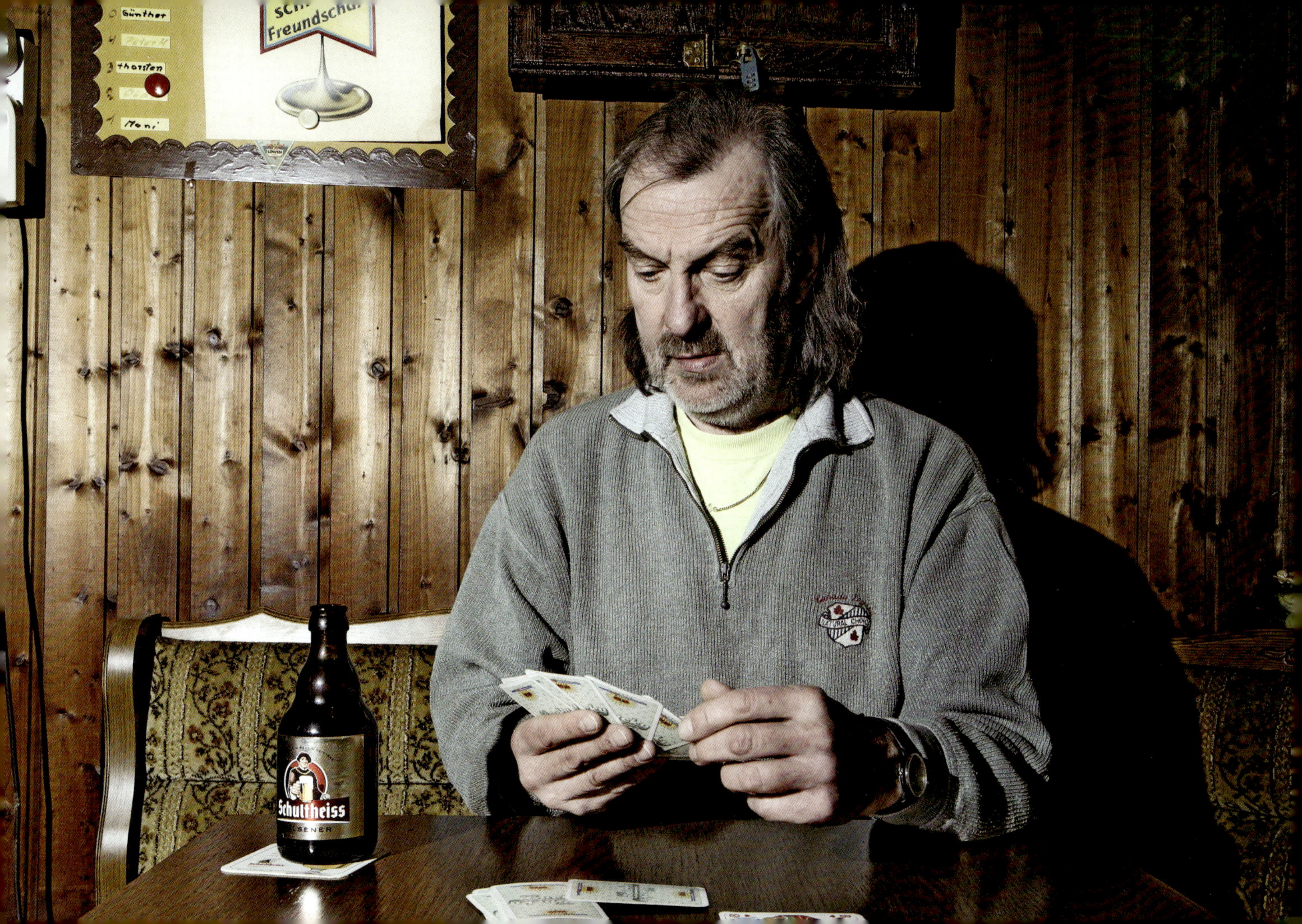

Günther
Moni
Freundscha
Schultheiss
PILSENER

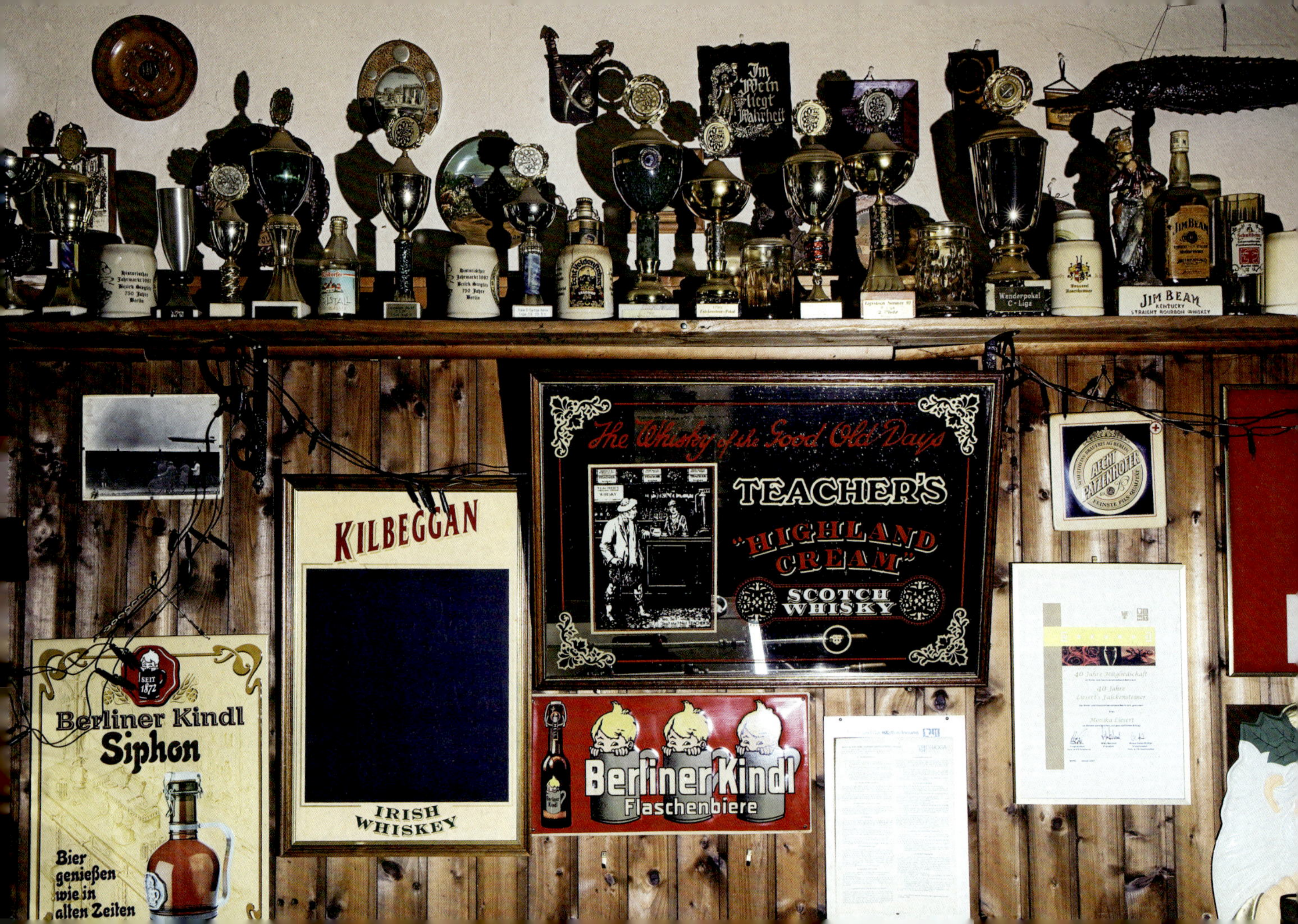
KILBEGGAN
IRISH WHISKEY
The Whisky of the Good Old Days
TEACHER'S
"HIGHLAND CREAM"
SCOTCH WHISKY
Berliner Kindl
Siphon
SEIT 1872
Bier genießen wie in alten Zeiten
Berliner Kindl
Flaschenbiere
JIM BEAM
KENTUCKY
STRAIGHT BOURBON WHISKEY
AECHT PATTENHOFER
Im Wein liegt Wahrheit

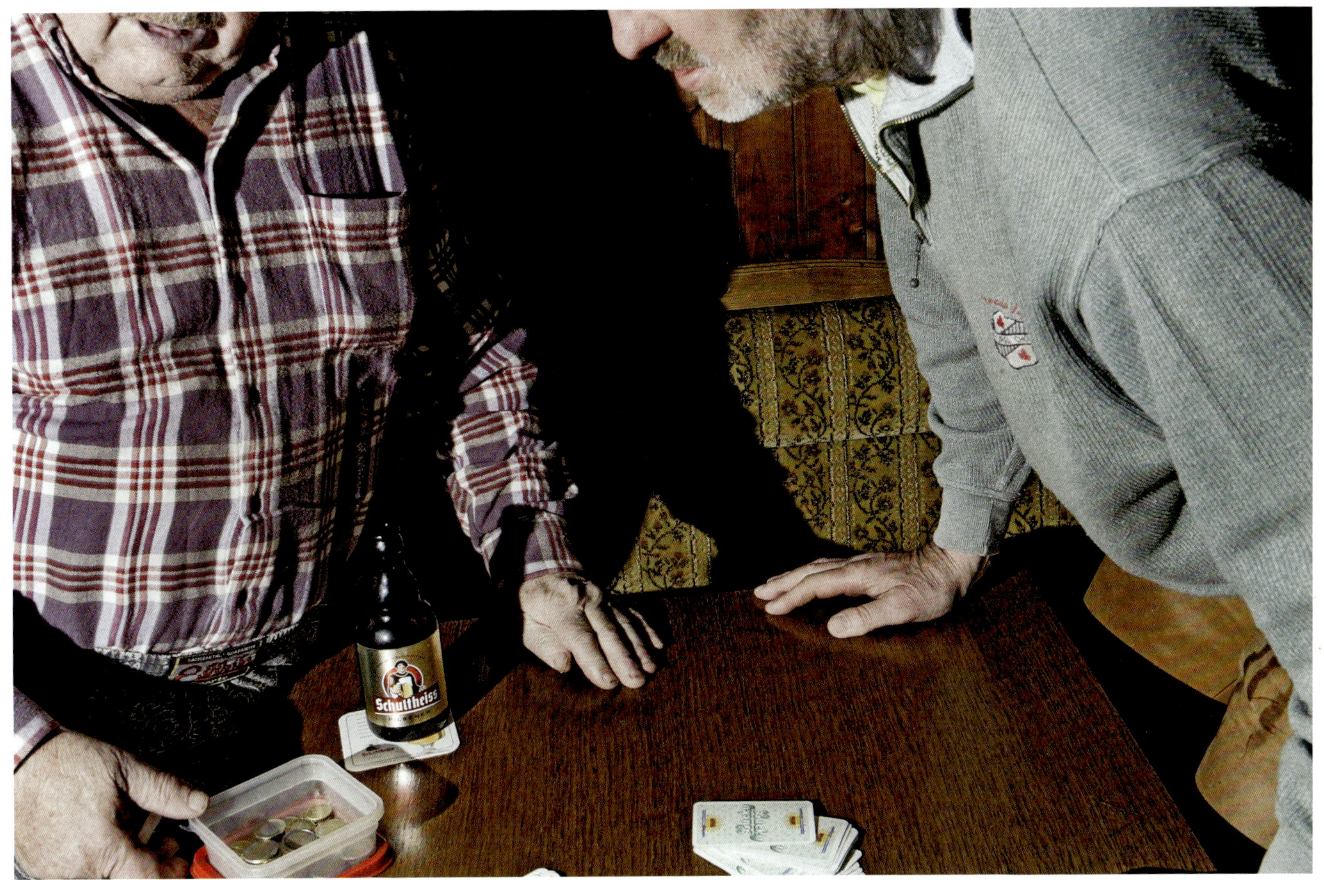

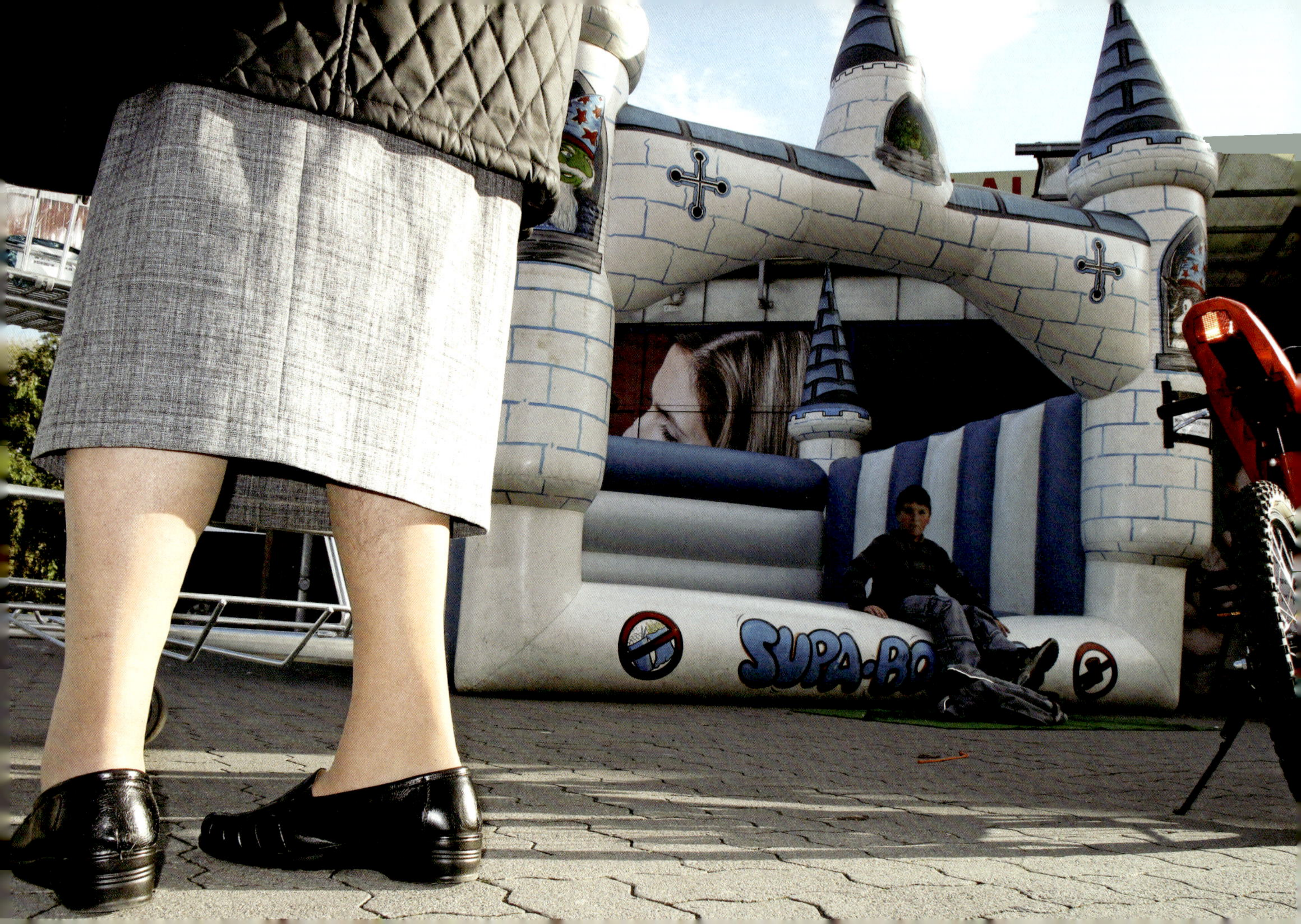

SUPA-BO

# CHARLOTTENBURG: BÜRGERLICH UND HERRLICH MONDÄN

## Charlottenburg:

## bourgeois and wonderfully glamorous

Charlottenburger Bürgertum, Rippchen im Eisbein-Eck, Büroetagen provisionsfrei zu vermieten, weiße Pudel in klassischer Modeschur, Tanztee im Café Keese, ein Schultheiss-Bier am Eichentresen, Businessmeeting in der Paris Bar, Rolf Eden, Hertha-Fans im Freudenrausch, Milljöh in der City-West.

*Charlottenburg bourgeoisie, spareribs in the Eisbein-Eck, commission-free office space for rent, classically styled white poodles, thé dansant in Café Keese, a glass of Schultheiss beer at the oak counter, business meeting in the Paris Bar, Rolf Eden, fans of the Hertha soccer club crowing in delight, old Berlin ambience in the Western half of the city.*

# »KREUZBERGER NÄCHTE SIND LANG.«

*"Kreuzberg nights are long."*

**50** U-Bahnhof Heinrich-Heine-Straße
*Köpenicker Straße 76 . Berlin-Mitte*

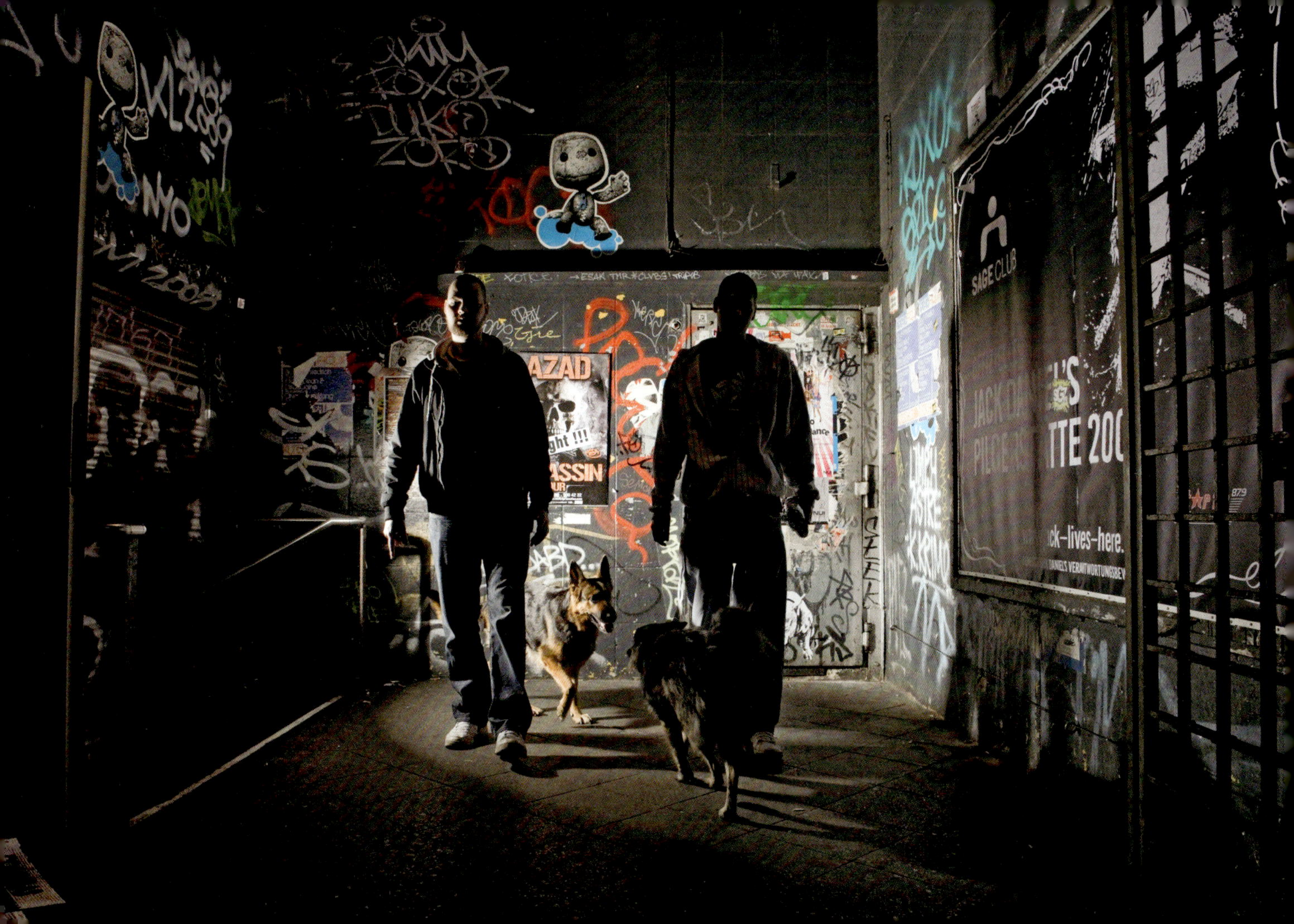

**ZWEI MÄDCHEN SITZEN NACHTS VOR EINER HÜTTE AM EHEMALIGEN MAUERSTREIFEN. SAGT DIE EINE ZUR ANDEREN: »DU, ES GIBT PLÄTZE, DIE ÄNDERN SICH NIE.«**

*Two girls sitting in front of a hovel at the former border strip.*
*One says to the other: "Listen, there are spots that never change."*

**51** **Alternatives Wohnen**
*Bethaniendamm 25 . Berlin-Kreuzberg*

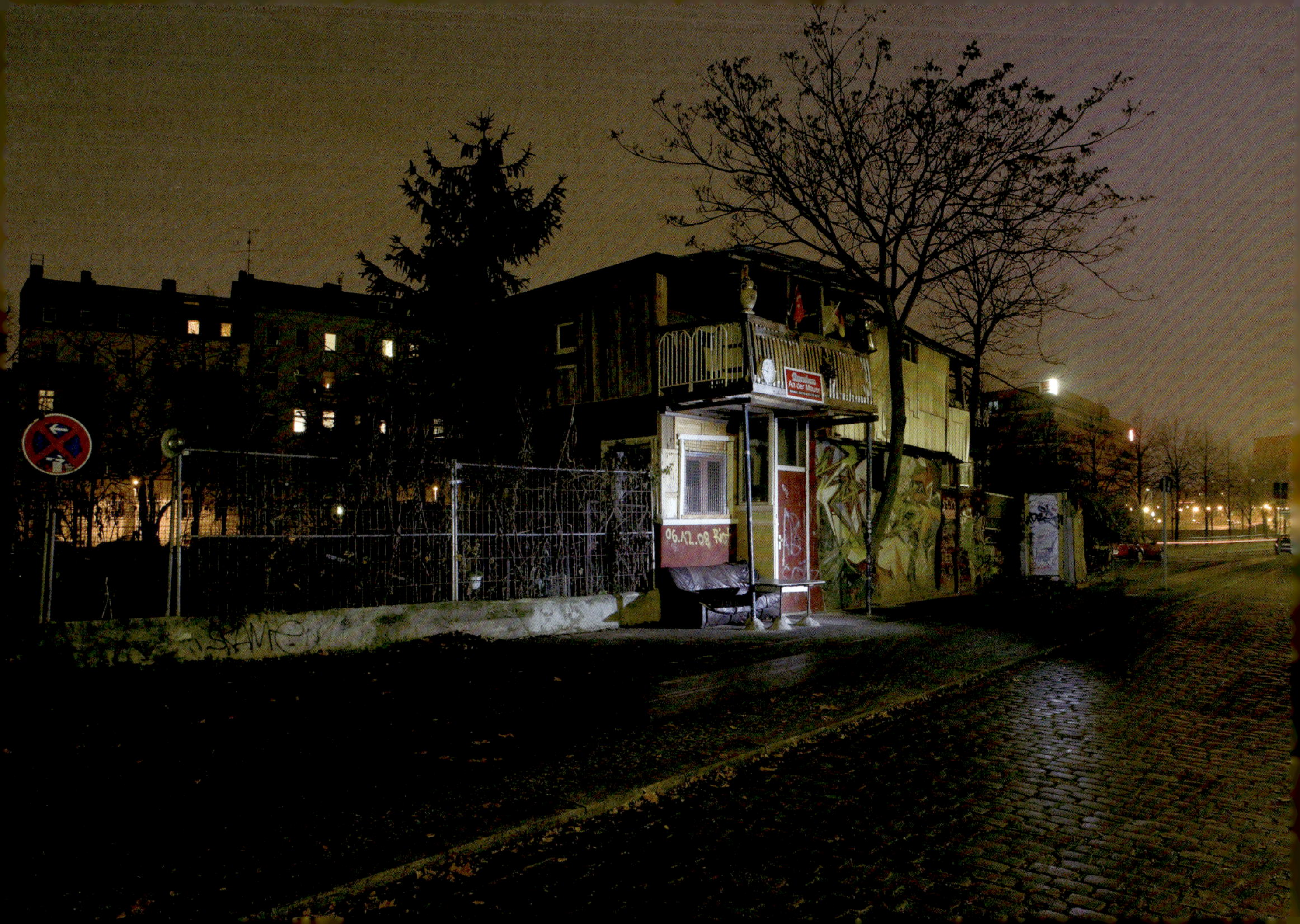
An der Mauer

# HARTE DROGEN, DER DUFT VON DÜRÜM DÖNER, TÜRKISCHE SÜSSWAREN UND LIEBE IM SCHATTEN VON HÄUSERFLUCHTEN.

*Hard drugs, the smell of Dürüm Döner, Turkish sweets, and love in the shadow of the house façades.*

**52** **Kottbusser Tor**
*Adalbertstraße 1 . Berlin-Kreuzberg*

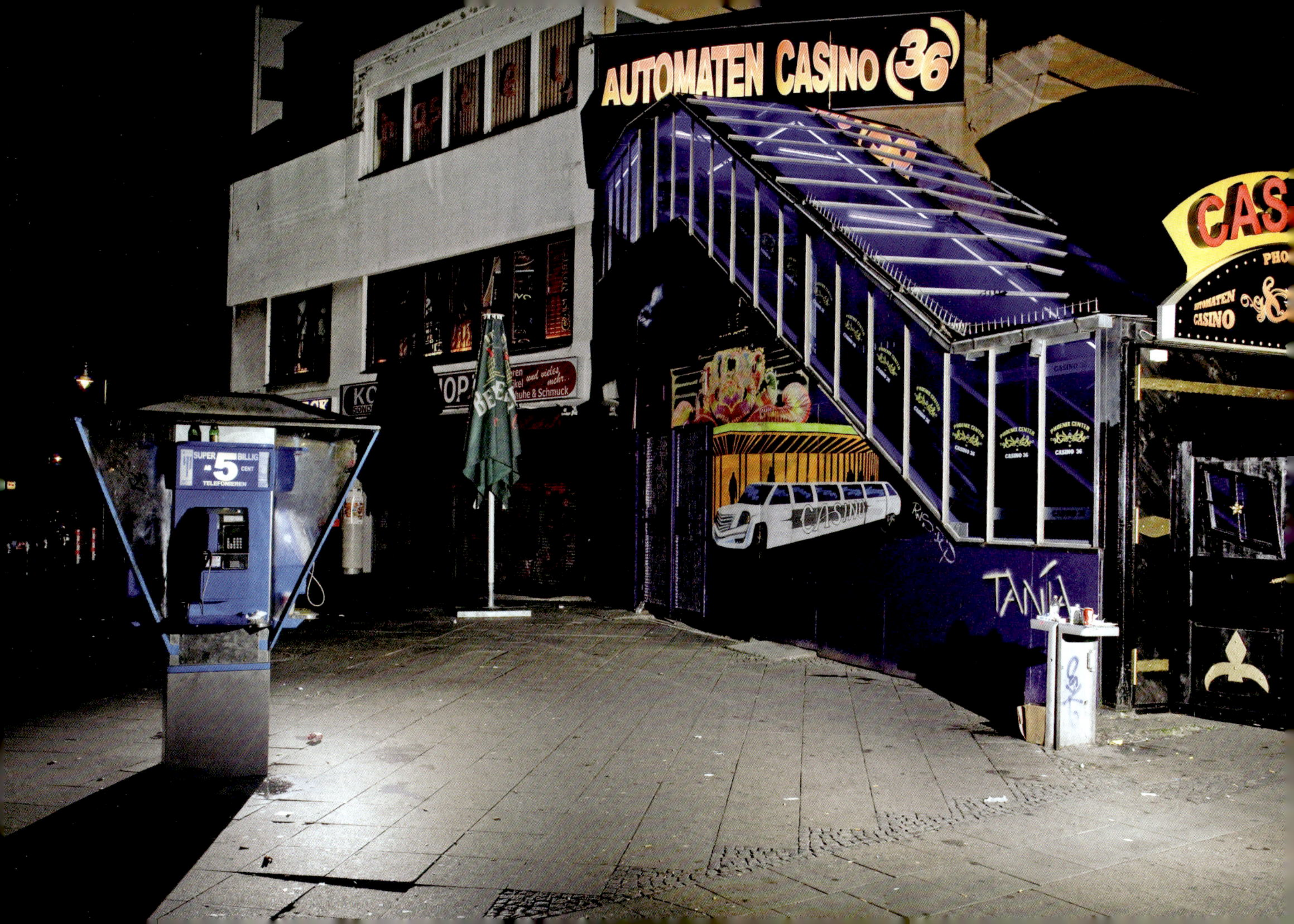

AUTOMATEN CASINO 36
CASINO
AUTOMATEN CASINO
SUPER BILLIG
5 CENT
TELEFONIEREN
BEES
und vieles mehr..
Schuhe & Schmuck
PHOENIX CENTER
CASINO 36
TANIA

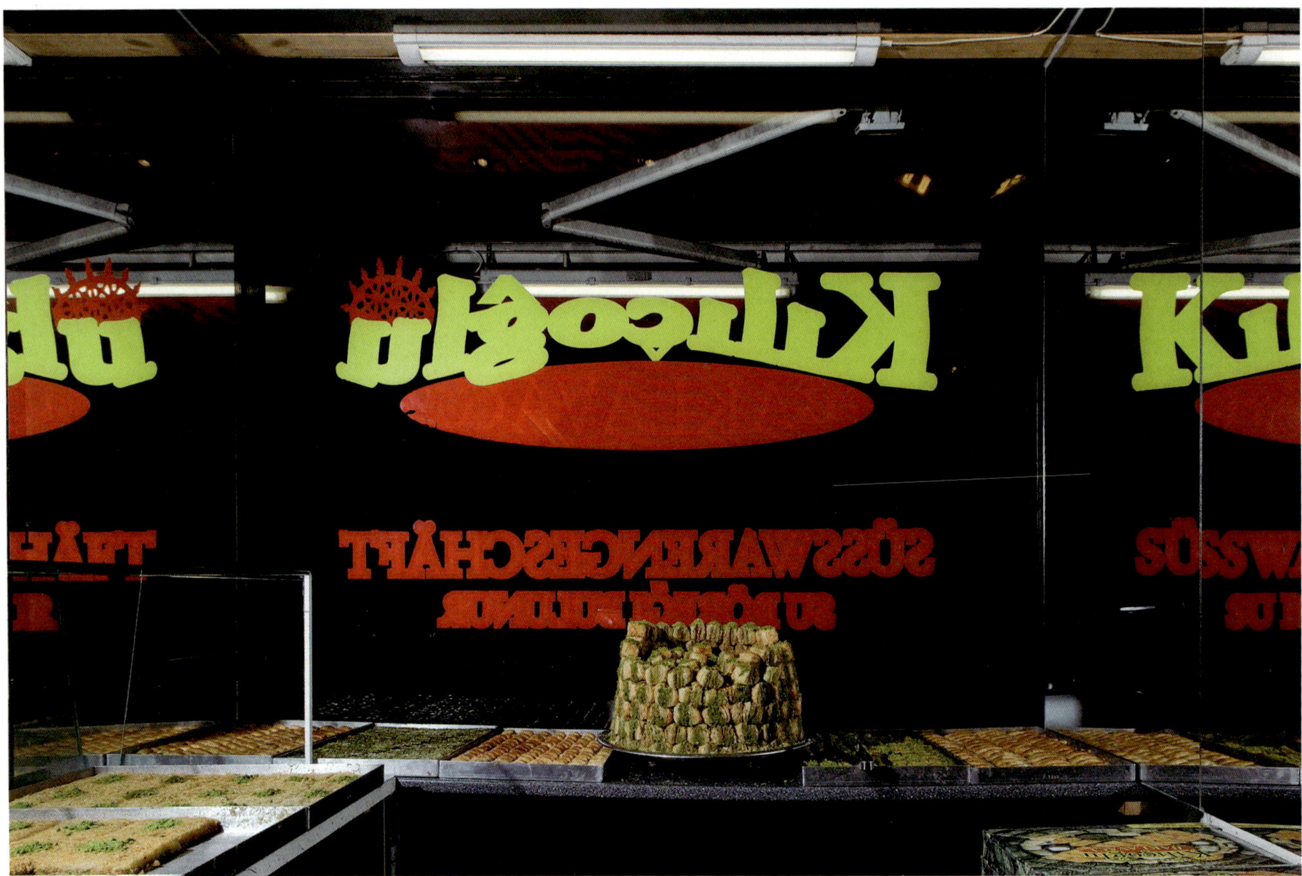
Kilıçoğlu
SÜSSWARENGESCHÄFT

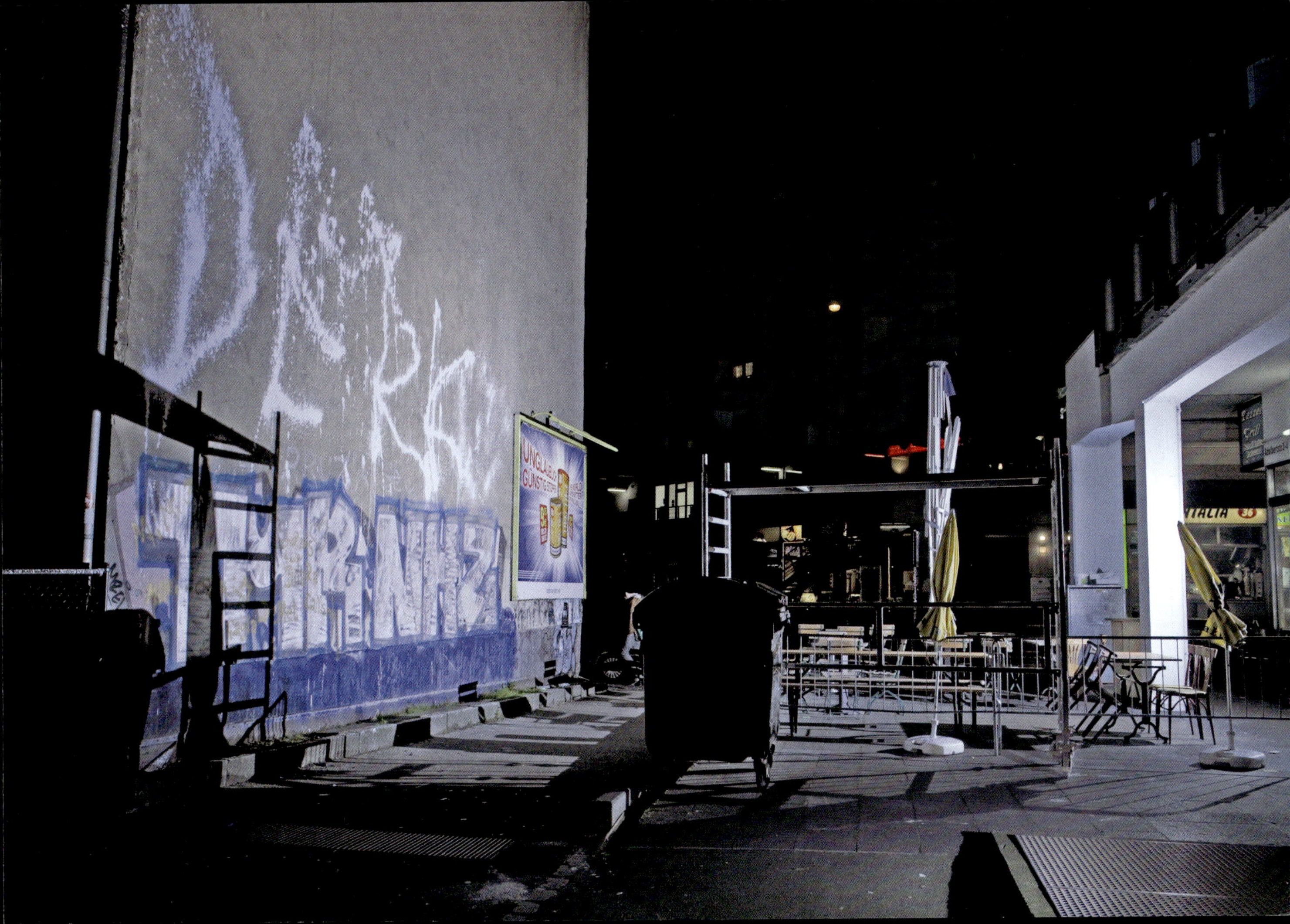

UNGLAUB
GÜNSTIG
ITALIA

# 'NE RUHIGE KUGEL SCHIEBEN
## Taking it the easy way



Freitagabend: In der Wiener Straße schieben sich die letzten Besucher aus dem Kino. Ein Mann in kariertem Holzfällerhemd sammelt Pfandflaschen aus Mülleimern und steckt sie in seinen blauen Sack. Im Firat, einem Café mit Tradition, erhellen Neonröhren den ruhigen Saal. Nur der Sound eines Spielautomaten dringt durch den Raum. Stammgäste und Betreiber sitzen an den runden Tischen beim Schachspiel, trinken Tee oder spielen Billard. Türkische Landschaftsbilder und ein Poster der Nationalmannschaft an der blassblauen Wand umgeben die Männergesellschaft. Im Fernsehen läuft eine türkische Nachrichtensendung. Am Billardtisch endet das Spiel frühzeitig durch einen gekonnten Stoß des Lokalmatadors.

*Friday night: The last moviegoers shuffle out of the cinema on Wiener Strasse. A man dressed in a checkered logger's shirt collects deposit bottles from garbage cans and puts them in a large blue plastic bag. In Firat, a café with tradition, neon lights illuminate the tranquil hall. Only the sound of a slot machine pervades the room. Regulars and owners play chess at the round tables, drink tea, or play billiards. Pictures of Turkish landscapes and a poster of the national soccer team hang on the pale blue walls. The television set is tuned in to a Turkish station. A game of billiards comes to a premature conclusion thanks to a skillful shot of a local hero.*

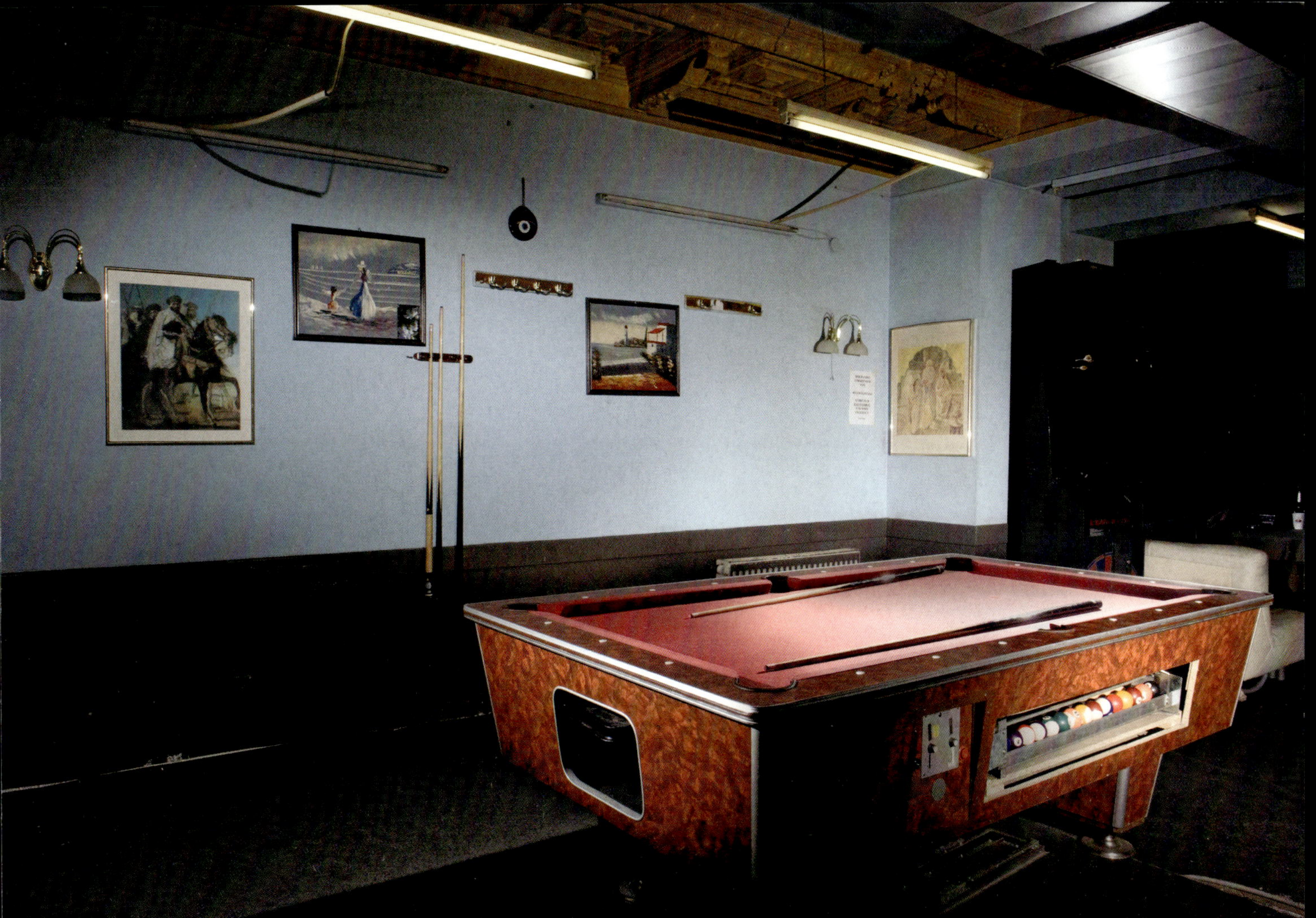

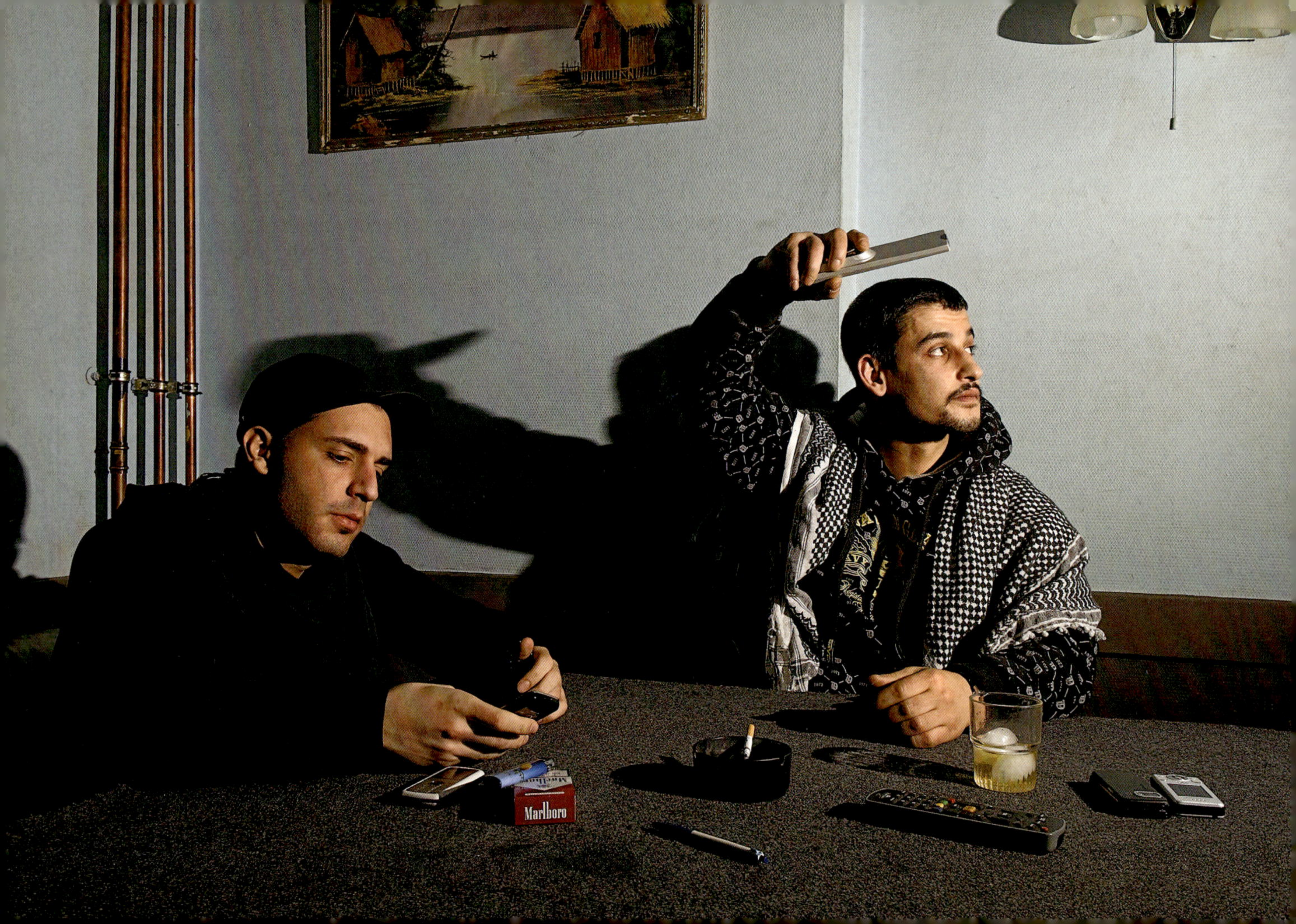

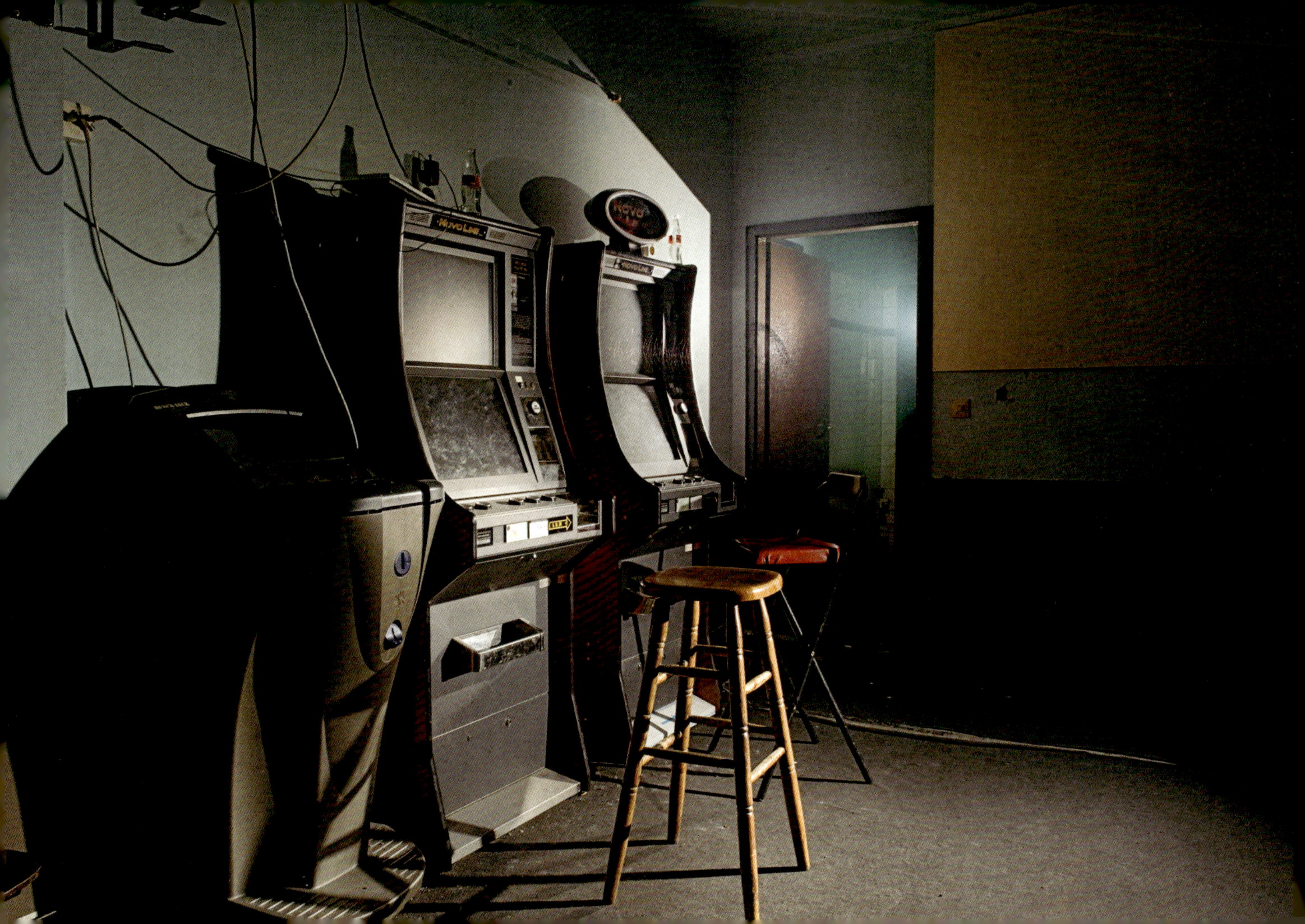

# VOR SEINER LAUBE SITZEND, BLICKT EIN KLEINGÄRTNER AUF EIN EHEMALIGES SOWJETISCHES MILITÄRAREAL. AGENTENTHRILLER GUCKTE ER HIER VOR 25 JAHREN.

*Sitting in front of his summerhouse, an allotment holder looks at a former Soviet military area. Twenty-five years ago he watched spy thrillers here.*

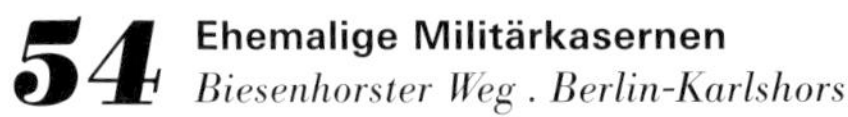

**54** **Ehemalige Militärkasernen**
*Biesenhorster Weg . Berlin-Karlshorst*

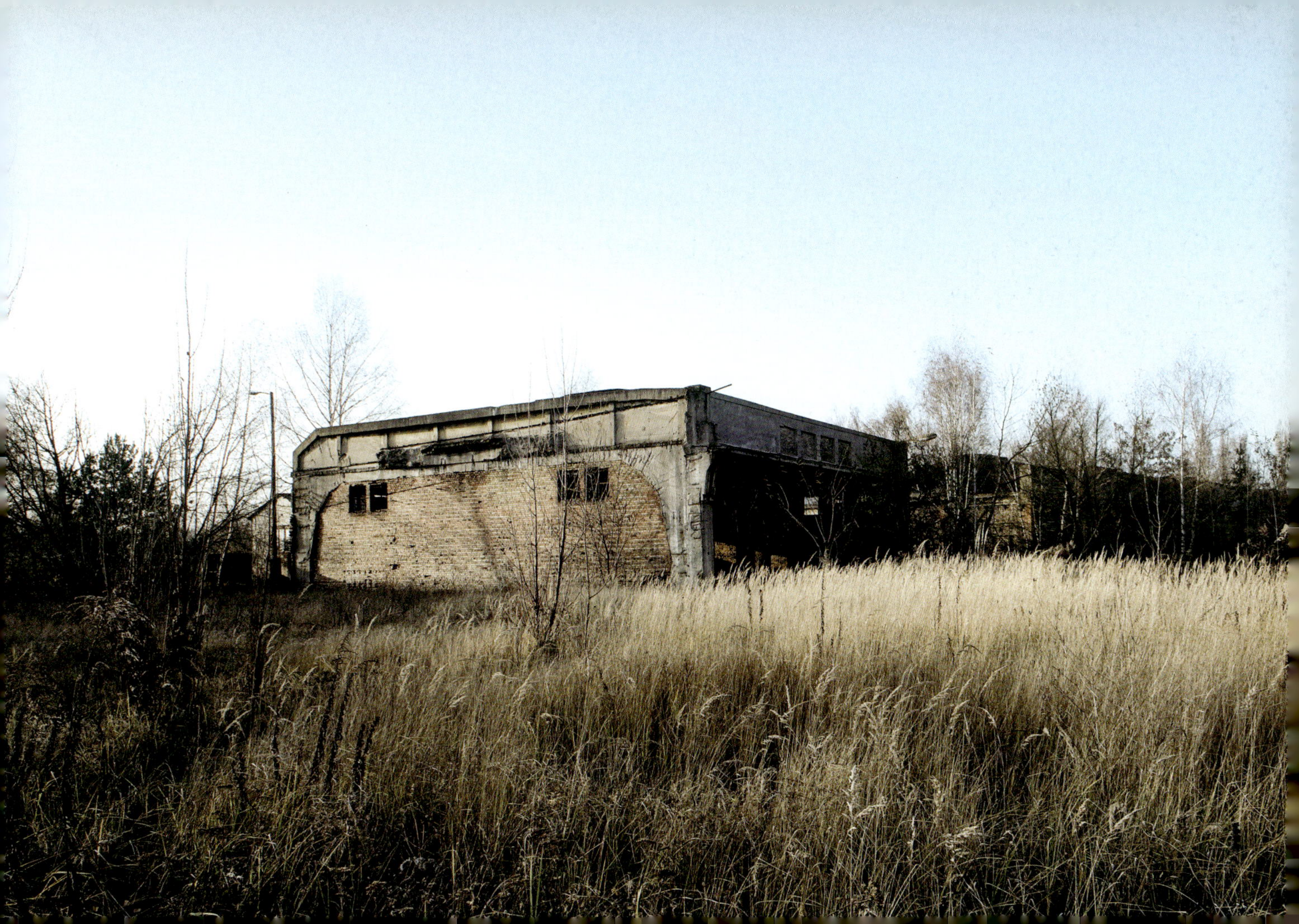

# KU'DAMM, KRANZLER, KADEWE

## Ku'damm, Kranzler, KaDeWe



Die Rolex für 17 000 Euro verschwindet aus der Auslage eines Schaufensters. Die stolzen Besitzer, Touristen aus dem Nahen Osten, verlassen den Laden und ziehen an den zahlreichen Boutiquen vorbei in Richtung Gedächtniskirche. Es beginnt zu regnen, hastig huschen Passanten unter die Vordächer der Geschäfte. Am Gehwegrand steht eine junge blonde Russin gequält vor einer Limousine, ihren Autoschlüssel suchend. Ihre Beute, Einkaufstüten von Luxusmarkenartikelherstellern, hat sie neben sich abgestellt. Einige hundert Meter weiter gegenüber dem Kaufhaus KaDeWe versucht sich eine Gruppe Rucksacktouristen an einer Biocurrywurst. Man blickt sich an und setzt nickend ein zufriedenes Lächeln auf.

*The Rolex at 17,000 euros a shot is taken out of the display case in the shop window. The proud new owners, tourists from the Near East, leave the store and walk past the numerous boutiques towards the Kaiser Wilhelm Memorial Church. It starts to rain; passers-by scurry ahead under the shop marquees. A young blond Russian woman with a distressed look about her stands on the sidewalk in front of a limousine, searching for her car keys. She has placed her spoils, shopping bags from luxury brand manufacturers, next to her. Several hundred meters down the street, across from the KaDeWe department store, a group of backpackers is trying out organic curry sausages. They look at each other and nod with a smile of approval.*

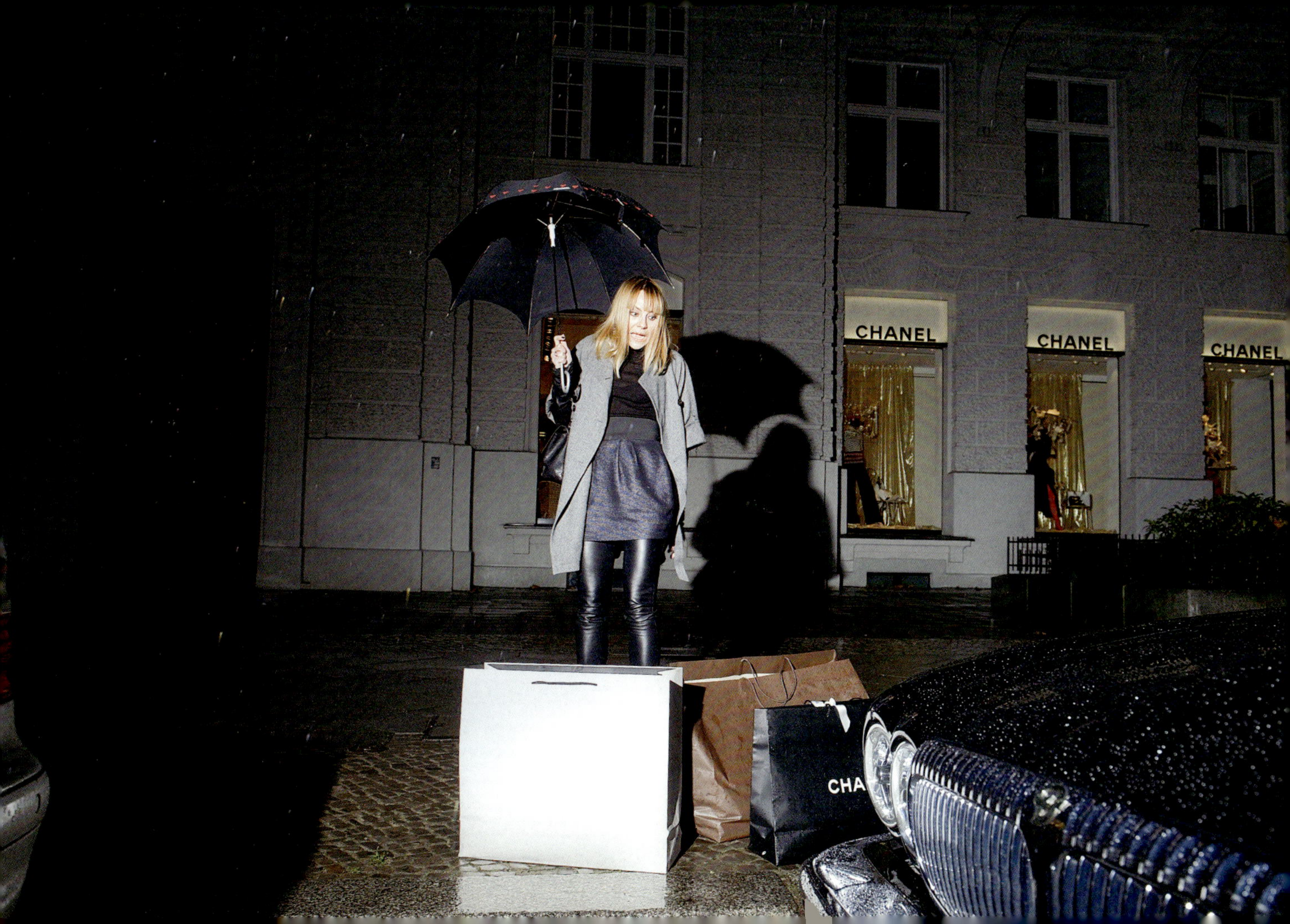

CHANEL
CHANEL
CHANEL
CHA

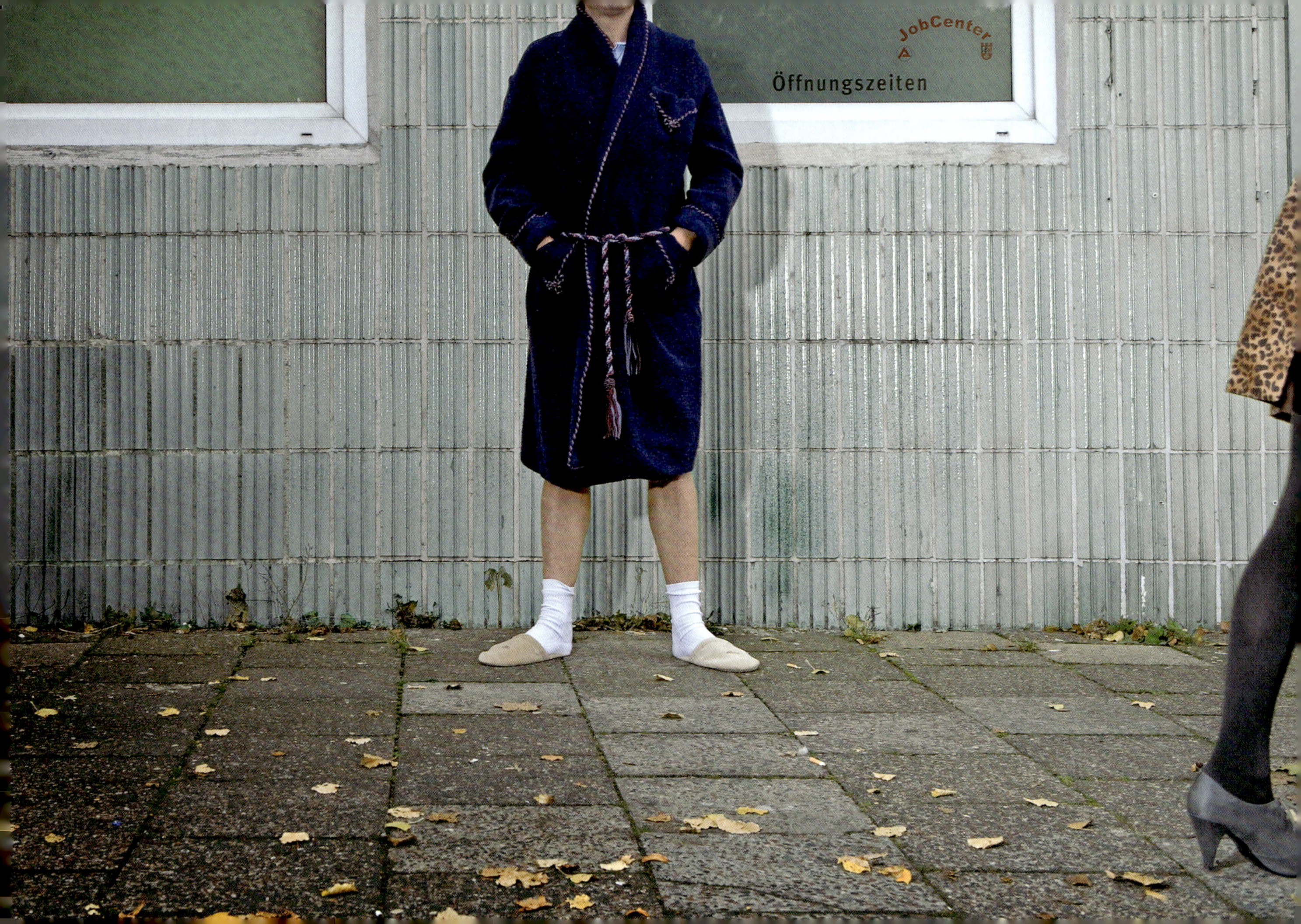
JobCenter
Öffnungszeiten

# NEUKÖLLN: PAMELA-ANDERSON-OUTFITS, AVANTGARDE UND PRÜGELKNABEN

## Neukölln: Pamela Anderson outfits, avant garde, and whipping boys

Weiße Siedlung und Körnerpark, Konsumwahn in den Arcaden, Wutzky-Center und Hermannquartier, Kiffen im Britzer Garten, kulturelles Getümmel und multikulturelle Nachbarschaftsgärten, Jobcenter und Breakdance-Crews, Haarverlängerung und Freitagsgebet, laute Musik und eine leere Kiste Bier.

*Weisse Siedlung and Körnerpark, consumption craze at the Arcaden, Wutzky Center and Hermannquartier, toking in Britzer Garden, cultural tumult and multi-cultural neighborhood garden, Job Center and break-dance crews, hair extension and Friday prayers, loud music and an empty beer crate.*

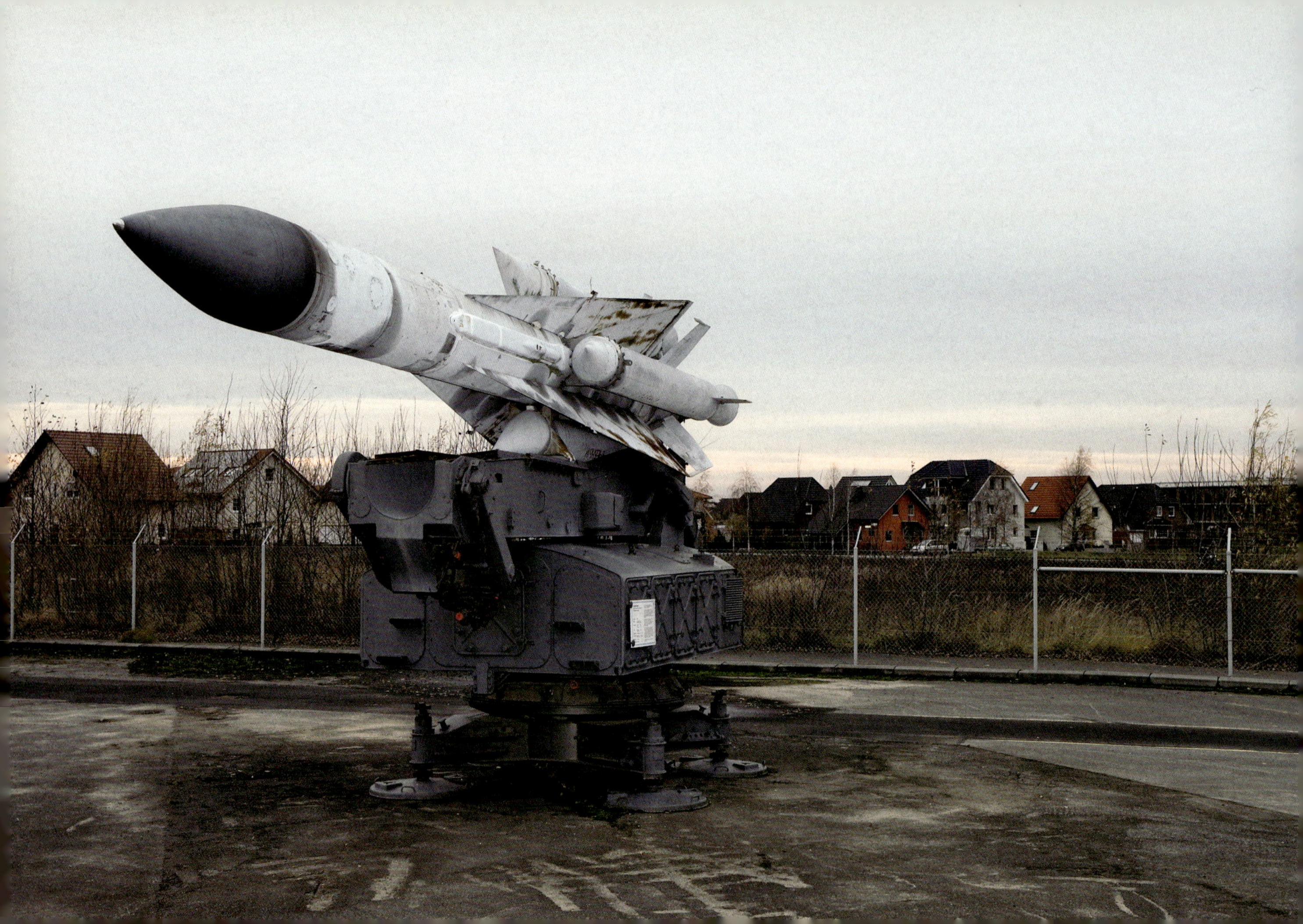

## IM ANGRENZENDEN WOHNVIERTEL ZIEHT JEMAND DIE GARDINEN AUF UND BLICKT AUF RAKETENWERFER UND HANGARS DES EINSTIGEN BRITISCHEN MILITÄRFLUGHAFENS UND JETZIGEN LUFTWAFFENMUSEUMS. EIN HAUCH VON KALTEM KRIEG IM EIGENEN WOHNZIMMER.

*In the adjacent residential quarter, someone is opening the curtains and looks out over the rocket launchers of the former British military airfield and present-day Air Force Museum. A smack of the Cold War in your very own living room.*

**56** **Luftwaffenmuseum der Bundeswehr**
*Kladower Damm 182–188 . Berlin-Gatow*

# OLYMPIA ANNO 1936

## Olympia anno 1936

**57** Olympisches Dorf
*Rosa-Luxemburg-Allee 69 . Wustermark*

Beinahe verwunschen wirkt das Areal des ehemaligen Olympiadorfs. Eine Besuchergruppe nimmt an einer Führung teil. Man wandert vorbei an leergeräumten Plattenbauten, errichtet für die sowjetische Armee. Im Hindenburghaus wartet ein Theatersaal mit einem Lenin-Wandgemälde auf seine erneute Nutzung, in den Seitentrakten erinnern Propagandamalereien an den Zweiten Weltkrieg. Der Weg führt weiter, vorbei an ehemaligen Sportlerhäusern, darunter dem von Jesse Owens in das ehemalige Speisehaus der Nationen, ein halbkreisförmiges Gebäude. Fetzen sowjetischer Tageszeitungen und Tapeten hängen von den Wänden. Die baufällige Schwimmhalle, die auf dem Rückweg passiert wird, wartet weiter vergeblich darauf, dass sich ihr Becken mit Wasser füllt.

*The area of the former Olympic Village seems somehow enchanted. A group of visitors are taking part in a guided tour. They wander past vacated prefabricated houses built for the Soviet Army. In Hindenburg House, a theater auditorium with a Lenin mural is waiting for its new use; propaganda paintings in a wing of the building bring World War II to mind. The path continues on past the former residences of the athletes, including Jesse Owens's, to the old Dining Hall of the Nations, a semicircular building. Remnants of Soviet daily newspapers and wallpaper hang from the wall. The dilapidated indoor swimming pool you pass by on the way back is still waiting in vain to be filled with water again.*

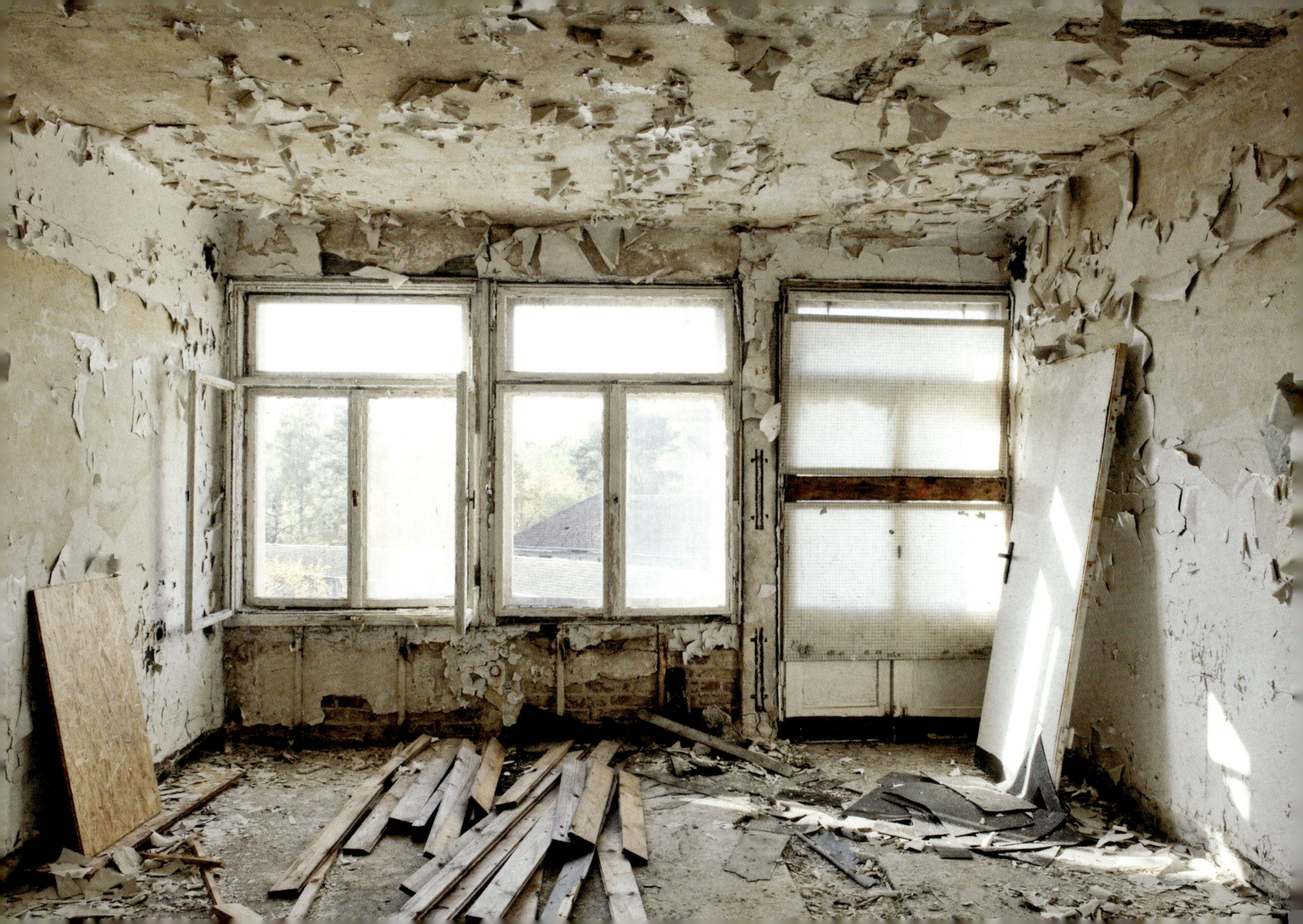

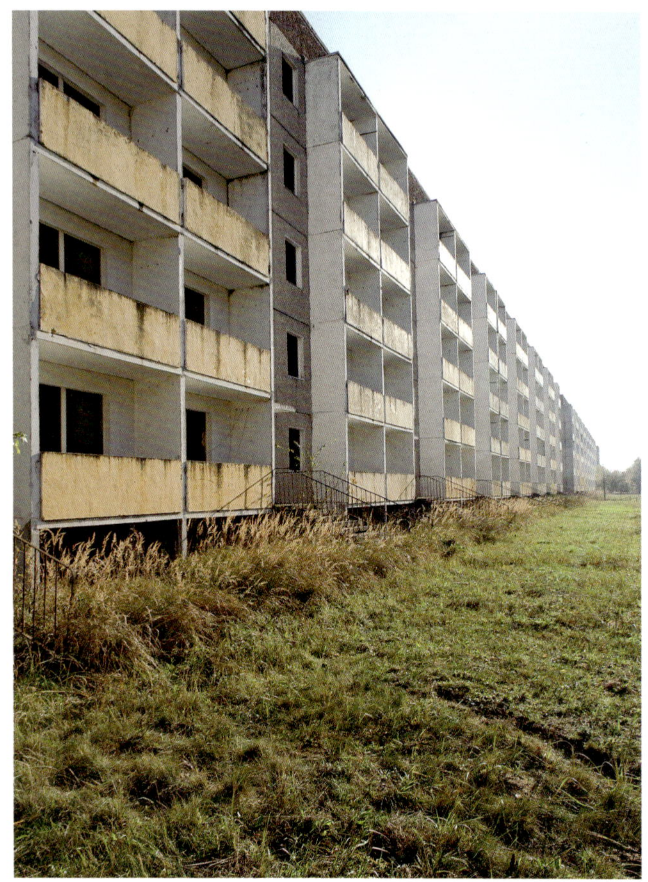

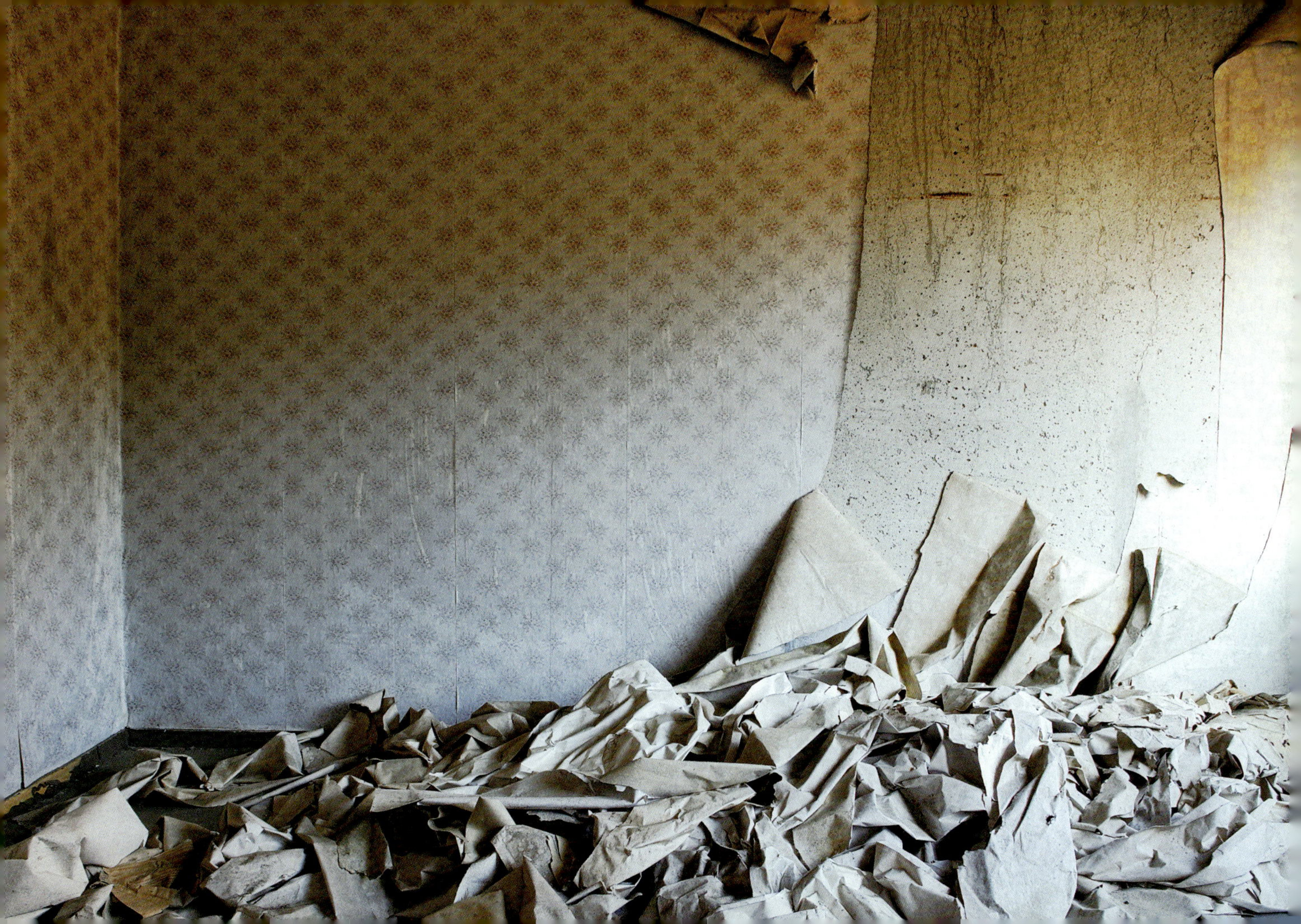

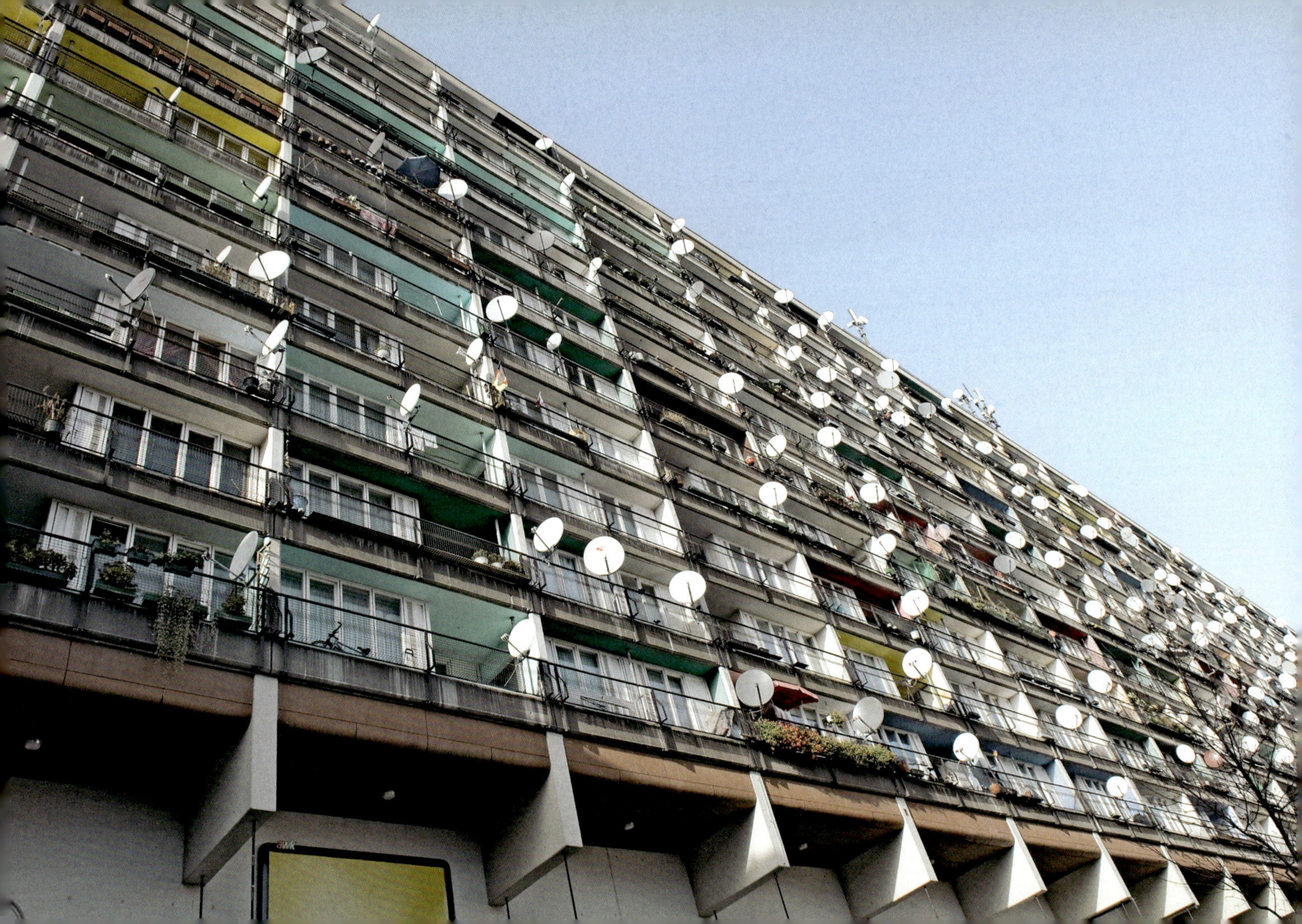

# WELTEMPFÄNGER MIT BLICK ÜBER BERLIN

*World receiver with view over Berlin*

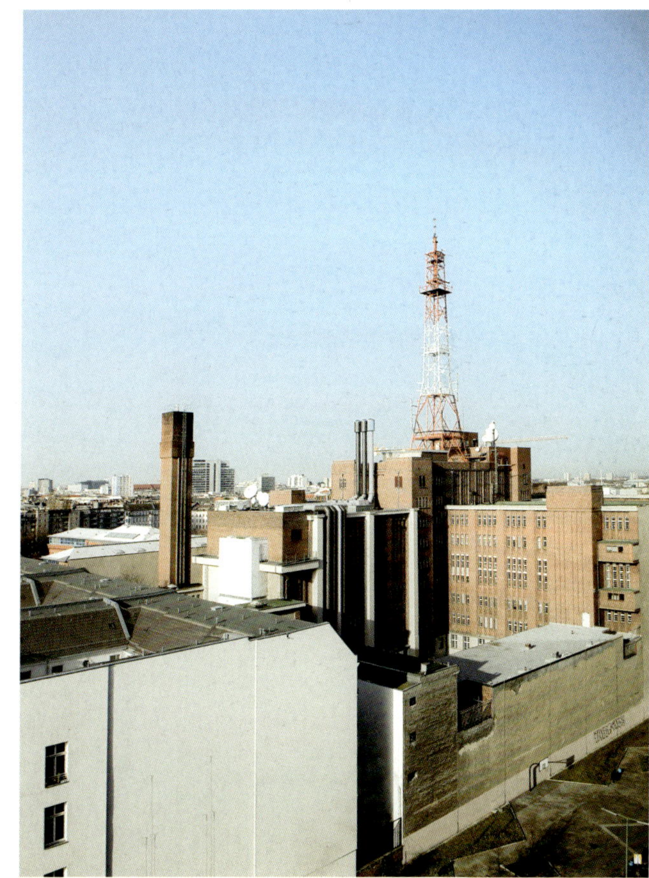

**58** **Sozialpalast Schöneberg**
*Pallasstraße 28 . Berlin-Schöneberg*

# MOSCHUS UND MAIGLÖCKCHEN
## Musk and lilies of the valley

**59** **Harry Lehmann**
*Kantstraße 106 . Berlin-Charlottenburg*

Der Duft betört, der Kunde atmet schwer. Der Mann mit Schnauzer im karierten Anzug genießt den soeben versprühten Moschus- und Maiglöckchenduft. Sein Wunsch: ein persönlich abgestimmter Duft in Erinnerung an eine Liebschaft. Das Parfum Eau de Berlin scheint zu süß. Der Verkäufer lässt ihn an seinen Eigenkreationen riechen, Sandelholz und russisches Eau de Cologne. Im Nebenraum steht eine begeisterte Dame zwischen Kunstblumen und Palmen. Nach kurzer Überlegung fällt ihre Wahl auf einen Strauß gelber Tulpen. Die Suche nach dem Duft nebenan ist erfolgreich verkaufen. Der Kunde entscheidet sich für das Aftershave Titano Man, einen intensiv grünen, holzig-blumigen Duft. Zum Einsatz kommt der gleich an der Kasse.

*The scent is beguiling, the customer breathes laboriously. The mustachioed man wearing a checkered suit is enjoying the just sprayed fragrance of musk and lilies of the valley. His wish: a personally designed scent in memory of a love affair. The perfume Eau de Berlin seems too sweet. The salesman allows him to sniff his own creations, sandalwood and Russian Eau de Cologne. An enthralled woman stands in an adjacent room between artificial flowers and palm trees. After a moment of consideration she chooses a bouquet of yellow tulips. Next door, the search for a fragrance has been successfully completed. The customer has decided on the aftershave named Titano Man, an intense green, flowery-woody scent. It is immediately deployed right at the cash register.*

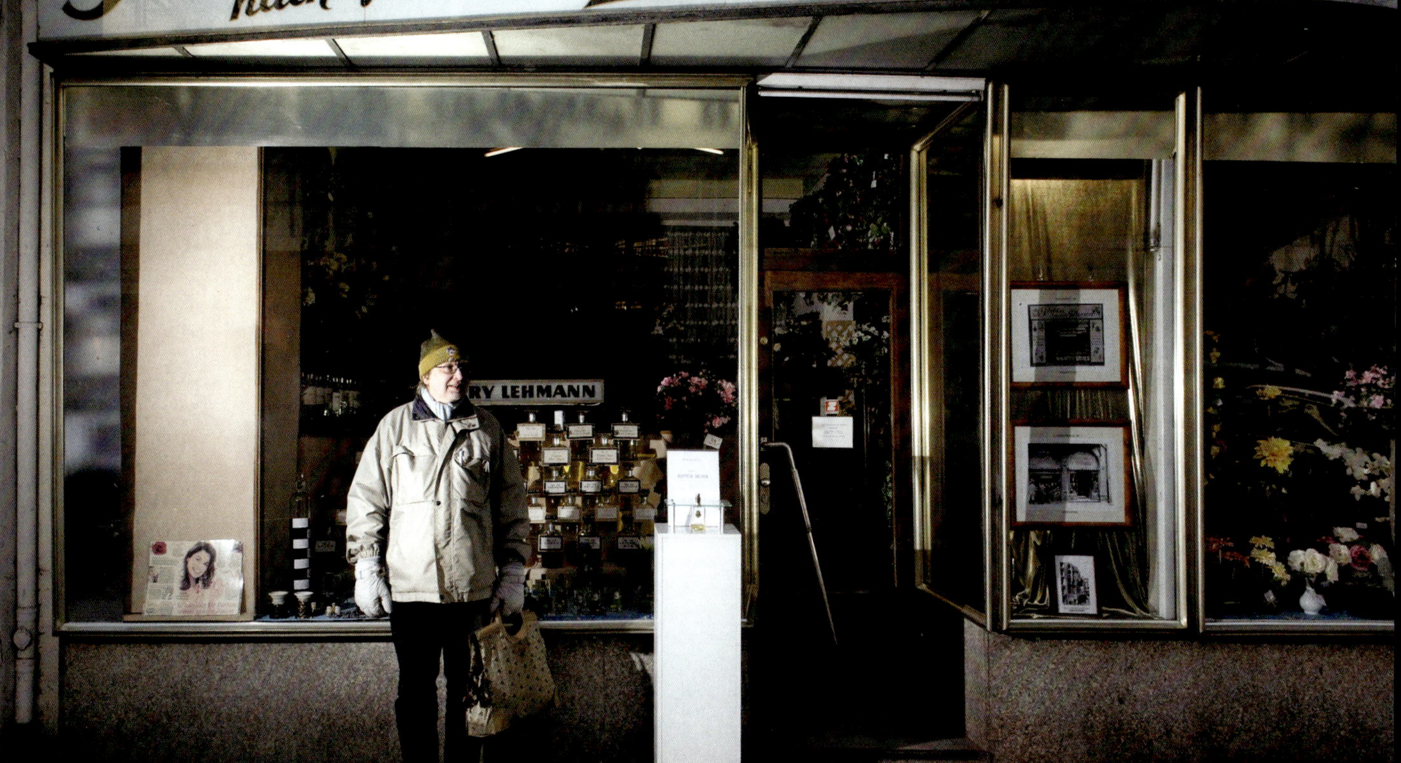

Parfums
nach Gewicht
Künstl.
Blumen
SEIT 1926
RY LEHMANN

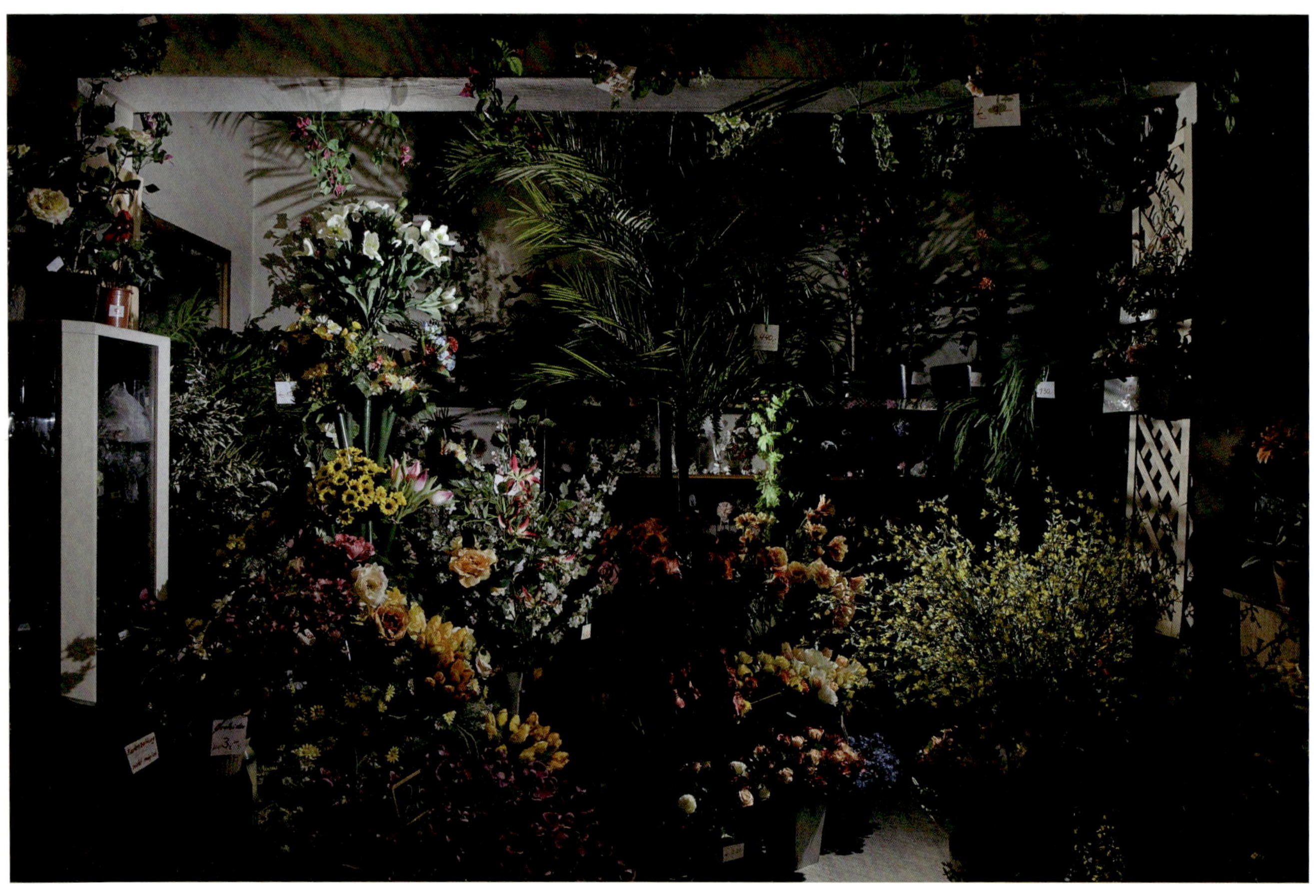

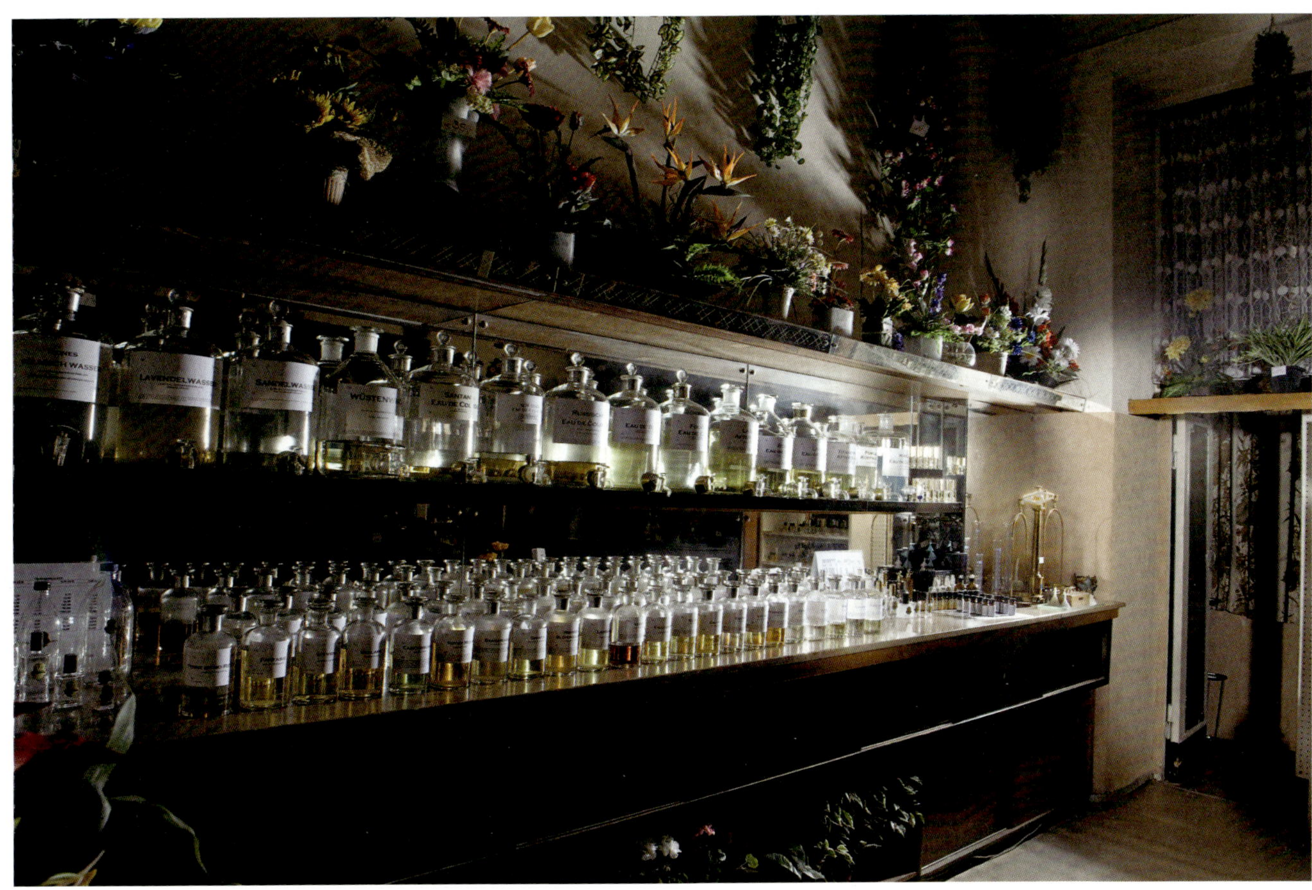

LAVENDELWASSE
SANDELWASSE
WÜSTENW
SANTAN
EAU DE COL
EAU DE COL
EAU DE
EAU DE COL

**IN DER ARENA TREFFEN SICH DIESMAL FREUNDE DER KÖRPER-BEMALUNG. SURREND ARBEITET SICH DIE NADEL ÜBER DIE HAUT EINER ZWANZIGJÄHRIGEN. NEBENAN FINDET EIN TATTOO-WETTBEWERB STATT. RAINER AUS MARKGRÖNINGEN GEWINNT MIT DEM GANZKÖRPERMOTIV »WERWOLF IM MONDSCHEIN«.**

*This time body art fans are getting together in the arena. With a buzzing sound, the needle moves under the skin of a twenty-year-old girl. A tattoo competition is taking place next door. Rainer from Markgröningen wins with the full-body "Werewolf in the Moonlight" motif.*

**60** **Arena Berlin**
*Eichenstraße . Berlin-Treptow*

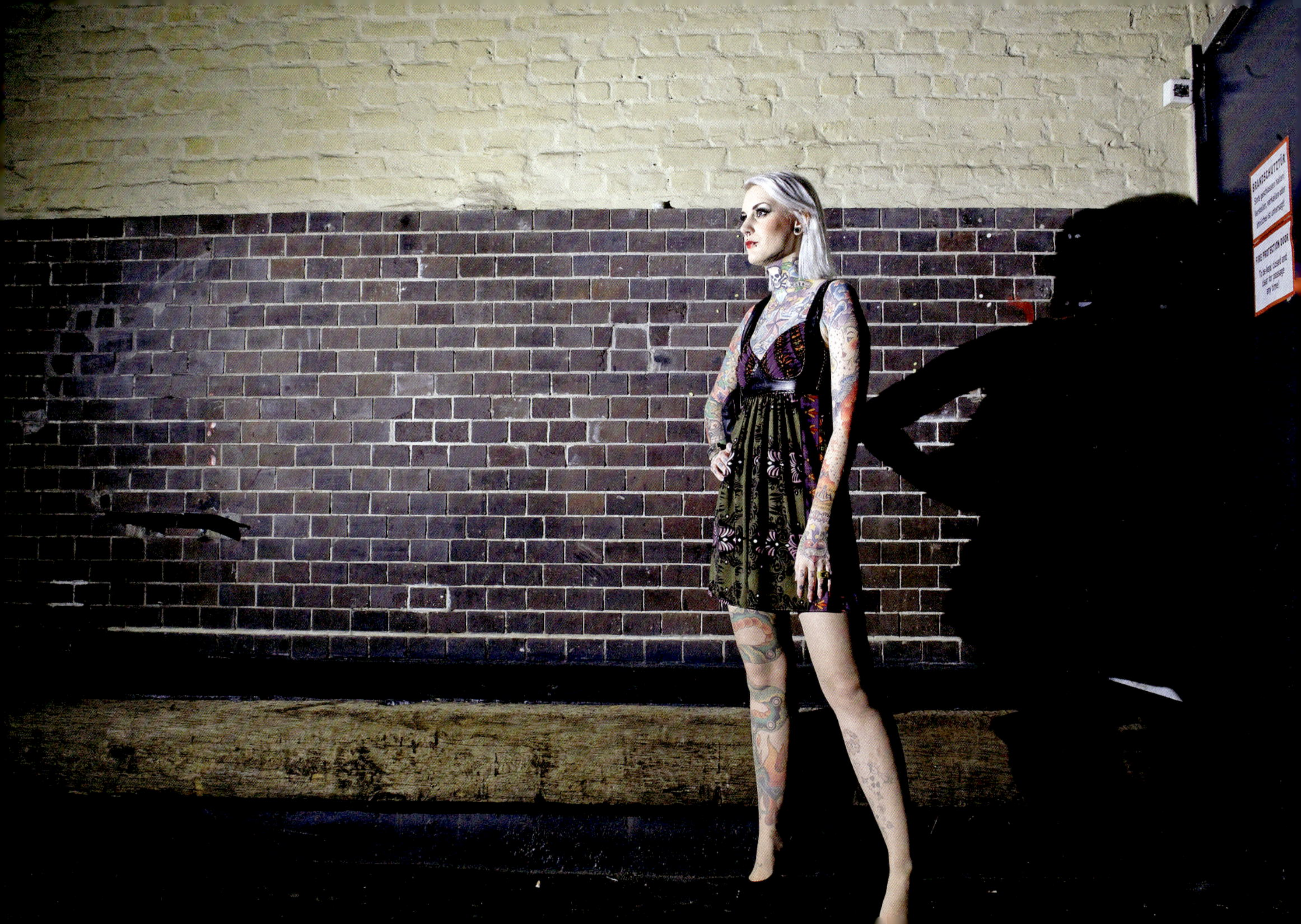

BRANDSCHUTZTÜR
FIRE PROTECTION DOOR

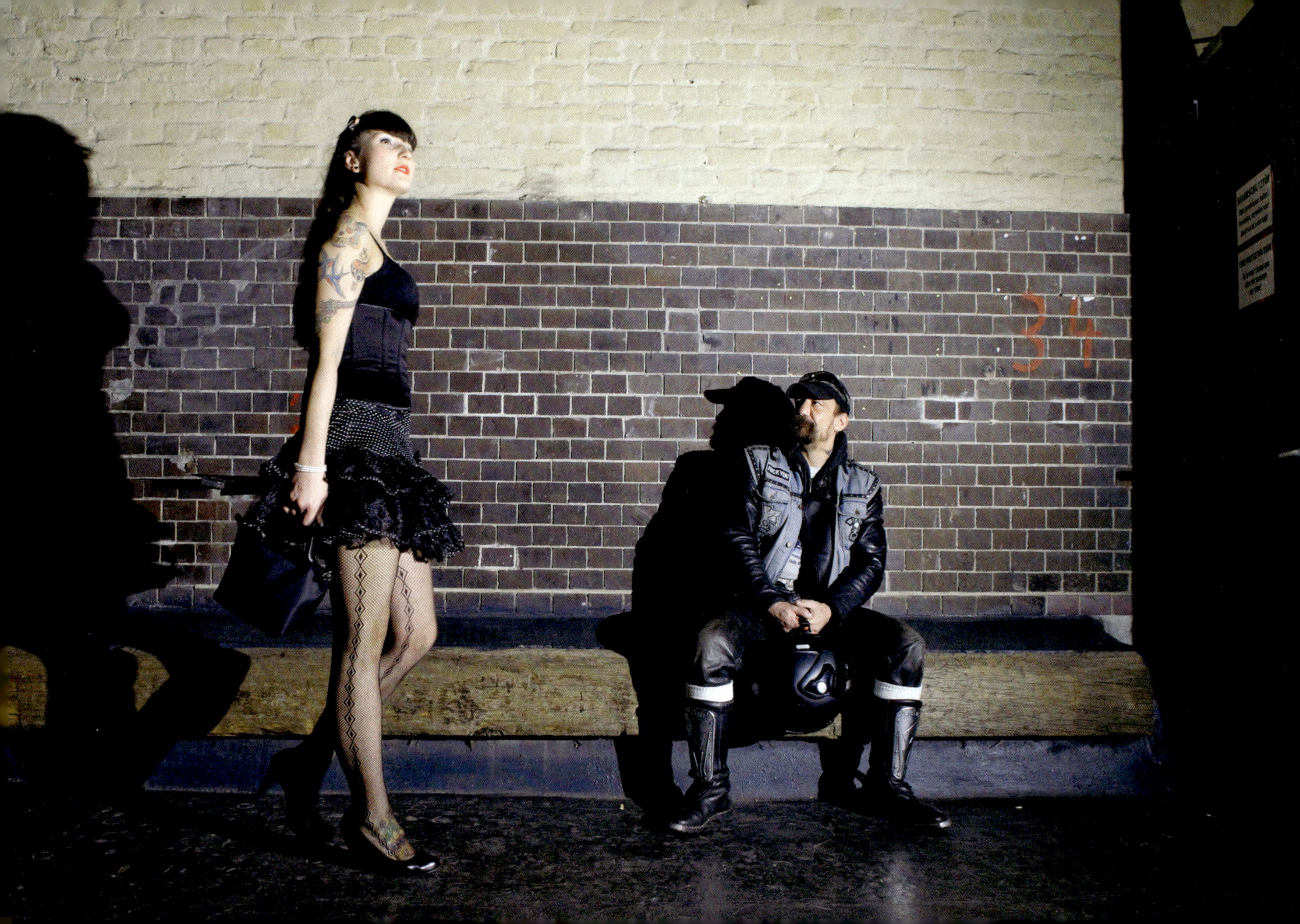

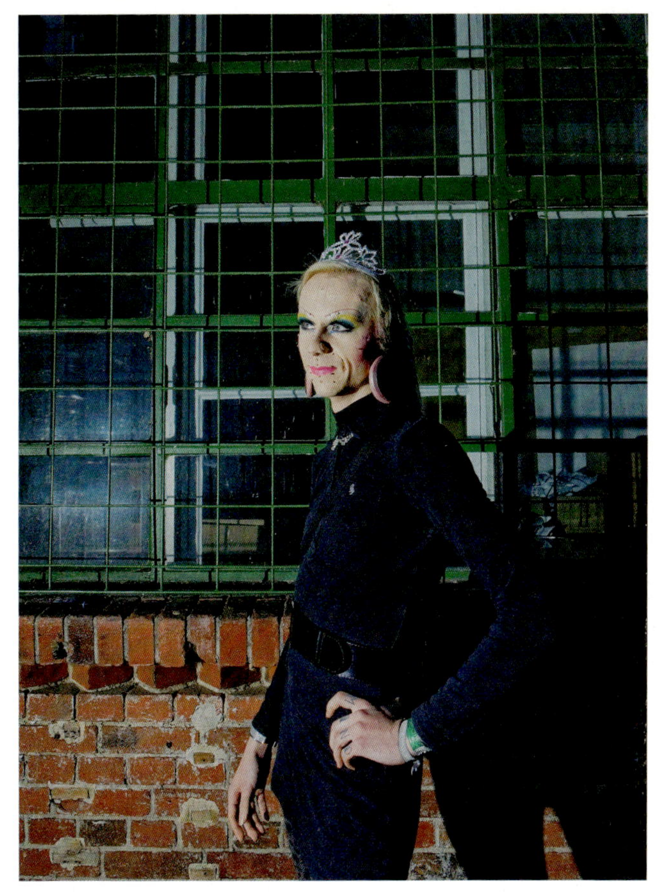

**EIN PASSANT ERINNERT SICH UND BLICKT HOCH ZUM TURM, DER WIE EIN ÜBERDIMENSIONALER FLEISCHKLOPFER ANMUTET. VORBEI DIE ZEITEN, ALS ER SÜLZE IN DER KANZEL SERVIERT BEKAM. DER TURM STEHT LEER.**

*A passer-by remembers and looks up at the tower that resembles an oversized meat mallet. The times when he was served headcheese at the pulpit are gone. The tower stands empty.*

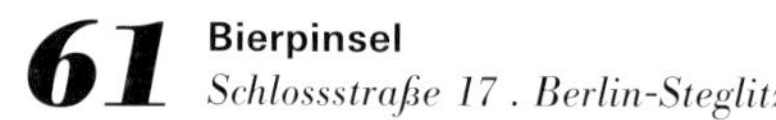

**61** Bierpinsel
*Schlossstraße 17 . Berlin-Steglitz*

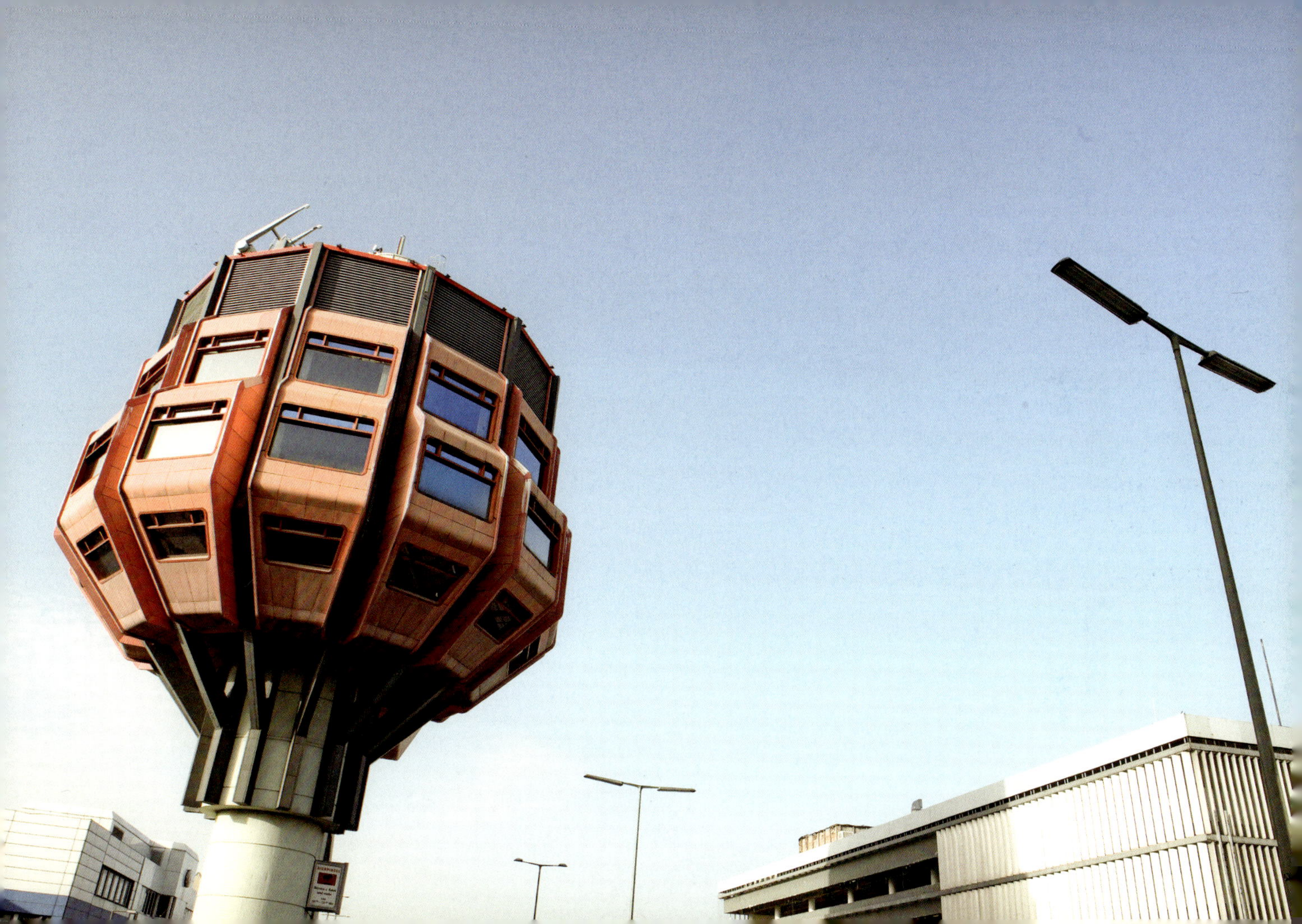

# MARZAHN: PORNOS AUF DEM HANDY UND KNUTSCHEN IN DEN GÄRTEN DER WELT

## Marzahn: cell phone porn and smooching in the Gardens of the World

Energisches Boulespiel auf Begrünungsflächen, blonde Dauerwelle, Handwerkertreff zum Skatspiel im Bezirkshaus, Berliner Göre in weißen Stiefeln an der Bushaltestelle, Knutschen in den Gärten der Welt, Schloss Biesdorf und Gutshaus Mahlsdorf, Shoppingtempel des Ostens.

*A spirited game of boules on the lawn, blond perm, workmen get-together for a game of skat in the district house, a cheeky Berlin girl wearing white boots at the bus stop, smooching in the Gardens of the World, Biesdorf Castle and Mahlsdorf Manor, shopping temple of the East.*

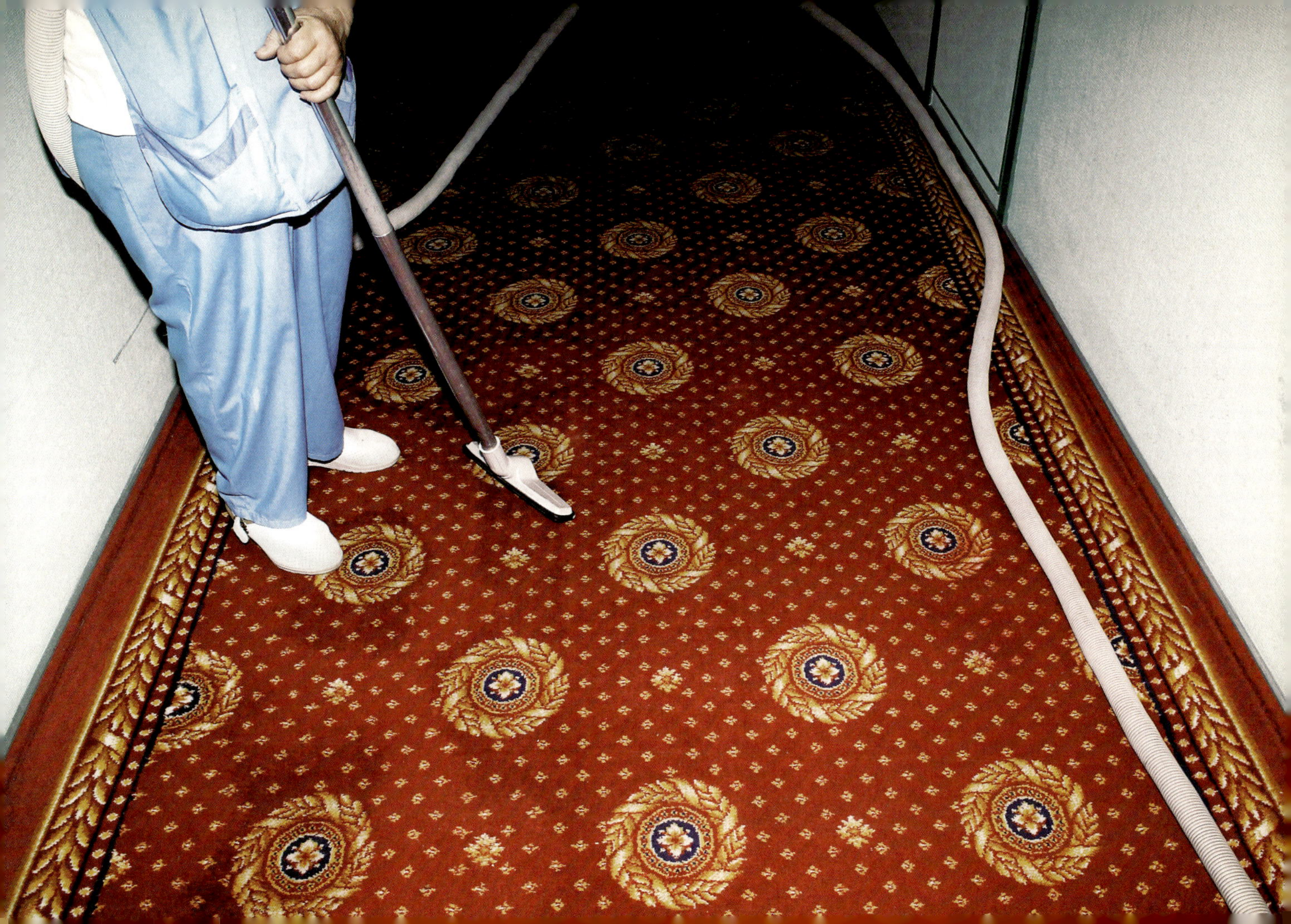

# BASS IM KRAFTWERK
## Bass in the power station

**62** **Tresor Club**
*Köpenicker Straße 70 . Berlin-Kreuzberg*

Die Nacht hat begonnen: Das junge, meist touristische Publikum trudelt nach und nach im ehemaligen Heizkraftwerk ein. Im kühlen Technokeller stapeln sich bei schummrig roter Beleuchtung Schließfächer aus dem Tresorraum des ehemaligen Kaufhauses Wertheim, in dem der Club früher seinen Sitz hatte. Weiter oben in einer schwarz schimmernden Lounge blasen Ventilatoren Luft in den menschenleeren Raum. Ein Außenbalkon überrascht. Der Besucher wähnt sich an der Berliner Luft, findet aber nur eine gewaltige Kraftwerkshalle vor, in die das Gebäude mit seinen Clubräumen eingebettet ist. Wie eine Mondlandschaft liegt die Halle da. Zwischen Dutzenden von Betonpfeilern dröhnt dumpf das Echo der Bässe.

*The night has begun: The young public, tourists for the most part, gradually enters the former heat and power station. Lock boxes from the strong room of the former Wertheim department store, where the club used to be located, are piled on top of each other in the dim reddish light of the cool rave basement. Further up in a lustrous black lounge, ventilators blast air into the deserted space. A balcony surprises. The visitor imagines he is outside in Berlin's air, but he only finds himself stumbling upon a enormous power plant hall in which the building with its club rooms is embedded. The hall looks like a lunar landscape. The thundering bass beats echo between dozens of concrete pillars.*

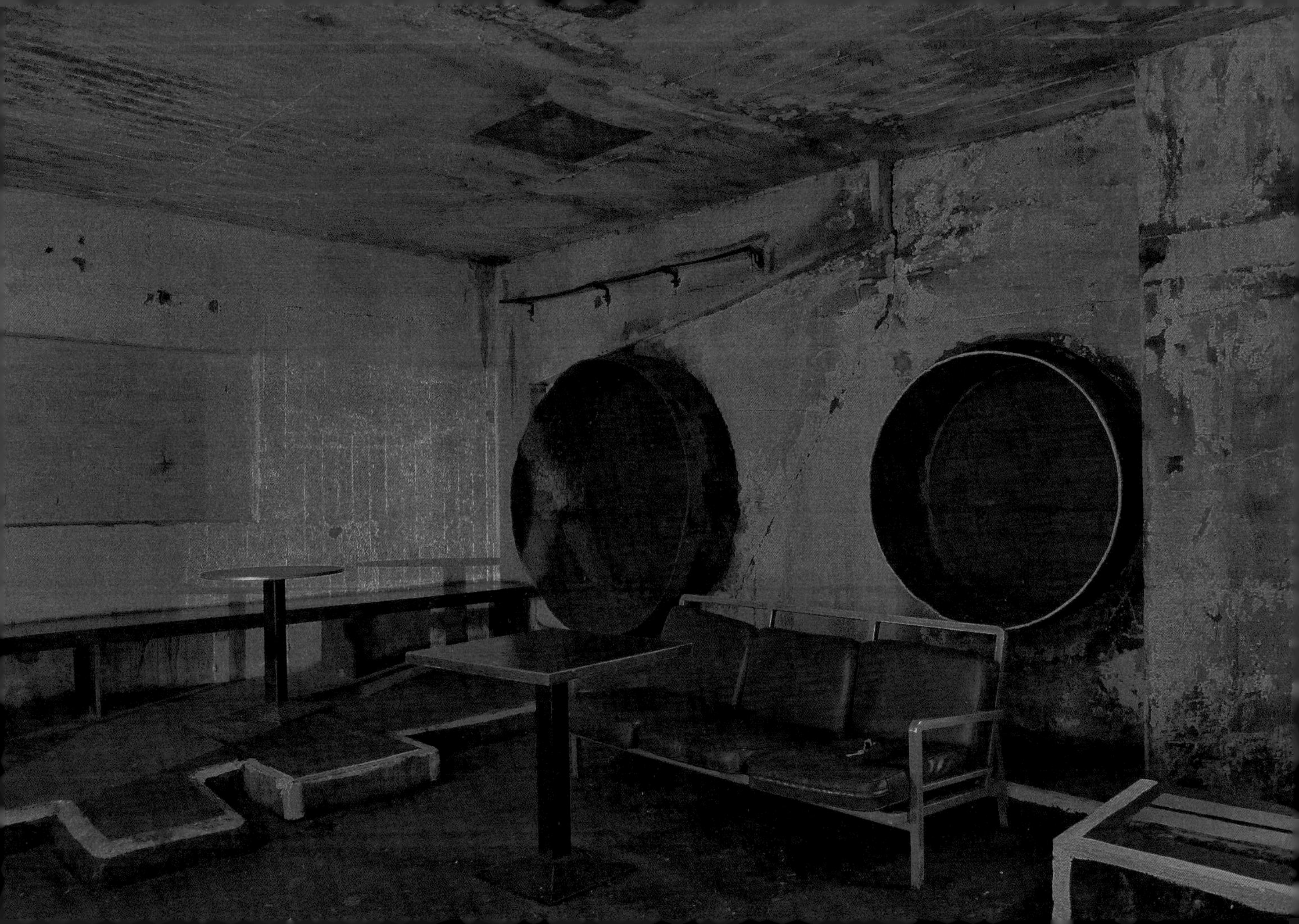

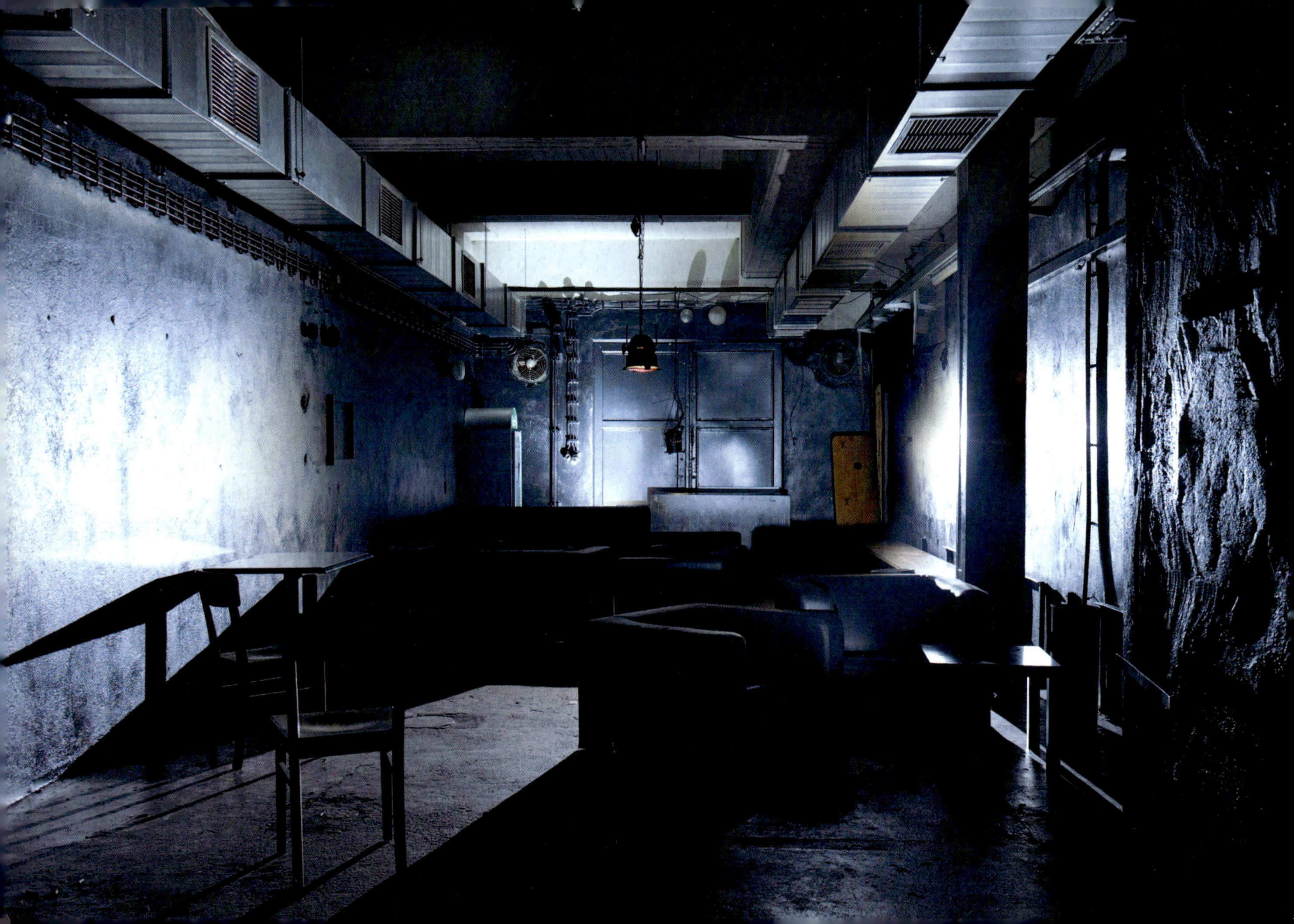

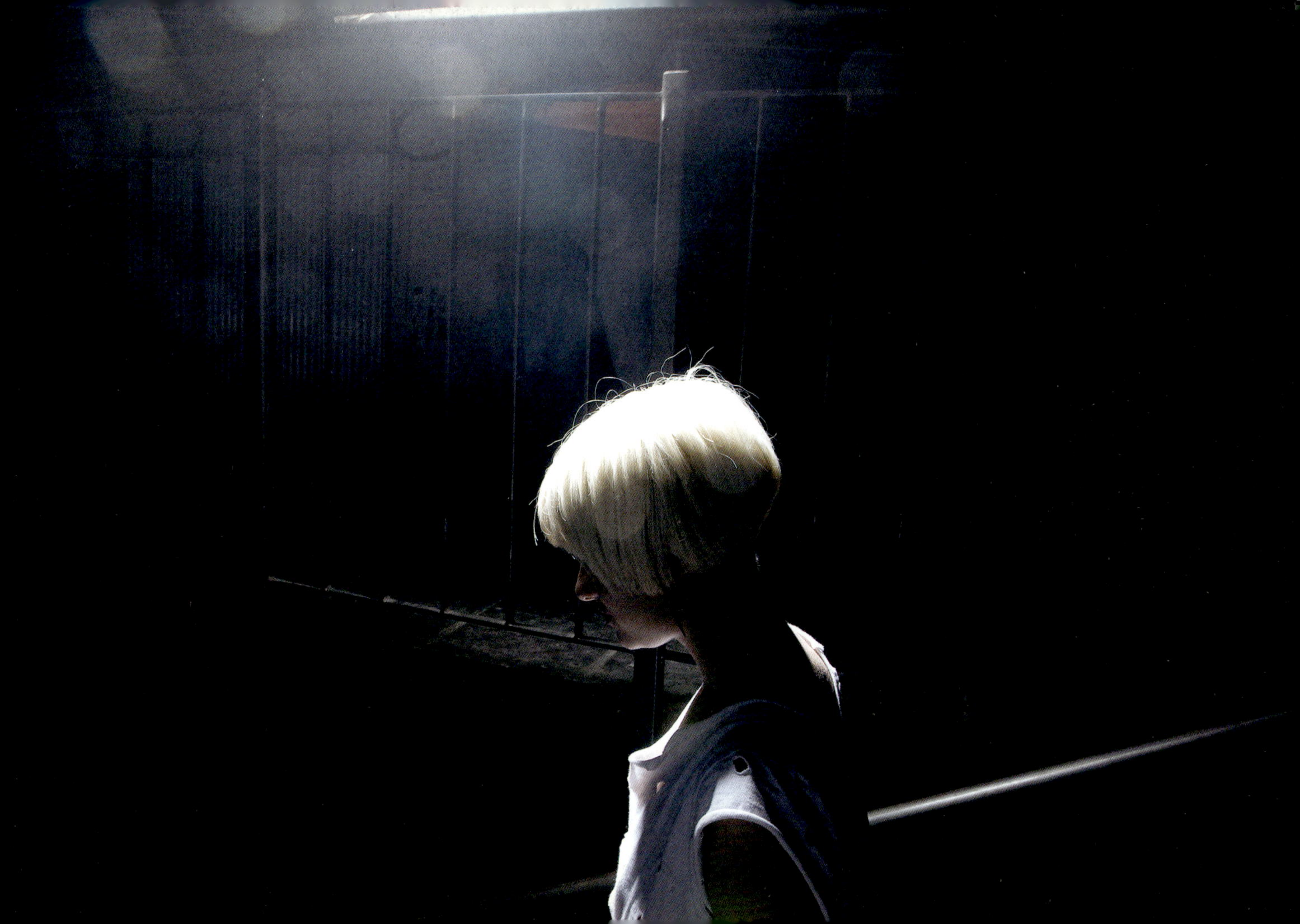

**WIR DANKEN ALLEN BETEILIGTEN,
DIE DIESES BUCH ERMÖGLICHT HABEN:**

*We extend our thanks to all who made
this book possible:*

HATJE CANTZ VERLAG: UTE BARBA, MARKUS HARTMANN, MARTIN WICHERT, ANNETTE KULENKAMPFF, CHRISTINE STÄCKER, ANJA BRELOH, DR. MICHAEL WOLFSON, DR. INGRID NINA BELL, MARTINA REITZ, TAS SKORUPA; THOMAS UND REGINE TAFEL, JENNY OREL, MICK OREL, INGEBORG OREL, FRANK OREL, FOTOSTUDIO OREL, ANDREA SCHUBERT, LAURA BERNHARDT, LISA TIEDJE, OLIVER KRÖNING, TEYMOUR TEHRANI UND DAMINA VERG, PANOS MAKRIS UND MICHAELA LEDER, CAFÉ FIRAT, CLUB AVALON UND AVALON-LADIES, FRAU CONDE UND HERRN WUSCHER (CLUB BEL AMI), FRAU BONNERMANN, LINA, XARAH VON DEN VIELENREGEN, ELENA SHYLINA, HANS JOACHIM FISCH, HORST LEDER, JENS MAESS (KONRAD TÖNZ), ROBERT UHDE UND TEAM (EQUIPAGE), SINTEQUE, ELWIRA UND JULI, HARRY POOLS, MICHAEL KRAFT, JACK HUNTER, ECKHARD PLATOW, HERRN UND FRAU KESSELRING (CCOT BERLIN 1950 E. V.), JOHN STEER (STASIMUSEUM BERLIN), FRAU PATTBERG (FRIEDRICHSTADTPALAST), JENNIFER GRÜNEWALD, ANDRE KOCKISCH (GEDENKSTÄTTE HOHENSCHÖNHAUSEN), HOLGER HAPPEL (UNTERWELTEN E. V.), BARBARA KRIJANOVSKY, GÜNTER SCHMIDTKE (CLÄRCHENS BALLHAUS), RAIMON MARQUARDT (E & M LEYDICKE), THERESA DÜHN (TROPICAL ISLANDS), MAGALI CAHEN, ALEXANDER SCHULZE (TRESOR BERLIN), ANGIE KOTRONI, SABRINA JANDA, MARKUS BECKER, ANNETTE LORENZI, RAINER RÜSSMANN, UDO BLANK, JÜRGEN METHNER, JERMAINE & ANDY (STENDAL), WILFRIED WEHR (BERLINER VERLAG), BARBARA EISENHUTH (DKB STIFTUNG FÜR GESELLSCHAFTLICHES ENGAGEMENT), HISTORIA ELSTAL E. V., JOCHEN KÜPPER (STADTBAD WEDDING), GENERALLEUTNANT A. D. DIRK BÖCKER (LUFTWAFFENMUSEUM DER BUNDESWEHR), H. JOACHIM LUDWIG (CAFÉ KEESE), BERJOZKA (RUSSISCHE LEBENSMITTEL), PRESSESTELLE DES KANZLERAMTS, JESSICA WOLF, DR. BLASZKIEWITZ (TIERPARK BERLIN), MICHAEL KRAFT, HENRY–JOSEPH POOLS, ANDREAS GLÄSER, GISA DIERKES, WARRANT OFFICER II BOB HOPE, SIEGFRIED THIEL (LUFTFAHRTMUSEUM FINOWFURT), MANFRED GRABOWSKI (CASTINGAGENTUR AUTSEIDER), HAUSMEISTER BENTHIN (WBM WOHNUNGSBAUGESELLSCHAFT), UWE EGGERS (VORSITZENDER WEST ALLIIERTE IN BERLIN E. V.), HERRN BAUDA, LUTZ LEHMANN (HARRY LEHMANN), MONIKA LIESERT (LIESERT'S FALCKENSTEINER), ROLF TREDER, ALEXANDER SCHELLBACH, HENRY KOLLIN, RENÉ ZABEL UND KOLLEGE, XRONIX FROM POLAND, LEXY HELL

SOWIE ALLEN WEITEREN PERSONEN, DIE HIER NICHT GENANNT WERDEN KONNTEN.
AS WELL AS EVERYONE ELSE WHO CANNOT BE NAMED HERE.

**32**
Stuttgarter Platz
*Berlin-Charlottenburg*

**33**
Ehemalige US-Radarstation
*Teufelsberg*
*Berlin Charlottenburg*

**34**
Flughafen Tempelhof
*Platz der Luftbrücke 5*
*Berlin-Tempelhof*

**35**
Trabrennbahn Karlshorst
*Treskowallee 129*
*Berlin-Karlshorst*

**36**
Equipage
*Nostitzstraße 30*
*Berlin-Kreuzberg*

**37**
Berliner Trabrenn-Verein e. V.
*Mariendorfer Damm 222*
*Berlin-Mariendorf*

**38**
Imbiss am Pla de Lü
*Platz der Luftbrücke*
*Berlin-Tempelhof*

**39**
Tierpark Berlin
*Am Tierpark 125*
*Berlin-Lichtenberg*

**40**
PanAm Lounge
*Budapester Straße 43*
*Berlin-Charlottenburg*

**41**
Spreepark Plänterwald
*Kiehnwerderallee 1–3*
*Berlin-Treptow*

**42**
Konrad Tönz (Bar)
*Falckensteinstraße 30*
*Berlin-Kreuzberg*

**43**
Nollendorfplatz
*Berlin-Schöneberg*

**44**
Berjozka (Russische Lebensmittel)
*Passauer Straße 4*
*Berlin-Schöneberg*

**45**
E & M Leydicke
*Mansteinstraße 4*
*Berlin-Schöneberg*

**46**
Cuvrystraße
*Berlin-Kreuzberg*

**47**
Tropical Islands
*Tropical-Islands-Allee 1*
*Krausnick*

**48**
Fichtebunker
*Fichtestraße 6*
*Berlin-Kreuzberg*

**49**
Liesert's Falckensteiner
*Falckensteinstraße 26*
*Berlin-Kreuzberg*

**50**
U-Bahnhof Heinrich-Heine-Straße
*Köpenicker Straße 76*
*Berlin-Mitte*

**51**
Alternatives Wohnen
*Bethaniendamm 25*
*Berlin-Kreuzberg*

**52**
Kottbusser Tor
*Adalbertstraße 1*
*Berlin-Kreuzberg*

**53**
Café Firat
*Dresdner Straße 19*
*Berlin-Kreuzberg*

**54**
Ehemalige Militärkasernen
*Biesenhorster Weg*
*Berlin-Karlshorst*

**55**
Einkaufsmeile Kurfürstendamm
*Kurfürstendamm*
*Berlin-Charlottenburg*

**56**
Luftwaffenmuseum
der Bundeswehr
*Kladower Damm 182–188*
*Berlin-Gatow*

**57**
Olympisches Dorf
*Rosa-Luxemburg-Allee 69*
*Wustermark*

**58**
Sozialpalast Schöneberg
*Pallasstraße 28*
*Berlin-Schöneberg*

**59**
Harry Lehmann
*Kantstraße 106*
*Berlin-Charlottenburg*

**60**
Arena Berlin
*Eichenstraße*
*Berlin-Treptow*

**61**
Bierpinsel
*Schlossstraße 17*
*Berlin-Steglitz*

**62**
Tresor Club
*Köpenicker Straße 70*
*Berlin-Kreuzberg*